KILLING WOMEN

THE TRUE STORY OF SERIAL KILLER DON MILLER'S REIGN OF TERROR

ROD SADLER

WILD BLUE
PRESS

WildBluePress.com

KILLING WOMEN published by:
WILDBLUE PRESS
P.O. Box 102440
Denver, Colorado 80250

WILDBLUE PRESS is registered at the U.S. Patent and Trademark Offices.

ISBN 978-1-952225-27-7 Trade Paperback

ISBN 978-1-952225-28-4 eBook

Cover Design by Villa Designs

Interior Formatting by Elijah Toten
www.totencreative.com

KILLING
WOMEN

This book is dedicated to Lisa, Randy, Martha, Marita, Wendy, and Kristine

"His persona is a disguise … the same disguise that he used before, both to get closer to his victims and to deny culpability. Miller's crimes identify him as a human predator, and there is no reliable basis to conclude he has changed."

—Eaton County Prosecuting Attorney Jeffrey Sauter
October 7, 1998

TABLE OF CONTENTS

ACKNOWLEDGEMENTS

I'd like to thank several people for contributing to this book: Mike Hocking, Ken Ouellette, Mike Woodworth, Gina Woodworth, David Bankhead, Rich Deer, Brent Morton, Neil O'Brien, Vince Green, Heidi Williams, Lesley Morgan, Douglas Lloyd, Peter Houk, Randy Gilbert, John Boggs, Vance Diggers, Dr. Frank Ochberg, Tom Bengston, Gene Miller, Kay Young, Rod Dropping, Dick Fitzgerald, Jane Sobleskey, Jeff Weiss, Don Ulrey, Ryan Wilkinson, and Jim Kus.

FOREWORD

In the summer of 1978, I had been an assistant prosecuting attorney in Eaton County, Michigan, for less than two years when I took a call in my office from a dispatcher at the Eaton County Sheriff's Department. That one call signified the beginning of a journey that would have a permanent effect on me both personally and professionally.

The dispatcher reported that two teenagers in Eaton County's Delta Township (the western portion of metropolitan Lansing, Michigan) had just been attacked in their home in broad daylight. I learned that the fourteen-year-old female had been raped and nearly strangled to death with her own belt, and her thirteen-year-old brother had been stabbed several times. The assailant had been confronted while leaving the residence by a passerby who had spotted a nude and frantic female running toward the road in front of her house. That passerby was not only willing to provide aid, but was astute enough to confront the assailant and accurately record the license plate number on his brown Oldsmobile Cutlass. The dispatcher informed me that the license plate came back to someone I was very familiar with: Don Gene Miller.

That call, and that day, were the beginning of the end for Miller, and it significantly changed the course of many lives, including my own.

Most everyone in law enforcement in mid-Michigan already knew who Don Miller was. He had been the prime suspect in the New Year's Eve disappearance of his girlfriend, Martha Sue Young, the previous year. Since Ms. Young's disappearance, the MSU/East Lansing community had endured the disappearance and murders of three more women.

The only crimes Don Miller was prosecuted for were the attacks on the Delta Township teenagers, and a later prosecution in Michigan's Upper Peninsula for possession of a self-made garrote while he served his Eaton County sentences. I was tasked with trying Miller on the teenager assault cases in Berrien County, Michigan, due to a change of venue granted because of intense pretrial publicity. During that process, I got to know Don Miller (a fellow graduate of MSU's School of Criminal Justice), as did the entire mid-Michigan law enforcement community.

As one of Michigan's first true serial killers, Don Gene Miller left a permanent imprint on my professional and personal life, as well as the victims, their families, witnesses, police officers, and court personnel involved in bringing him to justice. Although there have been less than a half dozen other such killers in this area since then, none have left their mark on the greater Lansing, Michigan, region like he did.

I have known Rod Sadler for over thirty years. He served with the Eaton County Sheriff's Department during my tenure as an Eaton County prosecutor, trial judge, and criminal defense attorney. In the narrative that follows, he'll provide you with both the publicly known details of the Miller cases, and intimate details of the investigation that the public was never made aware of. It will take you back over forty years to a time when life seemed much simpler – until, for those living in my hometown, it changed forever.

G. Michael Hocking
December 2019

PREFACE

There are very few cases more perplexing than those of a serial killer.

In the 1970s, names like Gacy, Bundy, and Berkowitz dominated headlines worldwide. Over a period of time, their cases have captivated us internationally. They were high-profile serial killers who had been caught. There were, and will always be, others out there.

Robert Ressler, a criminal profiler in the Behavioral Sciences Unit of the Federal Bureau of Investigation, is oftentimes credited with coining the phrase "serial homicide" in the seventies. Although the term had been used before that time in writings, it hadn't been widely accepted. Ironically, Ressler's alma mater, Michigan State University, would be the venue for a series of murders that would begin only three years after he first used the term.

Murders that involve a serial killer can occur over weeks, months, or even years. Several jurisdictions are likely to become involved, and finding a link between a suspect and his or her victim can be extremely difficult, if there even is one. There are obstacles and challenges faced by the investigators that have to be overcome. Information and leads can quickly build to a point where they become voluminous, and the investigators have to sort through it all, hoping to find that one piece of information to tie them all together.

In early January 1977, a missing person's case first appeared in the Lansing, Michigan, papers. Martha Sue Young, a coed from Michigan State University, had disappeared from her home after she was supposedly dropped off by her boyfriend in the early morning hours on New Year's Day.

Eighteen months later, with Martha Sue Young still missing, a second woman, employed on the MSU campus, was reported missing. Marita Choquette, who lived in the small town of Grand Ledge, was last seen at her home, yet her car was found in the early morning hours at her work place on 3241campus. She was nowhere to be found.

Two weeks later, a third MSU coed, Wendy Bush, was reported missing after she failed to show up to work on campus. A witness reported seeing her with a man near the MSU library late the previous night.

Two months after Wendy disappeared, Kristine Stuart, a Lansing area teacher, was reported missing as she walked home near the MSU campus.

While the investigating law enforcement agency in Martha Sue Young's disappearance suspected her boyfriend was involved in her disappearance, they weren't convinced he was involved in the others.

By August 1978, only one body had been found, and no one had been charged in that murder.

Two days after the fourth disappearance, a fourteen-year-old girl was raped in nearby Eaton County, and her thirteen-year-old brother was strangled, then stabbed. Police finally got the break they were looking for when a witness was able to copy down the license plate as the suspect fled from the scene.

Don G. Miller, the former boyfriend of Martha Sue Young, was arrested a short time later.

This is the tragic story of four women whose lives were viciously cut short, and it is the story of a courageous sister and brother who, as young teenagers, literally saved each other's lives in August 1978.

More than that, this is the story of a penal system that allowed for (what some would call) the unthinkable to occur with a plea deal that haunts mid-Michigan to this day.

My ability to document this case comes from a unique perspective. As I followed news reports of Martha Sue Young's disappearance, I had already chosen my career and began studying criminal justice in the fall of 1978, only three weeks after Miller's arrest.

I didn't realize it at the time, but as I continued my thirty-year career in law enforcement, I was fostering friendships with other officers, detectives, prosecutors, defense attorneys, civil attorneys, and judges, all of who had been intimately involved in the investigation of the murders and the prosecution of Don Miller.

When I began writing this book, I interviewed numerous people. I was fortunate enough to be able to speak with Martha Sue Young's sister, and before she agreed to answer any questions, she asked why I was writing this book. I told her that I believed it's a story that has to be told. Too many people have forgotten who Don Miller is and what he did. He's been eligible for parole several times in the forty years he's been in prison, but he will eventually have served his time, and he will be released from the Michigan Department of Corrections. What could be more frightening than the inevitable release of a serial killer from prison?

The only reason Don Miller remains in prison is for a 1998 conviction for possessing a homemade strangulation device, specifically a garrote, in his prison dorm. He has already served his time for the murders of two women.

Should the prosecuting attorney have made a deal with Miller in exchange for locating the other victims in 1978? Was the 1998 garrote case against Miller contrived? Should Don Miller be released from prison in 2031? These are questions the reader will have to decide.

Material for this book was drawn from interviews and other primary sources.

Rod Sadler
April 2020

1

The defense attorney's home phone rang at around ten p.m. A voice at the other end of the line said, "Are you representing Don Miller?"

The attorney, cautious now, responded, "Yeah."

The threat was immediate. "You're not going to live to see daylight."[1] The sound of the phone disconnecting was as sudden as the threat itself.

Everyone was apprehensive. They doubted their passenger would follow through on his promise. They had driven the forty miles from Jackson to East Lansing, and now the short caravan of cars was following a winding road as it curved around the east side of Park Lake. As the line of cars turned back toward the west along the north shoreline, the morning sunshine on the lake surface created a spectacular reflection. They reached Webster Road and turned to the north for just a moment before their final turn onto Drumheller Road. As the short motorcade moved slowly along the gravel surface, the shackled passenger in the lead car told the driver to stop and turn down a two-track trail on the south side of the road. It led into a heavily wooded area called Priggooris Park in Bath Township. The fact that the caravan had crossed from Ingham County into Clinton County never crossed anyone's mind, but it wasn't

---

1. Thomas Bengston, Interview by author, East Lansing, MI, October 12, 2018

a concern anyway. All of the police agencies in the tri-county area had already been notified that they would be out searching. They just didn't know where they would end up.

The cars moved at a snail's pace along the trail for a short distance before stopping. The group of police officers, attorneys, psychiatrists, and their passenger stepped from the cars and stood for a moment, looking around. They began slowly walking along the trail. After fifty yards or so, the handcuffed passenger, who was directing them, seemed puzzled and now unsure if he was in the right place. Some of the men began searching themselves by looking around the trees, under shrubs, and in the tall grass. The team of men searched for thirty minutes or so, but eventually gave up. It had already been a long morning, and the law enforcement officials were certain their passenger was playing games with them. Their original apprehension turned to frustration.

They were all too familiar with Priggooris Park. Named after Angel Priggooris, a former Michigan businessman and conservationist in the 1800s, the park covered over 260 acres of woodlands and marsh. Three years earlier, in June 1976, the Michigan State Police had led the search for two teenage girls from the nearby town of Charlotte. The girls had been camping in the park when they were reported missing by a friend. They were later found murdered, and their bodies were located miles apart. Two men had been charged with their murders. To area law enforcement, the park seemed to be a dumping ground for victims involved in the local drug trade too.

The park was also a short two miles from the site of one of the worst acts of domestic terrorism in American history. In May 1927, days before Charles Lindbergh celebrated his flight across the Atlantic, former school treasurer Andrew Kehoe bombed the Bath Consolidated Schools, killing thirty-eight school kids and six adults, in addition to killing his wife.

But today the investigators' focus wasn't on the historic crimes and murders in Bath Township. On this hot July day, with its bright sunshine and stagnant breeze, their sole focus was to find the bodies of Martha Sue Young and Kristine Stuart.

Ironically, law enforcement officials, family, friends and volunteers had searched the park for Martha's body several times over the previous two years, but the woods and brush were so thick that searchers had come up emptyhanded. Though apprehensive, there was still a small expectation that today would be different.

Earlier in the day, seven of the twelve men had met in Lansing at eight a.m., when an Ingham County judge signed a court order allowing them to pick up a man named Don Miller from Jackson Prison and drive him to East Lansing. Tom Bengston, Miller's attorney, and Bengston's assistant, Jonathan White, in addition to two psychiatrists from the prison, met the rest of the entourage there. After picking up their passengers, the three-car caravan continued back to the north along US-127 and into East Lansing before heading further north toward Priggooris Park.

Now, after their failed attempt, the investigators had had enough of their prisoner's games. Getting ready to take him back to the prison, they drove further east along Drumheller Road for a short distance, and the handcuffed prisoner told them to turn down a second wooded artery leading into the park. There was still a glimmer of hope. Maybe Miller had been confused. As the cars turned onto a second trail, they crept a short distance when he told them to stop. With cautious optimism, everyone got out, and the single-file line of men continued slowly walking along the new trail through the heavily-wooded park.

While hot, the shade from the trees and the slight breeze provided a brief respite from the summer sun. On this mid-

July day, the temperature averaged in the high seventies and was right where it should be, but to the men searching for two dead bodies, it seemed much hotter.

As the line of men walked slowly along the path, Miller walked up a slight hill with his escort and stopped. He stared straight ahead and pointed back to a small off-shoot trail they had just passed. He quietly said, "She's over there." With his wrists locked together by the steel restraints in front of him, he bent down and picked some small wild flowers as he began softly singing to himself, never looking back toward the trail.

Prior to 1977, Tom Bengston had never met the Miller family. Bengston had grown up in the town of Menominee in Michigan's Upper Peninsula. After graduating from high school there, he had already decided on a career as a lawyer. He attended his first year of law school at Wayne State University in Detroit and transferred to the University of Michigan in Ann Arbor before graduating in 1967, eventually joining the Hubbard Law Firm in Lansing.

Bengston's senior partner at the firm, Ellison Thomas, attended the same church in Lansing as the Miller family. Don's dad, Gene Miller, had contacted Thomas about Martha Sue Young's disappearance, telling him about Don and his relationship with Martha. With Martha missing, Don was being questioned by the police about her disappearance.

The accomplished attorney met with Bengston at their office in the Michigan National Bank Building in downtown Lansing and asked his younger law partner if he would like to get involved in the case. Tom Bengston agreed.

Tom Bengston was the last in the line of twelve men walking along the two-track trail.

When his client stopped and told the men where her body was, he was pointing to a small animal trail running perpendicular to the trail they were on. Since the line of officials had already passed it, they turned around, and Bengston was now leading the line. He started making his way down the trail. After twenty-five yards or so, he quickly changed direction and began heading back in the direction he had just come from. "She's over there," he said.[2] Ironically, the defense attorney representing the man who had killed Martha Sue Young was the first person to see what was left of her body after two and a half years. Her skeletal remains were scattered in a small area near a large oak tree.

Bengston and his client were quickly taken back to the three cars parked along the two-track, and the defense attorney had an immense sense of sadness at the discovery of Martha's remains.

The killer had agreed to lead police to the bodies of two women, but this was only the first. The deal wasn't complete.

The investigators who stayed with Martha's remains stood in a heavily overgrown area of the park. Her skeleton was lying on a downward incline sloping toward a marshy area. Her feet were pointed down the incline in a northeasterly direction. Her skull and arms had dislocated from the rest of her remains, and several of her teeth were missing from the skull.

East Lansing Police Lieutenant Dean Tucker had worked tirelessly for the previous two and a half years trying to find the young coed. He had become close friends with Martha's mother Sue, and he kept her updated at every turn in the

2. Michael Woodworth, Interview by author, Lansing, MI, July 18, 2018

investigation. As he stood over the remains of Sue Young's daughter, he was overcome with anger and sadness, and the veteran officer couldn't contain his emotions anymore as tears welled in his eyes.

The investigators knew ahead of time that if they were successful in finding the bodies, the crime lab would have to be notified. Captain Harry Tift, the lead detective from the Ingham County Sheriff's Office, and a few of the investigators stayed with the remains as the others left the scene and headed for a phone. The entire area was now considered a crime scene.

As the officers waited, their frustration turned to anger. They knew, as did everyone else in the mid-Michigan law enforcement community, that Don Miller had killed Martha Sue Young two and a half years earlier, yet law enforcement hadn't been able to find her body. They also knew Miller was the lead suspect in the disappearance of three other local women, yet only one of those victims had been found, and they still hadn't been able to connect him with her murder.

While they waited with Martha Sue Young's body for the crime lab technicians to arrive, the others drove to Tom Bengston's home in Okemos. Along the way, they stopped at a McDonald's to pick up lunch. Bengston, with his own family and the killer sitting at the same table, enjoyed a quick, fast-food lunch before heading back out with the officers to continue the search for another body.

Miller began directing the caravan again. At one p.m., they eased onto northbound US-127, quickly leaving Ingham County and continuing back into Clinton County, once again never thinking about having crossed the county line. The four-lane divided highway seemed to stretch on endlessly as Miller continued directing them. The cars moved north of the small city of Dewitt before finally reaching Jason Road.

The lead car slowed as Miller told the driver to turn west. After two-tenths of a mile, they passed a sign that read MUSKRAT LAKE ACCESS, and Miller pointed to a farm lane on the south side of the road. He told the driver to turn and follow it. The two cars drove slowly for six hundred feet along the grassy stretch of two-track before coming to a T-intersection with a second grassy farm lane, then turned back toward the east. Fields of soy beans waiting for the fall harvest lined both sides of the trail, and there was little to offer in the way of shade. The officers could see a farm house with manicured corrals located to the northeast, and they could see a drainage ditch lined with a heavy growth of underbrush and shrubs just ahead of them as Miller directed the driver to stop. He quietly told them the body would be lying in the drainage ditch along the row of shrubs and underbrush, and it would be about twenty feet south from where they had stopped.

Hazy sunshine and high humidity had taken over the day. Ingham County Prosecutor Peter Houk and Chief Assistant Dan McClellan were part of the remaining team. Along with the other men in the caravan, they began to make their way along the ravine and through the underbrush. The temperature had reached near ninety degrees and mosquitoes were everywhere. As Houk nearly reached the bottom of the drainage ditch, McClellan yelled at his boss. "You're about to step on her!" he said.[3] The prosecutor looked down to see Kristine Stuart's body at his feet.

Having grown up in Flint, Michigan, and working the line at Ford Motor Company, Peter Houk had come from a working-class family. While he worked at Ford, he attended Flint Junior College for two years before heading to the

---

3. Peter Houk, Interview by author, Lansing, MI, July 18, 2018

University of Michigan. Required to take Constitutional Law, he spent the summer getting it out of the way and realized he loved it.

Deciding on law school, Houk was told he had to take the Law School Admissions Test, and without ever opening a book, he scored a 94%.

After two years at the University of Michigan, he ended up at Wayne State University Law School in Detroit, and his first job after graduating was with the Michigan Attorney General's Office in the criminal division. He worked at writing arguments against appeals from inmates who claimed their rights had been violated or who wanted a new trial.

After three years, Houk took a job as the chief assistant city attorney in Lansing and knew he wanted to get involved in politics, but quickly realized he didn't have a knowledge base.

For the next five years, the future prosecutor learned a lot about practical law by sitting next to Lansing City Councilwoman Lucille Belin at the Lansing City Council meetings. After five years in the city attorney's office, he decided it was his time to run for prosecuting attorney, and he knew what his platform would be. Houk developed a twenty-six page strategy to enhance the prosecutor's diversion program for first-time offenders. More than that, if he was elected, he would abate plea bargaining. While the new prosecutor was out celebrating his victory in the early morning hours of January 1, 1977, Don Miller was murdering Martha Sue Young. Peter Houk never knew that in two and a half years, he would make a deal with the devil.

––––––––––

Almost two hours after the body of Martha Sue Young had been located, the investigators had found another of Don Miller's victims. She was lying face down in the nine-foot-deep drainage ditch that spanned thirty-two feet across. Her head was facing toward the east, and her body was badly decomposed. Her skull had separated from the spine and rested several inches from her body. Her jaw had separated from the skull, and some of her teeth were missing. The investigators noticed that several of her finger bones were also missing. A small amount of mummified tissue still remained on her upper body, arms, and legs.

As the team of investigators began to shrink with each body found, Officer Rick Westgate was left with another assistant prosecutor and Kristine Stuart's body. The others left to call for a second team of lab specialists from the state police. Lt. Tucker also called Sergeant Jim Kelley and asked him to help at the Stuart crime scene. Tucker knew what was next.

Lieutenant Tucker, ELPD's lead investigator, now had an even tougher job. After leaving the second crime scene, he returned to his office and called Sue Young, asking if it was okay to stop by. At 2:15 p.m., he pulled into the driveway at 1978 N. Harrison Road in East Lansing. Martha Sue Young's mother, already knowing in her own mind why they were there, became anxious when four neatly-dressed men, including Peter Houk and Dan McClellan, arrived at her door. As they were welcomed into her home, she offered them tea but they declined. Tucker spoke up, telling Sue they had some bad news. They had found Martha's body, and he quietly explained to her that while they were certain it was her daughter, there would still have to be an autopsy for a positive identification.

Sue Young thought she had prepared herself for that moment. She already knew of the deal offered to the killer in return for her daughter's body. Martha had been missing for so long, and Sue had reluctantly agreed to the deal, along with Kristine's husband Ernie. Knowing the likelihood Martha's body would be found any other way didn't make it any easier for her. As she stood in her living room with the men, she was numb.

Earlier in the spring, Sue Young had met with Lt. Tucker and Peter Houk at the ELPD. There was a third man at the meeting she didn't recognize. She learned it was Ernie Stuart, Kristine's husband. The media reports had already started to suggest that the disappearance of Martha in January 1977, Marita Choquette and Wendy Bush in June 1978, and Kristine in August 1978 were related. At that meeting with the three men, Houk explained the idea of a plea deal with Miller. It specified that if Miller would lead police to the bodies of Martha and Kristine, charges of second-degree murder would be dropped, and an amended count of voluntary manslaughter would be added for each death. Months earlier, Miller had been convicted in the sexual assault and attempted murder of Lisa Gilbert and her thirteen-year-old brother Randy, and he was already serving a thirty to fifty-year sentence for that conviction. Sue eventually agreed to the deal, as did Stuart.

Now having found Martha's body, Tucker knew he couldn't leave Sue alone. Sue Young also knew she couldn't be alone in her own home right now. Before the men left, he accompanied Sue to her neighbor's house. As Tucker left her with her close friend, Sue and her neighbor could only hug each other and sob.

After leaving Sue Young's house, the men drove the short distance to 1300 Basswood, and Kristine Stuart's husband Ernie met them at the door. Tucker told Stuart the same thing he had told Sue Young. Don Miller had led them to skeletal remains, and he believed they belonged to his wife Kristine. Kristine had been missing for almost a year. While they were certain the body belonged to the young school teacher, an autopsy would have to be conducted to confirm her identity. It was all that Ernie Stuart had hoped for. When the idea of a plea deal was first brought up, he quickly agreed to it, because the only thing he wanted was to have his wife back.

By 3:30 p.m., crime scene technicians from the MSP crime lab had arrived at the scene on Jason Road. Lab technicians Lincoln Gorsuch and Mike Sinke began processing the scene, with Westgate and Kelley helping them. Three more specialists from the MSP crime lab joined them.

The officers had realized by now that both bodies were located outside of Ingham County. Mike Woodworth, one of the Ingham County assistant prosecutors, left and headed north into St. Johns to look for the Clinton County prosecutor. Unable to find him, a call was made to Clinton County Sheriff Tony Hufnagel to let him know about the discoveries. Hufnagel knew the Clinton County medical examiner was out of town, so he agreed to act as the assistant medical examiner and handle both scenes so the bodies could be removed and taken to the morgue.

At 4:45 p.m., Sheriff Hufnagel arrived at the Stuart homicide scene along with two Clinton County assistant prosecutors, and after viewing the remains, he authorized the removal of the body to Sparrow Hospital for an autopsy.

By 7:30, both crime scenes had been processed by the MSP, and the remains of both Martha Sue Young and Kristine Stuart had been recovered. Martha's body was placed in a body bag, but because Kristine's bones were somewhat scattered, they were placed in a large paper bag, then unceremoniously secured in the trunk of an East Lansing police car. They were turned over to Sgt. Kelley, and he transported them to Sparrow Hospital, where they were locked in the morgue until the autopsy.

On July 14, Dr. Ron Horowitz prepared for both autopsies.

Before the start of Martha Sue Young's autopsy, Dean Tucker had already told Dr. Horowitz that Don Miller had admitted to strangling her.

As the autopsy started, Dr. Horowitz described the contents of the body bag as a skull, mandible, axial skeleton, and right and left upper and lower extremities. He noticed there were some missing finger and toe bones. The doctor began a very methodical look at what laid before him. He couldn't find any fractures in the bones or any penetrating or cutting injuries that might be consistent with the person being stabbed to death.

As part of the autopsy, the pathologist had asked two research assistants from the Michigan State University Department of Anthropology to assist him. As the two assistants looked over the bones, they came to a joint conclusion: the victim was a white female in her mid-twenties; she stood between five-feet-two-inches to five-feet-four-inches in height and had not been pregnant. The remains also showed no signs of trauma.

Dr. Horowitz had another specialist in oral and maxilla facial surgery assisting in the identification of the remains. Dr. Edmond Hagen examined the existing dental records of Martha Sue Young and compared them with the post-mortem dental records he had before him. Hagen was able to positively identify the remains as Martha Sue Young.

Dr. Horowitz couldn't find any evidence of disease or trauma, so his opinion was consistent with the history he had been given by Lt. Tucker. Martha Sue Young had died of strangulation.

After the first autopsy was done, lab assistants removed two paper bags from the cooler and placed them on the stainless steel table. Dr. Horowitz knew he wouldn't be able to perform any toxicological studies because there wasn't enough suitable tissue left on the remains.

Lt. Tucker gave the pathologist some historical information about Kristine Stuart regarding her disappearance, and statements made by Don Miller that he had strangled her.

As the two large paper bags were unsealed and opened, clear plastic bags containing several parts of a human skeleton were found inside. The investigators at the scene had placed the remains inside the plastic bags before putting them into the paper bags.

In one bag, the pathologist found a pelvis with a portion of vertebra attached to it. Still attached to the pelvis and vertebrae was a nine-inch-by-seven-inch mass of brown, leather-like mummified human tissue. The doctor could see maggots, worms, and insects on the remaining tissue.

Dr. Horowitz was going to rely on the two anthropology research assistants to establish the race, sex, and age of the victim, and both assistants agreed the victim was a female in her mid-twenties to mid-thirties who had stood between five-feet-two-inches to five-feet-five-inches. The two assistants were unable to establish a race of the victim, but they agreed that a previous pregnancy was likely based on the change to the left pubic bone of the skeleton.

As the pathologist examined the bones with the research assistants, he noticed a fracture across the lower vertebrae. Looking closer, he could see there was no evidence of the fracture ever having healed, and he found several faint cut marks on the victim's third and fourth left ribs. Like the fracture across the lower back, there weren't any signs of healing above those cut marks.

Once again, Dr. Hagen was asked to compare the existing dental records of Kristine Stuart with the dental x-rays taken during the autopsy, and he confirmed the remains were those of Kristine Stuart.

Much like Martha Sue Young's case, Dr. Horowitz was unable to determine an exact cause of death, but based on the historical information he had been given by Lt. Tucker, he opined that Kristine Stuart was also strangled. He also believed that she had been stabbed, and the fracture in the lower back was consistent with her having been struck by an automobile at or near the time of her death.

Two days after the bodies of Martha Sue Young and Kristine Stuart were found, Don Miller sat quietly in his cell at Jackson Prison while paperwork was drawn up so he could be taken to Wyandotte General Hospital near Detroit. Psychiatrist Dr. Gerald Briskin was waiting for him, and Miller would undergo regressive psychotherapy a second time. Having done so at the prison just three days before, he had confessed to the murders of Young and Stuart. This time, an effort was under way to see if Miller had any knowledge about the murder of Marita Choquette, whose body had been found near Okemos the previous year. She had worked on the Michigan State University campus.

There was also suspicion that Miller was linked to the disappearance of Wendy Bush, another MSU coed. She had been reported missing on the same day that Marita Choquette's body was found. The police hoped for a chance to link the deaths of Martha and Kristine to the deaths of Marita and Wendy.

At three p.m., the phone rang in Lt. Tucker's office. It was Harry Tift, and he had gotten a call from Dr. Briskin. Briskin told Tift that under regressive psychotherapy, Miller had confessed to killing Marita.

The following morning, Mike Woodworth stood with Harry Tift in the same room with Don Miller and his attorney at Wyandotte General Hospital. They were there to see if, after another session of regressive psychotherapy, Miller would confess to the murder of Wendy Bush. He had denied knowing Wendy Bush and denied having any knowledge of her disappearance.

Woodworth looked at Miller and told him he was going to have to find another job. Miller asked why. "They only hired me to work on these cases, and now that they're solved, they'll probably get rid of me." Miller looked puzzled, and

Woodworth was sly. He looked at Miller and told the killer he was going to charge him with Wendy Bush's murder. Miller's eyes widened as he turned toward Tift and asked if he could do that.

Tift replied, "He's crazy."[4]

Bengston and his client retreated to the therapy session. After some time, the doctor returned to the room where Woodworth and Tift were waiting. "He says he knows Wendy Bush, but he didn't kill her," the doctor said.[5] Tift and Woodworth looked at each other. They now knew beyond any doubt that Miller had killed the blonde coed. In the follow-up session, Miller admitted to killing her, and he agreed to take them to her body.

By 9:45 a.m. the following morning, many of the same investigators who had discovered Martha and Kristine's bodies met in Wyandotte and had Miller in a car heading back toward Lansing. They were confident he would follow through and lead them to Wendy Bush's body, just as he had led them to Martha Sue Young and Kristine Stuart. Since Wendy Bush had been reported missing from the MSU campus, Sgt. Larry Lyons from the MSU Department of Public Safety also joined the team.

Miller directed the caravan to Broadbent Road in Eaton County's Delta Township. They stopped at the intersection of Huckleberry Lane. Less than two hundred feet from the intersection was a trail leading to the southwest, and the start of it was hidden by a large pile of underbrush. Just as he had done a few days before, the killer directed them toward the trail. There were kids playing in the area, and they were told to leave.

Wendy Bush's skeleton laid only thirty-five feet from the start of the trail. Woodworth could see bright blonde hair glistening in the sunlight as they walked toward the remains.

---

4. Michael Woodworth, July 18, 2018
5. Michael Woodworth, July 18, 2018

As they got closer, reality quickly set in. The blonde hair was still affixed to a skull. They had found Wendy Bush.

The coed's skeleton was lying next to a fence row that separated the underbrush from a cultivated field. The skull was lying toward the south with her feet pointing to the north. Like Martha Sue Young and Kristine Stuart, some of Wendy's teeth had become separated from her skull.

The crime lab was called once again and two lab technicians were assigned. When they arrived, they diagrammed the location of the body. Wendy's remains were gathered and placed in a body bag, then taken to Sparrow Hospital for an autopsy.

A phone call was made to Mike Hocking, an assistant prosecutor in Eaton County, to let him know Wendy's body had been found in his jurisdiction. Hocking, who led the initial prosecution of Don Miller, was upset because his office hadn't been told the investigators were searching in Eaton County, and while he was angry, he was also relieved for the families of the all of the victims. He knew they would now have some closure, and he knew it provided an assurance knowing that Don Miller was the only person involved in all of the killings.

It was over. It had been a very long two and a half years as police searched for the missing women, hitting dead end after dead end. Now they had all been found, and police had confirmation Don Miller had killed them.

Since January of 1977, thousands of hours had been spent following leads, searching remote areas, and interviewing witness after witness in an attempt to locate Martha Young. A year and a half later, Marita Choquette, a student and employee on the MSU campus, was reported missing from the small town of Grand Ledge. Two weeks later, her body was discovered in a farm field. On the day Marita's body was found, Wendy Bush went missing from the MSU campus. Police had been unable to find her. Two months after Bush's disappearance, Ernie Stuart called the East Lansing Police to report his wife Kristine missing.

On August 16, two days after Kristine Stuart was reported missing, there was a sexual assault and attempted murder of a fourteen-year-old girl and her thirteen-year-old brother in Eaton County's Delta Township. That was the day Don Miller's reign of terror came to an end.

2

"Is your dad home?" the clean-cut young man asked. He walked from the kitchen and into the garage.

Fourteen-year-old Lisa Gilbert had noticed a brown car in the driveway as she walked around the house and came through the open garage door. She was used to an occasional contractor showing up to do finish work in the newly-built home. As she kicked off her tennis shoes inside the garage, she told him no.

"Do you know what time he'll be home?" the man asked.

"A quarter after six," Lisa replied.

Without hesitation the man asked, "Do you have anything to write his number so I can call him?"

Lisa started for the door leading into the house, saying, "Just a minute and I'll and get something." As she opened the screen door and walked in, he followed her.

The young teenager began to rummage for a pad of paper when she suddenly felt an arm around her throat. "Don't say anything," the man ordered. Gripped in fear, Lisa could see a knife in his right hand near her throat. He walked her into the living room, then began to lead her toward her parents' bedroom. Once inside the bedroom, he forced her to the floor, saying, "Lay down on your stomach and put your face on the ground."[6]

He left her alone for only a moment as he stepped back into the living room. Lisa heard the front door lock.

---

6. Eaton County Sheriff's Department, Statement by Lisa Gilbert, 78-2654-C, August 16, 1978

When he came back in the bedroom, he knelt next to her and took off her tank top and bra, tying her hands behind her back with nylons he had taken from the closet. Using a necktie he had also gotten from the closet, he gagged her so she couldn't scream and put her tank top over her head so she couldn't see. He groped her for a few minutes, then rolling her over onto her back, he took her shorts and panties off before tying her feet together with a second necktie. After restraining his young victim, he rolled her back onto her stomach and began groping her again. She heard the sound of a zipper and could suddenly feel the weight of his body across her entire back.

The rape was over very quickly. While Lisa was lying face down on the carpeted floor, he straddled her legs and rubbed her back. She could still feel his weight on top of her when she suddenly felt something around her throat. It felt like the thin belt she had been wearing around her shorts. She gasped for air. With her hands still bound behind her back and the man on top of her, she couldn't move. The belt tightened even more. She couldn't breathe. As she tried to struggle, blood vessels in her eyes began to rupture and her nose began to bleed from the pressure of being strangled. Her vision began to blur as she started to fade into unconsciousness. The man pulled the two ends of the belt tighter. Suddenly, it snapped into two pieces. A rush of air filled Lisa's lungs as she gasped. At the same time, she heard the back door that led from the garage to the house open. She instantly knew it was her brother Randy.

Life for the two Gilbert kids wasn't as they had planned. As the two youngest of six kids, they were the victims of their parents' divorce three years earlier. Their father had remarried, and because he had a steady job and a new wife, a court order gave custody of Randy and Lisa to him. After the new marriage, they moved from Mason to Eaton County's Delta Township on the west side of Lansing. Even with his father building a new home on Canal Road south of St. Joe Highway, Randy didn't want to be there. He wanted to be with his friends back in Mason, so he was a difficult student at school; not because he was a trouble maker, but because he just didn't care, and his grades were poor.

As the summer break of 1978 was coming to an end, he wasn't looking forward to starting the eighth grade at Hayes Middle School while his sister was going to start her freshman year at Grand Ledge High School.

The typical brother-sister rivalry was evident in everything they did, and Randy spent most of his summer outside. Finding new friends, riding his bike, and fishing in the pond behind the new house were everyday occurrences.

Along with spending most of his summer outside, he and Lisa still had chores each day. Like other kids their age, taking the trash out, setting the dinner table, and a myriad of other menial tasks were required. Each day at 3:15 p.m. they were required to call their stepmom at Michigan State University to let her know they were okay.

On this particular day, Lisa had left the house and walked out back near the pond to yell for Randy. Their stepmom would be expecting a call soon. Randy never heard Lisa yell for him. Something told him it was time to head for home.

It took a few minutes as Randy made his way back toward the house with his fishing pole. He walked around the front and in through the open garage door. Setting his fishing gear down, he walked into the house, through the kitchen, and into the living room when he met a man walking out of his parents' bedroom. The man had a knife in his hand. Although it seemed a little suspicious to the thirteen-year-old, like his sister Lisa, he assumed it was another contractor working on the house.

The man greeted Randy, saying, "Hi. How are you?" He walked directly toward Randy, then circled behind him and quickly grabbed him. The man held the knife to his throat. "I'm not going to hurt you. Where's your bedroom?" The thin teen was paralyzed with fear, but he was able to tell him the bedroom was upstairs. "Show me," the man demanded.[7]

He began to force Randy up the stairs to the second floor, but Randy decided he wasn't going willingly. He began to kick at the intruder, and the man fell backward briefly before regaining his footing and charged back up toward Randy. He took control of the boy again, forcing him into his own bedroom. Pushing him to the floor, the man sat on Randy's back and twisted the young teen's arm behind his back. Suddenly, Randy could feel the cold steel of the knife blade slicing into his neck, and he began screaming as he realized the man was trying to cut his throat. Randy tried to fight back. By now, his arms were free, and out of sheer terror, he was able to grab the knife and throw it under one of the twin beds in his room. The would-be killer quickly grabbed the teen around his neck and began strangling him from behind as he sat on the boy's back. Fighting for air, Randy continued to struggle, but the man's grip was too tight. As he fought for breath, his mind was racing, and he thought if he played dead, the man would stop, but it was too late. Randy began to see white lights as his vision quickly faded, and he passed out.

The intruder wasn't sure if he had completed his task. Grabbing the knife from under the bed, he stabbed the unconscious teen in his chest to ensure he was dead.

As Lisa lay dazed and alone on the first floor in her parents' bedroom, she was able to shake the tank top off from her head and loosen the bindings on her feet. The necktie

---

7. Eaton County Sheriff's Department, Statement by Randy Gilbert, 78-2654-C, August 16, 1978

used to secure a gag in her mouth had fallen around her neck. She quickly garnered enough strength to try to hide. She made her way to the bathroom in a futile attempt to hide under the counter. She quickly changed her mind. Hearing Randy screaming, she thought she might have enough time to escape. Still nude, with her hands bound behind her and blood running down her face, she made her way from the bedroom to the front door. Even with her hands bound, she was able to unlock the door. Terrified beyond anything she had ever experienced, she ran screaming from the house.

The new home sat on the west side of Canal Road just south of St. Joe Highway in Delta Township. The blue two-story Cape Cod with black shutters had a concrete drive that circled toward the side-entry garage, then back around to connect with the main drive. A basketball hoop stood at the edge of an extension to the driveway near the house for the young teens to pass the time.

The home was new enough that the front lawn had been seeded with grass but straw still covered a large part of it, while dirt was the only thing visible on the north side of the house.

Doug and Donna Gilbert had moved into the home with their small family only two months before. It was the only home in the stretch of Canal Road between St. Joe Highway and the I-496 overpass. Farm fields, woods, and swampy areas surrounded the house.

James Regan normally left from the Oldsmobile plant in Lansing at three p.m. But today it was only 2:45, and he had a dentist appointment. As he was getting ready to leave, he noticed an oil stain on his shirt. Not wanting to go to the dentist with the visible stain, he decided to go home and change before heading to the dentist, so he left work early.

As he turned south on Canal Road in his green three-quarter ton Chevy pickup, James Regan drove the one mile to the first stop sign on St. Joe Highway. As he came to a stop, then started through the intersection, the car ahead of him quickly braked as it neared a blue house on the west side of Canal Road. His eyes quickly focused on someone running. The person had run from the blue house. Regan was stunned when he realized it was a teenage girl, and she was nude. The car ahead of him sped up as he started to slow. Trying to comprehend what was going on, his gaze was fixed on the girl as she ran into the roadway and toward his truck, screaming. He could see she had something tied around her throat, and her hands were tied behind her back. Regan could also see blood on her face and down the front of her body as he slowed even more and she ran up to his truck screaming, "Help me! Help me! There's a man in there trying to kill my brother."

James Regan was trying to understand what she was saying. "What? What's going on?" he asked.

"He's in there trying to do something to my brother. My brother's in there. Somebody's trying to kill him!" she screamed. She was pleading with him now. "Get my brother."[8] The hysterical teen took off running, continuing northbound.

Regan could see a red car coming toward him. As the car slowed next to him, Regan yelled to the driver, "Cover her up and get her in your car." Without any hesitation, he stepped on the accelerator and pulled his pickup truck into the driveway as his tires squealed. He stopped behind

---

8. Eaton County Sheriff's Department, Statement by James Regan, 78-2654-C, August 16, 1978

a brown Oldsmobile parked in the drive, jumped from his truck, and started toward the house.

As Regan reached the small concrete front porch, a young man came walking out as if nothing were amiss. He was wearing sunglasses, and he casually slipped his hands into his pockets.

"Is there a little boy in the house?" Regan demanded.

"Yeah, I guess so," the man replied.

"Where is he?"

Keeping his cool, the man answered, "I guess he's upstairs."

Pressing him further, the Olds supervisor asked if he was all right.

"Yeah, I guess he's all right. Why shouldn't he be? I was looking for a fellow here."

Regan was anxious now when he said, "I don't know. I want to see him. You better wait right here until the police get here."[9]

As Regan took a step forward, the man jumped off the porch and ran by him. It took only a split second for Regan to realize he was trying to escape, and he turned to go after him. The man had a one-second advantage as he got into the brown Olds Cutlass and locked the doors just as Regan reached the car. Regan pulled furiously on the door handle, trying to get it open. The driver turned the ignition, threw the car into reverse, and turned the wheel as he backed up, hitting Regan with the side of the car in the process. He then sped forward, out around the basketball hoop, across the dirt in the front yard and south on Canal Road. Regan was able to see the license plate number and began repeating it out loud so he wouldn't forget it.

James Regan still knew there was a boy in the house, and he went in the front door to look for him. As he walked in, he saw a teenage boy standing near the center of the living

---

9. Eaton County Sheriff's Department, James Regan, August 16, 1978

room. He had come down from upstairs and was covered in blood. He was holding his right hand over the left side of chest, and Regan could see blood oozing from between his fingers.

"He hurt me," the boy said.

Trying to calm the bleeding teen, Regan reassured him, "He's gone, and there's going to be help here in a moment."[10] He helped lay the boy down in the vestibule and tried searching for a phone in the living room. Unable to locate one, he went back out into the front yard to try to find help.

Just as James Regan had seen the nude girl run from the house, Delta Township Fire Chief Ken Dorin was driving northbound on Canal. As he crested the overpass to I-496, he saw the young girl run from the driveway at the house and north in the southbound lane toward a green pickup. He could see her hands were bound behind her back, and after only a brief moment, she continued running north. Dorin was in his red 1977 Olds Cutlass fire chief's car equipped with a two-way radio, and as he slowed next to the green pickup, he heard the driver yell at him to get the girl into his vehicle, so Dorin pulled to the side of the road and yelled to get her attention.

She ran to Dorin's window screaming, "Oh my God. Help me. Help me. I've been raped."

While he didn't know her first name, he recognized her and knew her last name was Gilbert. Because her hands were tied behind her and she couldn't open the door, Dorin quickly helped her into his car and tried to calm her down. The hysterical teen pleaded with Dorin, "Please help me.

10. Eaton County Sheriff's Department, James Regan, August 16, 1978

There's a man in there stabbing my brother." The chief grabbed his radio and called for a deputy.

Chief Dorin had the young girl lean forward so he could loosen the bindings, but they were knotted too tight. As the chief desperately tried to free her, she glanced back over her shoulder.

"There he is!" she screamed. Dorin looked back at the house and could see two men standing near the driveway in the yard. One of the two was James Regan. He asked her which man it was and she quickly said, "The one in the green shirt."[11]

Dorin again tried to free Lisa's hands from behind her back, and then glanced back again as the brown Cutlass raced across the dirt in the front yard and sped out of the yard, heading south on Canal toward the I-496 overpass. Dorin grabbed his radio and called for an ambulance as another car pulled up behind him. Not realizing Regan had seen the license plate on the car, he told the driver to try to follow the Cutlass and get a license plate number. The fire chief quickly got back into his car and turned it around, pulling up to the driveway of the house. Another car was stopping behind Dorin's now. The chief moved Lisa to the second car because the driver knew who she was. As he did, James Regan approached Dorin and said, "This is the license number." Regan had it written on his hand. Chief Dorin had a small box with a shower head in it he had picked up from a surplus store in Lansing, and it was the first thing he could grab to write the license plate number down. He wrote GMV588 on a piece of masking tape across the corner of the box and headed for the house.

---

11. Eaton County Sheriff's Department, Statement by Ken Dorin, 78-2654-C, August 16, 1978

Only a moment behind James Regan, Barb Krapf and her daughter Cheryl were southbound on Canal Road, and Cheryl immediately recognized her friend Lisa Gilbert as she ran nude up Canal. She was screaming for help as Barb passed her. She could see the Delta Township fire chief trying to get Lisa safely into his car. Mrs. Krapf looked over at the Gilbert house and saw a green truck parked behind a brown Cutlass in the driveway and two men standing outside the vehicles. She stopped, got out of her car, and asked what was going on. The young man wearing a green shirt and sunglasses shrugged his shoulders and said, "I don't know." At the same time, Regan turned and yelled for her to go get the girl.

Barb Krapf quickly retreated and helped Dorin put Lisa into her car.

Lisa was still hysterical as Barb desperately tried to untie the nylons knotted around her wrists. As Mrs. Krapf continued to struggle with the bindings, the panicked teen kept saying, "He choked me. He choked me. He tried to kill me."[12]

It was only a moment after the suspect had fled the house when help began to arrive. As paramedics went to help Dorin, Regan came back from the house. Even though he had asked Dorin to write down the license number, he asked Mrs. Krapf to write down the number too. She grabbed a picture packet envelope in her car and wrote the number down. Regan, seeing Lisa's hands were still bound, took his pocket knife and cut the nylons off her wrists. Barb's daughter Cheryl said, "Here, Mom. We'll dress her with this."[13] She quickly grabbed some clothes from the back seat of their car. Mrs. Krapf took the brown polka dot necktie that had been used to gag Lisa from around her

12. Eaton County Sheriff's Department. Original police report. Statement by Barb Krapf. 78-2654-C. August 16, 1978
13. Eaton County Sheriff's Department. Original police report. Statement by Cheryl Krapf. 78-2654-C. August 16, 1978

neck and removed it. She laid it on the front seat and, in the chaos, forgot about it.

———————

Dave Bankhead considered himself a professional part-time student. The young deputy had only been with the Eaton County Sheriff's Department for two years, and he was attending Lansing Community College in hopes of getting his associate degree. He knew if he could get the degree, he'd get a four percent educational bonus in his salary.

Eaton County was made up of sixteen separate townships. The Eaton County Jail was in the small town of Charlotte, which served as the county seat. In the northeast corner of the county sat Delta Township, a fast-growing area on the west side of Lansing, and because of the township population, the sheriff's department had a substation with several deputies assigned to work out of an office in the Delta Township Fire Station on Canal Road at Saginaw Highway. Bankhead was one of them.

Working in the fire station like the other deputies, Bankhead had become friends with all of the firefighters, including Fire Chief Ken Dorin, whose office was adjacent to the sheriff's substation office.

On August 16, the sky was overcast as the deputy drove eastbound on St. Joseph Highway east of Creyts Road. There had been a heavy rain earlier in the morning, and the clouds had remained throughout the rest of the day. It wasn't unusually busy, and the occasional shoplifting call or accident took up his normal day-to-day routine. There were two other deputies patrolling the township, and each of the three was assigned to a specific district.

As Bankhead continued east approaching Snow Road, he heard the static of his radio and the dispatcher's voice sending him to an unknown trouble call on Canal Road south of St. Joe Hwy. He was just a little over two miles away. He'd been to similar calls like this over his short two-year career, and it typically involved a request for extra manpower to help carry a patient out of a house or some other mundane task.

Bankhead turned the black-and-white Pontiac Grand Prix around and began to speed up slightly. He wasn't breaking the sound barrier as he approached Creyts Road and flipped on the two single red-and-blue overhead lights and siren as he went through the intersection. His radio squawked again as the dispatcher asked him what his arrival time would be. He grabbed the microphone and replied he was a minute or so away. Even with his close proximity to the call, the dispatcher told him to step it up. Dave Bankhead knew there was trouble.

As the deputy turned south onto Canal Road, he could see the only house on the west side of the road, quickly taking note of a green pickup in the driveway and the cars stopped in front of the home. As he pulled up along the side of the roadway behind the line of cars, Dorin came from the house and toward Bankhead. The first thing he said was there had been a rape, and he wanted Bankhead to see how the young girl was tied. The deputy could see the hysterical young teen in the back seat of Barb Krapf's car, and he could see a necktie around her throat. He also noticed her eyes were extremely bloodshot, and her face was an unusual deep reddish color.

Bankhead looked toward the house and saw James Regan walking in circles in the front yard, and beyond what Dorin had just told him, he was trying to process everything that was happening. Regan came over and quickly gave Bankhead the license plate number, then told him there was a young boy who had been stabbed in the house. Bankhead ran toward the house. He found Randy Gilbert lying half in, half out of the front door. He tried to reassure the boy help was on the way, but the deputy really wasn't sure Randy Gilbert would survive before help arrived. Deputy Bankhead could hear the sirens from the ambulance and other police units getting closer, but out of sheer adrenalin, he still checked with the dispatcher to make sure help was on the way.

As the Delta Township ambulance pulled up, so did Deputy Mike Raines and Deputy Bob Placer. Dorin started to help the bleeding teen in the front door with the help of arriving paramedics as Bankhead and Raines quickly checked the interior of the house to make sure there weren't any more victims. The two deputies could see blood on the stairway leading to the second floor, and evidence of a struggle in the bedroom on the first floor. They sealed off the home so no one else could enter. With each piece of new information, Bankhead was able to start piecing things together, and he radioed the license plate number to the dispatcher in Charlotte. A moment later, the dispatcher radioed back telling him the car was registered to a Don G. Miller. To Dave Bankhead, at that particular moment in a very chaotic scene, it was only a name linked to a license plate.

At the Eaton County Sheriff's Department in Charlotte, Detective Jerry Woods was assigned to dispatch because he was recuperating from a back injury. The dispatch area was in the main lobby of the long, two-story brick building. Bars were clearly visible in the second-story windows, and the building sat adjacent to the old three-story courthouse at the corner of Lawrence and Cochran, which was still being used. A desk sergeant sat behind a sliding glass window with the dispatcher and whoever was assigned there on any particular day.

After a quick computer check, Woods knew immediately who the registered owner of the car was. He radioed the registration information to Bankhead, and hearing the deputy acknowledge him, he radioed a second time asking, "Do you know who you're dealing with there?"

Bankhead hadn't made the connection.

Woods quickly responded, "Martha Sue Young case."[14]

Like an epiphany, it suddenly became clear. Dave Bankhead had been following the media reports of the missing MSU coed for almost two years. He also knew suspicion in her disappearance had fallen on the young woman's boyfriend. His name was Don Miller.

Back at the house, as Chief Dorin leaned over the bleeding teen lying in the front doorway, he recognized the boy. It was Randy Gilbert, and now he remembered that the young girl was his sister Lisa. Randy had gone on a camping trip to the northern Michigan town of Grayling with Dorin and some others, and the chief had taken some stitches out of Randy's leg while he was there.

As Randy laid in the front door to the house, he held his hand over two stab wounds in his chest, and Dorin had his hand on top of Randy's. He was trying to stem the flow of blood from the boy's chest. The boy's entire shirt and much of his legs were covered in blood.

Trying to calm him, Chief Dorin asked, "Randy, what did you get yourself into this time?" It was a light hearted effort, and it seemed to work.

The boy calmed down as he recognized the chief. Not knowing the intruder had already retrieved the knife and fled, Randy told Dorin, "Chief, the knife is under the bed."[15]

By 3:11 p.m., only five minutes after Bankhead's arrival, the Eaton County Sheriff's Department had broadcast their first message over the radio and by computer to other area police agencies. The message read:

---

14. David Bankhead, Interview by author, Charlotte, MI, September 1, 2017

15. Eaton County Sheriff's Department, Ken Dorin. August 16, 1978

This department at this time investigating a rape and stabbing in Delta Twp of our county. Suspect vehicle left the scene southbound on Canal Rd from St Joe Hwy and is described as a maroon vehicle possible license GMV 588 78 Michigan registered to Don G Miller 530 Gainsborough East Lansing on 73 Olds 2 door. Stabbing victim is a male and rape victim female. Suspect only described as white male at this time. If vehicle located stop and hold or this department [sic].[16]

―――――――――

Fifteen miles to the southwest, Assistant Prosecuting Attorney Mike Hocking sat in his office in the newly-built Eaton County Courthouse. Norm Kelley, a detective with the Eaton County Sheriff's Department, sat across the desk from him as the two discussed a case. The building sat a mile from the old courthouse in downtown Charlotte and had only recently opened. It was so new even the courtrooms hadn't been finished. Court sessions were still held at the old courthouse downtown.

Hocking had been sworn in as an assistant prosecutor on January 1, 1977. It was the same day a Michigan State University coed was reported missing in the nearby town of East Lansing. Hocking and his colleagues were briefed regularly about that investigation and the investigation into the death of another woman who had been found murdered near Okemos in June. Her name was Marita Choquette, and she had been reported missing from Grand Ledge in Eaton County.

Mike Hocking's boss, Eaton County Prosecutor Paul Berger, was out of the office when Hocking's phone rang.

―――――――――――――――

16. Eaton County Sheriff's Department. Original police report. 78-2654-C. August 16, 1978

It was Jan Fisher, one of the dispatchers from the sheriff's department. She told the assistant prosecutor, "We've had a stabbing and attempted rape in Delta Township. Uniforms are on the scene. A witness got the license plate and the plate comes back to Donald Miller."[17]

When Kelley overheard, he was on his feet. "I've gotta go," he told Hocking, and he headed for his car.[18]

As the only attorney in the prosecutor's office who had a degree in criminal justice, Hocking was deeply committed to law enforcement. He not only wanted to be there, he knew he had to be. As he left the office, he told the other attorneys about the assault, and that the sheriff's department needed him there. He knew the part about being needed was a fib, but he wanted to be the one handling the case.

He didn't waste any time in driving the fifteen miles from Charlotte to the house in Delta Township. When he arrived at the scene, smoke was pouring from under the hood of his 1974 Cadillac Coupe de Ville, and one of the deputies thought the car might actually be on fire.

The young attorney had arrived before the state police crime lab technicians. Hocking found Norm Kelley, and the two quickly discussed what was known up to that point. Hocking wanted to talk with the witness, James Regan. The discussion between Kelley and Hocking turned to the possibility of showing a photo of Don Miller to Regan. Hocking knew if Regan wasn't able to identify Miller from a photograph, there would be no harm. If Regan did identify him, Hocking would have to prove in court that there was an independent basis for the identification. Hocking finally had the chance to speak with Regan, and James Regan described Don Miller to a T. Hocking decided to have Kelley show him a photo of Miller.

17. G. Michael Hocking, Interview by author, Lansing, MI, October 18, 2017

18. Norm Kelley, Interview by author, Charlotte, MI, December 5, 2018

Kelley knew James Regan was a key witness. He wanted a taped interview from Regan and wanted to show him photos of Miller in hopes he could positively identify him. Knowing East Lansing Police were leading the investigation into Martha Young's disappearance, Kelley contacted the agency and asked for photos of Miller before he left the scene with Regan.

The detective and the Olds supervisor left the house on Canal Road and drove to Colonial Village in Lansing where they met with Officer Benson from the ELPD. He gave some pictures to Kelley, and the two men left and headed toward the Delta Township substation at Delta Fire.

When Kelley's interview with James Regan was almost complete, he showed the pictures to Regan. There was no doubt in Regan's mind when he immediately identified Miller as the man who fled the Gilbert home. At about the same time Kelley was showing him the pictures, Don Miller was being arrested in East Lansing.

At the East Lansing Police Department, nine miles from the scene of the assault, Officer Rick Westgate heard the police radio broadcast about the rape and attempted murder in Eaton County, and like Detective Woods, he recognized Don Miller's name immediately. He knew Miller was the prime suspect in the disappearance of Martha Young. Along with Lieutenant Dean Tucker, Westgate had been working on Young's disappearance since January of 1977. After the radio broadcast, Tucker called Westgate and told him Miller had a new girlfriend who lived in the Edgewood Apartments north of Lake Lansing Road. Several other officers were already on the way to watch for Miller at his parents' home on Gainsborough Street in East Lansing, so

Westgate headed toward the Edgewood Apartments. Tucker also headed toward the apartments.

Westgate parked his car so he could watch the east side of the apartments. He hadn't been there long when he saw a brown Olds Cutlass at the intersection of Hardy Avenue and Raindrop. He knew immediately it was Miller. He had seen Miller's car numerous times. He grabbed the microphone to his car radio to let Tucker know and call for backup. In a split second, Westgate made the decision not to wait. He was not going to risk Miller escaping. As he pulled in behind Miller's Olds Cutlass, Westgate drew his gun as he stepped from the car. Identifying himself as a police officer, he ordered Don Miller to get out of his car.

Don Miller slowly opened the driver's door. "What's going on?" he asked. Westgate ordered him to face the vehicle with his hands on the top of car, and Miller persisted in his query, asking, "What's this for?"[19]

Officer Westgate was anxious as he shouted for Miller to spread his feet apart. As the suspect was moving his feet, Tucker pulled up with another officer from East Lansing and a detective from the Michigan State University Police. Tucker and the other officers drew their guns to cover Miller while Westgate approached him and handcuffed him. Before saying anything else to their prisoner, Westgate read Miller his Miranda rights, loaded him in the back of a police car, and drove him to the ELPD. It was a moment Westgate and Tucker had waited for over the past year and a half.

As Westgate left with the suspect in custody, Tucker knew the importance of preserving the car as evidence. There could be crucial evidence inside that could tie him to the Eaton County rape, or other cases across mid-Michigan. One of the officers called for a wrecker and Miller's car

19. East Lansing Police Department. Original Police Report. Assist. 2390-C-78. August 16, 1978

was impounded and towed to the East Lansing City Garage where it was held until it could be moved to Eaton County.

Less than two hours after Lisa and Randy Gilbert were viciously attacked in their own home, the man who would later become known as East Lansing's serial killer was in custody.

3

Along the Red Cedar, a lazy river stretching across two mid-Michigan counties, sits what was once known as the State Agricultural College.

In 1849, the Michigan Agricultural Society's goal was to establish an agricultural college in the state, and the society's secretary, John Clough Holmes, crafted a bill for the Michigan legislature to do just that. He travelled to Lansing from Detroit and spent a month pushing the bill through both houses. Governor Kinsley Bingham signed the bill in 1855. There were two stipulations: the cost per acre couldn't exceed fifteen dollars, and it had to be located within ten miles of Lansing. In an area east of Lansing, the first classes began at the college in May 1857.

By 1887, there were sixty-nine plots of land near the west end of the small campus, and the area was informally called Collegeville. It was intended for off-campus housing, and because of the eventual population growth in the area, the state granted a charter in 1907, establishing the city of East Lansing, which was one of the smallest in the state.

By 1909, the name of the higher educational institution was changed to the Michigan Agricultural College, and in 1925, the name was changed yet again to Michigan State College. Today, it's known as Michigan State University.

Nearly seventy-two years after the first classes, the National Crime Commission published a report emphasizing the need for better-trained police officers around the country. Michigan's own State Crime Commission (SCC) sent a delegation to the 1934 US Attorney's General Conference echoing the need for better law enforcement. Along with the Michigan State Police, the SCC was instrumental in pushing for a program to improve police professionalism, and it was decided that the program would be offered at the Michigan State College.

There were twenty-three freshman and a combination of eleven sophomores and juniors in the first School for Police Administration and Public Safety. The first three students graduated in 1938.

By the late sixties, given the air of protests against the government across the country, the word "police" seemed to denote a sense of hostility. MSU chose to rename their program in 1970 to the School of Criminal Justice. The degree program was one of the first in the entire country to offer police-community relations, industrial security, and traffic safety. Female enrollment had quadrupled by then, and overall, enrollment had continually risen since the late sixties.

Since the program's inception, there had been nearly three thousand graduates with students from all over the world. By the mid-seventies, a fundamental change had occurred in the program, and instead of requiring students to choose a specific career goal by their junior year, the school had adopted a generalist approach to their career path.

The MSU School of Criminal Justice had established itself nationally and was well-known and respected. It had become one of the oldest continuous professional programs in the country, focusing on criminal justice, and numerous graduates had proudly risen successfully to the highest levels in their profession, while one graduate would become a serial killer.

The neighborhood could only be described as modern suburbia in the mid-seventies. There were modest two-story homes with attached garages and neatly trimmed lawns accented with trees surrounding each home in a city with one of the wealthiest school systems in the entire state.

On the west side of the MSU campus, Harrison Road ran between the south end of campus northward to Lake Lansing Road. Intersecting with both Grand River Avenue and Saginaw Street along the way, it was a main artery for traffic. Only one half mile south of where Harrison intersected with Lake Lansing Road, Gainsborough Street ran east and west. Two blocks east of the intersection sat a well-kept home on the quiet residential street.

Born in 1954, Don Miller was the first of three kids born to Gene and Elaine, and to some, he appeared to be what every parent would dream of in a child. With two sisters, he was church-going and appeared sensible, serious and reserved, yet still sociable. His ideals were high, and some considered him a perfectionist. Having a closer-than-normal relationship with one of his sisters, he was content to be at home with the family rather than out with other kids his own age. He abhorred alcohol, didn't smoke, and never cursed.

His dad was a systems analyst with the Civil Service Department, and at one point had worked briefly with the Michigan Department of Corrections. His mom, Elaine, was a registered nurse and had been one of three nurses individually chosen to care for Ransom E. Olds. Taking leave of her career to raise her own kids, she had become a school crossing guard and a Scout den mother. Both of Don's parents had expectations for their children to be active in religion and humanitarian activities, and they were proud of their kids' accomplishments.

During the summer months, vacationing with the family, including his grandparents, wasn't uncommon. Don Miller's grandparents were like a second set of parents to Don, and occasional fishing trips with his dad and grandfather were part of his childhood. Don would often spend time on their farm, and the entire family would spend holidays together. A favorite summer activity was off-roading motorcycles with his dad.

His grandfather had come from a large family and was the oldest of nine children. Because of the number of brothers and sisters, he had been taken to an uncle's home to work for his keep, and he was beaten across the back to the point of leaving permanent scars. Leaving the uncle's farm, he walked barefoot back home, but his parents quickly returned him to the uncle. While his grandfather didn't have an education, by the time he had turned twelve, he was buying and selling horses. Having the chance to become bitter about his treatment as a young boy, Don Miller's grandfather had chosen to be a loving and tolerant father and grandfather and was very supportive of his own children and grandchildren.

Contrary to Don Miller's lifestyle, much of the previous generation was still prevalent in the early seventies.

At five-foot-nine and one hundred-sixty pounds, Miller was a quiet youth. He was conservative and deliberate in everything he did. Fellow students described him as introspective and said he often listened to spiritual jazz. Mixed with his devotion to God and his love of music, both seemed to offer him comfort. As a member of the Central United Methodist Church in Lansing, youth group activities were part of his routine, and at one point, he worked as a youth minister. He thrived on truthfulness, and according to one friend, over time his religion became dogmatic and was what one might expect from an elderly prelate with the zest of Billy Graham, but without the benevolence. Miller's religious beliefs were so strong that at a church group meeting, he once said it was necessary to test one's faith. He followed up on his statement by saying that if it was necessary, he would jump off a cliff, knowing that if his faith was strong enough, God would catch him.

As a high school student, he played first-chair trombone in the East Lansing High School Band, and was a rank leader in his section. Other students noticed he carried the instrument with him everywhere he went. The instrument was always at his side, and other students thought it was odd behavior.

Because of his ability to play the trombone, he attended Michigan's Blue Lake Fine Arts Camp, a 1,600-acre summer school for gifted musical students situated along Michigan's west coast during one summer break. When his parents visited, he surprised them during a performance when he played a solo of "I'd Like to Teach the World to Sing," a widely popular tune used in Coca-Cola advertising.

To most of his classmates, Don Miller was unassuming, and that's what made him noticeable. The gangly high school student's everyday attire consisted of a white shirt, dark pants, dark dress shoes, and white socks, while his hair was unstylishly short for the times, always greasy and slicked back.

Other than his foray into the high school band, the future serial killer led an undistinguished high school career. There was no senior picture in the yearbook, and his name was simply listed alphabetically. As a high school student, he was nothing more than a face in the crowd.

Close friends were few and far between. Bill Stoddard was a grade school friend of Miller's, and they were Boy Scouts together, in addition to going camping together. Miller eventually became an assistant Scout leader, and on one occasion when one of the Scouts called him to let him know he couldn't make it to a football game to raise the American flag, Miller began with a tirade of guilt on the younger Scout about God and country until the youth's dad took the phone, and the conversation ended abruptly.

After Don Miller's graduation in the spring of 1973, he started the fall curriculum at MSU, but he didn't declare a major. He auditioned for the MSU marching band in early '74 and showed up at the audition wearing a neatly-pressed shirt and dress pants, while other students wore faded blue jeans, t-shirts, and tennis shoes. He was teased about his dress, but he seemed tolerant of the ribbing. In fact, he seemed to be tolerant of everything that didn't follow his own beliefs, except religion.

By the summer of 1975, he declared Personal Administration as his major at MSU. By the fall term, he had changed it to Criminal Justice. His study habits were lacking, and cramming at the end of the semester became the norm for him. Spending time on music, art, and electronics were his preferred activities.

While being quiet and keeping to himself, Don Miller had taken notice of his sister's friend from their bible study at the church. She only lived a short distance from the Millers, and since they all attended the same church, the two families had become friends.

Born in Corpus Christi, Texas, Martha Sue Young had graduated from East Lansing High School in 1974. Early in Martha's life, she and her family had spent five years living in Lehore, Pakistan, where her father was assigned to help in building a hospital for the Methodist Board of Missions. Moving back to the United States in 1965, they settled back in Texas before moving to Michigan in late 1969, after her dad, Le, had found a job with an engineering firm in Lansing. As a young girl, Martha loved to brag about her family.[20]

After three years in Michigan, Sue and Le Young divorced, and Le moved back to Austin, Texas, while

20. Young, Sue, *Lethal Friendship*, iUniverse, 2004

Martha and her sister stayed in East Lansing with their mom.

At five-feet-five-inches tall and one hundred-twenty pounds, Martha Young's pretty face was highlighted by her shoulder-length brown hair and blue eyes. During her years at East Lansing High School, she was involved in a host of athletic activities, and she was also part of her church, in activities that included retreats and choir.

As her high school career came to a close, she had decided on Southwestern University in Georgetown, Texas, for her college education. The small school was close to her grandparents' home, and Martha had received a scholarship in addition to a work-program job. She couldn't turn down the offer, and she was looking forward to starting her collegiate years.

Enjoying her first year at Southwestern University, Martha made numerous friends and had made the Dean's List. She joined the Phi Mu sorority and became part of the French Honor Society, in addition to the school's student math group.[21]

During her return to Michigan for the summer, Don Miller, who had become fond of Martha, finally decided to ask her out, and the two began dating. A trip to the county fair in Ionia, Michigan, was their first outing as a couple. Teeming with people, the fair's midway was bustling with activity, and the smell of fair food permeated the entire grounds while carnival barkers shouted to lure patrons into games. Martha enjoyed every minute as she and Don rode the rides and talked. She was looking forward to him asking her out in the future.

After their first date to the county fair, it didn't take long for Martha to begin to wonder. Don would ask her out, but other than taking her to bible study, which she enjoyed, he never wanted to do anything more than that. Campus life

---

21. Young, Sue, 2004

was out of the question, as were movies and parties. There was so much more that the young coed wanted to do.

As the summer grew to a close, Martha headed back to Southwestern University to start her sophomore year, but there was still something missing. The young coed missed her mom and her sister, and she grew homesick. After each return visit to East Lansing, it became harder for her to return to Texas.

After Martha left for college, Don began to send her letters. It quickly became obvious he had a somewhat limited vocabulary and a hard time expressing himself. In his letters to his new girlfriend, he repeatedly used words like "wow" and "weird" with exclamation points. The letters were filled with small sketches of dark themes like crosses and graves, and were arbitrary, seemingly having nothing to do with whatever he was writing about. The letters were peppered with religious overtones, and there were numerous references to God.

Even before Martha had left Southwestern University, she had received letters from Don, and one letter upset her so much, she called her mom in tears. At some point prior, he had already asked her to marry him, and she had declined. In the letter, he told Martha it was "God's will" that they be married, and if she didn't, her family would "suffer horribly." Her mom tried to reassure her, and she suggested Martha simply throw away any future letters without opening them and to refuse any phone calls from him.[22]

Martha's mom knew she was homesick. Knowing she would lose her scholarship if she left Georgetown, Sue Young finally asked her daughter if she would rather finish her education back in Michigan, to which she quickly agreed. After finishing the spring term in 1976, Martha moved back home and was able to begin the fall term at

---

22. Young, Sue, 2004

Michigan State. Sue had asked if she wanted to live on campus, but her daughter insisted on living back at home in East Lansing.

After the move, it didn't take long for Martha to run into Don again. Even though the two of them weren't dating, Don asked if it was okay to still be friends. Never wanting to hurt him, Martha agreed. But slowly, over time, Don started showing up at the Young house without his sisters in tow.

In the summer of '76, he took a part-time job at the Murray Hotel on Mackinac Island, a tourist destination in northern Michigan. The correspondence with Martha began again, and she actually began looking forward to Don's return, even hoping he might introduce her to some other young men because she and Don were just friends now. She would be on the MSU campus, and since they had a simple friendship, maybe she could go to an occasional football game with him, or go out dancing, or take in a movie. Yet there was still something in the back of her mind about Don that bothered her.

In a peculiar letter Don wrote to Martha while he was working his summer job, he spoke of life on the island, and in the middle of the letter, he changed to the subject of a miracle. He described falling from a two-hundred-foot cliff on the island. He wrote, "It was about 200 feet down, but I miraculously landed safely." He then continued the letter, changing the subject without another mention of the "miracle."

In a separate letter, he wrote of his younger sister's visit to the island while he was working there, and how much he missed her. To Martha, the letter read as if he had reversed the role of girlfriend and sister.[23]

After Don's return, it wasn't as Martha had hoped. Nothing had changed. All he wanted to do was take her

23. Young, Sue, 2004

to bible study or come over to the house to sit with her. Martha wanted a social life, but Don was keeping her from it. He would show up at her classes and walk her to the next one, or show up at the library when she was studying and continually interrupt her.

To Martha, the Millers' lifestyle was so much different from what she knew. They never had guests over to their house, and she worried about Don spending so much time alone. He had told her the reason they seldom had guests was because their home was so messy.

Don continued his onslaught of affection to Martha by showering her with gifts, but the gifts were nothing more than curios from a discount store.

As the summer of the nation's bicentennial faded away, the vibrant fall colors Michigan is known for began to gleam in the sun. Unbeknownst to anyone else, Don Miller was slowly convincing Martha that their relationship was more than friendship. He persisted, again and again, until she slowly began to believe what he was saying. He had finally convinced her that by rejecting him, she would be rejecting God's plan for them.[24]

Kay, Martha's younger sister, knew better.

Three years younger than Martha, Kay and her sister loved to do things together as teens. If they weren't trying to eat an entire watermelon together, they were accidentally putting too much baking powder in their cookies and having to enlarge their recipe, but always seemed to stay out of trouble.

Kay could see through Don's charade. Normally, she was very quiet around the house, likely because Martha was so outgoing and gregarious. But when it came to her sister's boyfriend, she was outspoken and not afraid to make her feelings known. To her, Don Miller was an annoyance. When she was around him, she was seeing red. Kay had

24. Young, Sue, 2004

witnessed Miller's rage before: during a friendly snowball fight, and once as the young women teased him while he was driving. She sensed he was a ticking time bomb and never knew when he was going to explode. To Kay, the anger she witnessed was an anger meant to physically hurt someone. She didn't like Don Miller, and she knew he hated her.[25]

Sue Young sensed there was something wrong too, but she couldn't put her finger on it. He was always quiet and polite, yet he had an overbearing sense of religious conviction.

In late November, Don Miller came over to the Young home, but it wasn't simply to see Martha. He wanted to see Sue. Martha's mom was shocked when the quiet neighborhood boy asked her if he could marry her daughter.[26] On November 11, Don had gone to Zales in the Lansing Mall and picked out a 29-point yellow solitaire diamond ring. He put the two hundred-seventy-five dollar ring on layaway, and he came back the following day to pay the balance.

As Sue searched for words, Don told her the wedding would be in November of the following year. Much to Sue's surprise, Martha seemed excited about the proposal and accepted the engagement ring.

Martha's sister was more vocal about her disapproval. Even with Don nearby, she confronted her sister, asking Martha why she was going to marry him. She simply said, "Because he asked me." Kay tried to convince her sister to break off the engagement.

---

25. Young, Sue, 2004
26. Young, Sue, 2004

As the holiday season approached, a family friend from Pennsylvania had come to stay with Martha. Her parents had become friends of Sue Young and her ex-husband in the early sixties when they were missionaries in Pakistan.

Martha was excited her friend was visiting. As they enjoyed their time together, the holiday cheer continued to grow as they were planning to drive their friend back to Pennsylvania.

Once in Pennsylvania, the Youngs settled in for a short stay with their old friends. The family had three girls, and with Martha and Kay there, the five girls took over the basement of the home where they shared stories and laughter amongst themselves. They also shared their thoughts about Martha's impending marriage to Don Miller, and she began to have her doubts again.

On December 28, the return trip to East Lansing was delayed for a short time because of snow. As the roads began to clear, the Youngs headed out. After their return home, Kay already had plans to fly out the next day to see her father, and Martha had promised Don that she would go to a late birthday party for him at his grandparents' home. She didn't want to disappoint him.

After Kay's departure the following day, Martha finally had the chance to talk with her mom alone about the engagement. She could always count on her mom for another perspective.

Martha's concerns centered on reasons why she shouldn't marry Don. She was concerned about the way Don's dad treated his wife, thinking he didn't treat her with enough respect.

Martha loved to be around her friends, and she was concerned that her fiancé would cut off those friendships.

She explained to her mom that she had gone with Don to his best friend's house to ask him to be his best man at their wedding, yet the friend seemed shocked Don was asking him. While they had graduated together, Don hadn't seen him in three years.

Martha was also concerned that Don was twenty-two years old and had never had a real job. She wondered if she would have to work to support both of them after their marriage.

As the two women continued their discussion about her marriage reservations, Martha came to realization she should call off their engagement, but she wondered when would be the best time to tell him.[27]

With the next two evenings already planned with him at family parties, Martha didn't want to embarrass him, so her plan was to wait until the following week to tell him.

That Wednesday evening, Martha headed to the first party with Don. When she returned home, she told her mother she hadn't waited and had broken the engagement. She was surprised Don wasn't too upset, and he still wanted to stay friends with her, so she had agreed. She still planned to attend his belated birthday party the next night with him and all of his family.

It was New Year's Eve and there was excitement in the air. Sue Young needed to cash a one hundred-twenty-five dollar check for Martha before she headed out to go shopping and have lunch with a friend. The women sat at The Great Steak Restaurant in East Lansing when Martha stopped by. She was excited to show them the new shoes she had purchased to wear the following night, and she told her mom's friend of her plans to cook black-eyed peas the next day for good luck. Sue wanted to give her the money, but Martha was afraid she might lose it. She asked her mom to take it home and she would get it there.

27. Young, Sue, 2004

Martha had no plans for the evening. She simply planned to babysit for a young couple from church while they enjoyed a New Year's Eve dinner. Sue wasn't surprised when Don stopped by to pick her up and go with her to babysit. She knew they had remained friends after the engagement was called off two days earlier, and Don had told her to keep the engagement ring as a gift.

After leaving the couple's home, they stopped by Don's parents' home. They shared some pizza while watching the classic 1963 comedy movie *It's a Mad, Mad, Mad, Mad World*.[28]

As the two left the Miller home after the movie, it was bitterly cold outside.

———

Sue Young had gone to a late-night potluck dinner party with friends from church. It was a midnight dinner, and afterward, she toasted 1977 as the new year arrived. It was shortly after one a.m. when she arrived home to an empty house. Sue was surprised. She remembered Martha telling her she wouldn't be late, and that Don would drive her home after her church friends returned from dinner. Concerned, she thought about staying up until Martha returned home, or even calling the Millers to see if Martha had been there with Don. She decided against it, thinking that maybe her daughter had called to let her know she was going to be out later and discovered that her mom wasn't home yet.

It was almost two a.m. when Sue gave in and finally decided to lie down.[29]

The frigid night was a cold that only Michiganders could appreciate. With the temperatures hovering at eleven degrees, the snow crunched under the weight of passing car

28. Young, Sue, 2004
29. Young, Sue, 2004

tires. Sue was certain she would hear the sound of Don's car pulling into the drive to drop Martha off. She hadn't intended on falling asleep.

4

The only solace to a police officer starting a shift a 6:15 a.m. on New Year's Day when the temperature hovered at eleven degrees was the holiday pay. At the East Lansing Police Department, the dayshift was preparing for a bitter cold holiday morning with sixteen mile-per-hour winds that had been raging since before midnight.

Assigned to patrol, Officer Ken Ouellette had his briefcase in hand as he passed the front desk. The desk officer was missing, likely in the bathroom or grabbing a snack. The phone at the desk rang, and Ouellette reached for it. "East Lansing Police and Fire, Officer Ouellette," he said as he held the phone receiver to his ear with one hand while still holding his briefcase in the other. The officer, on the department for only two and a half years, immediately recognized the voice at the other end of the phone.

Ken Ouellette had graduated from East Lansing High School in 1970. Separate from his high school activities, he was part of a competitive rifle team, and Gene Miller was part of the same team. Both shot .22-caliber rifles from fifty feet in an indoor range.

Ouellette didn't care much for Gene's son Don, but in high school, still too young to drive, there were times when he couldn't get to a competition, so Gene Miller would swing by the Ouellette home on Durand Street and pick him up. Occasionally, Don would ride along and would sometimes shoot in the practice sessions. In the winter, they would practice at a shooting range in the basement of Demonstration Hall on the MSU campus, while in the summer they would go to the Capital City Rifle Club.

Don Miller was three years younger than Ken and also attended East Lansing High School. Ouellette knew of the sophomore because they were in the band together, but the future police officer considered Don nothing more than an acquaintance and didn't socialize with him at school. If they ran across each other at some sort of sporting event, they would simply exchange a "hi." To Ouellette, Don Miller was noticeable only because he was unremarkable. Wearing a white shirt and dark pants every day with dress shoes, Miller's hair was greased and combed over, and he always walked with his head tilted forward, looking down.

"Hi, Gene," Ouellette said.

Gene Miller had a serious tone to his voice when he said, "Martha didn't come home last night."

The young officer was puzzled. "Who's Martha?" he asked.

"It's Donny's girlfriend. She didn't come home last night," he repeated.[30]

Ouellette calmly asked what was going on.

Miller quickly told him they were at the Young home, and they had searched the house, but Martha wasn't there.

It was the officer's first call of the day. He jotted down the address and told the returning desk officer that he would run up to the Youngs' house and see what was going on since he knew Gene Miller.

The blue Ford Crown Vic patrol car was parked in the lot on the south side of the department. Ouellette loaded the briefcase into his car and headed to 1978 North Harrison

---

30. Kenneth Ouellette, August 22, 2017

Street. The car hadn't even warmed up by the time he arrived.

Working for the police department in a college town, it wasn't uncommon for the department to receive calls of students who hadn't returned from a night out on the town. Within a few hours after the initial "missing person" call was reported, the student would have returned, likely having slept a little late due to alcohol consumption, or a clandestine meeting with someone they were attracted to.

As Officer Ouellette headed north on Harrison, he thought to himself that he hadn't seen Don Miller since high school and that he hadn't shot competitively for three years.

Nearing Lake Lansing Road, he slowed as he checked for the address to the home along the east side of Harrison. Turning into the drive, he could hear the frozen snow crunching under his tires.

As he knocked on the door to the two-story home with large pillars across the front porch, he was greeted by a woman who had a look of deep concern and fear on her face. It was Sue Young. As Ouellette stepped inside the neat two-story home, he was greeted by Gene and Elaine Miller and their son Don. No one shook hands.

The mood inside the Young house was stoic. Don Miller stood emotionless as the young police officer began to ask questions about his missing fiancée. He didn't overtly offer information about where they had been the night before, but he didn't refuse to offer information when asked. The officer noted that he certainly wasn't being defensive.

Sue explained why the call had been made. Martha had been out the previous night babysitting for some friends, and Don was with her. She was supposed to be home at two a.m., but when Sue woke up at seven a.m., she checked Martha's bedroom, and her bed hadn't been slept in. She had quickly checked the house but she couldn't find Martha.

Fear gripped her. She knew something was dreadfully wrong.

Knowing the last person Martha was supposed to be with was Don, she had immediately called the Millers. Elaine had answered and Sue asked if Don was there. He was. She asked if Martha was there, and Elaine quickly said no.

Unadulterated terror gripped Sue Young. When Elaine told her her daughter wasn't there, it was at that instant she knew Don Miller had killed her daughter.

Gene and Elaine told Sue they would be right over.

As the Millers walked in the front door, Sue Young's first words were, "Don, what happened?"

Miller told Sue, in a very unemotional voice, that he had dropped off Martha Sue at 1:55 a.m. He said that she had sat down on the front porch, waved goodbye, and as he pulled out of the driveway, she was looking up at the stars.

Sue, Gene, and Elaine had quickly agreed that the police should be called.

Though he had only been on the department for a short time, Ouellette had already established himself as being thorough in everything he did.

He already knew that Don was the last person to see her. Using a sort of shotgun approach, he started with obvious questions: What was the time when he last saw her? What was she doing?

Sue Young described her own activities the previous night for the young officer. She told him she had gone to a party on Fairview Street in Lansing, but there was no alcohol at the party. She had been picked up at her house by another couple, and they drove her to the party. The three of them left the party at about 1:15 or 1:30 a.m.

When she got home, she yelled for Martha, and she went upstairs to see if she was home. Finding her bed was still made, she decided to stay up for a while longer, and she was certain that she was still awake at two before falling asleep.

Ouellette continued his preliminary investigation by asking Don what he and Martha had been doing before he had dropped her off. The officer was trying to establish some basic facts to see exactly what he was dealing with.

Don told the officer that after babysitting with Martha, they had gone back to his parents' home on Gainsborough and had shared pizza and 7-Up with his mother. Afterward, he had dropped her off at her house and walked her up to the porch. She turned, waved, and she sat down on the front steps as he backed out of the drive. He also told Ouellette that he had asked Martha to marry him on November 10, and he was certain she didn't have any other boyfriends.

After checking with the neighbors to the south, the officer returned to the house and asked Sue to check with all of Martha's friends in case she had decided to spend the night with one of them. Two more officers had joined Ouellette. Officers Dave King and Don Austreng continued to check with the neighbors. King and Austreng were able to track down a former boyfriend of Martha's who had broken into the Young home two years earlier. The boyfriend said he had several friends over at his house until three a.m. or so, and they would be able to vouch for him. He also said he would be willing to take a polygraph examination. He told the officers it would be very unusual for his former girlfriend to leave without letting her family know where she was.

Ouellette, now back at the house, checked Martha's room and found a small book with her friends' names and phone numbers in it. He gave it to Sue so she could start checking with the friends. While checking her bedroom, he took note of an address written on her calendar with the word COOKIES written next to it. He kept the address to check later. He asked Sue if her daughter had enough money to get a plane or bus ticket. Sue assured him she only had one hundred twenty-five dollars in cash. It was the money she had intended on giving her the previous day, but Martha had insisted she take it home and she would get it there. Sue checked Martha's top dresser drawer and found the money still in the bank envelope, and a new pair of shoes she had bought the previous day were still in the box in her bedroom closet.

When he spoke with Don again, Don told him that he didn't think Martha was depressed, and she hadn't mentioned anything about a party at the address written on her calendar. Ouellette asked specifically if he had seen Martha actually go inside the house when he dropped her off early that morning, and Miller told him no.

As Officer Ouellette was checking the house, he had been joined by a fourth officer. Ouellette's colleague began checking with some additional neighbors. Martha's blue 1968 Olds convertible was still parked in the drive where it had been the night before. There were no fresh tracks in the driveway, and no evidence that anyone had sat on the porch only a few hours earlier.

Ouellette needed one last thing before he left the Young residence. He needed a physical description of Martha, and he needed to know what she was wearing the last time she was seen. With great difficulty, Sue described her clothing. She had been wearing rust-colored plaid slacks, a blue ski jacket with a fur collar, and a green scarf. There was a matching jacket to the slacks, but it was too cold for Martha to wear that, so it was still hanging in the closet. Sue thought of giving that to the officer so he could see the pattern, in addition to a matching wool hat.

Sue described her daughter as petite when she gave her daughter's height and weight. She said Martha was five-feet-five-inches tall and one hundred-twenty pounds. She gave a photo to Ouellette, but she quickly realized Martha had been wearing contacts in the photo. The previous evening, she had worn her glasses. She found a second photo of her beautiful daughter wearing her glasses.

As Officer Ouellette's initial investigation continued, Don asked Sue if he could make her some tea. She declined, and began to wonder what he really knew about her daughter's disappearance.

After the Millers left Sue Young's house, Ouellette and his partner quietly discussed the investigation by themselves. The other officer suggested going over to the Miller home, only a few blocks away, and seeing if they could look in Don's car. They both thought it was crucial to get a look inside, but they also didn't want to try to get a search warrant because it might appear they were focusing on Don as a suspect. They both realized, as they prepared to leave Sue Young's house, they had not been able to establish if Martha Sue Young had ever been back inside the house after Don Miller had dropped her off.

The two officers agreed it was a good idea to try and get permission to look in Don's car, and after leaving Sue Young's house, they drove directly to the Miller home on Gainsborough Street.

As the two officers casually spoke with Gene and Don Miller, they asked if they might be able to look in the car.

"What do you want to do that for?" Gene asked.[31]

Ouellette told him they wanted to see if there was a possibility Martha had dropped her keys inside the car. If that were the case, then it would explain why she might not have been able to get into her house after Don left. The car belonged to Don, and he agreed to let them look.

Sitting at the corner of Gainsborough and Roxburgh Avenue, there was a driveway on the east end of the house,

---

31. Kenneth Ouellette, August 22, 2017

and a small driveway on Roxburgh. Don's car sat in the drive on Roxburgh.

Ouellette's partner opened the driver's door. Taking an overall look at the front seat, he narrowed his focus to the seat area, then quickly glanced under the driver's seat and between the seats. His glance under the front seat was so quick, he didn't see the pair of women's glasses. They were lying under the front passenger seat. After the quick glance, he focused his attention on the seat cushions, where he could see a blue thread and some light-colored hairs. The officer asked Miller if the blue thread could be from Martha's coat or if the hairs could belong to her. He said the hair could be hers, but the thread was the wrong shade of blue for her coat. As both officers looked closer, they noticed a reddish stain on the front seat. It was on the passenger side, just to the right of center and about six inches back from the front edge. Ouellette's colleague asked Miller if he knew what the stain was and told him it looked like it could be blood. He asked if he could take a sample of it, and Miller agreed. The officer also saw white scuff marks on the inside passenger door panel. The officers thought the scuff marks could have been caused from someone's feet being up against the door.

As the second officer was collecting the sample, Don Miller quickly said the blood could be from a nosebleed he'd had a few weeks earlier. A small sample was collected and put it into an evidence envelope.

As the two officers talked quietly about what they had found, they decided to check with the chief of detectives. Because of the holiday, he had the day off. After finding what appeared to be blood on the front seat, both officers now wanted to see if they could get a search warrant to look a little deeper into Don Miller's car. While Ouellette stayed at the Miller home, his colleague drove to his own home only two blocks away from the Millers' house. After a quick synopsis of what had happened up to that point, Detective Lanny Laskowsky suggested they check with the on-call Ingham County prosecutor. The officer called the prosecutor and was told they didn't have enough probable cause to impound the vehicle, but as long as they had permission, they could continue to take any evidence they found.

After his partner returned to the Gainsborough address, Ouellette checked with Don Miller again to see if he would allow them to take some additional small items from the vehicle, and Miller agreed.

Ouellette's partner took a larger sample of the reddish spot on the front seat, and he took some small hairs from the passenger side of the back seat.

While his partner was taking the larger sample from the front seat, Ken Ouellette was looking at the outside of Miller's car. He noticed two fresh scratches along the passenger side of the car. They were about a quarter of an inch apart and two feet from ground level. The officer thought they were peculiar because they were in the winter road salt that had accumulated on the surface of the paint, but not in the car's paint itself. He pointed the scratches out to his partner, and when he looked closer, he noticed sand and mud in the right rear wheel well, but not the left. Ouellette's partner also took a sample of the sand and mud.

The scratches on the passenger side of the car intrigued both of the officers. They looked as if they could have been caused by trees or brush scraping along the side of the car. Ouellette asked Miller if he would be willing to show them everywhere he and Martha had been the night before, and Don agreed.

The two officers and Miller got into a patrol car, but before they left, Ouellette took the opportunity to read Miller his rights. They were read from a form the officers carried, which Miller signed after his rights were read to him.

The three men started off, and while Miller said he couldn't remember the names of the roads they had gone on, he could still remember where they had gone. Ouellette thought it was odd that a young man who had lived in East Lansing his entire life didn't know the names of the major roads in the area. He filed his suspicions away.

As the car moved north along Park Lake Road in Meridian Township, Miller directed the officer to turn on Raby Road. As they headed east, he told them that he and Martha had turned off on two small two-track drives on the south side of the roadway and parked for no more than five minutes or so. It was clear to the officers that a car had been parked right where he said they had been parked because the ground had thawed as if a running auto had been parked there, and the ground had re-frozen. Ouellette noticed there weren't any trees or brush near where the vehicle had been parked, nothing that might have caused the scratches on the side of the car.

Their passenger also directed them to the Trinity Church on Timberlane in East Lansing and the East Lansing Water Treatment Plant on Burcham just east of Park Lake Road.

The two seasoned officers were satisfied that Don Miller had been at each location the previous evening, but weren't convinced he was telling them everything.

It was mid-morning by now, and the officers were still not able to convince themselves that Miller wasn't involved in Martha's disappearance. Their focus began to narrow and shift more towards him.

Ken Ouellette's partner dropped him back at the police department, and the officer did some additional checking with Sue Young's neighbors, including the address where Martha was supposed to attend a party Saturday night. Afterward, he headed back to Sue Young's to see if he could get some more information about Don.

Sue told the officer that while Don was quiet, he often inserted himself into conversations about family problems, offering his own solutions. Yet even before the officers had arrived, when he was confronted with Martha's disappearance, he offered no information other than simple yes or no answers when directly asked.

Because the Youngs and the Millers attended the same church, the officer suggested the minister try to contact Don and see if he might be able to gain some more information.

Sue called Pastor Howard Lyman. The pastor had already heard about Martha's disappearance. He had already contacted Don on his own and was told he didn't care to go for a drive, and he didn't want to talk to the pastor either.

Checks were also made at Lansing's Capital City Airport to see if anyone with the name of Martha Sue Young had flown out that morning. Two airlines confirmed no one had. The officer also checked the local Greyhound bus station and numerous restaurants in the area that had been open all night.

Back at the police department, Ouellette conferred with the other two officers who had come to the scene to help search. Officers Dave King and Don Austreng, along with Ouellette, decided a formal interview with Don Miller should be done. Ouellette called and asked if he would be willing to come to the station to make a formal statement, and Don agreed.

It was just before two p.m. when Don Miller showed up at the station for his interview. The four men sat together in an office across from the front desk, and Ouellette started off with basic questions about how long he'd known Martha and what their relationship was.

The officer moved into the subject of marriage when he asked, "Do you have any plans on getting married?"

Don replied, "Yeah, we do. We haven't set any date or anything, as we have finances and school to get straight, and we want to make sure that we both are grown up in these two areas before we set a date."[32]

---

32. East Lansing Police Department, Interview with Don Miller, 6-C-77, January 1, 1977

Dave King interrupted. He made sure that Miller was aware of his Miranda rights by reading them before there were any more questions.

Resuming his questions, Ouellette focused on the pair's activities the previous night. Don Miller described their original plan of watching a movie at his house all evening, but Martha had changed the plans when she had been asked to babysit for a couple from the church. Don told the investigators that he went along with her, and after babysitting, they had returned to his house at about 9:15. They finished watching the movie and had some pizza and pop, and they left his house to go for a drive to look at Christmas lights.

Ouellette interjected, "How long was that drive, approximately?"

Don replied, "The drive, approximately? Probably a good hour."

The young officer now began to focus on the time Miller said he had dropped her off. "A couple minutes to two," Miller said. When asked how he knew the exact time, he said he always checked his watch when he dropped her off because Martha's mom was sometimes peculiar about what time she would get home.

Ouellette became even more specific by asking, "Okay, you said you let Martha out. Did you walk her up to the door, or did you stay in your car?"

Miller replied, "I, um, you know, opened the door." The officer clarified that it was the car door he was referring to. Miller continued, "Yeah, I opened her door and I kissed her goodbye there, and then she walked up and I got in my car and waved, you know, and backed out, and she just sat on the edge of the step like she was going up."

The officer wanted to be sure, so he asked, "Front step?"

"Yeah, in a couple of seconds, just on the edge, just on the very tip edge, not really being seated almost, just the edge, anyways, she smiled and I drove on home," Miller said.[33]

The three officers all knew Miller's story didn't make any sense. The low temperature was at eleven degrees with sixteen mile-per-hour winds. It seemed unlikely that Martha would have sat on the front porch at all.

"How long were you in the driveway?" the Ouellette asked.

"Not very long. It was too cold out there to kiss that long."

Austreng decided to take a more direct approach to the questions. He asked, "Did you have an argument with her last night?"

"No, I didn't."

Austreng continued his hardline approach. "Did you hit her?"

"No, I've never hit her."[34]

The officer never realized how close he was to the truth when he asked Miller, "Did you drive to a park in another area and mess her up and leave her out there?"

"Nuh-uh," Miller grunted.

Officer Dave King interjected, "Isn't it a little unusual not to walk a girl right to the door?"

"Well, I've never walked her right to the door. Sometimes I walk her up to the door, sometimes, you know, since the car is right there almost by the door anyway; it's only a few feet," the suspect said.

"Do you ever wait until she gets into the door before you leave?"

Miller replied, "Not in the winter."

As the questioning continued regarding the outside temperature the night before, Miller offered, "When I'm

---

33. East Lansing Police Department, January 1, 1977
34. East Lansing Police Department, January 1, 1977

with Martha, sometimes I don't think of temperatures and that like."

"Didn't it strike you a little bit unusual that she would sit down on a step rather than go in?" King asked.

Miller agreed.

"Did you think about that at all?"

"Yeah, I did, but sometimes she doesn't think about things like that right off," he answered.[35]

As the interview came to an end, the three officers thanked Miller for coming in, and he left. The investigation into the disappearance of Martha Sue Young was about to ramp up.

---

35. East Lansing Police Department, January 1, 1977

5

Ken Ouellette came into work on January 2 with Martha's disappearance on his mind, as well as the other officers. It was still bitterly cold outside.

It had now been over twenty-four hours since Martha Sue Young had been reported missing. At nine a.m., Ouellette asked the dispatcher to enter her information into the Law Enforcement Information Network (LEIN) as a missing person.

Ouellette and his partner met with the dayshift lieutenant for a briefing about the previous day's events. The lieutenant told Ouellette's partner to contact the MSP crime lab to see if they could analyze the sample of the dark stain he had taken from the front seat of Miller's car. After a brief phone discussion with MSP, Ouellette's colleague was on his way to the lab, which was in East Lansing. The lab specialist did a preliminary test and determined it was blood, but it would be a couple days before he would be able to conclude if it was human or not, and what the blood type might be. The officer also turned over the thread and hair he had collected the day before.

Ouellette, still with his supervisor, had suggested a polygraph examination for Miller, and the lieutenant agreed, telling him to see if he could set one up. Ken Ouellette contacted Lieutenant Markham by phone, and Markham agreed to do one at one p.m. that afternoon. Ouellette called Don Miller, and he agreed to come in.

While the two officers suspected Don Miller wasn't being truthful in what he'd told them, other leads were still being pursued.

Sue Young had been contacted by her neighbor to the south because they had heard about Martha's disappearance, and they had found a Jewish prayer cap in their driveway the following morning. Sue immediately called the East Lansing Police, and it was turned over to them. Martha's sister, Kay, told the police her sister had one friend of the Jewish faith, so the investigators tracked him down. In a short interview, Martha's friend told them he had been to her house a few times, but hadn't seen Martha in at least six months, and he hadn't attended a Jewish service in several years. That prayer cap didn't belong to him. Investigators found another couple living nearby who were of the Jewish faith and had gone out on New Year's Eve, but couldn't identify the cap as belonging to them.

Later that afternoon, Ken Ouellette met with Sue Young again, but this time it was with Detective Lanny Laskowsky. Both men wanted more information regarding Martha's finances, and wanted to know if there was any possibility she might have left home voluntarily.

Sue was certain Martha hadn't left voluntarily. Martha had a new job at American Bank and Trust that was supposed to start on January 3, and she had over five hundred dollars in her bank account. She also said Martha's relationship with Don Miller was up and down. Sue told the men she and Martha had a casual conversation while returning from Pennsylvania on December 27, and Martha had told her she was considering breaking the engagement off and giving the ring back to Don. She added that her daughter had broken the engagement and tried to give the ring back at one point, but Miller had told her to keep it, and they could remain friends. Ouellette immediately remembered the interview the day before. Miller had said their relationship was strong with no signs of breaking up.

Sue also relayed the events of her own activities on New Year's Eve again to the investigators.

After the interview with Sue Young, Ouellette contacted Don's mother Elaine to see if they could interview her too, and she agreed.

Elaine told the officers that she remembered Don and Martha leaving the home on Gainsborough at around 11:30 p.m. She said they were supposed to go to the Trinity Church on Timberlane to see if Don's sister was there. If she was, they were going to bring her back home. They didn't return to the house, and Elaine remembered Don finally getting home just a few minutes after two a.m. on January 1. She said when he got home, he appeared happy, and she had asked him what they had done. Don had told her they drove around looking at Christmas tree lights, and added he had dropped her off, kissed her goodnight, then left her sitting on the front steps. Even Elaine thought that was odd, and when she asked Don about it, he said, "Oh, we always do that. It's not uncommon for her just to go up and sit on the steps before going in."

The first time Elaine realized anything was wrong was when Sue Young had called her at around seven.

The *State Journal,* Lansing's local paper, published their first report about the pretty missing coed on January 3. On page B-3, the title read EAST LANSING HUNTS MISSING WOMAN. The short article said only that her boyfriend had dropped her off at two a.m., but her mother had said she never came in the house. It ended with a brief description of Martha.

That same morning, a briefing had been scheduled with several members of the East Lansing Police Department. Officer Rick Westgate was included the in the first meeting, and afterward, he was assigned with Tucker to do a follow-up interview with Sue Young. The officers were looking for information about Martha's family, friends, doctors, dentist, and even her classes at Michigan State University.

After the interview with Sue Young, Tucker and Westgate headed to American Bank and Trust. It was supposed to be

Martha's first day there. The bank president confirmed that she was indeed supposed to start working there again. She had been a trusted employee in the past, and they had re-hired her, though she was only supposed to show up for a meeting on this particular day to fill out personnel forms. The president told the men that if she showed up, he would give them a call.

Later in the day, Westgate made a call to Martha's close friend in Pennsylvania. She was one of the family members the Youngs had stayed with over the holidays. He was trying to find out if Martha had said anything to her about the relationship with Don Miller. Martha's closest friend said that she had confided that she wasn't sure about her engagement with Don, but he wasn't aggressive at all, adding he wasn't even sure about when to kiss her.

After stopping at the bank, the two men went over the Miller residence, and the Millers offered some photographs of Martha.

By one that afternoon, Ouellette was meeting with Lt. Markham about Miller's polygraph. He went over the details of the initial report, and Markham listened to his interview from the previous day.

Just before one, Gene Miller left his home and headed to the ELPD with his son for a polygraph examination.

When Markham sat down with Don Miller, he first read him his Miranda rights, and a pre-polygraph interview was done. Miller relayed the same basic information he had told the investigators during his taped interview the day before. It included the stops where he parked with Martha for approximately five minutes each time and his returning her home at exactly two minutes before two a.m. He spoke of the discussion with Martha about her parents' divorce, and how he and her sister disagreed on things, but it was just a normal conversation. He said Martha didn't appear to be upset, and nothing had occurred that upset her.

As the polygraph examination began, Markham centered it around five questions. He asked Don Miller:

1. On January 1, 1977, did you deliberately lie to the police about where you last saw Martha Young?

2. Did you deliberately lie about leaving her home at her home at approximately 2 a.m. on January 1, 1977?

3. Do you know for sure where Martha Young is at now?

4. Did you directly cause Martha Young's disappearance?

5. On that night, did you physically harm Martha Young?[36]

Each time Miller answered a question, the instrument would measure his respiratory rate, blood pressure, heart rate, and the sweat on his fingertips. Each time a question was asked, Don Miller's answer was no. After an analysis of the data, Markham was sure he wasn't telling the truth.

Part of the corporal's procedure was to share his findings with Miller and to conduct a post-exam interview, which lasted several hours. During that time, Miller spoke with not only Markham, but with Officer Ouellette and his partner, in addition to Lt. Tucker. He also spoke with his parents several times.

Markham shared his findings with Don by telling him he didn't think he was being truthful. He also spoke with Gene Miller about the process, what the findings were, and explained the reason for the lengthy interview afterward. After listening to Markham, Gene Miller agreed to speak

---

36. East Lansing Police Department, Supplemental Report, Maynard Markham, 6-C-77, January 2, 1977

with Don privately to see if he would share any additional information he might be withholding.

Suddenly, Miller's story changed. Now he told the investigators he and Martha hadn't simply discussed her family. He said she was upset about her family. In fact, he said she was so upset that she had used profanity at one point, and he knew that wasn't her nature. While they were riding around, she had even asked at one point to stop so she could get out of the car and pray. Miller had refused to let her, and he told her he would take her home and she could pray there.

Lieutenant Markham was concerned. Don Miller's girlfriend had only been missing for a day, and he was suddenly subjected to a polygraph, then changed his story when he was confronted with the corporal's opinion he wasn't being truthful. Markham wanted to do a second polygraph.

After Miller left, Markham wanted to validate his findings. He drove to the Michigan State Police post and met with their polygraph examiner. He shared his findings, and the MSP examiner agreed; it appeared Don Miller had been deceptive in his answers.

After Markham's return to the police department, he and Tucker told Gene Miller they thought Don had been interviewed long enough, and he should go home and get some rest. Before leaving, even Elaine Miller spoke with her son to see if would share any more information, but he didn't. He told her he had already told everything to the police.

The same day, Martha's dad, Le, arrived in East Lansing from Texas. Sue had called him almost immediately after reporting Martha was gone. He needed to see what he could do to help find his daughter. He and Sue quickly headed to the police department so he could find out more about the investigation.

When they arrived, the two headed toward Tucker's office, and they passed the room where investigators had been questioning Don. Sue made eye contact with Don as they passed. It was the first time Le had seen the man who at one time had been considered his future son-in-law.

As they stepped into Tucker's office, Gene and Elaine Miller were also there. When the discussion began, Gene began to complain about how Don was being treated, never once mentioning Sue's daughter. As he continued to express his concerns about his son, he mentioned the possibility of hiring an attorney.

After a short briefing on the investigation, the Youngs left the police department, and they saw Don briefly in the hallway. He spoke to Sue for only a moment, telling her the police wanted him to bring in his underwear. He never asked about Martha, and she thought that was very odd.

An ELPD lieutenant went over to the Miller residence on Gainsborough, and Don went into his bedroom alone, then came out with blue dress pants, a short-sleeve white shirt, a tan pullover sweater, and a pair of white socks. He gave them to his mom, and she placed them in a paper bag. She handed them to the lieutenant. When he returned the items to the police department, he tagged them as evidence and secured them.

While the Youngs were at the police department, Ken Ouellette met with a Lansing police pilot, and an air search was done in the East Lansing area, looking for any signs of a recent grave, or any indication of something having been dragged through the snow. Most of the search was centered around the areas where Don had told the investigators he and Martha had been on New Year's Eve.

Ouellette's partner had been able to get a search warrant for Don's car, and it was towed to the city garage and placed on a hoist so it could dry out from the snow. Ouellette's colleague never knew Miller had taken the women's glasses from beneath the front passenger seat and destroyed them before the second search.

The officer was met by the same lab technician he had met with the day before, and the two of them began a methodical search of the 1973 Oldsmobile with 20,126 miles on the odometer.

The lab technician removed several small hairs from both the front and back seats. He also took an additional sample of the red stain that had been found two days earlier. The state police lab technician found another small stain that appeared to be blood on the inside of the passenger door, and a sample was taken.

As the East Lansing officer photographed the car, the lab technician noted the Uniroyal Fastrak Belted F-8-14 tires on the front and rear. When the search was complete, the car was returned to the Millers.

As word spread about Martha's disappearance, some possible sightings of the missing coed started coming in, but none could be substantiated. Police began to contact her professors at MSU to let them know she was missing, and if she showed up at class, to contact them. The same information was given to the employees at the bank where she held her checking account. The police contacted her dentist to ensure her dental records were on file should they be needed, and they also contacted her doctor to let him know she was missing.

Martha's dad was able to track down information about her blood type, and he passed that information on to the police. They in turn contacted the MSP crime lab and passed along the information so it could be compared with the blood taken from inside Miller's car. Martha's blood type was AB positive.

On January 5, four days after Martha Sue Young was reported missing, Lt. Markham arranged to have a second polygraph examination done. Gene Miller brought Don back to the police department for the exam. Markham had similar questions:

1. On January 1, 1977 did you deliberately lie to the police about where you last saw Martha?

2. Do you know for sure where Martha is at now?

3. Did you deliberately lie about leaving her at her at her home about 2 a.m. on January 1, 1977?

4. Did you directly cause Martha Young to become missing from her home?

5. Did you plan with Martha to have her missing from her home?[37]

As expected, all of Don Miller's answers were no. Again, Markham was sure Miller wasn't being truthful in his answers, and he wanted to be certain, so he took the results to two polygraph examiners from the state police, and both agreed with his findings.

The following day, Westgate and Tucker interviewed Martha's dad, and her sister Kay. Le told them Martha might still be in possession of a money order he had sent to her, originally for her to give to Don Miller as a birthday gift. It was in the amount of twenty dollars. He had told Martha that if she chose to not give it to him, she could keep it for herself. Kay was able to share some information about some places where her sister and Don would occasionally park and talk near Lake Lansing.

Le Young also passed along Martha's hairbrush to the investigators. As difficult as it was, he knew it might be needed later for some sort of comparison.

Part of Rick Westgate's investigation included following up with Southwestern University in Texas. In addition to

---

37. East Lansing Police Department, Maynard Markham, January 5, 1977

notifying the police department in the city of eight thousand people, he contacted the radio station to ensure they would air the story of the missing woman, and he attempted to confirm Martha's blood type by tracking down doctors in the area to see if Martha had any lab work done before she had returned to Michigan.

Reports of women being followed around East Lansing began to slowly trickle in as the days progressed, and while they may have been legitimate, none of them were connected to Don Miller.

It had now been ten days since Sue had reported Martha missing. Her ex-husband was in town trying to support the investigation, and while communication between the ELPD and the suspect had started to falter, Sue believed if she kept communication open between her and Miller, maybe some information about Martha's whereabouts could be learned.

But Sue was living in a fog. Every day was a struggle, and every day she thought of a new, haunting theory about where her daughter could be. She decided to call Gene Miller and see if Don would agree to drive them on the route he had last taken with Martha. Gene immediately denied her request. He said his son had been through enough with the repeated interrogations by the police. Sue begged with Gene to allow Don to do it. Her hope was the drive would trigger something in Don's memory. He finally agreed to allow Don to go along, but it was made clear that Gene would drive.

When the four met, Sue and Le got into the back seat, while Gene got in the driver's seat and Don got in the front passenger side. The four headed to the Trinity Church in East Lansing.

After they left the church, they headed back to Burcham Road, following it to the dead end where Don had said he and Martha had parked. Sue remembered that Officer Ouellette had told her he hadn't seen any sign of a car having been parked there. She kept it to herself.

At one point, Miller directed his dad to head back toward the East Lansing MSU campus. He said that on New Year's Eve, he had wanted to see how many students were back on campus by checking to see how many dorm lights were on. Sue thought that was a bit odd, but again, she kept it to herself. As their trip with the Millers ended, both Sue and Le were still at a loss for information about their daughter's whereabouts.

The day after the trip around East Lansing, Officer Westgate met with the Youngs, and the three retraced the route Miller had taken the night before. Westgate taped the route on a recorder.

Sue Young's days were difficult. Even more so when Le had to return to Texas after only being in East Lansing for a couple weeks. They still had no definitive answers, and each day became harder. There were times when Sue had to rely on her friends for day-to-day activities.

Though they suspected Don Miller had something to do with Martha's disappearance, police still had to follow up on every tip or lead they received, and they explored every theory in her disappearance, including the possibility she had run away.

Westgate had spoken with the newspaper delivery man who had delivered the morning newspaper on January 1. He told Westgate he had delivered the paper between 1:30 and 1:45, and the front porch light was on at the house. He said that when he dropped off the paper, there were several people leaving a party from across the street. Miller had told investigators that when he dropped off Martha, there weren't any lights on at the house.

On January 11, Markham called Don Miller and asked that he come in for another interview so they could discuss his polygraph results. When Miller showed up at the police department, he was interviewed by both Markham and Tucker in Markham's office. Before starting, Don Miller was read his Miranda rights again.

Much to the investigators' surprise, Miller had his own agenda. He had a list of topics written down and wanted to know if the police had followed up on any of them. Did they have any information on the blue car seen in the Young driveway when the paper was delivered at 1:30 on New Year's morning? Who owned the Jewish prayer cap found in the driveway next to the Youngs? Did they find any information on a sorority that Martha was supposed to be connected with? Had they found any information on another missing girl from the Lansing area? The two investigators assured him all of the leads were being pursued.

After his first round of questions to the investigators, he also wanted to know when his clothing would be returned to him, and he asked if the entire police department was just sitting around in the office to conduct their investigation into Martha's disappearance.

As the two officers settled into the interview, Markham asked a hypothetical question about Martha either running away to spend time by herself or joining a cult, and if Miller knew about her doing that, how long would he keep that secret. He said, "About two seconds."

Markham asked Don Miller if he had broached the subject of Martha's disappearance in any of his criminal justice classes to see if anyone had any ideas as to what might have happened to her. Miller assured the veteran officer that he only had one criminal justice class during this particular term and hadn't done that.

The officer asked the suspect whether or not he and Martha had fought prior to her disappearance. He followed up by asking Miller that if he felt responsible because she was now missing, would he keep that from the investigators? Miller assured Markham he wouldn't keep anything from the police.

The final hypothetical dealt with Miller's religious beliefs. Markham asked if there was a conflict about divulging information, and if it would prevent him from sharing information about Martha's disappearance. Like before, he assured them it wouldn't.

After the series of hypothetical questions, Lt. Markham moved onto more basic questions about the investigation.

The suspect told Markham the car he drove was registered to him, and it was driven mostly by him and his mom. His sister only drove it occasionally. Miller told Markham there were no other tracks in the driveway at the Young house when he dropped Martha off, and he would have noticed if there had been. The next question centered around Martha's request to get out of the car to pray. Don Miller said he couldn't recall what time it was, but it was when they were driving around campus near Spartan Village, the on-campus married housing complex. He reiterated that she was upset about her parents' divorce, and she didn't want to end up divorced like them. He also mentioned she became upset when he had asked her if her sister wanted her to break off the engagement. He told Markham that Martha had told him the only way she would break the engagement was if God directed her in another direction.

Markham continued the interview, but went in another direction. He asked if Don was upset that Martha hadn't given him the twenty dollar check her dad had sent to her for his birthday. He seemed surprised about the check, but not about Martha not discussing it with him.

The questioning moved to religious groups he and Martha might have been involved in. He told Markham the only group he had been involved in briefly was called The Way, and he hadn't had any contact with them since his return from Mackinac Island.

Lieutenant Markham had been trying to build trust with Don Miller. It was time to focus even more on minute details. He asked about the blood on the front seat and passenger door of the car, and if it turned out to be Martha's, how would he explain that? Miller quietly said the blood could have been caused from their heavy petting, and if she was menstruating, the blood could have been on her hands. He told the investigator that he and Martha were "all over the front seat" and that he had had her pants and panties down to her knees, so that could explain it. He added that he hadn't noticed any blood on his hands when he got home at two because he had a sandwich and washed his hands before that.

When Don Miller described going to Trinity Church, he said the two of them went inside, looked over the congregation for his sister, and when they didn't see her, they left. Markham wasn't satisfied. As a seasoned investigator, he wanted more details. He asked what was going on in the church with the congregation, and the question caught Miller off guard. He hesitated. He seemed evasive. The suspect finally told the detective the congregation was standing and singing when they had gone in.

The corporal decided it was time to discuss the polygraph results. He asked the suspect why the answers indicated deceit. Miller told him that any questions of an accusatory nature bothered him.

Markham confronted Don with information that several people had told him how Martha had thought about breaking off the engagement. Miller quickly countered Markham's statement by saying he too had thought about breaking it off because his fiancée had expressed an interest in the Mormon religion, and he felt there was a possibility that Martha had been kidnapped.

While the interview was being conducted, Gene Miller had contacted Officer Westgate and provided the blood type of Don. Both Don and Martha's sister had gone to a doctor separately because of the ongoing investigation and had their blood types identified.

Following up on the interview with the suspect, Markham also interviewed the pastor from Don's church. The pastor had interviewed Don on two separate occasions, and he told Markham he didn't see anything in Don's personality that would lead him to believe he wasn't being truthful, yet he told Le Young that he didn't think Don was being completely truthful about Martha's disappearance.

By the end of the week, Markham had learned that Miller's grandparents used to own a farm near Carson City, Michigan. It was about an hour from Lansing, but they had sold it in 1970. Don had taken Martha there at some point, so the investigators met with the Gratiot County Sheriff's Office where the property was located and searched the house and abandoned buildings around the property for any sign of Martha. They found nothing.

In a follow-up interview with Martha's parents, Markham learned that Miller had not told them about Martha wanting to get out of the car to pray, or that they had parked on Raby Road. Sue also told the corporal that it was possible Martha could have been menstruating because the time would be very close to her normal cycle, but her cycle wasn't always regular.

Le Young told Markham that he had spoken with Don for about twenty minutes, and Miller still hadn't mentioned that Martha had wanted to get out of the car to pray, and Miller's main concern seemed to be Le heading back to Texas.

Gene Miller stopped by Sue Young's house on January 13, and during their conversation, he told her that he felt Don's rights had been violated by doing so many interviews. He was going to consult with an attorney.

The following day, Tucker and Markham began following up on the investigation with more interviews. It had been two weeks and there was still no sign of the beautiful coed. They interviewed the pastor from the Campus Action Group Martha was a part of. It was a "born again" type group, and Don Miller started attending in July of 1975. Martha had attended three or four meetings that summer before she returned to school in Texas. The pastor was certain Martha wouldn't run away. It wasn't in her nature, but did tell the investigators that Martha had felt Don was too domineering. She liked to have lots of friends around, and she thought he was more of a loner. The pastor couldn't help but agree with Martha. He too felt Miller was a loner. For the pastor, it was hard to understand Miller's thoughts.

After leaving the interview, the investigators stopped by a dental office on the west side of Lansing to pick up Martha's dental records in case they would be needed later.

Heading to the Lansing Mall, the officers went to the jewelry store where Miller had purchased the engagement ring. The manager at Zales Jewelers showed the detectives photos of the engagement ring and told them there would be an identifying number inside the ring: **JTC 969**.

The officers were beginning to get frustrated. In spite of all the interviews and follow-ups, Martha Sue Young was still missing. Air searches had been flown over Bath Township, where two other young women had been found murdered the year before, but there was no sign of Martha's body. Yet everything still pointed toward Don.

Tucker contacted the friend who had spent Christmas with Martha in Pennsylvania. She told him that Martha had told her she was afraid to go through with the engagement. She felt she was much smarter than Don and he was weak. Martha confided to her close friend that if she married him, she would have to wear the pants in the family.

Tucker also contacted the pastor at the Trinity Church where Don said he and Martha had gone on New Year's Eve to look for his sister. The pastor told Tucker there were no young students meeting at the church. They were at a high school coach's house for a New Year's Eve party. He also told Tucker that the adults were meeting in the basement of the church from nine to around midnight. There was a pot-luck supper, and games were set up. At around 11:30, the nearly one hundred adults were facing the east basement wall in a semi-circle while singing. At around midnight, communion was given. The pastor said there was no activity at all in the main portion of the church on the first floor.

Tucker and Westgate wanted to interview Gene and Elaine Miller about their activities on New Year's Eve, but a wrench had been thrown into the works. Gene Miller had hired Lansing attorney Tom Bengston to represent the Miller family. He had followed through on his promise about legal representation. The two officers headed to the Hubbard Law Firm on the eleventh floor of the Michigan National Tower in downtown Lansing to meet with Bengston. The men asked the attorney if they could interview Gene and Elaine, in addition to interviewing Don again. Bengston told them he would have to think about it. He simply wanted to protect Don's rights.

Now past the two-week mark, Sue and Le Young were becoming more frustrated. Maybe offering a reward would help bring out some information. On January 19, Tucker provided a statement to be distributed through the ELPD, that a one thousand dollar reward was being offered for information about the whereabouts of Martha. Tucker suggested that Sue Young do a press conference at her home to let the media know about the reward. Eight separate media outlets showed up at her home. Sue was petrified at the thought of standing in front of the media, but knew she had to do it. She read her prepared statement, letting them know of the reward being offered. Three days later, the Central United Methodist Church offered an additional thousand dollars to the initial reward.

After the announcement of the reward, Tucker and Westgate had a chance to clarify a couple things with the Youngs. Sue provided a description of Martha's purse, which was missing along with her, and the things she would have in the purse. Sue also gave the two men a letter Miller had sent to Martha before her disappearance.

By January 24, Westgate and Markham were able to interview Don's parents, but they weren't able to do it alone. Tom Bengston, their newly-retained legal counsel, sat in on the interview. Their only purpose was to gather a timeline for both Elaine and Gene on New Year's Eve.

As the initial investigation began to slow down, Tucker, Westgate, Markham, and several other officers thought another ground search near some of the places Miller had said he was on New Year's Eve should be done. The men searched the area around Raby Road again, along with an area around the East Lansing Water Treatment Plant and the Trinity Church. Still nothing.

The flier distributed by the ELPD described the circumstances of Martha's disappearance, provided a description of her, and showed pictures of her with glasses and without. It was posted everywhere and was shared with numerous police departments and organizations around the state.

As the story of the missing coed grew, astrologers, psychics, and a dowser contacted the police with maps showing where they felt Martha's body might be found. As far-fetched as it seemed, Tucker knew they had to follow up on it. Another helicopter search, this one in Shiawassee County, northeast of Lansing, was done, in addition to using tracking dogs from MSP, but like so many other searches, nothing was found. Checks were also made with numerous cemeteries in the area, with searches in the mausoleums and crypts.

With Le Young now having returned to Texas, Sue Young was living in a haze. Her mail accumulated on her table without her opening it, and each day became even more difficult for her.

Martha's mom had one hope. Even though Don wouldn't talk to the police, there was still an open line of communication between her and the man suspected in her disappearance. She decided to try and take advantage of the situation. She would script some questions and invite Don over to the house. Her only concern was her safety. She convinced a friend to come over also, but to arrive early, then stand out of sight but within hearing distance so she could confront Miller, hoping he might admit to something.

As Sue readied her plan, she saw Miller coming to the house, but her hopes were dashed when she saw his sister accompanying him. Miller's sister believed him and spoke for him as Sue tried to ask him questions. Her plan had failed.

By late January, Rick Westgate wanted another interview with Miller, but had to contact Tom Bengston. Miller's attorney scheduled the interview, but told Westgate there would be stipulations. The questions they had of Miller would have to be submitted in a written form. Don Miller would answer them with the advice and guidance of his attorney. At the end of the awkward interview, Westgate had a short discussion with Miller that lasted two minutes. Bengston was there when Westgate was able to ask again about the activities at the Trinity Church on New Year's Eve. The investigators knew there were no activities on the main floor of the church, yet Miller stuck to his story. He maintained it was the main floor of the church, and he didn't have to go down any stairs. The interview had ended, but they had caught him in a lie.

As the investigators continued to follow up on leads, they issued a plea to the public on February 7. A statement was issued to residents in the greater Lansing area asking them to check any abandoned buildings and area fields in an effort to find the missing coed. The statement read:

> The East Lansing Police Department requests all great Lansing residents to check abandoned buildings and fields in an attempt to locate Martha Sue Young, missing from East Lansing since January 1, 1977. East Lansing Police have no evidence of

foul play at this time. However, due to the length of time Miss Young has been missing, they wish to pursue every possibility. Persons locating anything of a suspicious nature are asked to notify their local police agency.[38]

They knew it was a long shot but they had to try.

By mid-February, police thought they might have another lead. A sweater had been found along a dead-end road in neighboring Eaton County. Tucker contacted Sue Young and asked her to go with them to the scene. A state police trooper was waiting there. Sue looked it over cautiously but it didn't belong to Martha.

The ELPD continued, day after day, following up on any tip or clue that might lead to Martha.

The winter of 1977 was quickly drawing to an end, and in mid-March, Tucker decided another search of the Sleepy Hollow State Park, located northeast of Lansing, should be done. As the helicopter searched back and forth, Tucker couldn't believe what he was seeing. In an area of heavy brush and shrubs, he spotted a body. As the helicopter circled closer toward the ground, Tucker could see blonde hair. His heart began to race. He was certain they had found Martha.

As investigators approached the body on the ground, they could still see the blonde hair, but as they got closer, it was clear the body was black. Tucker wondered if there was a possibility that it might still be Martha, and maybe her body had decomposed to a state where it had turned black. When the investigators looked closer, they discovered the blonde hair was a wig. The hair on the body they had discovered was black. The police had found a body they weren't even looking for.

---

38. East Lansing Police Department. Supplemental report. 6-C-77. February 7, 1977

Desperate, Tucker decided to use their discovery in an effort to lure Miller out. While he formulated a press release about their discovery, his plan was to simply indicate that a woman's body had been found, but not indicate the location. The police would maintain surveillance of Miller for twelve hours in the hope he might head to wherever he had hidden Martha's body. Tucker relayed the information to Sue Young, and he told her the body was definitely not her daughter's. While law enforcement staked out Miller, the press had learned the location where the body had been found and quickly let the public know the location. The plan had failed.

By the end of March, Tucker was becoming increasingly frustrated. He knew a change in seasons might bring a break in the case because people would begin working outside as the weather warmed. He was also discouraged because Tom Bengston had created a road block to any further interviews with Miller. Tucker penned a letter to the attorney:

> It has been brought to our attention that it is your position and that of the Don Miller family that the East Lansing Police Department is satisfied with the cooperation of Don Miller in the case of the missing Martha Sue Young…We would like this letter to be your written notice to inform you and your client, Don Miller, that the position of this department remains the same as it was on 2/7/77 and that is as follows. Our investigators would like to interview Don Miller at the East Lansing Police Department as soon as possible and as many times as might be needed to assist this department in attempting to locate the missing Martha Sue Young.[39]

The letter was nothing more than letting Tom Bengston know the position of the investigators.

---

39. Dean Tucker to Thomas Bengston, March, 30, 1977

As spring arrived, Sue Young dreaded the month of April. Martha's birthday, April 27, was quickly approaching. As she sat home on that day, she tried to keep busy, but she noticed a floral truck pull into her driveway. She was suddenly anxious. Someone had sent her flowers. Her excitement quickly changed to anger when she opened the card attached the bouquet. It read, "Martha was a rose." The flowers were from Miller. There was no way she would keep them, yet on her daughter's birthday, she decided the beautiful flowers shouldn't go to waste. She removed the card and took the bouquet to a neighbor in hope they might enjoy the flowers. She was appalled that Don Miller would even think of sending them.

In early May, the reward for information about Martha's disappearance had expired. Both Sue and her ex-husband Le were broken. The offer of two thousand dollars hadn't produced any information about their daughter's whereabouts. They decided not to extend the reward, and the money they put up for it was returned.

Toward the end of May, the East Lansing police had received some additional tips about possible sightings. One witness was sure he had seen Martha at a YMCA in Chicago, Illinois. Coincidentally, Le Young had a brother who lived near there, but it was another dead end.

Another tip was passed on through an informant. The person called the East Lansing police and told them he knew of a person in Florida who could have physically harmed the missing East Lansing coed. A handwritten letter was received by the police, and they quickly turned it over to the FBI. It was another lead that never panned out.

As the months passed slowly, the tips coming into the police department became fewer and fewer. The investigation, while still very active, seemed to slow to a snail's pace.

6

The two friends had a plan to spend the afternoon doing what they loved the most. It was almost one p.m. as the two men headed toward Clinton County's Bath Township. With the temperature hovering near sixty degrees, it was a perfect day; the fall colors were spectacular, but the terrain was difficult as the two friends made their way into a thicket covered with low-lying brush and small trees. After parking on the north side of Potter Lake, Earl McCafferty and Jerald Butler trudged into the woods, circling to the west of the lake, and the two hunters loaded their shotguns and walked into the field to pheasant hunt. The two men worked the day shift at the Oldsmobile Plant in Lansing. On their day off, their favorite fall pastime was hunting.

It was 1:30 as the two made their way through a swale between the road and Potter Lake. McCafferty was a short distance from Butler, and as he glanced at the ground ahead, he could see clothing in the grass and underbrush. He was almost on top of it. He called to Butler, and the two men closed in on the garments. As they looked closer, they could see the clothing was laid out like a body, as if someone had been lying in it and simply vanished.

Lying with the coat were orange-and-red-colored plaid pants. The bottoms of the legs were facing toward the west. The stitching had deteriorated, and the pants were in pieces, held together by one remaining set of threads. The pantyhose were inside the pants, and white cotton panties inside the pantyhose. It was obvious to both men that the clothing had been there for some time because grass had grown over the toe of the pantyhose. The coat was lying at the waist line to the pants, and under the coat were two sweaters. The outermost was a blue turtleneck, and inside that was an off-white crewneck. Both sweaters had been turned inside out. A bra, scarf, and turquoise mittens were also placed as if they had been on whoever had been wearing them. The bra was unclasped, and a young tree sapling was growing through the scarf material. There were shoes at the bottom of the pant legs, but only one was untied. Two feet beyond the neck of the coat was a purse.

The two men picked up the purse and looked inside. They found a myriad of small items one would expect to find. There was a small leather wallet, and when they looked inside, they found a Michigan temporary driver's license, a Michigan State University identification card, and an East Lansing High School graduation card. Each piece of identification had the name *Martha Sue Young*.

Though McCafferty knew something was wrong, he didn't make an immediate connection to the missing MSU coed. The two men stacked the clothes in a small pile and decided to finish their hunt before calling the police.

It was nearly four when the two hunters made their way back to their find. As they got to the clothes, McCafferty looked at the identification again. It was only then he realized who the purse belonged to. The hunters took the purse with them and quickly headed for a phone. They knew they had to notify the police.

McCafferty and Butler drove to a nearby party store and used the phone to call the state police. They told the store owner about their discovery as they made their call. Waiting outside the store for the state police to arrive, store owner James Spagnuolo made a quick call to the Bath Township Police Department.

Dave Hall, a young officer who had only been with the department for a short time, took the call from Spagnuolo and quickly headed for the store.

When Hall met with the two hunters, they explained their find to him, and one of them reached behind the front seat of the pickup to retrieve the purse. Officer Hall could tell the purse had been exposed to the weather for some time simply by looking at it. He grabbed his radio and contacted the dispatcher, asking for the East Lansing Police be notified. The young officer knew the two hunters would have to be interviewed, so he directed them to the township offices where they could meet with the other investigators.

It was after 4:30 when Hall made his request to have the East Lansing police notified. All of the detectives had gone home. They called Dean Tucker's direct number to his desk, but he was gone too. The dispatcher called the chief. The chief told them to contact Sgt. Kelley. He couldn't be found either. After more futile attempts, the chief told them to contact Westgate and Markham. In a matter of minutes, both men were on their way to Bath Township. Shortly afterward, a patrol officer was able to track down Lt. Tucker, and he too was on his way to the scene. Tucker asked the dispatcher to notify the state police and have them respond, not realizing they had already been notified.

Detective John Boggs from the state police was sent out to the scene to assist the two local police departments. While the state police had been involved in a support role in the search for Martha, this was the first time they had become directly involved in the investigation. When Boggs arrived, he met with Tucker at Bath Township Police Department. The two investigators were briefed by the Bath Township police chief, and the three headed to the location where the two hunters had made their discovery. McCafferty had only brought the purse back, so the clothing was still in a pile in the underbrush.

Boggs and Tucker made their way off the road and soon discovered the pile of clothing. Another officer was already there, securing the evidence so it wouldn't be disturbed before Tucker and Boggs' arrival, and taking some photos before the MSP detective took the clothing and placed it in a plastic bag for transport to the crime lab.

Tucker knew the discovery of Martha's clothing and her purse would be big news. He was certain the discovery was the break they had been waiting for. He also knew they might be able to use the discovery of the clothes to their immediate advantage.

Tucker, Boggs, and East Lansing Police Chief Steve Naert decided to issue a press release from Westgate and Markham. The press release would only say that a purse was discovered near a residential area in Bath Township, and it had been identified as Martha Sue Young's. There wouldn't be any mention of her clothing in the initial statement put out by the police. Beyond the press release, Markham would run surveillance on the area where the purse and clothing were found, while the state police would run surveillance on Don Miller at his residence. Their hope was curiosity would get the best of Miller and he might return to where the clothing had been left; or, better yet, unknowingly lead the trailing officers to Martha's body. The men also decided that if their plan didn't work, MSP tracking dogs would be brought in the following morning to search the area. Afterward, a complete search of the area by investigators could be done before the press converged on the scene.

———

Tucker and Westgate had a difficult task ahead. They had to tell Sue Young about the discovery of her daughter's clothing and purse. A little after seven p.m., the two men arrived at the Young house. Sue welcomed the two officers, and knowing that Tucker had kept her up to date on a regular basis, she wasn't surprised when he had called and asked if they could stop by. She hadn't seen the local news, so she knew nothing about the discovery of her daughter's purse and clothing.

As Sue was starting to make some tea, Tucker spoke and told her they'd made a major discovery in Martha's case; he explained the critical discovery of the clothing.

Sue was quick to ask why they were certain the items belonged to Martha. Tucker told her about the identification inside purse. Sue wanted more. She asked question after question.

Tucker explained how the clothing had been laid out. He described the scarf at the neckline of the coat, the pants positioned at the waistline, and the bra inside the sweaters, which were inside the coat.

Everything Dean Tucker had told Sue Young confirmed to her that her daughter was dead.

———

Detective Boggs took the clothing recovered from the Potter Lake area to the crime lab. When the lab technician took a look at one of the sweaters, he saw a large stain on the front. Initially, the two men suspected it was a blood stain, but a quick analysis showed it wasn't blood. The technician thought it might be some sort of grape juice, and he forwarded samples on to a second technician.

———

As the investigation continued into the next day, disappointment set in for the surveillance officers. Miller never headed to the Potter Lake area or anywhere near there.

At nine a.m., Boggs met Tucker at the scene, along with Trooper Bill Flower and his tracking dog. A search of the entire area by the dog was fruitless.

Detective Boggs had also contacted the MSP post commander the previous afternoon and asked him to contact the Community Radio Watch Volunteers, a group whose members all had citizen-band radios, for help in searching the area.

At one p.m., fifty members of the CRWV were assembled in a parking lot near Potter Lake. After a briefing, the volunteers met at the scene, and under the direction of Boggs, they did a methodical search of a large area from east to west. A command truck was set up for constant radio communication with the volunteers but nothing was found. The following day, thirty more CRWV members showed up and another search was conducted in the same area from north to south, still hoping to find Martha. Much like the search the previous day, the searchers came up empty handed.

Boggs also conferred with another detective at MSP who specialized in techniques used by killers. Given the information about how Martha's clothing had been arranged when it was found, he told Boggs it was possible her body might be within a half mile of the clothing; in some cases, the top portion of the clothing might point in the direction of where the body is located. Given the information, Boggs contacted the state police dive team and had their coordinator fly over Potter Lake, paying particular attention to the western shore. As the coordinator searched from the air, he could see the lake was too shallow to actually conduct a dive operation, and suggested the lake be searched by dive team members wearing waders and using rakes.

When the news finally broke that Martha's clothing had been found, Tom Bengston paid close attention. He wondered why someone would take the time to lay them out like the press had described. He knew, at that point, it was more likely that Martha was dead, and whoever had laid her clothing out probably had psychological problems.[40]

As each day passed, nothing more had been found, but the entire area still hadn't been searched.

On the east side of Potter Lake, the terrain was much more difficult. Boggs and Tucker decided to utilize the Michigan National Guard. On November 6, a contingent of national guardsmen arrived and searched the area along the east side of the lake. The men bivouacked overnight, and on November 7, they continued their search, but after eight and a half hours, nothing had been found.

The following day, the MSP dive team searched Potter Lake. It was another dead end.

After the discovery of Martha's clothing, the local news printed the story. Police were hopeful it might spur some new information in the case, but by November, the local news media had stopped printing stories about Martha's disappearance. Sue Young became convinced the discovery of the clothing was just another dead end in her daughter's disappearance.

Law enforcement refused to give up. Late in December, almost one year after Martha had last been seen, the ELPD received information from the Ingham County Sheriff's Office in Mason that an inmate there was making admissions to murders in the area. While Lt. Tucker was certain Don Miller was responsible for Martha's disappearance, he knew he had to follow up on the information he had received. He and Det. Boggs headed out to Mason and met with two detectives there.

Detective Dick Fitzgerald was a seasoned veteran at the sheriff's office, and after briefing Tucker and Boggs, he told them the inmate lived in the 600 block of Gainsborough in East Lansing, only two doors from the Miller home. That information piqued their interest.

---

40. Thomas Bengston, October 12, 2018

The interview began with the inmate telling the detectives about a woman he and a friend had picked up in the south end of Lansing around the first week of January. He was sure of the date, because it was the day after his birthday. The two had supposedly picked up this woman named Debbie at a local pool hall in Lansing, and after driving around for a while, they ended up in Clinton County, near Ovid. The inmate continued, telling the officers that his friend had bludgeoned the girl to death, and they had poured gasoline on her body and burned it. He also told the officers it was all he could remember about it.

The inmate said he didn't know why he had done it. When Boggs asked him about the statement, he said, "I don't know why I did that to Martha Sue Young." He wasn't referring to the first murder he had just confessed to, even though Boggs doubted his story.

Tucker led the questioning about Martha. As he started, the inmate said, "I cut up Martha with a chainsaw. How could I do that?"

Like Boggs, Tucker doubted his story but pressed him further by asking, "Did you take her clothes off?"

"No."

Tucker continued, "Where is Martha now?"[41]

He told the two investigators he had left her in a field at the end of Marfit Road. He continued by telling them she was wearing a yellow jacket and slacks. The inmate changed his story, telling them he had picked up Martha on December 24, 1976. Describing the evening, he said he had left his house on Gainsborough, driven to the intersection of Harrison, then turned north. He said he saw Martha sitting on her porch, and described the house as white with a front porch and attached garage. After seeing her sitting on the porch, he stopped, backed up, then pulled into her

---

41. East Lansing Police Department, Supplemental Report, January 9, 1978

drive and asked her what she was doing. She supposedly told him that she was just enjoying the night, and he asked her if she wanted to go for a ride. She did, and they drove to the nearby 7-11 store and bought some Stroh's Beer. After leaving the store, they drove to Rose Lake, and he described the route he took to get there. When the two reached Rose Lake, he told the detectives that he took a wrench from beneath his front seat, and he knocked her out with the wrench and removed her clothes.

The inmate said Martha was wearing glasses when this happened, but she wasn't wearing any long underwear, and she wasn't wearing any jewelry. He described her as wearing brown high shoes and no gloves. He also told the investigators that after he had hit her, there was blood on her clothing.

Boggs still wasn't buying it, nor was Tucker.

As the man continued to confess, he gave a third version of events, and he became confused as he described taking her out of his car and removing her clothes. He said he drove back to his house on Gainsborough, got a chainsaw, then returned to Rose Lake, where he dismembered her body and placed the pieces in large garbage bags, then into his trunk. He said he drove back home and went to bed, then took his car to the store the following morning and bought some oil, returned home, and changed the oil in his car.

Boggs asked what he had done with the plastic bags. The inmate became more confused at that point, and he told Boggs he buried the bags. The detective asked him to describe what Martha was wearing when he picked her up. Not to anyone's surprise, in yet another version of events, the clothing he described didn't match what Martha had been wearing on the night of her disappearance.

Not leaving any stone unturned, Boggs asked exactly where he had taken Martha on the night he supposedly killed her. The inmate was sure he could show the detectives.

Arrangements were quickly made with the sheriff to allow two uniformed officers to accompany the inmate to retrace the route he had taken for the two detectives. The four law officers and the inmate drove to Gainsborough in East Lansing. Starting from there, the inmate told the officers to drive west and to turn on Harrison. He pointed to a house on Harrison, telling the officers that that is where Martha lived. Again, not to anyone's surprise, he pointed to a house one and a half blocks south of where the Young home was, and on the wrong side of the street.

Their quest continued as the inmate directed them to the entrance to Mud Lake at the Rose Lake Wildlife Station. They turned on to a two-track trail heading south, and as they moved along the trail, the inmate suddenly denied any part in the disappearance of Martha Sue Young.

The detectives were tired of the games. The inmate told the officer driving to head out to Center Road near Potter Lake. They stopped near where Martha's clothing had been found, and got their passenger out of the car. As they started to question him again, the inmate repeatedly denied any knowledge of Martha's disappearance or her death, admitting he was only familiar with the area because he used to come out there as a kid and drink.

Boggs and Tucker were absolutely convinced he had nothing to do with Martha's disappearance, so they took him back to the jail. Once back, the inmate began bragging once again about how he had killed Martha, so they continued questioning him. His story changed again, along with the description of the clothing that Martha was wearing on the night she disappeared.

Sadly, it was another dead end.

By the spring of 1978, new leads had slowed to a trickle, yet each one was pursued. At one point, a lead developed through a nationwide broadcast on the Law Enforcement Information Network regarding a fugitive who had been arrested in Maine. He had numerous photos of beautiful women, along with a copy of the book *The Michigan Murders*. On the chance that one of the girls in the pictures might be Martha, Detective Sue Brown asked for copies of the pictures. None of the women resembled Martha.

The investigation seemed to have stalled.

7

As a young woman who supported herself going through college, she wanted to write for a law magazine, or maybe edit some sort of government publication. Marita Choquette, already with her BA in English, was a forthright woman who was determined to finish her journalism degree, while juggling classes with her full-time work schedule to do so. Still very close with her family in Freemont, they spoke frequently by phone.

While business-like, she was also witty and funny, and very giving. Marita had two sisters, the younger living in the Lansing area, and they would spend time together a couple of times each week.

Since her brief two-year marriage, then divorce, the college coed spent her free time with the Episcopal church she attended in East Lansing, and the minister was one of her confidants and closest friends. She would often call Reverend John Mitman for advice and spiritual counseling.

Marita loved to go to restaurants with friends, and she would watch other people around her, trying to guess who they were and what they were doing. At twenty-seven years old, she was a young lady who preferred to go to quiet restaurants rather than the popular East Lansing bars like Dooley's or Alley Aye.

In early June, Marita had developed a runny nose, and she wondered if she might have developed allergies. Setting up her appointment with an allergist on June 14, she took the day off work at WKAR on the MSU campus. The appointment was scheduled to last for most of the day. At the conclusion, her doctor suggested she begin allergy shots, but she had immediate plans, so the shots were put off for a couple weeks.

That evening, she was looking forward to meeting her friend Myrna Russell at the Cork and Cleaver restaurant on Abbott Road in East Lansing. It was a quick twenty-three-minute drive from her apartment in Grand Ledge, a small town west of Lansing. When she arrived at the restaurant, Myrna wasn't there yet, so she waited in the front foyer. When Myrna finally showed up at 5:30, Marita seemed unhappy that she was late. Her mood quickly changed when they were joined by another acquaintance, Rod Volma, and the three of them went inside the restaurant for a drink.

As the three friends sat there, the discussion turned from Marita's allergy appointment to her planned trip to Chicago in a few weeks. Her sister Ann had just moved there, and she was planning a visit over the Fourth of July holiday. The conversation turned to a man Marita had become interested in. She had met him at a local tire repair store and had considered going out with him. She was impressed by him, and he had asked if she might join him for coffee sometime. Marita told her friends that she had discovered he was married. Volma offered his advice to her, suggesting she forget about any relationship with him.

There was a light rain by the time they decided to leave the restaurant at 7:30. In the parking lot, Marita stopped briefly to admire Volma's '76 Corvette, and after a minute or so, the three left separately; Myrna pulled out of the lot first, followed by Marita, and then Volma. The three cars headed west along Saginaw Street, and as Myrna slowed to turn right onto Chestnut Road just past US-127 in Lansing Township, Volma followed her. Marita waved at her as she passed her on the left of the four-lane road.

When Marita arrived back at her third-floor apartment on Pine Street in Grand Ledge, she grabbed the trash and carried it outside to put in the dumpster. Seeing her elderly neighbors, she smirked as she asked, "Are you out for your beauty walk?" It was eight p.m., and Mr. and Mrs. Tasker had just returned from dinner at the Ponderosa Restaurant. They had considered going to a movie at the local theater because it was dollar night, but decided on taking their evening stroll instead.

"Yes, that's what makes me so pretty," Mr. Tasker jokingly replied.

Not to be outdone, in her witty manner, Marita shot back, "I think you're handsome."[42]

The young woman finished emptying her trash and headed back into her apartment.

The Taskers thought their young neighbor was the happiest they had ever seen her as they continued on their way.

At around eleven, another of Marita's neighbors arrived back at the small apartment complex. She and Marita always parked next to each other, and she casually noticed her neighbor's car wasn't there.

As Willa Gritter turned into the parking lot at the WKAR studios on the MSU campus, she thought she recognized the yellow 1974 Opel sports car parked under the locust tree. It belonged to one of the other employees. She must have come in to work early. Willa noticed that the young assistant editor's car wasn't parked where it normally would be.

When she saw Marita two days earlier, her colleague had been in a bad mood. Willa had even suggested that she go home early because of her moodiness. She knew Marita had had a long phone call with her friend Myrna Russell. When she asked about the phone call, Marita had told her

---

42. Grand Ledge Police Report. Missing Person. 192-3-78. June 15, 1978

something happened, but didn't specify what it was. It turned out that she was upset about not being invited to a wedding.

With Marita having the previous day off, Willa was hoping she would be in a better mood. She entered the building expecting to find her colleague already working, but she wasn't.

As Marita Choquette's supervisor, Willa shared an office with her. She checked the entire building and when she couldn't find her, she thought she might have been mistaken about the car in the lot belonging to Marita. Maybe it was someone else's car.

By eleven a.m., Marita still hadn't shown up, and Willa became concerned. Knowing she had had a doctor appointment the day before, she thought Marita may have overslept, so she called a friend of Marita's and asked that he go over and check her apartment. It was twenty miles west of the MSU campus. Willa was hoping Marita was there.

The friend, a local minister, called her back and told her no one had answered the door. She became even more concerned, but she was sure Marita would show up eventually. Waiting most of the day, she slowly came to the realization that her co-worker wasn't coming in, so she called Marita's dad, a soon-to-be retired Episcopalian minister in Fremont, to see if he had heard from her.

―――――――――

It was early evening when the phone rang at the Grand Ledge police desk. Officer William Smith answered at 6:50 p.m. On the other end of the line was Reverend Henry Choquette, and he was calling to report his twenty-seven-year-old daughter missing. She was supposed to call him the previous night about his upcoming retirement party, and he hadn't heard from her.

As Reverend Choquette told the officer about his concern, Smith wrote the information down and dispatched Officer Rick Risk to the small apartment complex at 1225 Pine Street. The small, brick apartment building was part of the Whispering Pines complex, and Risk pulled into the parking lot that circled around to the east side of the building. He went to the third-floor apartment and knocked. After several attempts to raise someone, it was clear no one was going to answer the door. He headed back to the police department and met with Smith. Smith told him a friend of Choquette's had been to the apartment that morning and had knocked on the door, but was unable to raise anyone either.

Other than simply trying to see if someone would answer the door, Risk thought she might be injured or sick, so he called all the hospitals in the Lansing area to see if she might have been admitted. Still nothing. Marita's dad had given the officers a list of her closest friends, so the officer tried calling each one of them, but no one had seen or heard from her. At a dead end, the officer called Marita's father back and told him he hadn't had any success in trying to find her.

Reverend Choquette's concern multiplied, and he told the officer he would drive down the following day.

The following morning, Marita's dad walked into the Grand Ledge Police Department and met with Smith, giving him two pictures of Marita. He told Smith he'd be staying at her apartment all day and through the night. If the police were able to find out any information on her whereabouts, they could find him there.

Late in the afternoon, Risk came back on duty, and his first order of business was a return to the Pine Street apartment. Meeting with Reverend Choquette, they searched inside for anything that could indicate where his daughter might be.

The only thing he found was a small book from the doctor's office she had gone to on June 14.

After talking with Marita's dad, Risk returned to the department. Officer Smith had received a call from MSU about Marita's car being found the previous day at WKAR studios where she worked as an editorial assistant. Risk and Assistant Chief Ron Flitton decided to head for campus.

The car, still parked under the locust tree where it was discovered the day before, was locked. Flitton used a device to unlock the door, and the two men searched through the front seat hoping to find anything that might give them clue as to where she might be. Risk removed the rear seat so they could check the trunk, and nothing appeared to be out of the ordinary. Still not sure of what was going on, the officers asked Sgt. Jim Dunlap of the MSU Department of Public Safety to have the vehicle towed to the DPS office and secured. As Dunlap waited for the wrecker, the two Grand Ledge officers headed into the WKAR building.

The officers met with Willa Gritter, who remembered that her colleague brought lunch to work every day. They checked the refrigerator to see if her lunch was there. It wasn't. To Willa and the two Grand Ledge police officers, it only confirmed their suspicions: Marita had never been inside the building on the morning of June 15.

The following day, the GLPD contacted local media outlets to have them air the story of the missing Grand Ledge woman. In the next day's paper, the *Lansing State Journal* had already started to suggest a possible link to another missing woman: Martha Sue Young.

Following the media reports about Marita's disappearance, Risk met with a detective from the Clinton County Sheriff's Office, as well as Chief Gene Reno of the Bath Township Police Department. Hoping he would be wrong, he wanted to check some of the areas where other bodies had been found in Bath Township, and he also wanted to check the area where Martha Young's clothing had been found the previous October. Officer Dave Hall, along with a couple police cadets, accompanied Risk to the locations but nothing was found.

Risk knew from his initial investigation that Marita had been married for a short time. He also knew she was divorced and briefly had a boyfriend following the split with her husband. When the ex-boyfriend heard about her disappearance, he called the Grand Ledge police.

The missing woman's former boyfriend told the officer that he and Marita had dated in early 1977, but the relationship had been brief and only lasted for two or three months. The two had met through the church they attended in East Lansing. He also told Risk that she had a sister in Chicago, but he was certain that she wouldn't leave the area without having told someone.

Both Marita's former boyfriend and another witness who had called to speak with the police told them that Marita had made the statement at some point that she would be "out of Lansing" by August. Beyond that, the missing woman had never elaborated any further. Her former boyfriend had even asked her if she had a job lined up, and she had told him no.

Risk was leaving town for a week, so he asked Officer Steve Starr to continue working the case. Risk would be out of town from June 22 to 28.

Starr, along with Sergeant Larry Lyon of the MSU DPS, continued to interview friends of Marita, both in Grand Ledge and on campus, as they tried to piece together clues about where she might be.

They spoke with Willa Gritter a second time. She told the officers that she felt Marita wasn't happy with her job or her personal life. Marita hadn't had a boyfriend in some time and wanted one. She also felt that her colleague would take any flirtation from a man very seriously. She considered Marita very vulnerable and extremely naïve.

While Risk was out of town, Lyon and Starr also interviewed Marita's former boyfriend a second time. He told the officers that while they had dated for a couple months, it was Marita's idea to break off the relationship, and the two remained close friends, both in and out of church, from that point on. To her former boyfriend, Marita was a woman who needed male companionship. He described her as independent yet occasionally insecure, and he even thought at times she was desperate to find male companionship. In spite of that, he felt Marita maintained her sense about her and wouldn't do anything that might place herself in any danger. The officers asked if he had seen any recent unusual activity from her, and he said she had left in the middle of a church service on June 4. He respected her privacy, and the next time he saw her, he decided not to ask her why she had left. Trying to think of anything that might help the investigation, he told the two officers that she would often call him over minor decisions she had to make, and she seemed to spend a lot of time on the phone. He thought that seemed to cause some financial problems for her.

On June 27, the temperature reached eighty-five degrees by noon. It had fluctuated between the mid-seventies and eighties for the previous two weeks, and it had turned out to be a beautiful summer day.

A surveillance team was keeping tabs on Don Miller during the day. It was something they tried to do every day. On this particular outing, they took note that he appeared to be scrubbing the back of the front passenger seat in his car.

Ten miles away in Ingham County's Alaidon Township, Clifford Nichols made his way back through a field that ran south off Willoughby Road, west of Okemos Road. Clearing the field of rocks, he dumped them near the small grove of trees in the middle of the farm field. It was almost 12:30 p.m., and he was making his way back toward the road. As the farmer approached the small patch of woods, he was overcome by a putrid smell. Thinking there was probably a dead animal nearby, he continued back toward the farm.

Nichols had some quarry stone he wanted to move back to the wooded area, so he loaded it into the bucket on the front of his tractor. He was going to put the stone with some concrete silo slabs that had been left back in the field. As he neared the corner of the grove, he started down a trail leading into the woods, and he could see a large pile of bricks a hundred feet or so from the edge. It hadn't been there three weeks earlier, and he knew it wasn't supposed to be there.

As the farmer drove the tractor past, he glanced down and could see maggots and flies covering the bricks. The smell was insufferable. He continued for a short distance and unloaded the quarry stone he had in the bucket. He began debating whether or not he should go back to see what was under the bricks. He knew there had been some poaching in the area, but wondered why someone would take the time to bring a dead animal that far back from the road and conceal it under bricks. He was trying to get his courage up to go back and take a look. He finally made the decision.

As the farmer climbed down off his tractor, he walked around the stacked blocks a couple times. He could see a couple of the cement silo slabs stacked with them, propped up almost like a tepee. Nichols noticed a handful of dead weeds were coving something near the edge, and he reached down to pull them back. Staring up at him was a decaying human skull.

Wasting no time, Clifford Nichols got back on his tractor and headed back toward the farm. He quickly headed for the house and called the Ingham County Sheriff's Office. The operator put him through to Captain Harry Tift.

———————

Harry Tift walked into the detective bureau at the Ingham County Sheriff's Office in Mason. Detectives Dick Fitzgerald and Steve McGuire were both there, and Tift told the two to head out to the farm on Willoughby Road. There would be a man by the name of Clifford Nichols, and he had found a body on the property. Knowing there were two missing women in the Lansing area, the two detectives hurried to their car.

Nichols waited patiently at his farm for the two detectives. When they arrived, the farmer calmly described his gruesome discovery and told them to follow him back in their car through the field.

Nichols got back on his tractor, and the three men headed back on the two-track lane toward the woods with Nichols leading the way. They drove for one-fifth of a mile before coming to the edge of the trees. They stopped shy of the wooded area and continued to walk to the north for another fifty yards. As the two detectives got closer to the grove of trees, they immediately recognized the rancid odor of decomposition.

As they walked with Nichols, he stopped them when they reached the pile of cement cinder blocks. Fitzgerald and McGuire looked closer, and could see why Nichols had called. Beneath the stack of cement blocks and silo panels, the men could see the decomposing body.

Nichols told the two detectives he hadn't moved anything and had quickly returned to a phone, where he called the police.

After McGuire and Fitzgerald roped off the area, Fitzgerald left his partner at the scene and headed back to the sheriff's office to brief Tift. Captain Tift assigned a third detective, Dennis Shackelford, to act as a medical examiner, and by three, both Shackelford and Fitzgerald had arrived back at the crime scene.

Captain Tift had called for the MSP crime lab, and shortly after the request was made, he contacted Lt. Tucker. Tucker jumped in his car and headed for the scene. He needed to know if they had found Martha Sue Young.

After Tucker's arrival, even though the body had started to decompose, the men were confident that it wasn't Martha.

After Tift's request for the crime lab, he and a fourth detective headed for the Nichols house. Fitzgerald met them, describing what Nichols had found, and he took Tift back to the scene.

The stench of the rotting corpse was overpowering in the summer heat. Members of the Ingham County Prosecutor's Office had arrived by now, including Mike Woodworth and Stuart Schaefer. Woodworth was anxious yet apprehensive. He'd never been to a homicide scene before. As they approached the wooded area, they could see one of the investigators vomiting from the overpowering smell of decomposition.

Shackelford used a polaroid camera and took seven photos of the victim. He also called Dr. Larry Simson, the forensic pathologist at Lansing's Sparrow Hospital. Simson would be on his way.

Sergeant Larry Lyon and Officer Brett Bean from the MSU police had also come to the scene after hearing of the discovery. Could the human remains be those of Marita Choquette?

Needing to see the remains before they were disturbed, Dr. Larry Simson arrived at around four. The smell didn't bother the seasoned pathologist as he looked at the decomposing body. After a cursory examination, Simson told Tift that he felt the body had been there for at least four days, but no more than two weeks. His rough estimation was seven to eight days.

After conferring with Simson, Tift met with Lyon and Tucker, and while Tucker was satisfied the body wasn't Martha Young, Lyon thought it might be Marita Choquette.

Captain Tift left the scene and headed back to the sheriff's office while technicians from the crime lab began to process the scene. Each brick and each concrete silo panel was photographed, carefully removed one by one and documented before the next piece was removed. The body slowly came into view.

She was lying with her head toward the west. Her head was turned to her right. She was partially clothed, nude from the waist up. Her legs, bent at the knees, were tucked under her thighs. As the eight bricks and two concrete silo panels were slowly moved, the body was photographed, and the investigators made an even more grisly discovery. Her hands had been cut off. Hidden under some additional blocks to the left of the victim, police found the severed hands. A ritual? A sacrifice? Or perhaps something more elementary?

Speculation was immediate. The blocks and silo slabs were stacked in a way that could be interpreted as an altar of some sort. The severed hands were found in a praying position. Surely there had to be a religious connection to the murder. Simson looked closely at the severed hands, and the cuts appeared to be almost surgical. The incisions made to remove the hands followed the cartilage and bones in the wrist. Simson was amazed at the precision. Now, in addition to the possibility of a religious murder, the investigators began to wonder if the killer might be someone in the medical profession.

As evidence was gathered, the hands were packaged separately from the body. The technicians found a metal braided ring on the right hand and a metal knot ring on the left hand.

The crime lab technicians also gathered maggots from the scene, both alive and dead, to help in determining a time of death. They also took small beetles from inside the victim's skull. Dirt and leaf material from around the body was packaged. Everything would be sent to the state crime lab.

Hopefully, the lab technicians could get a set of fingerprints from the hands to aid in identification. They would also remove the rings in hopes of helping identify the victim.

Back at the sheriff's office, Tift called Sgt. Lyon. He asked Lyon to contact Marita Choquette's dentist in Fremont to see if he could get her dental records. He also described some of the clothing the victim was wearing: panties, a girdle with a flower design, and culottes. He asked Lyon to also check with Reverend Choquette and his family to see if their daughter had clothing similar to that.

Lyon began working immediately on the request, not realizing that MSU would soon have another missing person.

———————

By eleven p.m., the eighty-five degree day had cooled to the mid-sixties. The detectives were staking out the murder scene on Willoughby Road in hopes the killer might return. It was a beautiful night.

Ten miles away, a brown Oldsmobile eased along Chestnut Road on the MSU campus. As the car neared Munn Ice Arena, the driver noticed the pretty blonde walking. She looked familiar. He thought he might have met her at some point before, so he pulled his car alongside her and stopped. The two began talking. The young coed told him she was walking to her dorm in North Case Hall, and he asked if she'd like a ride. The pretty young blonde,

Wendy Bush, loved to make new friends, and she agreed to the ride, never knowing two other women had been murdered in the same car.

The driver slowly pulled into the circle drive at Case Hall and into a parking lot near the loading dock.

As the two talked in the car for ten minutes or so, the young blonde seemed flirtatious. It was her personality. He hated that. It angered him. He was certain she was trying to seduce him, and his anger began to build. Her perceived attempts at seduction reminded him of his former girlfriend.

Casually, he slowly put his hand on her shoulder as she talked. Suddenly, it was around her neck, and he squeezed her throat as she fought for air. She never had a chance to scream.

He knew he would have to hide her, just as he had done with the others. He would have to find a quiet place to leave her body. In a daze, he had no idea where he was going as he left campus.

Driving for thirty minutes or so with her body still in the front seat, he found a small trail into a brushy area in a newly-developed subdivision. Carrying her body for a short distance along the trail, he laid her down and removed her clothes. He left her body there, and after returning to his car, he found a trash can and disposed of the clothing before heading home.

By nine a.m. the following morning, Detective Dennis Shackelford had arrived at Sparrow Hospital and made his way to the morgue. Using the phone in the hall outside the secure door, he spoke with a lab assistant, who came and unlocked the door to let him in. He only had to walk a short distance before he reached a small, refrigerated room on his right. He made a quick check, ensuring the evidence tape left as a seal on the morgue cooler was still intact. After checking the tape, he continued down the short hall and turned to an open area referred to as the autopsy suite. A small office with a large window overlooking the suite was on one side of the room.

Dr. Simson arrived, and as the body was brought from the cooler to the autopsy suite, he could tell it was the same body that had been at the scene on Willoughby Road the previous afternoon. While they all suspected the body was Marita Choquette, they also knew there was another possibility. On June 16, Beverly Gold was last seen at two p.m. in a house she shared near the University of Michigan campus in Ann Arbor. The U of M coed was still missing, and investigators knew there was a chance the body could be Beverly.

As the autopsy began, Shackelford left and headed to Fremont to meet with Marita Choquette's dentist and get her dental records.

The morgue was crowded with investigators. As Simson began the autopsy, he knew it would likely be the following day for dental records to try to make a positive identification. He could tell the victim was a female, likely between twenty-five and thirty-five years old. It was quickly apparent to the pathologist how the victim had died. Even with the decaying flesh that remained, he counted seventeen stab wounds across her back, abdomen, and thighs, the largest of which was the nine-inch stab wound across her back.

Detective Shackelford didn't return until late in the afternoon, and it wasn't until the following day when he turned the dental records over to Simson. Afterward, he headed to the crime lab, where he picked up the rings recovered from the victim's severed hands.

The state police crime lab was in East Lansing on Harrison Road next to the MSU campus. Shackelford didn't have far to go.

After picking up the rings, he met with Marita's supervisor Willa Gritter and another co-worker at WKAR studios, but neither could identify the rings as belonging to Marita. The two women suggested another co-worker might be able to say whether or not the rings were Marita's. The detective tracked down the co-worker, and she knew immediately that the rings belonged to Marita. She had seen her wearing them on June 13, the day before she disappeared.

While Shackelford was showing the rings to co-workers, Fitzgerald and Baldwin were interviewing a witness who used the wooded area where the body was found to produce maple syrup. He told the two detectives that he was sometimes in and out of the wooded area five or six times per day, and that on June 18, he had taken his father and a friend for a ride on his tractor. Because he was in and out of there so many times, he was certain he would have noticed if the large pile of bricks had been moved because they were next to where he drove his tractor. He was steadfast in his belief that the body was not there on June 18.

Back at the crime scene, detectives checked and found the tire prints from the tractor. They were within one foot of where the body had been found. While the officers were there, they collected more insect larvae.

The detectives from Ingham County were certain the remains belonged to Marita Choquette, but they still needed an expert to match dental records. The police weren't going to wait for a positive ID. They were going to search both her car and apartment again. The victim's 1974 Opel was still being held at the MSU public safety office, and lab technicians from the state police were processing it by gathering fingerprints and paperwork strewn about the floor, along with some clothing.

As the investigation began to move forward, both Clifford Nichols and some of his neighbors reported seeing a van parked back by the wooded area where the body was found. One witness was certain the van was there on June 14. She described it as a 1977 or '78 model van, and she told detectives it was boxy looking. She thought the time was about 9:20 p.m. when she saw it parked back in the field near the wooded area.

Nichols had seen a van, but during the daylight hours, and he described it as a white van with a large window behind the driver's door. He also said the van had a large hockey stick-shaped stripe across the side of the van. He just assumed it was a young couple who wanted to go parking. He was certain he saw the van on June 19.

The following morning, Dr. Edmond Hagen was able to positively identify Marita Choquette's remains using the dental records that Shackelford had picked up in Fremont.

Up to the point of identification, Marita's case was listed as a missing person. Now it became a homicide investigation, and Marita's apartment was searched again by Detective Fitzgerald and state lab technicians. The apartment was as neat as a pin. The investigators took contents from the bathroom wastebasket, a notebook, and two hairbrushes.

There were two main theories about the murder of Marita. The first revolved around a religious killing; the second was it was committed by someone in the medical profession. Fitzgerald and the other Ingham County detectives weren't convinced the murder was related to Martha Young's case, but they weren't discounting it either. By that time, there still wasn't any confirmation Martha was even dead, though many suspected she was.

Fitzgerald met with Lt. Tucker and discussed the idea of Don Miller being involved with the Choquette homicide. Both were convinced that Martha Young's disappearance was a boyfriend/girlfriend homicide, and Marita's murder wasn't related.

Don Miller's attorney Tom Bengston had heard about the Choquette homicide. No one ever suggested to him that it could be related to Martha Sue Young's disappearance, so he never considered it. There was nothing significant about it that led him to believe his client was involved in any way.

Fitzgerald was suspicious of the van reported near the site of Marita's body and wanted more information. The suggestion was made to have Nichols hypnotized, but Fitzgerald wasn't in favor of it. He didn't believe in hypnosis and thought it was nothing more than hocus pocus. To the detective, a hypnotist was someone who was paid money to make people say things that weren't true.

In spite of his beliefs, Fitzgerald took Nichols to see Damon Reinbold, a hypnotist who specialized in therapy sessions to make people stop smoking, or to diet. He did occasional hypnosis shows for entertainment purposes too, and he was always willing to help out the police in missing person cases. Trying to help the detective understand the process of hypnosis, he explained that as the client relaxes, their eyes begin to flutter as they closed, and that was the point he would zero in on a specific timeframe. Fitzgerald watched closely as the hypnosis began and Clifford Nichols began to relax. The detective was even more amazed when Nichols' eyes began to flutter while they were closed, and he began to describe the van he had seen. It was just as Reinbold had described.

Under hypnosis, Clifford Nichols was able to recall the words "LEISURE VAN" written on rear of the vehicle. He also remembered the stripe on the van was gold, brown, and copper colored. There was a chrome bumper and a chrome ladder on the rear of the van. The farmer recalled the license plate was red and white, but he couldn't recall the numbers.

Beyond Nichols' report of the van, there were other reports that a car had pulled into the farm lane and sat for several hours, but witnesses couldn't provide any other details about the car.

Leads began to come in about Marita's murder, and while each one had to be followed up, most turned out to be dead ends.

After Nichols' hypnosis session, investigators focused their interviews on Marita's ex-husband. They interviewed her family members for the names of old boyfriends or acquaintances. They were grasping at straws, and they were coming up empty handed.

One promising lead was from a witness who knew Marita personally, and thought she had been behind her after Marita had left the Cork and Cleaver restaurant on June 14. As she was following Marita, she turned onto Saginaw Street from Abbott, and she saw a car similar to Marita's pull over and open her door to pick up a hitchhiker. Fitzgerald took the witness for a hypnosis session with Reinbold, and she was able to recall that the hitchhiker had dark, shoulder-length hair, and a beard. To her, it looked as if he had a sunburned complexion too. Beyond the hypnosis, police were never able to verify it wasn't actually Marita the woman was following.

After the crime lab had searched Marita's car, her family asked that her friend, Reverend Mitman, pick it up for them. The car was still at the MSU Public Safety, and when Mitman arrived, the battery was run down. When it finally started, he discovered a hole in the gas line, and there was gasoline spraying onto the engine. A grounds employee from MSU was able to repair it, and Mitman left with the vehicle. He stopped by a Shell station in East Lansing and left the car overnight to get the battery recharged.

The next day, he stopped back at the station to pick up Marita's car. When he took the car back to the church parking lot to start cleaning it up for Marita's dad, he found a knife lying in the seam of the front passenger seat. The knife had a serrated blade and a wooden handle. The length of the blade was about six inches long, and it was lying with the blade pointing forward. Mitman picked it up, then realized the implications of what he had just found. He slid the knife inside a glove to protect it, went home and he placed it in an envelope, then called the police.

Detective Cliff Oakley picked up the knife from Mitman, took it back to the sheriff's office, and tagged it as evidence. He wondered if it might be the murder weapon. After tagging it as evidence, Oakley took the knife and headed for the state crime lab. He knew the car had already been searched and wondered how anyone could have missed something so obvious. At the crime lab, the knife was checked for blood and fingerprints, but nothing was found.

After dropping the knife at the lab, Oakley contacted the MSU police to see who could have been in or around the car. Each officer who had been inside the car was certain the knife couldn't have been there when the car was initially found. The detective also spoke with the grounds person who helped repair the gas line, but he had used a jack knife. Oakley continued his follow up by contacting the state lab technicians who had searched the car. They said the knife was definitely not in the car when they searched it.

By mid-afternoon, Oakley and Fitzgerald headed to the Shell station where Reverend Mitman had left Marita's car. After checking with some of the employees, they discovered that one of them could have left a knife inside Marita's car as they worked on it. As a promotion, the station owners offered steak knives to customers as gifts, and they were able to find one of them and give it to the detectives. Oakley and Fitzgerald took the knife and headed back to the crime lab to compare the two. They knives were identical. It was another disappointment in the investigation.

Without any solid investigative leads into Marita's murder, Fitzgerald and Baldwin began to speculate about the possible religious connection as they recalled how the bricks and concrete slabs were placed over the body and how her severed hands were found in a praying position.

They wondered if Father Mitman might be able to offer some insight.

Mitman had already been interviewed by Sgt. Lyon at MSU. The priest told Lyon that he had known Marita for years and had counseled her with some of her problems. He described her personality to the detective as bitchy and manipulative, but she was also predictable. Mitman thought she was a very lonely person and was someone who had a big desire to have another relationship with a man.

Mitman was asked if there was anyone he might suspect in Marita's murder. He said there was only one person, and his name was Andrew Kensington. He described Kensington as a flake. He thought he was antagonistic and weird. Mitman recalled that in the past, Kensington had said, "A basic human right is to take the life of another."[43] He also suspected the man had made some sort of advances toward Marita in the past.

In an effort to help Ingham County investigators with their investigation into the murder, Father Mitman did a taped interview with Fitzgerald, Baldwin, Shackelford, Oakley, and Clyde Stevens. Wanting to be sure the five men had reference material during the interview, he brought a number of bibles with him.

During the interview, investigators provided Reverend Mitman with a sketch of the murder scene, showing how Marita's body was positioned. With that, Mitman began by telling the men that after looking at the sketch, he had some possible ideas about the murder. He referenced a book called *The Concordance,* saying it was a book containing lists of words that appear in the Bible, and the reader can then look up the meanings of those words. The words that came to mind for him were *stone, hand, eye, divorce,* and *adultery.*

---

43. Ingham County Sheriff's Office, Supplemental Report, Interview with John Mitman, 8279-78, July 17, 1978

Before getting too far into the discussion, he queried each investigator about their own religious beliefs. He told the men the words he had referenced in *The Concordance* were accounts of severe judgement. "Very, very heavy, very, very judgmental," he said. "With the homicide involved, it's playing God in terms of this whole judgement, judge, jury, execution."

To Father Mitman, the entire scene and how Marita's body was positioned were suggestive of one thing. "And this whole business about the stones, the picture there is, to me, what comes across is a semi-walled surface tomb," he said. He felt that Marita's burial place was an altar, saying, "Now, an altar, the definition, the traditional definition of an altar is that an altar is the place, the locus of sacrifice, and that sacrifice is an animal, a human being, ah, a bird, whatever, but is the place of sacrifice."[44]

The men shared a detail known only to a very few about a large stick laid between a rock and the young woman's body. To Father Mitman, that suggested the possibility of a kneeler.

The priest discussed one particular stone found on Marita's body. He confirmed with the investigators that the stone didn't lay on her genitals and it was not over her navel. Because of its position, he believed it represented pregnancy because it covered the womb.

Baldwin wanted to know the significance of her hands being cut off, and Mitman sidelined the question for a moment to stay on track. To him, the placement of the stones on top of Marita's body was significant, in that it could also represent being stoned to death because she was divorced. Everyone knew of her connections to the church, and several people knew she had sexual relations after her divorce, and to some, that represented adultery.

---

44. Ingham County Sheriff's Office, July 17, 1978

The police officials were intrigued by his analogy of the murder based solely on the description of scene. While they still had questions, Father Mitman said, "Almost certainly, it was done by someone who has an experience of the Bible. There are lots of people who use the Bible very selectively, to prove their case, whatever the case, and that's the kind of thing I see coming off here." Mitman was certain the killer was someone who was into judgement. That is, a judgement in vengeance and execution.

Detective Oakley's interpretation of what Father Mitman was trying to say was that the killer could be someone who went to church on Sunday, attended meetings with the church, talked about the church and the religion, but yet still committed adultery himself.

Mitman agreed, saying, "This is a person that has these kinds of problems himself, but the way they work them out, is you lay them on somebody else."

Oakley asked if the killer's problems would be something he had currently, or something from the past, and the priest told him it was likely from the killer's past, but still on his mind.

Fitzgerald was listening intently as the priest outlined his theory. As Father Mitman got deeper into his analysis of the murder scene and his religious profiling of the murderer, Fitzgerald spoke up and said, "Yup. Right. Boy, that's creepy there."

Baldwin was getting it. He understood exactly where Father Mitman was coming from. He told Mitman, "This guy that did this, if he's coming from this angle, probably feels in his own mind that he's going to be forgiven for what he's done, because he could say, 'Marita, she was sinful and everything else.'" Father Mitman agreed.[45]

At the end of the interview, no one could have realized how close the clergyman had come at profiling the killer.

---

45. Ingham County Sheriff's Office, July 15, 1978

The discussion turned to the man mentioned earlier, who was a parishioner at Father Mitman's church. Andrew Kensington was someone who Mitman was sure wouldn't give him the time of day. He described him as a troubled soul. The priest remembered him being in church the Sunday before Marita's body was discovered and that her name was bought up during a discussion following the church service.

Detectives began digging into Kensington's background. They discovered he had come from a split family. His parents divorced when he was ten, and he was sent to a military institute before eventually attending Illinois State University. His father worked as a consultant in Washington, DC, and his mother and step-father lived in the Chicago area. They would occasionally send money to support him, but when he moved to Michigan, they stopped.

In 1974, he was arrested for assault and was briefly committed to the Kalamazoo State Hospital. He had ended up in Michigan because of a girlfriend who was involved in a radical political party called the United States Justice Party. He was considered a transient because he couldn't obtain welfare. The detectives spoke with several people who considered Kensington a chronic schizophrenic who suffered from temper rages to explosive hostility. He had even admitted to some friends that he had to push his temper back to prevent himself from hurting someone. At one time, he had even refused to seek professional help because he had an illusion that he had a personal duty to kill someone, and he considered himself a genius.

The detectives knew they would have to interview him next. Within a few days of interviewing Father Mitman, Fitzgerald had received word that Andrew Kensington was being evicted from his apartment in Lansing.

That evening, Fitzgerald and McGuire met with Kensington at his apartment. When the detectives told him they wanted to speak about the possibility of involvement in Marita Choquette's homicide, he became upset and asked them to leave, yet continued to offer them information at the same time. The three ended up outside the apartment, and Kensington told them he knew Marita through the All Saints Episcopal Church in East Lansing and had given her a ride home on one occasion. In turn, she had also given him a ride home on occasion. He told the veteran investigators that he had no idea what happened to her, but that whoever had committed the murder was probably someone who was angry with the Episcopal church. He offered to do anything he could to help out the investigation and they suggested a more formal interview the following day.

The next day, the two detectives picked up Kensington to take him for the interview, and they bought him lunch on the way. While they were talking over lunch, Kensington told them the reason he had left the Episcopal church in East Lansing was because of Father Mitman. He admitted to them he had some angry feelings toward Mitman and had little respect for him.

After lunch, the three men headed for the sheriff's office for the interview.

As the taped statement started, the detectives began to ask Kensington about his impressions of Mitman again. Kensington told them he thought Mitman was a womanizer, and he thought the priest had several women he was attracted to, including Marita Choquette.

As their suspect spoke, he sat cross-legged and smoked cigarettes continuously. Kensington would smoke a cigarette down to the point where it would burn his fingers, then immediately light another one. Both investigators thought he was very strange.

Kensington continued talking and described an evening when Marita had given him and several others a ride home from the church during a snowstorm. The detectives were interested in details and asked him if she had come on to him. He said she hadn't and described her as one of the "fickle ones." McGuire, seizing on that answer, began to press him, and Kensington admitted they had had some sharp words. He said she had been in a bad mood that particular night, and he had made some comments about her car and whether or not she had paid for it. He had also criticized her driving. Marita had become very defensive, but quickly recognized that he hadn't meant anything by the questions and calmed down.

The detectives began to focus on Kensington's means of support. He admitted that he had several commercial interests, but received his financial backing from the Department of Social Services. The more Kensington spoke, the more doubts they had about the possibility he was involved in Marita's murder, but something was still lingering.

As their questioning came to a close, Kensington said, "I'm glad that I'm an innocent man."

McGuire shot back, "Innocent of what?"

"Innocent of all crime."

The two bantered back and forth. McGuire asked, "Are you talking about the death of Marita Choquette?"

"I'm talking about guilt, I think, in a general sense. I mean, we are dealing with a murder case."[46]

The detective suggested to him that maybe Marita's death was a suicide, but Kensington quickly disagreed, and he reiterated that he was glad he was an innocent man.

It became clear from the start of the interview that a lot of Kensington's answers were babbling and incoherent. While the detectives tried to pin him down on several things, they couldn't. They also knew they wouldn't be able to have him take a polygraph examination. In their minds, he was just too weird.

---

46. Ingham County Sheriff's Office, Supplemental report, Interview with Andrew Kensington, 8279-78, July 20, 1978

While Kensington was being interviewed, Detective Oakley was meeting with a waitress at the Howard Johnson's in East Lansing about another tip. The waitress recalled that around mid-June, a man had come into the restaurant, and as she was waiting on him, he asked if she had heard about the girl who was missing. "Her name is Marita," he said. The man had said that Marita's parents had hired him because he's an attorney, and he was expecting to be contacted by the Nazis about the missing woman. He told her Marita's disappearance was directly related to the Patti Hearst case and finished the conversation by saying that Marita was a nice person.

When Oakley asked more specific questions about the man, she said whenever she saw him, he always appeared to have law books. She described him as having a beard and mustache. She also said he wore dark-rimmed glasses, and he always wore a plaid shirt with a sweater vest over it. More specifically, she said he wore a copper bracelet and two rings. She also thought he smoked Chesterfield cigarettes and described exactly how would stub them out when he was done smoking them. She told the detective that she had seen him in the restaurant three separate times, and he would usually stay for two or three hours. She also mentioned he never looked anyone in the eye when he talked with them and had a peculiar odor about him.

Oakley knew exactly who she was referring to. He contacted Fitzgerald and McGuire and got a photo of Andrew Kensington. Detective Oakley showed it to the waitress, and she identified him as the person she had spoken to. By that time, the detectives had already discovered he had an alias.

Surveillance was set up on the apartment where Kensington was being evicted. As detectives watched Kensington hand the keys over to the apartment manager and leave, they approached the manager. Explaining their reason for being there, they were able to get permission to search the apartment. The keys were handed over to the detectives, and they made sure the apartment was secure. The following morning, they returned with lab technicians from the MSP crime lab and Kensington's former apartment was processed to see if there was any evidence. While the apartment was empty, a hair brush and some clothing were found and seized and sent to the lab.

Fitzgerald, Baldwin, and McGuire, along with other detectives in the bureau, continued working on Marita's murder through the month of July and into August. While working on their investigation, they heard about a new missing person case from the MSU campus: Wendy Bush had last been seen on the day Marita's body had been found, and the campus police were handling the investigation.

8

By July 5, and the discovery of Marita's body, a growing concern had developed with the MSU police about Wendy Bush's disappearance. The department averaged one thousand missing person reports per year, and the majority of them were quickly resolved, but this case was different. Wendy Bush's lifestyle differed from the predictable lifestyle of other missing woman from Michigan State.

Wendy Bush had spent June 27 hurrying around campus, trying to get registered for classes. Her short-term loan had been refused and she couldn't get into the classes she wanted. She owed money to Michigan State and she was certain they were going to kick her out of her dorm in Case Hall. She was nearly in tears.

At the cafeteria on campus, she had a paycheck waiting for her.

On June 28, the Agricultural Economics major was scheduled to start work at noon. She was very reliable because she needed the money, and she never missed a shift. That's what concerned Marcia Evans, the cafeteria supervisor who called the MSU police when Wendy didn't show up for her shift.

Evans relayed to Officer Brett Bean that a few days before, the blonde coed had been sent home early because she was spending too much time talking with people rather than working. She returned to work a day or two later and seemed a little depressed. The supervisor also told the officer that Wendy liked to make short-term relationships with men and would talk with anyone.

Initially, the campus police suspected she might have simply left campus for the long Fourth of July holiday.

At twenty-one years old, the five-foot-five-inch, one hundred-forty-five-pound coed's bright blonde hair was a stark contrast to her green eyes. From St. Louis, Michigan, she was the oldest of five children. Two of her brothers suffered from muscular dystrophy, and as a child, Wendy had suffered from red measles and encephalitis. After recovering, she began having a mild form of seizures, and as a young adult, regularly took medication to prevent them. Because of her seizures, Wendy never learned to drive and didn't have a driver's license.

In high school, she was an A student, and held a 3.5 GPA at MSU.

After taking down information for the report, the MSU officer left the Union Cafe and headed to the seventh floor of Case Hall. When he arrived at Wendy's room, he met with her roommate. Wendy's roommate hadn't seen her since the previous evening when she had picked up her linen. She also told the officer that Wendy's boyfriend had stopped by the dorm room at about 8:30 and had asked where Wendy was.

Officer Bean was able to track down Wendy's former boyfriend Brit Wilson. Wilson said that he and Wendy had previously dated but had broken off their relationship in the first part of June. He had run into her near the library on June 27 at around eleven p.m., and she was with another man. Wilson described him as a little taller than Wendy, who looked to be in his mid-twenties. He was wearing a collared shirt and pressed pants. He also thought the man was wearing some sort of a necklace. To Wilson, the man looked as if he should be carrying a briefcase. As Wilson spoke briefly with his former girlfriend that night, the man seemed to disappear into the shadows. He suspected the man was Wendy's new boyfriend, and if she wasn't at the dorm, she was probably living with him.

Bean followed up with a phone call to Wendy's father in St. Louis. He hadn't seen or talked to Wendy since before her disappearance was reported, and he told the investigator that he had received a phone call from the *Lansing State Journal* that afternoon. The person calling was inquiring about his daughter's disappearance, and he thought it was prank call so he hung up on them.

As the police began to piece together information about Wendy, a disturbing portrait began to emerge about her relationship with her parents. Wendy Bush had been told not to return home by her mother. Their relationship had deteriorated to a breaking point because she was constantly changing her major, and was seeking independent status on her financial aid. Her mom had asked her to drop out of college until she decided what she wanted to do, but when she refused, both her parents decided to stop paying for her education. That didn't matter to Wendy. She borrowed the money to continue. Her mom hadn't seen her for the two months prior to her disappearance.

The college lifestyle was something Wendy seemed to enjoy. Her lifestyle was described as less regulated, free spirited, and she seemed to think nothing of short-term, casual relationships while still wanting to put her life in order. She would talk to anyone. Even an academic advisor of Wendy's described her as being naïve in terms of being realistic about the dangers of being in short-term relationships with people she didn't really know.

As word began to spread about Wendy's disappearance, MSU police received a phone call from an acquaintance who told them Wendy had mentioned the possibility of going to Ann Arbor to see a friend of hers, who was from Africa, or maybe even going to see friends in Indiana. While that would certainly explain her hasty departure, there was one problem with that theory: she hadn't taken anything with her when she left. Her purse was still in her dorm, all of her personal items were still in the dorm, and her medication to prevent her seizures was still in her dorm.

By July 5, MSU police decided another interview with Wendy's former boyfriend was in order. As they began the interview, Brit Wilson began to shake and became very nervous, but as the interview progressed, he slowly began to calm down. He told the officers he had known Wendy for approximately two and a half years, and they were sometimes lovers. That would only last until she would see someone else she might want to have a relationship with, and they would break up for a short time. He knew she had several relationships, and that made him jealous at times. Brit and Wendy had also discussed the possibility of marriage, but she had told him she enjoyed living too much to be married.

By the end of the spring term, Brit was tired of being used by Wendy, and while he still had deep-seated feelings for her, they broke up. He told the officers again how the last time he had seen Wendy was on June 27 at around eleven p.m. near the library, and he gave another description of the man she was walking with. When he last saw her he thought they were walking toward Grand River Avenue on the north side of campus.

As the investigation entered its second week, Officer Bean told the media, "It's been two weeks. The longer she's missing, the more serious it gets." They were now labeling the missing coed's case as extremely serious.

Tips trickled in. MSU investigators were able to identify and interview the friend from Ann Arbor who Wendy had mentioned. When contacted by the police, he told investigators that he and Wendy had become friends and were close, but there was nothing more to their relationship than that. He had last seen her the day before she was reported missing.

In another tip, investigators were told that Wendy had said she might move to California and perform in porn movies, but police doubted the tip.

The investigators also spoke with a campus counselor who knew Wendy. The counselor offered an opinion based on Wendy's personality and believed she had staged her own disappearance. She felt Wendy was seeking attention.

In yet another tip, an acquaintance of Wendy's had contacted the police and told them Wendy had mentioned going to Philadelphia because she had a boyfriend in the orchestra there. Detectives were able to contact the musician, and he told them the orchestra had played at MSU two years prior. After the show, Wendy and her boyfriend had approached him in the lobby and struck up a conversation. She seemed very forward. He ignored her, and later that night, he and some other members had gone to the Pantry restaurant in East Lansing for a bite to eat. He ran into Wendy there, and she was alone. They talked and ended up exchanging addresses. A year or so later, he received a letter from her indicating she wanted to come see him in Philadelphia, and she spoke in the letter of sleeping arrangements with him. He thought it was very strange and never wrote back to her.

While police worked on that, another tip came in that Wendy was seen in Northport, Michigan, at the tip of the Leelanau Peninsula. An arrangement was made with the Michigan State Police to contact the witness there and show the person a photo of Wendy in an attempt to confirm the sighting. It was another dead end.

The MSU police considered Wendy the "odd woman out." Her case didn't fit a particular pattern like they might expect. From the information they were gathering, they considered her lifestyle impulsive and rootless. All indications were that she was talkative to the point of being compulsive. She had been fired from a job at Arby's in East Lansing the spring before her disappearance, and she attached herself to men who showed even the slightest interest in her. One high-ranking officer at the MSU police considered her a troubled young woman who was in need of counseling.

Wendy's mother had become less than optimistic about her daughter's disappearance. She was certain her daughter was dead. She had gone to Case Hall to pick up all of Wendy's things, including her clothes and medication. Nothing was missing from her room. She was steadfast in her belief that Wendy hadn't planned to leave. There were still two paychecks in her room, plus her student loan paperwork. Mrs. Bush was also concerned about her two handicapped sons finding out about their missing sister. She dearly hoped no one would tell them about her disappearance.

In late July, police had run out of leads to follow up on, and in early August, possibly anticipating the worst, detectives from MSU had received dental records of Wendy Bush to keep on file.

———————

Harold Duncan enjoyed working for Ernie Stuart. Duncan was working on job site #123 at the end of Fairoaks Court in East Lansing on August 14. He needed more carpentry supplies and knew he'd have to run to Erb Lumber to pick them up. As he got into his pickup truck, he headed west toward Coolidge Road. As he began to slow for the stop sign, he recognized Ernie's wife, Kristine, walking north on Coolidge as she turned onto Fairoaks. He stopped short of the stop sign and rolled his window down.

"What's the matter? Did Ernie take the car away from you?" he jokingly asked.[47]

———————

47. East Lansing Police Department, Original police report, Missing Person, 3268-C-78, August 14, 1978

The five-foot-four-inch teacher laughed as she stopped briefly. She told him the car was in for repairs. Duncan laughed at her response and continued up to the stop sign. He glanced to the north and could see southbound traffic, but he had enough time to make his turn. As Harold Duncan headed south on Coolidge, he passed a northbound car driven by Nancy Daniels.

Nancy Daniels was supposed to meet her husband but was running late. The two were meeting in Lansing at ten.

As she left her home on Wolf Court, just one block south of Fairoaks, she headed west toward Coolidge Street, stopped, then turned northbound. As she started north on Coolidge approaching Fairoaks, she glanced to her right and could see a car parked on the side of the street. To her, it looked as if two people were arguing. She quickly turned her attention back in front as a car turned left in front of her and she had to slam on her brakes. She came to an abrupt stop. She looked to her right again at the car on Fairoaks. The man backed away from the car a few feet and stood for a few seconds as he turned and looked directly at her. She quickly accelerated to leave and drove immediately to Center Street in Lansing to meet with her husband. She was in a daze.

When Nancy arrived to meet her husband, she wanted to tell him what she had seen, but he was in a hurry, and she never had the chance.

As a seventh grade Life Sciences teacher, Kristine Stuart was hired by the Lansing School District in 1975 after working for St. Gerard's Catholic School in Eaton County's Delta Township. She started in the Lansing schools on a part-time basis, but that only lasted three weeks before she was offered a full-time position. She gladly accepted it.

Kristine was dedicated to her students, and often times could be seen with her arm around one of them. She had a great concern for them and was considered an outstanding teacher. She was deeply caring; not only to her students, but her co-workers too.

She and her husband were married in the early seventies, and they had yet to have any children. There was a desire on her part to have kids, and she had visited her gynecologist a year earlier to discuss her fertility. Still, she was a very happy woman who enjoyed crafting and gourmet.

On August 13, Ernie and Kristine Stuart arrived back at their home on Basswood Court at around 5:30 p.m., returning from a canoe trip in northern Michigan near Roscommon with Kristine's parents.

The following morning, as Kristine was still lying in bed, Ernie got up to get ready for work. He was heading to his office on South Waverly Road in Lansing. Ernie left without getting her out of bed.

Much like the other school teachers in Lansing, Kristine was off for the summer. As she laid in bed awake, she knew she'd have to get up pretty soon because she had to take her 1977 MG to Herm's Body Shop in Lansing for some repairs. Her plan was to take a bus back home.

———

At 6:30 p.m., Ernie Stuart arrived back home on Basswood Court. The house was locked, and as he walked inside, he noticed the dog was anxious. It was obvious the dog hadn't been let out for quite some time. Calling for Kristine and getting no answer, he noticed the bed was unmade. She surely would have made the bed during the day. He found a bus schedule on the bedroom dresser.

Concerned, he began to call Kristine's friends and other family, hoping she might be visiting someone, but no one had heard from her. By 11:30, Ernie was more concerned than ever. This wasn't like Kristine. They had been married for eight years and had never been apart. They hadn't had any disagreements or fights. This was out of the ordinary.

At 11:40, Ernie made a call to the East Lansing Police Department to report his wife missing. While the desk officer took down the information, he told Ernie that little could be done until morning. Since there wasn't any evidence of foul play, he was told an area broadcast would be radioed to the police units to keep an eye out for her, and if she hadn't shown up by morning, he should call back to have an officer dispatched to the house.

The longest night of Ernie Stuart's life followed as he waited for daybreak to call police again. At about 7:40 a.m., he made the call, and an officer was dispatched to the Stuart home.

When Officer Bob Fisher began the initial interview of the frantic husband, Ernie described the previous morning and told him Kristine was still in bed when he left the house at around 5:45. He knew she had an appointment at Herm's Auto Body in Lansing that had been made several weeks prior. He described her car to Fisher and told him she was planning on taking the bus back home.

Officer Fisher had taken missing persons reports before. He needed to know if they had had an argument or disagreement of some sort and quickly learned they hadn't. Was she a heavy drinker? No. Did she take any medication? No. Ernie told him he had called everyone he could think of to locate his wife.

After Fisher took the initial information, he drove to Herm's Auto Body. He met with two employees, and they remembered Kristine coming in the previous day. She had gotten there around 8:30 and had spent no more than fifteen or twenty minutes in the shop. She dropped off the car, and one of the employees remembered seeing her leave. To him, it looked as if she was heading for the bus stop in front of the Boron gas station, but no one could say whether or not she actually got on a bus.

After finding out she had actually made it to the body shop and dropped her car off, Fisher headed back to the Stuart home. When he arrived, he found that Ernie Stuart had already organized some family and friends and had begun to search the area around his home. Ernie had also learned that one of his employees, Harold Duncan, had seen Kristine the previous morning and had spoken very briefly with her. Fisher needed to talk with him.

By 9:30, Fisher had already requested a helicopter from the state police to begin an air search for Kristine. East Lansing's deputy chief arrived at the Stuart home along with Dean Tucker. Concern began to grip everyone.

Martha Young was still missing. Marita Choquette had been missing and was found dead. Wendy Bush was still missing. While some local police believed the Martha Young case was an isolated murder between Don Miller and his former girlfriend, others in the law enforcement circle now believed they were dealing with a serial killer.

Officer Fisher obtained some family photos of Kristine, and copies were made and distributed to numerous police officers who had been dispatched to help canvass the area. The officers, armed with her photo, began going door to door in search of the school teacher.

Rick Westgate was assigned as an observer in the helicopter, and as the chopper circled the area between Saginaw Highway and Lake Lansing Road, the police department's afternoon shift was called in early to help in the door-to-door search. If Westgate saw areas that couldn't be searched from the air, he notified the deputy chief on the ground, and officers were assigned to check the area on foot.

Officers from the East Lansing police bike patrol were dispatched to help in the search, and the MSU police sent additional manpower to the area to help out.

The search for Kristine had been underway for two hours. Officers continued going door to door in hopes that someone saw something the previous morning. At around 11:30, an East Lansing officer was walking along the south side of Fairoaks, just east of Coolidge, when he noticed something lying in the grass just off the street. It was a pair of sunglasses. He called for Sgt. Jim Kelley.

As officers documented the location of the glasses lying in the grass, three-hundred-thirty-five feet east of the intersection, they also noticed a skid mark on the road surface that also began three-hundred-thirty-five feet east of the intersection. They had no way of knowing whether or not the skid was related to the missing woman. The position where the glasses was found was recorded, and they were collected as evidence by Kelley. Tucker headed to the Stuart residence because he needed to know if the glasses belonged to Kristine.

Officers searching the area also found a woman's brown shoe behind a residence on Coolidge. The Bass brand shoe was also plotted, then taken as evidence.

Tucker could tell from markings on the glasses they had been purchased at Nu-Vision. To confirm his suspicions, Tucker asked Ernie where Kristine had purchased her glasses. He checked his records at the house and found a billing statement from Nu-Vision Optical. There were two numbers on the billing statement that he pointed out to Tucker. Those numbers (528634 and 528135) represented receipt numbers. The billing number on both receipts was 1139148, and the paperwork showed they were delivered to a K. Stuart on August 1, 1977, and August 12, 1977, just a little over a year earlier.

Z52, representative of the size, appeared on the frames. The Z represented the color brown. When investigators checked at the NuVision Optical store, the clerk was able to tell them the delivery number was 1139148, and it belonged to Kristine Stuart. Each lens was checked with the prescription sheet, and the clerk was able to say with certainty they belonged to Kristine. Each lens was assigned an identification number, and those numbers coincided with the frames. When a lensometer was set to the prescription numbers, they were matched against the lens and they matched. The police were now certain the glasses belonged to Kristine Stuart.

Officer Fisher was busy checking with the CATA bus service. The Capital Area Transportation Authority operated the public transportation busses around Lansing, and Fisher was able to find one driver who was sure he picked up a woman at around 9:30 a.m. near Herm's Auto Body. He recalled the woman was wearing a blouse and shorts, and she was wearing sunglasses. The driver also said she had told him she was having her car repaired. He remembered her because she was the only passenger he had picked up near downtown Lansing that morning. He told Fisher he had dropped her off at the Kroger store in the Frandor shopping center and told her she could catch the Pebblebrook bus to Coolidge Road.

As bits and pieces came in, police began to theorize that Kristine had dropped her car off at Herm's Auto Body, taken a CATA bus to Frandor, then to Coolidge, where she walked up to Fairoaks.

The following day, officers began to compile a list of all the construction workers working at the job sites on Fairoaks.

By 8:15 a.m. on August 16, investigators from the ELPD were meeting in the chief's office. They were being briefed on the Kristine Stuart case and what Tucker wanted them to do for the day. Their instructions were clear and concise: follow up on the tips phoned in the previous evening about Kristine's disappearance.

After the early briefing, Westgate went with Tucker to the Stuart home. With Kristine's parents already at the house, they wrote a list of what would be in Kristine's purse should it end up being found. Westgate also set up a phone recorder at the home in case there was some sort of a ransom demand.

While at the Stuart home, Tucker learned Kristine was originally from Port Huron. Her parents said they had been on a canoeing trip with Ernie and Kristine, and had returned to their own home on August 13, late in the afternoon, just as their daughter and son-in-law had. They told the detectives there was no animosity during the trip, and there was no apparent trouble between Ernie and their daughter. On the morning when Ernie first reported Kristine missing, he had called them at about six to ask if they had heard from her since last seeing her on August 13. When he told them she was missing, they immediately left for East Lansing. Kristine's mom said her daughter was a science teacher at Lansing's Gardner Junior High School, and she was a very organized person. Because she taught school during the summer also, she only had a short two-week break before beginning the fall term.

The two detectives also interviewed Ernie Stuart again, and he told Tucker the same thing he had told Officer Fisher. He added that if his wife were going to be somewhere, she would leave a note telling him where she was.

After Tucker finished speaking with Ernie Stuart and Kristine's parents, he met with Harold Duncan. Duncan agreed to hypnosis to see if he might remember anything additional. The two men headed to Damon Reinbold's house.

As Reinbold began the hypnosis session, Duncan described exactly what he had told Officer Fisher. He had recognized Kristine as she walked around the corner on to Fairoaks from Coolidge. He stopped to talk briefly, made a left turn onto Coolidge, and continued to Erb Lumber. He was able to recall one additional detail: Kristine seemed to have something on her shoulder. More than likely it was her purse. He was asked specifically if he had seen anyone else walking on Coolidge or making a turn onto Fairoaks, and while he wished he had, he could only tell the investigators no.

While Tucker was finishing his interview with Duncan, Westgate was busy continuing his follow-up. He had no idea that his first tip would be crucial in the disappearance of Kristine Stuart, and no way of knowing that later that day, he would arrest her killer.

———————

After leaving the Stuart home, Rick Westgate went to Kristine's dentist, and he was given her dental records so police would have them quickly available should they be needed. After picking up the dental records, he looked at his first tip sheet. He saw the name Nancy Daniels.

He drove to Wolf Court, which ran off Coolidge, only a block south of where Kristine was last seen. Westgate looked at the tip sheet again. Nancy Daniels had called in the previous evening, and the tip sheet said she had seen something at Coolidge and Fairoaks on the day Kristine had disappeared.

The detective turned onto Wolf Court and slowly made his way down the quiet residential street looking for the house number. As he pulled into the drive, he took another look at the tip sheet before walking to the front door.

After a quick knock, he was greeted by Nancy Daniels. She already knew why he was there. She had been told an officer would be contacting her.

As Westgate took a seat in her living room, Nancy began to tell him what she had seen only two days earlier; on August 14, around ten a.m., she had seen a car stopped on Fairoaks near Coolidge, and a man had been standing alongside the car. She thought the car was gold. She also told the officer she would be willing to undergo hypnosis if he thought it might help her recall more details.

Nancy finished relaying her information to Westgate, but never realized she had unknowingly suppressed key details about what she had seen on the morning of August 14.

After leaving the Daniels residence, Officer Westgate drove into Lansing to meet with Kristine's gynecologist. He had hoped to find out her blood type but it wasn't available.

Westgate drove to the state crime lab after leaving the doctor's office. He met with a technician and they drove back to the Stuart home to replace the original phone recording equipment with something more advanced. While at the house, the officer picked up some items from Ernie that would likely have Kristine's fingerprints on them so they could be used for identification purposes if they were needed. Ernie Stuart gave him a bottle of lotion, a magazine, a notebook, and a stapler.

Officer Westgate continued his follow up by contacting Kristine Stuart's bank to see if there had been any purchases on the Stuarts' joint credit card in the previous three days, but there hadn't.

Morning passed quickly into the afternoon as the officer kept busy and hoped for one small clue that might help pinpoint the whereabouts of Kristine Stuart. He was in his car when the dispatcher's voice on the radio caught his attention. It was an area broadcast about the rape and attempted murder of two teens in Eaton County's Delta Township. When he heard the description of the car and who the owner was, he headed toward the condo where Don Miller was living with his fiancée.

9

As Detective Norm Kelley was finishing his interview with James Regan, the man who had witnessed Lisa Gilbert run from her home with her hands bound behind her back, a deputy poked his head in and interrupted. He told Kelley that Don Miller had just been arrested by the East Lansing police.

Kelley knew there was much to be done. Like everyone else, he knew Miller was the prime suspect in the disappearance of Martha Sue Young, and now he was in custody for the rape and attempted murder of fourteen-year-old Lisa Gilbert and the attempted murder of her thirteen-year-old brother Randy.

Detective Kelley told the young deputy to tell the East Lansing police he was on his way. Lieutenant Ken Dedafoe was with Kelley, and the two men headed for East Lansing.

At the ELPD, Kelley looked over the booking sheet. It was standard procedure that the officer verify the prisoner's property taken from him when he was booked in. He read what had been taken from Miller when he was arrested: one watch, an identification case, scissors, a pen, a comb, his wallet, a belt, and $24.41. At 6:11 p.m., Miller was turned over to Kelley and Dedafoe.

As the three made their way back toward Eaton County, Miller didn't say much. He spoke briefly in the car about some sort of powers controlling his mind. Rather than heading directly to the Eaton County Jail in Charlotte, Kelley felt he might have better success with an interview at the Delta Township offices. It would be less intimidating in an office setting. He could take him to the jail in Charlotte afterward.

As Kelley and Dedafoe were heading to the Delta Township fire station with their prisoner, work had already begun at the Gilbert home. Crime lab technicians from the MSP had arrived and were starting to collect the evidence necessary to convict Don Miller.

When the two detectives arrived at the fire station, they walked their handcuffed suspect into Ken Dorin's office where they planned the interview. Miller had already been read his rights at five p.m. by Lt. Murray in East Lansing, but Kelley was going to read them again, and he started by turning on the tape recorder. He began by identifying the suspect as Donald Gene Miller.

"No, it's just Don," the suspect said as he interrupted the detective.

Kelley corrected himself and said he was going to read him his rights. He asked that Miller initial next to each phrase after it was read to him. He added that the initials weren't an admission to anything and would only indicate he understood each phrase read to him.

As Kelley got to the second phrase, he told Miller he was going to make a slight change to the form, saying, "The words are 'may be used against you.' I'm going to put in there 'will be used against you.'" He continued, "I also understand that any statements, or any answers I might give to questions, and it says now on the form, 'may be used against me in court.' I've crossed that out and put 'will be.'"[48]

Miller said he understood.

After the detective finished reading the Miranda, Miller was asked if he understood each of them. He said he did.

"My throat's kind of dry," Miller said.

48. Eaton County Sheriff's Department. Supplemental Report. Interview with Don G. Miller. 78-2654-C. August 16, 1978

Kelley offered the suspect a Coke, explained to him that he would be allowed to use the phone, then asked Miller to sign the form and indicate on it whether he would or wouldn't speak with the officers.

"I think I'll wait until I make my phone call," he said.

At 6:47, the detectives allowed him to use the phone.

After the call was made, crime lab technicians came into Dorin's office and interrupted Kelley. They needed to take some evidentiary samples. The two technicians looked over Miller's body to see if there were any scratches or marks, then took fingernail clippings and a swab before leaving.

Norm Kelley was a patient man. As the two technicians left the fire chief's office, Kelley finished explaining the last part of the Miranda form and told Miller they would be taking him to the jail in Charlotte.

At 7:28, the rights form was completed and signed by Miller and Kelley. As part of every interview, Kelley asked his suspect if he had any questions he wanted to ask.

"My mind is so boggled. It's hard for me to remember," Miller said.

"What is it you're confused about?" Kelley asked.

"I don't know why I've been arrested. I mean, because I wasn't, you know, wasn't doing anything. I was just shopping."[49]

Kelley asked him where he had been shopping.

Don Miller said he'd been shopping in East Lansing and at the mall. He was looking for a present for his girlfriend's daughter, but hadn't found one. He told the detective that it was around 2:30 when he was shopping, and he'd driven to his girlfriend's place. He said after he got to his girlfriend's at 4:30 or so, things got weird.

The officers continued their casual conversation by asking Miller if he remembered which stores he had gone to

---

49. Eaton County Sheriff's Department, August 16, 1978

in the mall. He said he'd been at the Knapp's store and then to the Frandor Shopping Center, and finally to Meijer's.

Norm Kelley knew what he was doing, and he wanted to be up front with Don Miller. He said, "Okay, Don. I'm going to explain a little bit why you are here today, okay? Right up front. I'm going to tell you, okay, I feel you got a right to know."

Before Kelley was able to say anything else, Miller was quick to reply. "It must have been somebody else. It was somebody else's car."

Kelley kept the calm demeanor he was known for when he confronted Don Miller with the facts. He told him they had his license number, witnesses had seen him leave, and he had even talked to one of them. Miller acted like he didn't know what Kelley was talking about, and Kelley told him the witnesses could identify him.

"I don't see how," Miller said.

Kelley pressed him. He told him he needed to provide some names of someone who could verify his story. He knew there was no way Miller could do it, but he asked the suspect if he could help him out.

"I might be able to, but I'd have to go over to Sears and see if that person is there. I don't know because I was in Sears. I don't know if the person would be there or even remember, but I can try."[50] He said the cashier might remember him, but he wasn't sure.

The two detectives asked if there was anyone else who might remember him, and he said he couldn't think of anyone.

"Can you explain to me why they wrote down your license number?" Kelley asked.

The detective knew the witnesses had written down the correct license number. He pressed the suspect a little more when he asked if he had loaned his car to anyone. Kelley

---

50. Eaton County Sheriff's Department, August 16, 1978

knew Miller couldn't claim it was stolen because he'd already told them he'd been shopping, and the police had seen him driving it.

"It couldn't have been stolen, could it?"

Miller was beginning to withdraw a little when he asked if he could call his girlfriend.

Kelley promised him a call as soon as they arrived at the jail in Charlotte. He told the suspected rapist that he wasn't buying his story. "It's not concrete enough, there's no names, there's no places for me to check out. And I got to believe what the witnesses told me, the witnesses that got your license number and they can identify you. They saw you, the description, the clothing, everything."

"Something is haywire somewhere," Miller said.[51]

Kelley agreed, and he told Miller that only he could clear things up.

Don Miller still insisted on going to Sears to see if they might find the cashier who could remember him.

Kelley thought if they had just a few more minutes, he could get Miller to confess, so he redirected him by asking about a muffler repair Miller had mentioned on the way to the Delta office, then about where he'd spent his vacation. Miller said he'd gone over to Holland, south of Grand Rapids, and Kelley asked him if he had relatives or friends over there.

Their suspect told them no, then said he'd like to use the phone as soon as possible.

Kelley knew the strategies used in an interview were dependent on the suspect. He had talked with Miller on their way to the office, and though it was outside of his Miranda warnings and might not be admissible, they would still have information to help in the investigation. The detective knew there was a sort of dance he had to play with a suspect during an interview. He didn't think Dedafoe

---

51. Eaton County Sheriff's Department, August 16, 1978

had enough experience as a detective to know that, but still deferred to the lieutenant by asking if he had any questions for Don Miller.

Ken Dedafoe had remained quiet thus far. He had wanted to take Miller to Charlotte from the start, but Kelley thought it best to do the interview at their Delta Township office. The lieutenant had a particular way he wanted to question the suspect, and it was in direct conflict with Kelley's proven techniques. He was still anxious to get the prisoner to the jail, but now offered the chance to ask some questions, he jumped on it.

Dedafoe told Miller about the witnesses again, and described how James Regan had pulled into the drive behind him. He told the suspect the witness had already described him, and other witnesses had written down his license number. He finished by saying, "There is no doubt in my mind, right now, at this time, that you're the person that attempted to stab this boy and attempted the rape on the girl."

Kelley calmly interjected, saying, "We'd like to hear it from you, Don."

"You keep asking me questions."

"No, we're not asking you particular questions. I'm telling you what took place," Dedafoe said. He wasn't giving up, and he told Miller they had to go with what the witnesses had told them. He mentioned the license plate number again and even mentioned the photographs shown to one witness.

"I don't know how they could have gotten my license plate number," Miller said.

"We think you do, Don, and we'd like to have you tell us," Kelley said quietly. He felt he might be close to a confession when he added, "I mean, you can sit there and tell us about Sears and all this other stuff, but I think that you know right now that that's just not true. I think you know. I can sense by your reaction. I'd rather that you would tell me."[52] The detective was playing on Miller's soft side.

"It must have been somebody else that looked like me."

"It's your car, your license number," Dedafoe said.

Don Miller knew they had him, but he wasn't giving up. He tried searching for some explanation in hopes the two seasoned police officers would buy it. "Maybe they stole my plates. I don't know, I'm not sure," he said. "I'm trying to think how they could have gotten my license number."

Kelley was gentle yet persistent. "Well, we think you know, Don. You know you would know, I think you were there. I know you were there. I think you want to tell us."

Just as quickly as the interview had started, it ended. "I'd like to tell you, but I refuse to talk," Miller said.

Norm Kelley thought if he'd have had just a few more minutes with him, he could have had a confession.

Tom Bengston's firm was hosting a shrimp dinner for the Ingham County Bar Association when he heard the news of Don Miller's arrest. Up to that point he had used an ad hoc approach in dealing with his client, taking any developments one day at a time. "This could be a problem," he said to himself when he heard the news.

Since his firm was hosting the dinner, he decided not to leave the gathering suddenly. He needed time to digest what options he might have. After the dinner was over, he talked with one of his law partners about what he might do next. His colleague met him later that night over coffee to discuss the arrest. Bengston didn't know a lot of the details and wondered why the police were looking at his client for the rape. He needed some answers.

----

52. Eaton County Sheriff's Department, August 16, 1978

As the two lawyers spoke, Bengston continued to wonder what options he might have. Maybe it was a case of mistaken identity. Could someone be mistaken about the license plate number? At that point, Don Miller's defense attorney simply didn't know.

The old Eaton County courthouse, built in 1867, towered over the center of Charlotte with stately charm in the center of the small city. The tall white pillars on both the south and east sides of the building were a stark contrast to the orange brick as they marked two entrances to the grand structure.

Sitting next to the courthouse was a two-story brick building with bars across the windows on the second floor. Built in 1961, the jail had replaced an antiquated building that had been connected to a large Victorian residence which had once been home to the sheriff. The new jail, built separate from the old sheriff's residence, sat in virtually the same location.

Detective Kelley turned onto the main street dividing the east and west side of Charlotte, then quickly slowed for the left turn into the sheriff's department parking lot. The small, fenced area at the rear of the building was limited to eight patrol cars. As he made the turn, the garage door at the far end of the lot began to slowly rise, and the detective eased the unmarked car inside. Kelley and Dedafoe had arrived with their prisoner.

Locking their weapons in a lockbox before entering the building, the two detectives followed Don Miller up a small set of concrete steps inside the garage. The dark orange paint on the bars was peeling and dirty as the three men turned immediately to their right and made another quick turn to the left into a caged area facing the booking counter.

The cage was lined with a heavy mesh screen with a small opening at desk height to pass paperwork through.

Dedafoe told Kelley he would book Miller. As he was taking the handcuffs off the suspect, Kelley left to meet with Assistant Prosecuting Attorney Ray Buffmeyer to get the search warrants. They would need two of them: one for Miller's car and one for evidence from Miller's body.

Each search warrant had to be very specific, and each affidavit outlined Kelley's probable cause for the warrant. The first called for the seizure of hair, blood, saliva, perspiration, and urine samples from Don Miller. The warrant for Miller's car specified blood, gloves, ropes, belts, fingerprints, soil samples, hair, any bodily fluids, knives or other weapons, clothing fibers, and cigarette butts. It went on further to list other trace evidence, female shoes, female clothing, men's neckties, and glasses.

While Kelley was working on the search warrants, Don Miller was answering a series of monotonous questions asked of every prisoner brought into the jail. After, he was photographed, fingerprinted, and placed in a holding cell near the booking area.

Ninety minutes after meeting with Ray Buffmeyer, Norm Kelley tracked down District Court Judge Ken Hansen at his home and had him sign both search warrants.

While Dedafoe and Kelley were transporting Miller to the jail, his car had been towed from East Lansing back to the fire station. After having the car placed in an apparatus bay, yellow crime scene tape was placed around the entire exterior so the integrity of the secured vehicle could be maintained. A deputy was assigned to guard the car until the following morning.

By one a.m., the two detectives had their prisoner in the car again, and they drove three blocks to the local hospital. Miller, in shackles, was taken into the emergency room, and Kelley showed the search warrant to the emergency room doctor on duty. He examined Miller and collected the items outlined in the search warrant. He began by collecting blood samples, hairs, and a urine sample. He examined the inside of the suspect's thighs for any evidence of blood, but didn't find any.

The doctor packaged the evidence and turned it over to Det. Kelley. It was imperative the evidence be available to state lab technicians the following morning, so Kelley turned it over to another deputy for transportation to the crime lab.

With Don Miller back at the jail and the first search warrant complete, both Kelley and Dedafoe headed for home for a quick night's rest.

By 9:30 that morning, Kelley was back at the prosecuting attorney's office to pick up Mike Hocking. Hocking knew there was only one district court judge available for Miller's arraignment, and that judge also worked in neighboring Barry County. He wouldn't be available until the afternoon, so the arraignment would have to wait.

While waiting for the judge, the two headed for the fire station to watch while lab technicians searched Don Miller's car. The search of the car took several hours, and technicians seized numerous pieces of evidence. Beginning in the trunk, they found several pieces of men's clothing, including dark green pants, a green shirt, two pairs of men's white underwear, sunglasses, and a pair of black pants with underwear tucked inside the pocket, as well as two tents. From inside the tents, they were able to find several human hairs, which were collected and packaged separately. There was also a box in the trunk that had a tow chain with some wire attached to it. The small wire held the chain together in loops. It looked as if it could be used to strangle someone. There was a second box with a white jumpsuit in a clear plastic bag and rubber gloves.

Inside the passenger compartment, they found numerous fingerprints and an Intercept Security notebook. They also retrieved hairs from under the headrests. Everything found was packaged as a piece of evidence and taken back to the crime lab.

By the early afternoon, Kelley was back in Charlotte with Hocking. After dropping Hocking at his office, Kelley headed back to the jail to pick up his prisoner for his first court appearance. At two p.m., before the arraignment even began, Hocking asked Eaton County District Court Judge Bauer to clear the courtroom of any reporters and courthouse employees who didn't need to be there. He also asked that friends and relatives of other people being arraigned leave the courtroom. Hocking's request was based on a new Michigan statute protecting the identity of sexual assault victims. Tom Bengston, now in the court to represent Don Miller, agreed with Hocking's request.

After the courtroom cleared, Bauer began by reading the charges outlined against Don G. Miller: two counts of attempted murder, one count of first-degree criminal sexual conduct, and one count of breaking and entering. Ensuring that Bengston was Miller's legal counsel, Bauer set a date for Miller's preliminary examination for August 29.

Hocking asked Judge Bauer for a half million-dollar bond, but Bengston argued the bond should be much lower because Miller had strong ties to his family and the community, and he shouldn't be considered a flight risk. Bauer weighed the two arguments and decided to grant Bengston's request instead of Hocking's. Don Miller's bond was set at one hundred thousand dollars.

As Hocking left the courtroom, it was clear he was disappointed in Bauer's decision about Miller's bond. While Bengston refused to speak with reporters, Hocking took a difference stance. He chose to answer questions from media, and when asked if his office was making any connection between Miller and the disappearances of four other Lansing women, Hocking said it was natural to suspect there was a connection to the Choquette case, but said nothing more.

After Miller's arraignment, he was taken back to the jail. Having been formally arraigned, he was now assigned a specific cell on the second floor of the jail, in maximum security section 11. A second inmate was doing his time at the jail as a state prisoner and was also in the max 11 section. He was only housed at the small county jail because there wasn't enough room at the state prison in Jackson, and because Eaton County had extra bed space, the state paid the county to house prison inmates.

Between the barred cells of the jail, staff had placed a television in the hall for inmates to watch. The state prison inmate watched the local news as the story of Don Miller's arrest made the headlines. The reporter described the charges against Miller and where he would be held. The inmate watched with passive interest until later in the evening when a new prisoner was brought into max 11. He recognized Don Miller from the news report. As the two men began a casual conversation, the state inmate's interest piqued.

The next morning, the inmate stopped Ron Rainey, a seasoned jailer and military veteran. Rainey, known for his colorful vocabulary, was well respected by the inmates.

The inmate told Rainey about his discussion with Miller from the night before, and the corrections officer immediately took him to Captain Richard Dye's office on the first floor of the jail. Dye was the jail administrator, and after speaking with the inmate, he called Norm Kelley. He knew Kelley would want to talk with the inmate.

At 3:30 that afternoon, Detective Kelley sat down with the state inmate for a formal interview.

When asked to relay how the conversation went between the two, the inmate said he and Miller had started talking about the young girl and boy he was accused of assaulting. Miller told him that if he'd have stabbed and killed the boy, he never would have been caught. Countering Miller's claim, the inmate told him dogs would have "sniffed him out." Miller continued a brief discussion with the inmate, and told him he had problems with his girlfriend and had done away with her.

Kelley asked the inmate about overhearing one side of a phone conversation Miller had with someone, presumably his new girlfriend. The state inmate said he had heard part of the conversation, and said Miller became angry because whoever was on the other end of the phone wasn't planning on coming to his preliminary hearing.

Kelley was definitely interested in what the state prisoner had to offer because the inmate wasn't getting any favors or special treatment in return for his statement. He was already sentenced by the state and wasn't asking for any preferential treatment in exchange for information about Don Miller. To Kelley, it made him much more credible.

By August 18, the 1973 Oldsmobile had been taken from the fire station to the Eaton County Sheriff's Department in Charlotte. Kelley had suggested the possibility of having Don Miller's car vacuumed by the crime lab for minute trace evidence. A second search warrant was drafted and included many of the same items listed in the first search warrant, but included human tissue, fabric samples, fiber samples, soil samples, and bodily fluids

The car was vacuumed, and an additional small piece of clothesline rope was found.

With the search of Miller's car complete, detectives in neighboring Ingham County were busy typing out their own affidavits for a search of the Miller home in East Lansing.

Lieutenant Darrell Pope had been with the state police for twenty-two years and was head of the Sex Motivated Crimes Unit. Pope had spent eleven years of his career studying sexually motivated homicides, including profiling thirty-two men who had committed murder for sexual gratification. In each of the cases he studied, the victims were either strangled or stabbed to death, and of those who were stabbed, each had between seven to fifteen stab wounds. An additional finding in Pope's study was the stabbing of the victim was an extension of the suspect's penis, and the blood flowing from the stab wounds represented the suspect's semen.

In the search warrant affidavit prepared by Pope, he wrote that he believed the man who killed Martha Sue Young was Don Miller, and believed the way her clothes were found was "symbolic and ritualistic." He also believed the large stain found on the front of her sweater was blood. He believed Miller had stabbed her to death, and even though her body had yet to be found, the person who had murdered her was psychopathic.

Pope had also studied the case of Marita Choquette. He thought the disfigurement of Marita's body suggested a degeneration of the killer's mind, and the murderer required more sadism to stimulate his mind. The number of stab wounds in her body suggested the "penis syndrome." By taking some of the items from Marita's body, the detective believed the killer was acquiring items to satisfy his sexual desires.

In the affidavit, Pope wrote that the grave of Marita Choquette and the way it was constructed was symbolic of a ritualistic sacrifice, and he believed it led directly to Don Miller's involvement. He believed the way Martha Sue Young's clothing was positioned and the ritualistic nature of Marita's murder suggested the two crimes were committed by the same person.

Pope also reviewed the Gilbert case and found similarities to the Young and Choquette cases. He described how Miller had laid items meticulously in the master bedroom of the Gilbert home prior to the assault, and how afterward, Miller had tried to strangle Lisa Gilbert. The strangulation would create a tortured look on Lisa's face, which provided physical satisfaction for Miller. Pope believed Miller would have eventually stabbed her several times. Because there was semen found on the carpet where he had assaulted Lisa, Pope believed Miller ejaculated upon seeing the tortured look on his victim's face when he began raping her. He wrote that Miller was not only capable of these crimes, but that he had kept items from Martha Sue Young and Marita Choquette, and likely would have kept items from his fourteen-year-old victim had he not been interrupted.

According to Pope, men who commit sexually motivated murders often keep items from the victim and use them to trigger their memory as they masturbate. The killer's ability to remember is lessened, and they have to kill again. Because their memory gets shorter, the killer has to commit the crime again, only more frequently.

Pope opined that Kristine Stuart's disappearance could be related to Don Miller because it was exactly two months after Marita Choquette's disappearance and murder. He believed Miller's mind was beginning to degenerate faster and faster.

Having worked quietly with investigators in profiling the killer, Pope said that he believed Don Miller would have trophies from the murders, including jewelry, clothing, purses, glasses, shoes, and maybe even body parts, and those items would be kept at his home.

Even Miller's demeanor after his arrest was mentioned by Pope. Miller was relaxed. The lieutenant wrote that it wasn't unusual for someone who had just committed a crime like the assault on Lisa Gilbert. He believed a person that relaxed was an expression of a man who had killed in the past for sexual gratification.

As Pope was typing his affidavit, Dean Tucker was too.

Tucker began from the beginning by describing the disappearance of Martha Young, and continued with details of his interview with Don Miller about the disappearance.

He wrote that Miller had been given two polygraph examinations by Lt. Markham, and Markham had said Miller wasn't being truthful when he answered the question about doing harm to Martha.

The detective described Miller's car being seized and processed by the state police only days after Martha's disappearance, and how blood had been found on the front seat and door handle of the '73 Olds, in addition to several pubic hairs. The blood had been identified as Type A human blood, and the pubic hairs had similar characteristics to Martha's known hair samples. Tucker wrote that there was not enough blood to identify it as Martha's, but it was similar to hers, and not to Don Miller's or his sister's.

Tucker also mentioned Miller's different versions of what might have caused the blood in his car.

Moving to discredit the suspect's version of events on New Year's Eve, Tucker described how detectives had checked with the Trinity Church, and there had been no activity in the main service area of the church on New Year's Eve.

Mentioning the way Martha's clothing had been displayed in the field where it was found, Tucker wrote that there were still two things missing: her eye glasses and engagement ring.

In the affidavit for the search warrant, Tucker continued by describing the circumstances surrounding the disappearance of Kristine Stuart. Like he'd done in the disappearance of Martha Sue Young, he began from the beginning with Kristine's disappearance.

Tucker mentioned Harold Duncan having spoken with her, and a witness on Basswood Street had seen a vehicle in the area of the Stuart residence on August 14 around ten a.m., and when that witness saw Don Miller's picture on the news, she believed it was the same person. Tucker wrote that the Miller house was less than one mile from the Stuart home.

The detective described the arrest of Miller. He wrote that Miller was very calm and he showed no emotion other than to ask, "What's going on here? What's happening? Why are you doing this to me?"

Detective Ty Strong was representing Eaton County's interests in the search of the Miller home. In his affidavit for the search warrant at the Miller home, he wrote that he had been working with Norm Kelley on the assault of the Gilberts and had personally witnessed the search of the Miller vehicle at the fire station.

Strong wrote that Fire Chief Ken Dorin was allowed to look into the trunk of the vehicle when it was opened and had identified a shirt in the trunk as the same shirt he had seen Don Miller wearing when he was leaving the Gilbert home. Strong also wrote that when Lisa Gilbert was in Dorin's car, she had pointed to Miller as he was standing in front of the house and told Dorin, "That's the guy...the one in the green shirt."

The last detective to include an affidavit for the search warrant was Dick Fitzgerald. Fitzgerald, leading the investigation into the murder of Marita Choquette, described the circumstances of her disappearance and the discovery of her body, and mentioned each of her stab wounds. He wrote that when Marita's body was found, there was one pearl seashell earring found under her body. The matching earring had yet to be found. He also wrote that her glasses hadn't been located yet, nor had her identification.

The veteran detective also put that on or about June 27, 1978, Don Miller was observed by an ELPD surveillance team scrubbing the front passenger seat of his car. On the same day, Wendy Bush, a Michigan State University student, was reported as missing and had yet to be located.

While the officers from multiple jurisdictions worked on their affidavits, Rick Westgate and Officer John Benson drove to the Intercept Security offices on Chandler Road in Bath Township. They had been told by detectives from

Eaton County that when Don Miller was booked in at the jail, an identification card from Intercept Security had been found in his wallet. Miller worked as a store detective, and with that information, they wanted to check his time card for the day Kristine Stuart had disappeared.

The two officers made contact with a supervisor and were allowed to look at Miller's personnel file. They learned he had been hired by Intercept Security on May 30, 1978. Westgate made notes as he saw Miller's references on his application: a pastor and another woman were listed, both of whom lived in Petoskey, Michigan. Westgate knew Miller had worked in Petoskey the previous summer as a youth counselor.

As the men looked over Miller's time card, Westgate noticed that on August 14, he didn't punch in until 11:28 a.m. The reason given in the file was a flat tire. Miller had worked at three separate locations for Intercept Security. In addition to the Paramount News on South Washington Street in Lansing, he also worked at two other bookstores: the Community News Center in the Meridian Mall and at the Frandor News Center. Westgate and Benson went with the second supervisor to the other two locations so they could physically gather the time cards. On August 14, he had only worked at the Lansing store. The information was relayed back to Tucker.

The East Lansing police had the Miller home at 530 Gainsborough secured, and no one was home as the officers watched it. When Elaine and Gene Miller finally arrived, Detective Westgate had returned from Intercept Security and met with them to explain the reason for having the home secured until the search warrants arrived. Gene Miller became angry, and the situation began to escalate until Westgate could calm things down.

The Millers were told the police would be searching the home for at least two days, and they would have to stay at a hotel. After their departure, the police began the arduous task of searching the entire home at 530 Gainsborough.

Dividing the house into sections, each detective was given a separate area to search. They continued past midnight, and at two a.m., the detectives quit for the night. With officers securing the exterior, the detectives left but were back at the house early in the morning to continue their search.

When the search was finally over, the search warrant required a document called the "Return" to be left at the home, and it had to list each item taken by the officers. The detectives listed several items: two women's nylons tied in a knot; a drawing of a blindfolded woman; newspaper clippings about Martha Sue Young and Marita Choquette; a separate newspaper clipping about death with a photo of a coffin; a painting of an angel in chains; and a disposable jump suit. The investigators also listed a bible, handcuffs that were double-locked, hair samples, a small tin box with nylons in it, magazines referencing Satan, monster comic books, a paper written about rape and voodoo, some miscellaneous newspaper clippings about a scout's murder, numerous other news clippings about Martha Sue Young's disappearance, a shovel with some hair on it, some hair in a bra that was found in a kitchen cupboard, and some other newspaper clippings.

The next two days were taken up by more ground searches, and an air search had been organized again in hopes of finding Kristine's body yet nothing was found.

Tucker and Westgate also tried to interview Don Miller's girlfriend at the bank where she worked, but she refused to speak with anyone until she spoke with an attorney. She called Tom Bengston, and he told her not to say anything until she could speak with him.

Fitzgerald was now working alongside the other agencies trying to piece together a timeline for Miller's activities between August 14 and August 16. He contacted the store manager at Paramount News in Lansing. It was where Don Miller had worked on August 16 from ten a.m. until two p.m. When Fitzgerald asked her what Miller had been wearing that day, she described a dark green short-sleeve shirt.

The following day, Dean Tucker and Rick Westgate finally had the chance to interview Miller's girlfriend, Janet, at a park in Okemos.

Janet told the two detectives she had met Miller when he was a youth counselor for the Petoskey United Methodist Church during the summer of 1977. As a youth counselor, Miller would work with kids between the ages of thirteen to college age. Janet had transferred her church affiliation to Petoskey from a church in Milan, Michigan, in early 1977. She told them that after Don finished his nine weeks as a counselor in Petoskey and returned to East Lansing, she kept in touch with him by mail until she finally moved to the area in the spring of 1978. When one of the investigators asked about Don Miller's activities around August 14, she told them he had come over on August 13 and left at around two a.m. on August 14 to go home. She didn't see him again until about five p.m. when he came back over to the apartment for dinner. He only stayed an hour because he had to be to work at the Meridian Mall as a store detective, and he returned about nine and spent the night with her. The following morning, she left for work at around 8:30 and Don was still at her apartment. He picked her up for lunch, and after he dropped her back off at two, she saw him again at 5:30 when she got home. Later that night, they went to a movie. Janet said they got back to her apartment at around 12:30 a.m. on August 16. She also told detectives that Don had a key to her apartment because they were unofficially engaged to be married.

After the interview, Tucker and Westgate headed back to the office. There was a joint meeting with representatives from East Lansing Police, the Michigan State Police,

Lansing Police, the FBI, the Ingham County Sheriff's Office, the Eaton County Sheriff's Department, the Clinton County Sheriff's Department, and the Ingham County Prosecutor's Office. The sole purpose of the meeting was an exchange of information regarding the missing women and the assaults in Delta Township.

Ernie Stuart, lost without his wife, made a personal plea for her safe return at a press conference to the public the following day. The East Lansing police chief also fielded questions from reporters about the ongoing investigations.

On that same day, Rick Westgate had made the arrangements to accompany Nancy Daniels for a hypnosis session at Damon Reinbold's home office. When prosecutor Peter Houk heard the East Lansing police were using Damon Reinbold to do hypnosis sessions, he wondered why they weren't using a psychologist from the state police. His main concern was they were doing hypnotically regressed recollections, and each witness could have been picking up bits and pieces of information on a regular basis from the news outlets. The media was running frequent stories about the cases, and it was a legitimate concern.

After the suggestion was made, Nancy Daniels was taken to Dr. Donald Rossi for a second hypnotic session. Even before Dr. Rossi began the session, video tape equipment was set up so the session could be recorded.

Dr. Rossi began the session at 9:55 a.m. by simply talking with her to get some background information. Tucker was in the office with them, as was a police composite artist. Lt. Markham was also present.

After being hypnotized by Dr. Rossi, Nancy slowly began to recall what she had seen on the morning of August 14. She said she was driving northbound on Coolidge Road when a car suddenly turned in front of her onto Fairoaks. In order to avoid an accident, she had to brake suddenly. As she stopped, there was a brown car on Fairoaks facing to the east alongside the street. She had seen the car just prior to having to hit her brakes. As she looked toward the car, she could see some sort of a scuffle between a man and a woman. She could see the man pushing the woman into the front passenger seat.

Dr. Rossi slowed her down and had her describe the car. She said the car was completely brown with light colored interior. She recalled the sun was shining brightly on the windshield, and she could see some sort of small object on the dash. She even recalled a reddish pencil on the dash. When Rossi asked her the make of the car, she told him she didn't know individual makes very well but it was smaller than her Ford T-Bird. She recalled the car had chrome strips around the door windows, and locks that had to be manually lifted. The back of the car was square, and the license plate was in the bumper.

Rossi wanted to concentrate on the woman that she had seen. Under hypnosis, she described the woman wearing a black top that resembled a polo shirt. The woman was wearing blue shorts and brown sandals. She had reddish brown hair, and it was messed up. She also recalled the woman was wearing nail polish.

Nancy Daniels' attention was shifted to the man she had seen scuffling with the woman. She described him as white, with medium-length brown hair that, although it was messy, appeared to be trimmed. He wasn't wearing glasses, and he appeared to be about twenty-five years old. She focused even more. He was wearing a white t-shirt. He had a medium build, but he wasn't muscular.

As Nancy was describing the person under hypnosis, the composite artist was drawing a sketch based on her description.

She could see the man and woman appeared to be wrestling. The passenger door was open, and to Nancy, the man appeared to be shoving the woman backward toward the open passenger door. The woman was kicking and fighting as she was pushed into the car, and the man held her down with his left hand. He reached toward the dash to his right and grabbed a knife. Nancy Daniels could see the woman's left hand grabbing the hair of her attacker. She saw the man's arm come down again and again with the knife, and she could see blood on the blade as the woman's left hand fell limp.

Slowly, she focused on the knife in the man's right hand. The knife had a dark brown or black handle and long blade, and she could see it as the man was holding the knife up above him.

As the session ended, Dr. Rossi began to bring Nancy out of hypnosis. He told her that at some point later in the day, or even the week or month, she might remember other small details she could have neglected to mention in the session. He told her that was normal and not to be alarmed. She should simply make a note of what additional details she remembered and contact the police.

Afterward, Nancy was asked to look at the police sketch. After some subtle changes, she was satisfied it looked like the man she had seen on the morning of August 14. Her only criticism was the drawing didn't depict him looking as angry as he had looked when she saw him.

Later that afternoon, Tucker received a phone call from Nancy, and she was crying. She had remembered another detail and wanted to let him know. The woman was wearing a bracelet of some sort; it was silver with some sort of links. She had also read the local paper and saw a photo of Don Miller. There was no question in her mind: he was the man she had seen on the morning of August 14 on Fairoaks at Coolidge.

Tucker was concerned because Nancy was so upset. After hanging up, he called Dr. Rossi. Rossi told him to call her back and reassure her. He also told Tucker to let her know that that sort of emotional response was not uncommon.

By August 30, a reward had been set up for information leading to the whereabouts of Kristine. The reward totaled eight thousand dollars, and Ernie Stuart read a prepared statement to the press to publicize the reward money, desperately hoping it would lead to his wife. A week later, an additional twenty-five hundred dollars was added to the reward by the Lansing School Education Association.

The investigators searching for clues about Kristine's disappearance were not leaving any stone unturned. On September 5, they interviewed Gene Miller about his son's whereabouts on August 14.

Gene told Tucker that he and his wife had returned to their home on Sunday, August 13 after a weekend trip. Don was at the house, and had mentioned that his muffler had come off over the weekend. He had taken it to K-Mart near the Meridian Mall on Saturday, August 12 to get it repaired. Gene Miller continued by telling the detectives that on Monday, August 14, he had left the house at 7:30 a.m., and Don was still asleep in his room. He had spoken with Elaine, and she said that Don had gotten up and driven to Lansing to deliver a note to his grandparents because their phone was out. When Don got back to the house at around nine, he got cleaned up, and left for work at around 9:45. Tucker informed Gene Miller that his son hadn't punched in at work until 11:28 on August 14, and Gene was surprised at the discrepancy in times. Tucker asked him if he had been communicating with his son or talking with him, and he refused to answer the detectives.

It was clear to everyone by now that Wendy Bush's disappearance could be related to the other missing women. Investigators from MSU met with the East Lansing detectives to share information on their missing person case.

By September 1, a lineup had been arranged to be done at the Ingham County sheriff's office. Nancy Daniels would be taking part, as would a second witness who had observed the brown car in the neighborhood.

Ingham County Assistant Prosecutor Lee Atkinson drafted a writ to have Miller moved from the Eaton County jail to the Ingham County jail for the lineup. To be certain the witnesses didn't speak with each other beforehand, they were driven separately to the jail.

There were six men in the lineup, and Don Gene Miller was in the number five position.

After viewing the men, the witnesses were taken to a separate room and given a form which had six spaces on it. The witnesses were instructed that if they had seen anyone who might have been involved in the incident on August 14 to mark the lineup position of that person.

Both Nancy Daniels and the second witness marked position five.

On September 11, Detective Sue Brown was working on the case with Tucker and Westgate. She headed to K-Mart in Meridian Township to follow up on the muffler repair Gene Miller had mentioned. A receipt was located showing Miller had been in for repairs. When the detectives spoke with the technician who wrote up the work order, he said the tail pipe had separated from the muffler, and the muffler was pretty beat up. Of interest to Detective Brown was the mileage written on the work order. The technician had written 40,064. The detective asked the technician how accurate that was, and she was told it was written exactly. Brown called Detective Kelley to let him know what the mileage was, thinking that if there was a large discrepancy before the car was seized by the police, it might give them an idea as to how far Miller had driven. Kelley told her that when Miller was arrested, the mileage was 40,543. From late afternoon on August 12 to late afternoon on August 16, Miller had added 479 miles to his car.

Thus far, the police had been able to track Don Miller's movements for several days prior to Kristine Stuart's disappearance. They were able to determine that on Wednesday, August 9, he had been to Holland State Park along the west side of the state, camping for two nights. He paid five dollars per night and stayed in campsite 96. The camp permit showed he used two pup tents.

On Sunday, August 13, an officer who was familiar with Miller and had helped with the Martha Young investigation saw Miller walking near his girlfriend's apartment. The officer had always tried to be friendly with Miller, so when he saw him, he stopped and said hello. Without saying a word, Miller turned toward the woman he was walking with and began to kiss her. The officer thought it was weird and drove around the parking lot to look for a couple suspects in a bike larceny. As he circled back around and drove by the two again, Miller quickly turned and started kissing the woman again. It seemed very odd to the officer at the time.

Based on their interviews, the investigators knew where Don had worked over the weekend, and they also knew when he had been at Janet's apartment. They knew what time he got out of work on August 16, and what time the attack had occurred in Delta Township. With that information, they began to check the distances. From the K-Mart auto center on August 12 to Miller's return to Janet's apartment after the attack on Canal Road, Miller's car should only have had an additional ninety-two miles.

As Detective Brown was checking on the muffler, Tucker made phone contact with both of Don's references listed on his job application. He was told that the pastor had contacted Don at the Eaton County jail over the Labor Day weekend, and asked him specifically about the charges against him, and Miller told him he was sure he couldn't do something like that. The pastor asked the former youth counselor if he had a split personality, and thought that maybe he couldn't recall what had happened. Miller told him he didn't have a split personality, and he could remember everything that happened in his life.

As the investigations continued on several fronts, there were daily foot searches around Ingham, Eaton, and Clinton counties, and daily air searches using the Lansing police helicopter Air 80 and the MSP helicopter. Officers continued to follow up on every tip that came in.

With Don Miller in custody, law enforcement investigators throughout the tri-county area searched for a connection between the cases. Other than the disappearance of his former fiancée, investigators wondered if he had stalked his victims and planned their kidnapping and murder, or if they were simply random. Now convinced Miller was responsible in all of the disappearances, a meeting was held involving each police agency.

Key components of each case were laid out for the investigators so they could compare them, and each case highlighted listed missing items and a possible connection to Don Miller.

Martha Sue Young's disappearance was the first to be discussed. Details outlining the facts in her case were given in staffing notes and distributed. The notes described her clothing and how it was found laid out near Potter Lake in Bath Township. Missing were her glasses and the engagement ring Miller had told her to keep.

Marita Choquette's case was discussed next. Though she lived in Grand Ledge, her car had been discovered at her work place on campus the morning after she was last seen at her apartment. Two weeks later, her body was discovered in a field between Okemos and Mason, covered with cement blocks, and her hands had been severed. Items that were missing when her body was discovered were her glasses, her purse, and her shoes, and as the investigators looked into her background, they discovered that prior to working at WKAR, Marita had worked at the MSU library as an assistant to William Stoddard. Stoddard lived across the street from Martha Sue Young, and his son was asked by Miller to be the best man at his wedding to Martha. On

Sunday, June 18, a witness observed a chocolate brown car parked thirty feet east of an intersection near where Marita's body had been discovered. She saw a male bent over in the front seat, flailing his arms, and as they drove by, he looked up at them with a contorted look on his face. She recalled the letter G in the license plate. Don Miller was not working on June 18.

Moving to the disappearance of Wendy Bush, they noted her disappearance coincided with the day Marita's body was found. Looking for any connection to Miller or the other women, investigators noted for a short period of time, Wendy had been involved in the Campus Crusade, and The Way; the same group Don Miller had been associated with for a short time in 1976 when he and his sister attended a few meetings.

Last was Kristine Stuart's case. She was last seen by an employee of her husband as she walked around the corner from Coolidge onto Fairoaks. The employee, Harold Duncan, spoke briefly with her and continued on. Her glasses were found three-hundred-thirty-five feet east of the intersection in the grass on the south side of the street. A skid mark was located on the roadway, three-hundred-thirty-five east of the intersection. The state police determined the wheel base of the vehicle that made the skid mark was one-hundred-twelve inches. Don Miller's car had a one-hundred-twelve-inch wheelbase, but so did several other makes and models. Going into more detail, the notes mentioned a neighbor on Basswood, where the Stuarts lived, saw a brown two-door car cruising through the neighborhood sometime between 9:30 and eleven a.m. on the day Kristine disappeared, and the car had turned around in the Stuart driveway. The neighbor even said the driver resembled Don Miller. In looking for some sort of connection to Miller, the investigators found that Kristine Stuart shopped regularly in Carriage Hills ShopRite, and

Miller occasionally worked there as part of his employment with Intercept Security.

The last case to be discussed was the Gilbert case. After a description of the assault, the notes mentioned that Donna Gilbert, Lisa and Randy's stepmother, was attractive and could have been the intended target. She frequented Goodrich's ShopRite on Trowbridge Road in East Lansing near the university campus, and Miller had worked there in the course of his employment with Intercept Security as well.

After having reviewed each case, the discussion turned to the suspect. East Lansing police had been aware of Miller's new girlfriend, Janet, since July 19, 1978. She was divorced and had two children, ages three and five. Miller came to know her when he was a youth counselor in Petoskey during the summer of 1977. Miller was arrested as he drove into the parking lot at her apartment and was calm during the arrest.

A lab technician from the state police discussed the results of the searches and the evidence thus far against Don Miller: Miller's fingerprint had been found inside the Gilbert house; the wheelbase of Miller's car matched the wheelbase of the car the suspect had fled in from the Gilbert home; semen had been discovered inside the Gilbert home and was still being analyzed; and finally, foot impressions lifted by technicians at the Gilbert home were still being analyzed.

The technician said the search of Miller's car had yielded fingerprints on the driver's side. In the trunk, investigators had the two pup tents, and each of those had hairs inside them. A chain was found in the trunk, with small wires attached and fashioned as a strangulation device, in addition to a roll of galvanized wire. There were red stains inside the trunk, in addition to some clothing and a disposable jump suit. There was also a map of Michigan with several cities circled.

On the day of Kristine Stuart's disappearance, Miller had punched into work at the Community News Center in Lansing at 11:28 a.m. and listed his reason for being late as a flat tire. The crime lab had examined all four tires and the spare after his arrest, and there was no evidence any of the tires had ever been off the vehicle or been flat.

The detectives also discussed the scratches on the top of Miller's hands when he was arrested. He told them the scratches were from wiring up his muffler on his way back from camping in Holland.

The lab tech mentioned the double-lock handcuffs found in the search of the Miller home had small traces of blood on them, and it appeared the handcuffs had been washed or cleaned.

The meeting then turned to Miller's movements just prior to Kristine Stuart's disappearance. On the morning of August 14, Miller left his grandparents' house on South Washington Street in Lansing to return to his own home to change clothes and get ready for work. The detectives assumed he would have had to leave his grandparent's home by 8:15 to return to East Lansing, then be at work in Lansing by ten. They knew he didn't arrive at work at Community News until 11:28.

He punched out of work at 1:02 p.m. from the South Washington location, drove to the Frandor Shopping Center on the east side of Lansing, and punched in at 2:04. At 4:58, he punched out from the Frandor branch and drove to the Meridian Mall, where he punched in at 5:58. At 9:51, he completed his shift and punched out from that location and headed for his girlfriend's apartment.

Don Miller had August 15 off, and he took Janet to lunch, then later spent the night at her apartment again.

On August 16, he was scheduled to work at Paramount News, and he punched in at 9:56 a.m. His time card showed he punched out at 2:01, and at 4:47, he was arrested at Janet's apartment by Rick Westgate.

There was a time period of almost three hours between the time Miller left for work and the time he was arrested, and there was only a brief window the police could account for. Miller tried to convince them otherwise.

10

As the investigators in East Lansing tried to link Don Miller to their missing person cases, detectives in Eaton County were following up on their case with the prosecuting attorney's office. The preliminary examination of their suspect had to be within twelve days of his arrest.

As the prosecutor was preparing for the exam, so was Miller's attorney. Tom Bengston knew what he was up against. He knew it would be an uphill battle. His first option was to have his client sent to the Center for Forensic Psychiatry in Ann Arbor for a competency evaluation.

On August 29, the scheduled day for Don Miller's preliminary examination before District Court Judge Ken Hansen, Bengston stood before the Court with Miller. After conferring with prosecuting attorney Paul Berger and assistant prosecutor Mike Hocking, all three men agreed that Bengston's client should be evaluated at the Center for Forensic Psychiatry.

The following day, Don Miller was transported to Ann Arbor by deputies from the Eaton County Sheriff's Department to begin his evaluation.

Three weeks after the order was issued by Judge Hansen, the director of the Center for Forensic Psychiatry, William Meyer, along with Dr. Lynn Blunt, sat down with Don Miller for his evaluation. It would be the first of several interviews with other doctors, but it would be the only interview evaluating his competency for the preliminary exam. Dr. Harley Stock also sat in on the interview.

Neatly dressed in casual clothing, Miller wore a sport coat and dress shirt as he sat with the three men in the small interview room. To the doctors, Miller looked younger than twenty-three.

They began the interview by asking Miller if he knew why he was there, and he told them he was there to be checked regarding his ability to assist Tom Bengston in his defense.

Miller let the doctors know that he knew he was charged with breaking and entering, rape, and two counts of attempted murder. He added that he didn't really understand the charges against him. He said when he was first arrested, he didn't know what happened but was finally told it was an assault, and he was supposed to have been in a house where a girl between fourteen and sixteen years old had been raped. He also said that her brother was supposedly stabbed, and the girl escaped, got some help, and the person responsible for the assault had come out and left before the police arrived. He knew the police had a visual identification, a description of the car, and his license number.

The doctors shifted the conversation from the charges to Miller himself. Miller told them he wasn't involved, and he didn't know anything about what had happened. He gave a detailed description of what he had done on the afternoon the assaults occurred. He had gotten up after sleeping over at Janet's house and saw her off to work. He had to work that morning, and at ten, he punched in at the Paramount News on South Washington Street in Lansing, explaining to the doctors that he was a store detective there. He added that he had made five or so apprehensions since he started there in May. He told them he had left work at two p.m. and had stopped at his church in downtown Lansing to use the bathroom to change into different clothing.

Before heading into the church, he said he was looking in his glovebox for a comb when he suddenly felt light headed, and as he stood up, he felt a pain in his chest and bumped his head on the car. He said he didn't black out from the bump on the head and continued into the church to change his clothes. When he returned to his car, he put his work clothes inside and drove to the Frandor Shopping Center to look for a gift for his girlfriend's young daughter. After leaving there, he stopped to buy three dollars in gas, and he drove over to the nearby Sears, then out to the Meridian Mall in Okemos, and finally to Meijer. He added that he was sure he saw some people he knew while he was shopping, and as he drove back to Janet's apartment, he was arrested.

He was adamant he knew nothing about what the police said he did. He couldn't have done any of the things because he was very religious and came from a Christian family.

Dr. Blunt asked Miller about Martha Young, and he quickly told the three that his attorney had told him not to answer that question.

With each question, Miller paused, carefully thinking about his response before saying anything. Other than declining to answer certain questions that Tom Bengston had told him not to answer, he was very cooperative. He reiterated to the doctors that he remembered everything about the afternoon, and there was no time when he blacked out. It was very clear to him that he had gone shopping and was exactly where he said he had been.

As the doctors watched his behavior and mannerisms and listened to his answers, it became clear to them there was no evidence of any disturbance in his thought process, and no evidence of any psychotic symptoms such as hallucinations or delusions.

As their sixty-five-minute interview with Don Miller concluded, the three were in agreement: there was no evidence of any mental illness. There was nothing they could see that would interfere with Don Miller's ability to understand the charges against him and assist his defense attorney in a rational manner. They also came to the conclusion that there was no evidence of any illness that would cause Miller to be unable to recall the events of the day that led to charges against him.

Dr. Blunt sent his report to Judge Hansen, in addition to Mike Hocking and Tom Bengston in late October, and Hansen quickly set a date for the hearing.

Ingham County Prosecutor Peter Houk had an open file policy at his office for defense attorneys. He adopted the policy the day he took office, thinking the best way for a defense attorney to know what the prosecutor had on his or her client was to allow them access to the file. It was part of the reason Houk didn't get along with some of the other prosecutors around the state.

While Miller's competency was being evaluated, Tom Bengston was in the middle of another murder trial and Peter Houk was prosecuting the case. As the two men sat together at the Ingham County courthouse waiting for a verdict from the jury, Bengston asked Houk why he was after Miller.

"Tom, I don't get it," Houk said. "If you were talking about me chasing him around for Martha Sue, I can understand that, but the kids out there in Eaton County? His fingerprint is in blood on the wall. What makes you think we're chasing him around?"

Bengston was taken by surprise. He hadn't known anything about Miller's fingerprint being found inside the Gilbert house. He thought for a moment, and in a joking manner he asked, "Is there any way to transplant a fingerprint?"[53]

On November 1, Dean Tucker and his chief met with Peter Houk in Lansing. Tucker had the entire files for both

---

53. Peter Houk, July 18, 2018

Martha Sue Young and Kristine Stuart with him and turned them over to Houk.

It was already common knowledge that over the previous several months, there had been a citizen grand jury empaneled in Ingham County. The grand jury had been set up for two specific reasons. The first was to investigate a large heroin ring in the Lansing area, and the second was to look at several fraud cases. Houk thought it would be an easy way to attack those because a grand jury could be used as an investigative tool. Knowing there were still three missing women in the area, Houk decided the grand jury would be a great way to question Don Miller's sister about what she knew.

It wasn't a hard decision for the prosecutor. Peter Houk knew she wouldn't be allowed to have an attorney in the room when she was questioned, and it would be as simple as having her sitting in a conference room for the questioning.

On November 3, Don Miller's competency hearing was brought before Judge Hansen in Eaton County District Court. Mike Hocking was going to present Dr. Blunt's testimony to show Miller was competent for his preliminary examination. Bengston was ready too.

When the hearing began, Bengston asked the judge to clear the courtroom. For Miller's previous court appearances, the motion had been granted, and Bengston expected the judge to grant it again. Hocking had no objection as long as the defendant's family was also sequestered from hearing the testimony. Hocking did ask that law enforcement be allowed to remain in the court for security reasons and to assist in case preparation. The judge agreed.

Hocking's witness, Dr. Lynn Blunt, was called to the stand. The assistant prosecutor knew he had to qualify Dr.

Blunt as an expert witness so he would be able to offer an expert opinion about the defendant, and began by asking the doctor about his qualifications.

Dr. Blunt said he was the clinical director at the Forensic Center, and part of his job consisted of the evaluation of people referred through the courts from around the state and the treatment of them. He added that he'd evaluated over six hundred people in his career, and fifteen to twenty percent of those had been deemed incompetent to stand trial. His definition of competency was a person who had the necessary mental faculties to understand they were being charged with a crime, as well as being able to cooperate with the defense in a reasonable manner.

Hocking had his questions methodically written in order, and he asked what type of exam had been done on Miller.

Blunt said Miller's examination was a standard clinical evaluation, and he'd been given the Minnesota Multiphasic Personality Inventory test, known as the MMPI, by Dr. Stock. He told Hocking the examination was a series of questions about whether Miller understood the charges against him, a time accounting during the period of the crimes, and questions about any mental illness in his family history. He added that Miller understood all three charges and had been very cooperative.

"Let me ask you this," Hocking said. "Would you define what mental illness is?"

"Well, it's defined by law under the Michigan statutes. It's a defect, a condition in which the person's judgement, or his ability to appreciate reality, or there is a defect in mood which is affected. That's not the exact wording, but generally."[54]

Mike Hocking referenced mental illness and psychosis by asking the doctor if they were synonymous, and if they

54. People v Don G. Miller. Transcript of Competency Hearing. January 10, 1979, 13

would have an effect on a person's ability to understand the charges against him and his ability to assist his defense counsel.

The doctor said they weren't synonymous. Mental illness included disorders other than psychosis. He felt it might have an effect on someone's ability to cooperate with their attorney, but would be dependent on what areas of their functioning it might affect.

According to the doctor, Don Miller didn't feel he was competent. When Hocking pressed him for more information, Blunt said that Miller felt that he wasn't competent because he claimed he knew nothing about the charges against him. He understood what they were, but he didn't have any knowledge of the events occurring.

Hocking cut right to the chase. He asked the doctor if there was any sign or symptom that would indicate mental illness or psychosis that would affect Don Miller's ability to understand the charges and assist his attorney.

Tom Bengston was prepared to cross-examine, and as Hocking took a seat, he began by asking Dr. Blunt if he could explain the term "organic brain dysfunction."

Dr. Blunt said that based on his clinical interview, there wasn't any evidence of memory loss or difficulty in thinking. He found out that Miller had been told by the police what he had supposedly done, but he didn't know anything about it, and he wasn't involved.

When Bengston asked if the threshold question was whether or not there was mental illness, Blunt said yes, and added that for the purposes of competency, without mental illness, a person would be competent. He added that the basis for his opinion was his training and experience, in addition to the dialogue with the person he was evaluating.

When the doctor explained the MMPI test that had been given to Miller, he described a personality profile, or a screening test that could sometimes indicate the possibility of mental illness or personality characteristics. It was a standard test for competency evaluations, and it was used in all cases where they determine criminal responsibility.

Blunt said the outcome of Miller's test showed a person with brittle defenses. There wasn't any obvious mental illness, but there was a possibility of decompensation under stress.

Making the explanation simpler for Bengston, he said, "It showed that the person's defenses are such that if he were pushed hard enough under some adverse circumstances that he might de-compensate in a psychotic condition."[55] He added it was a process of going psychotic over a matter of a few days.

Other than the MMPI test, both Dr. Blunt and Dr. Stock didn't think any further testing was necessary after their interview with Miller; tests don't determine competency to stand trial.

When Tom Bengston asked about Miller's statement to the doctor that he didn't think he was competent, Blunt said that Miller felt that way because he claimed that he didn't know anything about the charges against him, and therefore, he couldn't be competent. He clarified that Miller was competent if he understood what he was charged with, and the burden of trial was whether or not he knew anything about the crime.

Tom Bengston was looking out for Don Miller's rights as a defendant. He knew the courts addressed two issues when it came to a defendant's competency, and asked the doctor to address the second issue regarding Miller's ability to assist his attorney.

The doctor didn't see any evidence of any mental illness that would prevent Don Miller from cooperating with defense counsel.

Bengston shifted back to the MMPI test. "If I understand correctly, you are not persuaded by the MMPI result

---

55. People v Don G. Miller, January 10, 1979, 26

whereby, apparently, Mr. Miller has the possibility of being pushed or drove psychotic. Is that correct?"[56]

Blunt explained that many people in the community would show the same findings as Miller if they were tested. One in every one hundred people was schizophrenic, and it was one of the biggest mental health problems.

Because Miller had described everything he did after leaving work on the day of the assault, and even mentioned specific times, Blunt was certain Miller had not blacked out.

"So absent mental illness in this case, as you have told us, it's your determination that this Mr. Miller is not voluntarily telling what he wants to tell me and no more, is that right?" Bengston asked.

"That would be in my conclusion."

Mike Hocking had a chance to clarify a few things.

"Dr. Blunt, did Don Miller ever decline to answer any questions?"

The doctor said he had and he'd been instructed by his attorney to answer certain questions, which showed Don Miller thoroughly understood instructions from his attorney.

Bengston wasn't letting go. He asked the doctor if he understood that the test isn't whether or not a client understands his attorney, but, rather, whether or not he can communicate with his attorney, and Blunt agreed.

The defense attorney continued, "Okay, now with respect to my client apparently cooperating, except to the extent that his attorney informs him not to talk about, is that about Martha Sue Young?"[57]

Dr. Blunt couldn't recall her name, but agreed with Bengston that the conversation was about Don Miller's missing girlfriend. He told the attorney that Miller had told him his attorney had instructed him not to discuss anything about her.

---

56. People v Don G. Miller, January 10, 1979, 31
57. People v Don G. Miller, January 10, 1979, 38

Bengston wanted to know if that influenced his opinion about Don Miller's competency, and for Blunt, it had. It showed Miller understood what was going on, and what he was, and was not, to talk about. He felt that Don Miller's competency was part of following his attorney's instructions.

Both Mike Hocking and Tom Bengston had tried to make their case before the Court, and Hocking was fairly confident Judge Hansen would rule in his favor.

Hocking's statement to the Court was short. He told the judge that through Dr. Blunt's testimony, it was clear that Miller was competent to sit for his preliminary examination, and Hocking felt he was competent to stand trial too, but he wasn't sure if the Court had the ability to declare him competent in the circuit court.

Bengston's reply was just as brief. "I don't think the Court has the power to say he's competent to stand trial; it's a jurisdictional matter: Insofar as the proofs go, the testimony of Dr. Blunt, I think there is sufficient evidence for this Court to find that my client is in fact competent, but I would further suggest that's not."[58]

Judge Hansen had been in the legal profession for a long time, and knew the preliminary examination was a critical stage to a defendant in any criminal matter. It was the reason he had agreed to Bengston's petition to have Don Miller sent to the Center for Forensic Psychiatry for a competency evaluation. At the end of the testimony from Dr. Blunt, he agreed: he didn't see any evidence that Miller suffered from any mental illness which would interfere with his ability to understand the charges against him or to cooperate with Tom Bengston in his own defense. Judge Hansen ruled Don Miller competent for the preliminary exam.

---

58. People v Don G. Miller, January 10, 1979, 40

The judge also knew that Miller's exam had been delayed for the evaluation, and he wanted to get it scheduled as soon as possible. The date was set for two weeks later.

By November 9, with all of the investigative reports turned over to Peter Houk's office, Dean Tucker had been asked by Houk to re-interview the inmate who had been in max 11 at the Eaton County Jail with Miller. Norm Kelley had passed on his report, but a second interview was in order in case he was brought before the grand jury.

Tucker headed to the jail in Charlotte.

A corrections officer brought the inmate downstairs to the basement of the jail where the detective bureau was. The men walked down the dimly lit hallway toward the office. Across from the detective bureau was a large area that served as a squad room, locker room, and lunch room all in one.

The detective bureau was cramped with three desks but it would have to do.

As Tucker began the interview, he asked the inmate to recount the conversation he'd had with Miller when he was brought up to max 11 after his arraignment.

The inmate told the same story to Tucker that he had told Norm Kelley. He said that on the evening when Miller was brought into the jail, the news was on the TV that had been put between the cells for the inmates to watch. He said he joked with Miller by telling him he was a celebrity, and Miller said he should have gotten rid of the boy and the girl like he did his girlfriend. The two had talked about Miller's girlfriend, and Miller had said that she made him mad.

Tucker asked if there was anything else he might have heard from Miller.

He told the detective, "Well, that he could have gotten rid, should have gotten rid of the boy and the girl, and his girlfriend aggravated him a lot, and he got rid of one, he done away with her."

Tucker was surprised when he asked the inmate if there was anything more he wanted to add to his statement.

"Yeah, I was threatened Sunday. I believe it was his father," the inmate said. "I didn't know at the time it was his father or not, but I was standing, I had just got a visitor, and I was standing by, by the front of the building."

As he continued the discussion with Tucker, he described being threatened by a man he assumed was Don Miller's dad while he was doing trustee work at the jail. He'd been out in front of the jail, and Miller's family was out there. The man he believed to be Don Miller's dad had started asking him questions about the trustees, and he even mentioned the inmate's state prison number. When Gene Miller mentioned the inmate's name, he mispronounced it. The inmate knew it was his own name that Miller was trying to pronounce, and then said that if he got his hands on whoever had said that about Don, "He's going to break up his fucking head."

Tucker interrupted, asking, "Okay, this conversation you had with this man, you believe this to be Don Miller's father?" The inmate was certain it was.

There was genuine concern on the inmate's part. He figured that Miller's dad had checked the files at the prison because he had mentioned that he worked in both Marquette and Jackson prison. "He wants to get his son off in any way he can, and I believe it's his son."

Asked once more if he wanted to add anything to his statement, he said, "No, just that I'm not getting anything for it, and I just think it's my duty, you know, if I heard something, that's my duty to reply what I heard."[59]

The new courthouse on the north end of Charlotte looked more like a modern office building than the old, ornate structure at the center of town that had served the county for over one hundred years. Two courtrooms on the first floor served as the district court and two courtrooms on the second floor served as the circuit court.

On November 17, three months after Don Miller's arrest, his preliminary examination began in the 56th District Court in Charlotte.

With his hair neatly combed and wearing a suit, Don Miller was shackled with his hands in front as he was loaded into a car for the mile ride from the jail to the new courthouse. Deputy Dave Bankhead, along with Detectives Kelley and Reusch, walked him from the rear parking lot to a door at the back of the building that led directly to two holding cells behind the first-floor courtrooms.

Inside the courtroom was a small seating area for the public and a waist-high wooden partition separated it from where the judge and attorneys conducted business. To one side of the courtroom was a jury box; the prosecution and defense tables were in front of the judge. Compared to the stately old courthouse downtown, the new courtrooms seemed almost sterile.

The defendant was led in from one of the holding cells and took a seat at the defense table with Tom Bengston. His boyish looks were highlighted by a white shirt, tan sport coat, and brown tie.

---

59. East Lansing Police Department. Supplemental Report. Interview with Ernest Boillard. 6-C-77. November 9, 1979

Before beginning, the courtroom was cleared of any reporters, witnesses, and other police officers who would be testifying.

As Don Miller's preliminary examination finally got underway, the first witness to be called was Doug Gilbert, father of Lisa and Randy Gilbert.

In preparation for the exam, Mike Hocking had visited the Gilbert home. He wanted to physically see how the house was laid out rather than relying on a diagram. His strategy worked, and his questions were brief and to the point.

Hocking began by showing Mr. Gilbert a diagram of the house and asking if it was accurate. The young prosecutor then identified each of the bedrooms in the house, including Mr. Gilbert's, and the two second-floor bedrooms that belonged to Lisa and Randy.

After having Mr. Gilbert describe the doors used to enter the house, Hocking had finished his questioning.

When Tom Bengston asked him about the sliding glass door to the house, Mr. Gilbert described it and said there was no deck yet, and because of the elevation, the door was kept locked. When he'd gotten back home that night after leaving the hospital, the door was intact. He added that the front door of the home wasn't used very often. The door most used was the door from the garage that led into the house.

Bengston asked Mr. Gilbert about his belts. He said he'd been wearing one on August 16, and when he returned late that night from the hospital, his other two belts were still in the closet. He had about twenty ties, and when he'd gotten home after leaving the hospital, one was missing.

When asked about the cutlery in the kitchen, Mr. Gilbert said there was none missing.

Gilbert described the carpeting, the size of the bed, and eventually the blood on the carpet. He also told the defense attorney there were three phones in the house.

At the close of Bengston's questions, Mike Hocking stood and asked if the house had been ransacked, and where the blood was found. Mr. Gilbert said the house hadn't been ransacked, and the blood had been found in both the master bedroom and in Randy's bedroom.

Doug Gilbert's daughter Lisa was the key witness against Don Miller. She was quietly brought into the courtroom as the next witness.

Lisa Gilbert was apprehensive and scared as she took the stand. When she answered her first question, her voice was barely audible. Mike Hocking told her she would have to speak up a little.

There were several times Lisa would answer questions by simply nodding. The prosecuting attorney gently reminded her that she had to verbally answer the questions so the court reporter could record what she was saying.

As each question was asked, Lisa would quietly answer.

Lisa began her testimony by describing the layout of the home and where the doors were located. She began to describe what had happened on that day, and said she had gone out to the back of the house to yell for Randy, and no one was in the house at the time. When Hocking asked if the door had shut behind her when she went to go get Randy, Tom Bengston began to object.

"Excuse me, if I may, I would like to, mindful that the witness is not an adult and the Court is prompted to give latitude, I would like to object; improper foundation insofar as whether or not the door closed," he said.

"I don't understand the objection, Your Honor," Hocking said.

"Neither do I," the judge replied. Judge Hansen wasn't feeling well, and the tone of his voice was lower than normal.

Bengston said, "The question is on what basis does the witness indicate that the door closed? Did she hear it? Did she see it, or how does she know?"

When prompted by the judge, Lisa answered, "Because I heard it slam behind me when I went out."[60]

The questioning moved beyond the defense attorney's objection, and Lisa continued her description of the day. She said she was listening to the radio in the living room and walked through the dining room and kitchen and out through the garage. She hadn't seen anyone when she went outside, and there weren't any cars in the drive. She walked out the side door leading into the yard and walked back to the lagoon where Randy was fishing. She yelled his name because it was time for them to call their stepmom.

Lisa said she had come through the door she had just used to leave the garage when she saw a car in the driveway. She described the car as brown with a sort of slanted back, and it was facing the house. She briefly wondered if it was a friend's car, so she walked back out toward the lagoon to see if anyone was out there.

Continuing to describe what she had done, she said she came back through the same door a second time to re-enter the garage and slipped off her shoes as she stopped at the screen door leading into the house from the garage.

Hocking asked her if the door was still closed, which it was.

Lisa told the prosecutor she looked up through the screen door leading into the kitchen and saw a man standing in the hall leading into the kitchen. She didn't know the man, and he walked from the house into the garage, asking about what time her dad would be home.

Lisa described the brief conversation with her attacker and how she had gone back into the house to find a piece of paper to write down her dad's number for the man. Prompted by each question, she quietly described him grabbing her

---

60. People v Don G. Miller. Transcript of preliminary examination. November 17, 1978, 29

around the throat with his left hand while holding a knife up to her with his right hand.

Her voice was fading, and she was talking softer than before; the judge asked her to speak a little louder.

Lisa said she was led her into her parents' bedroom and forced to lay on the floor. She told Hocking how her attacker had left the bedroom very briefly, and she heard the front door to the house shut. He had returned to the bedroom almost immediately.

It was a very difficult time in the courtroom as Lisa described what Miller had done to her. At one point, she only answered by nodding, and the Court had to ask her to answer out loud.

The fourteen-year-old girl described every detail of the assault by Don Miller, including how he had bound her hands and feet with nylons, and she told the Court how he had taken her belt, wrapped it around her neck after raping her, and how he began to strangle her. She vividly described lying on her stomach with her hands tied behind her back and her neck being pulled back as he tightened his grip. She said it lasted for only a few seconds before the belt broke into two pieces, but Miller began choking her from behind with his bare hands. As he squeezed harder, she heard the back door open, and she knew it was her brother Randy.

It was difficult for Mike Hocking to ask the questions, but it was even more difficult for Lisa to answer them.

The prosecutor asked her what she had done when he left the room, and she told him she was able to make her way into the master bathroom. With her hands and feet bound, she tried to hide in the linen closet.

Hocking asked if she could hear anything at that point, and she said she could hear Randy screaming. She said she was able to free one of her legs from the bindings and decided to escape by going through the front door. She ran for the street without any clothes on.

Mike Hocking had only three more questions. "Would you recognize him if you saw him again?"

The teenage girl answered, "Yes, I think."

"Is he in the courtroom?"

"He's over there," she said, describing what Don Miller was wearing and pointing directly at him.

"And that's the person who held this knife up to your neck?"

"Yes."[61]

It was noon, and Mike Hocking had finished questioning Lisa Gilbert. Judge Hansen ordered a lunch recess and instructed everyone to return at 1:30 p.m.

As the afternoon session began, Lisa took a seat back on the witness stand.

Tom Bengston began by asking Lisa how she was able to know what time she had gone out to call for Randy, and she told him she had looked at the clock before she went outside.

"What prompted you to go out and call for Randy?" he asked.

Lisa said that she and Randy were normally in the house together when they made the afternoon call to their stepmom.

After Lisa described what she had done that day and answered a question about how long the garage door had been open, Bengston asked her to describe the person she saw in the garage when she came back in from calling for Randy.

Calling for specific details about the suspect, he asked her if the brief conversation she had with him was in the garage, and if she had noticed where his hands were when she spoke with him.

61. People v Don G. Miller, November 17, 1978, 52

There were some things she couldn't recall, but she was able to say that the man who raped her had on a green short-sleeved shirt.

He asked Lisa if she could remember anything else about his clothing. She thought his pants were green, but she couldn't recall his shoes.

Tom Bengston's strategy was to move directly into the house with Lisa's testimony. "And then he indicated to you that he would like to have something to write on, to copy down the telephone number of your father?" he asked. When Lisa confirmed that, the defense attorney asked, "And he made that request to you in the garage, correct? And then you proceeded into the house. You opened the door? And then he followed you?"[62]

Lisa said yes.

Step by step, the defense attorney had Lisa account for everything she had done while getting a piece of paper to write down the telephone number.

As she described looking for the paper in a drawer, Bengston asked, "Where was this person at the time?"

"Behind me."

"Were you concerned at that point? Were you scared?"

When Lisa said she was a little scared, he asked why, and she told him she didn't know.

"Is this the time of that incident when the arm around your neck developed?"

When Lisa said yes, he asked, "How do you recall it was the left arm that was around your neck as opposed to the right arm?"

Lisa became frustrated. "I don't know. I just, guess, I don't know. I guess it was because his body was right back in there, and I don't know. I just know it was the left arm or the left hand."

---

62. People v Don G. Miller, November 17, 1978, 61

"How much time went by from the time this person had the arm around your neck and the time in which you saw the knife?"

Lisa regained her composure, saying, "Not very long. A few seconds."[63] The knife never touched her neck, and she couldn't describe it for the defense attorney either. She never saw the knife during the rape, and Miller never said anything to her about what he was going to do with it.

Bengston asked Lisa if she had suffered a nose bleed. Lisa said she had, and it was caused by Miller choking her.

During the questioning, Lisa said that she had given a statement to Deputy Denise Keena and hadn't looked at any photos of the suspect nor had she seen any newspapers.

Bengston avoided any questions about the rape and moved to when Randy came into the house. He asked how she knew it was Randy, and she told him she didn't know until she heard his screams.

"There came a time, you told us this morning, that you fled the house. You went outside without any clothing to summon assistance, is that right?"

"Yes," Lisa said, but she told him she couldn't recall how long that had taken.[64]

Before Bengston asked Lisa any other questions, he told her he wasn't asking them to embarrass her, but needed to get some things on the Court record.

Once more, Tom Bengston walked Lisa through the entire sequence of events related to the rape, so after Lisa described what Don Miller had done to her, Bengston said, "That is to say, the whole thing took ten or fifteen minutes, isn't that fair?" and asked her if she knew how he had gotten into the house.

"Probably just walked in. The door was not locked or anything," she said.

63. People v Don G. Miller, November 17, 1978, 63
64. People v Don G. Miller, November 17, 1978, 69

"So in conclusion, from your testimony that the person who did this, the only thing he asked you to do after he put his left arm around your neck was 'don't say anything' or words to that effect, is that correct?"

"Yes."

Bengston reaffirmed her answer by asking, "He said absolutely nothing else to you?"

"Right."[65]

Asked how she had gotten up and moved to the bathroom after the suspect had left her to go after her brother, she told him she had stood up, made her way into the bathroom off the master bedroom and closed the door. She thought she waited thirty to forty-five seconds before making the decision to run with her hands were still bound behind her back.

"Initially, I think you told us that something was inserted into your mouth, a cloth or something, so that you couldn't scream," Bengston said. "Do you remember what it was, Lisa, that was in your mouth?"

"A nylon."

"Did the presence of this nylon in your mouth, did that prohibit you from screaming?"

"I don't know. I didn't try screaming. I mean, I don't know if I could have," she calmly answered.

"This morning you told us that there was a belt. I think you told us, was it a belt around your neck, please?"

When Lisa said yes, he asked her if she knew where it had come from.

"I think it was mine, that I had on my jeans." The belt was leather, and she told the defense attorney it was blue and white.

"And it's your recollection that this belt broke?"

"Yes," she said.

---

65. People v Don G. Miller, November 17, 1978, 77

When Bengston asked her how she could tell the belt broke, she said, "'Because I heard it, like when he was tightening it, it broke and you could, you know, then it loosened. Plus, I heard like a snap."

"Okay, so you didn't see it break but rather you heard it break, is that the idea?"

"Yes."

Bengston needed her to clarify if something else was around her neck when she ran from the house, and she said, "The thing that was around my mouth."

"Okay, so actually, it wasn't around your neck?"

"It was not."

"So the only object around your neck was this belt that you think was your own belt?"

When Lisa answered yes, Bengston asked, "And then hands were applied around your throat, right?"

When she answered yes, he continued along that line of questioning by asking her why she felt it was her own belt that had been wrapped around her neck.

She began to get frustrated again. "I don't know, I think I just felt, like, I don't know, it felt like, you know, a smooth leather kind of belt."

"Could you hear the belt being removed from your pants?" When Lisa said no, Bengston asked, "How long was the belt being tightened around your neck by this person?"

"Only a few seconds. It wasn't very long before it broke."[66]

Bengston asked Lisa if she had ever passed out from being choked and she said no, but her vison began to get blurry. She said Miller had pressure on her neck with his hands after her belt broke and she couldn't breathe. She added that she just laid there and didn't try to fight back because Miller was sitting on her back.

---

66. People v Don G. Miller, November 17, 1978, 81

Tom Bengston circled back to the suspect's position as he tried to choke Lisa. She described to him again how she was on her stomach, and Miller was sitting on her legs as he tried to strangle her with the belt and his bare hands.

"And so, from behind you, this belt was applied to your neck, is that correct?" When Lisa said yes, he said, "And that's what caused you earlier to tell Mr. Hocking your neck was arched back like so." The defense attorney demonstrated by arching his own back.

"Not very far, but a little. My head wasn't back like that when he was choking me with his hands."

"And the person is saying nothing to you as he is choking you, is that right?"

"Right."

Tom Bengston was nearing the end of his questioning. He asked Lisa if she had been menstruating. She said she had, and he asked if the suspect had to remove anything. She told him she had a sanitary napkin in her underwear.

It was almost three p.m. Lisa had been under cross-examination for almost ninety minutes when the defense attorney asked for a short recess. Eleven minutes later, her testimony resumed.

Lisa said she didn't see any glasses on the suspect, he didn't have a mask of any kind, and he wasn't wearing any gloves.

She added that the necktie used to bind her legs was still tied around one of her legs when she fled the house.

Mike Hocking knew Lisa had been through enough, and as Bengston finished, he called his next witness. It was Lisa's brother Randy.

The terrified eighth grader took the stand and was asked by Judge Hansen if he knew what it meant to tell the truth. When he answered yes, Hansen asked if Bengston and Hocking were satisfied that he would, and they both agreed.

Mike Hocking began walking Randy through the afternoon of August 16, 1978. Randy remembered it vividly. He had heard Lisa calling his name while he was out in back of the house fishing.

Still apprehensive, he told the Court he had just come in and saw a man coming from his parents' bedroom.

"Is he in the courtroom?" Hocking asked.

"Yeah."

As the prosecutor began having the eighth grader describe what Don Miller was wearing in the courtroom, Bengston interrupted, saying, "I'll stipulate."

Mike Hocking asked the youth what the man did when he first saw him.

"Well, he said hi and all that and I just kind of said hi, like, you know. I didn't know what was happening because a lot of people have been coming in the house to fix it, and I thought that's what he was and all that, and he just came up from behind me and grabbed me."[67]

Judge Hansen asked him to repeat what he had said.

Randy repeated it. He said the man had come up from behind him and put a knife to his neck. The boy clarified what had happened when he said, "Well, he came up in front. I saw him first and then he walked past me, kind of, and came up and grabbed me from behind."

"How did he grab you?"

"With his arm around my chest, around there," he said as he pointed to his chest.

Randy described the knife as being somewhere by his neck.

"Did you go anywhere from the living room after this man grabbed you?" Hocking asked.

"Yeah, he took me upstairs in my room." Randy described the brief struggle on the stairway with Miller and said the two of them ended up at the top of the stairs. "He put me down on the floor and put my arm around my back and started pulling on it."

---

67. People v Don G. Miller, November 17, 1978, 93

Describing the assault, Randy said he was face down on the floor, and his left arm was pulled up behind his back in a hammer lock.

"What did he do then?"

Randy was hesitant, but said, "He started cutting my throat."[68]

Randy said he could feel the knife slicing into his neck, and the blade felt sharp even though he never saw it.

"I just started yelling and I took, I don't remember what I did, but I kind of remember taking my arm around and getting the knife or something like that and throwing it. I think I threw it under the bed."

After the knife was thrown under the bed, Randy said Miller started to choke him and said he started getting a tired feeling as he was being strangled.

Hocking asked the eighth grader if he remembered seeing anything when he woke up.

"Just blood. All over, just about, on the carpeting and on me."[69] Again, he pointed to his chest. Randy's said after he woke up, he got up, ran to the bathroom and tried to use the phone. He described running down the stairs and going toward the front door as he saw the suspect leaving in a car.

Mike Hocking wanted an identification in the courtroom. As he pointed toward Don Miller, he asked Randy Gilbert, "Okay, and is this the same person, the defendant?"

"Well, it looks like him, yeah," he said.

"Is that the same person that approached you in the living room in the house?"

"Yes," the boy said, confident now.

Randy described standing at the front door when a man came up and told him to lie down. He was talking about James Regan and said the man kept repeating some numbers. Randy guessed it was a license plate.

---

68. People v Don G. Miller, November 17, 1978, 96
69. People v Don G. Miller, November 17, 1978, 98

Tom Bengston had been taking notes as Randy testified. When Hocking took a seat, Bengston stood to question Randy.

When asked, Randy said he couldn't recall what the suspect was wearing.

Bengston showed him the diagram of the house and asked him which door he had come through. Randy told him he had come through the large garage door.

The defense attorney asked if the suspect was wearing sunglasses when he encountered him, and Randy told him no.

When Bengston asked about the car he had seen the defendant leaving in, the eighth grader couldn't remember much about the car other than it had a crack in the windshield, and Randy told him it looked purple, but it was actually a different color.

"And in the course of these events, you never saw a knife until such time as you took it away from him upstairs?"

"Yes."[70]

Tom Bengston went over the details of Randy coming into the house, how the suspect had grabbed him, and whether or not Randy had seen his sister.

After Randy had confirmed he had not seen his sister, Bengston moved to the struggle on the stairs and the assault in the bedroom.

Randy said he'd been stabbed twice in the chest, and his throat was cut.

After Bengston's cross examination, Judge Hansen asked Mike Hocking if he had any motions.

The young assistant prosecutor stood up from the table, buttoning the suit he was wearing as he addressed the Court.

He began by taking the counts against Don Miller. Beginning with the charge of breaking and entering, the prosecutor pointed out that "breaking" didn't necessarily

---

70. People v Don G. Miller, November 17, 1978, 104

mean great force. He argued the breaking of the curtilage was sufficient and pointed out to Judge Hansen that Lisa had testified that when she left the house to go get Randy, the house was empty, and there were no cars in the drive. When she came back, there was not only a car in the drive, but a person standing in the kitchen. When she spoke with the person, he brandished a knife and took her into her parents' bedroom. Hocking argued it was sufficient to show the breaking and entering.

The prosecutor moved to the charge of assault with intent to commit murder. He described Lisa's testimony about the belt being placed around her neck and pulled to the point where it caused her to arch her back before breaking. He told the Court that the defendant then took his hands and began choking her to the point where her vision became blurry and things around her started getting hazy.

Mike Hocking moved to the rape of Lisa up to the point where her brother Randy came into the house. He described Randy's testimony to the Court and how he struggled briefly with the defendant before being choked to the point where he passed out, then woke up to find himself covered in blood.

Hocking finished his motion to have Don Miller bound over to circuit court, saying, "I believe the People have shown there were four crimes committed, and I believe the People have shown there is probable cause to believe this defendant committed them, and I ask the Court to bind him over to circuit court."

Tom Bengston knew the Court was prepared to bind his client over to the circuit court.

As he addressed Judge Hansen, he said that while he felt there was sufficient evidence to bind his client over on something, he disagreed with the prosecutor on the breaking and entering charge. He told the Court that there was no breaking because there was no force used, and it was clear that Lisa had opened the door for him and implicitly "consented to his entry into the house."

As Bengston spoke, Hocking was thinking to himself that it was Lisa who was outside and saw Miller already inside the kitchen when she came back from calling for her brother, yet Bengston was arguing that his client shouldn't be bound over on the breaking and entering charge.

Tom Bengston had nothing to argue about the rape of Lisa. He moved to the assault on Randy, suggesting if Miller had wanted to kill Randy, he would have. Therefore, a more appropriate charge might be assault with intent to great bodily harm less than murder, or even an aggravated assault rather than the original charge.

Mike Hocking had the burden of proof. He stood to address the Court one last time before the judge would make his decision. He pointed out that Miller was already in the house when Lisa came into the garage. Clearly, he must have opened a door at some point to enter the house. He also mentioned the assault on Randy, telling the Court that a knife to the throat, being choked to the point of unconsciousness, and two stab wounds to the chest abundantly showed an assault with the intent to commit murder.

Judge Hansen was quick and concise. Don Miller was bound over to the circuit court on all charges.

While the preliminary examination was over, Tom Bengston wasn't through. He wanted a reduction in Miller's bond. Hocking also had a motion regarding the same thing.

Tom Bengston began by telling Judge Hansen that there was no way Don Miller had the means to post the one hundred thousand dollar bond set by the Court, and said he believed it was set at that amount for another reason. "The prosecutor was concerned that my client may be involved in the Martha Sue Young case and other people in the Lansing area, and I suggest that there is no evidence to hold that way. I think the prosecutor, at that time, talked in terms of there being a ritual with respect to this case and that the ritual had occurred in the Choquette case in Lansing, and therefore, the two were done by the same person."[71]

Hocking stood to address the judge. He told the Court that he had originally asked for a half million dollar bond on Miller, even before the proofs had been heard. He continued by telling Hansen the crimes committed against Lisa and Randy were heinous, and the kids were fortunate enough to escape. He argued the bond was reasonable, and Miller certainly had every reason to flee the state, or even the country, given the charges against him. Hocking added that he feared for Lisa and Randy's safety if Miller's bond was reduced.

It was Judge Hansen's turn. As he spoke, he told both attorneys that he was not the one who set the original bond; Judge Bauer had done that and Hansen wasn't going to reduce it. "It's interesting to note that between the time of this defendant's arraignment and the original setting of bond, public policy in this state, as declared by its citizens, is to allow Courts in these sorts of cases to deny bond absolutely. Motion is denied."[72]

Don Miller, the twenty-three-year old criminal justice graduate from MSU, would stand trial for breaking and entering into the Gilbert home, the rape and attempted murder of Lisa, and the attempted murder of her brother Randy. It was only the beginning.

---

71. People v Don G. Miller, November 17, 1978, 113
72. People v Don G. Miller, November 17, 1978, 114

11

With Don Miller's preliminary exam over, his case was moved to the circuit court for arraignment.

Tom Bengston had withdrawn as Miller's attorney after the preliminary exam. He had originally been retained by Gene and Elaine Miller, but now it appeared that the charges were more complex than Bengston had originally anticipated. For Bengston to continue on the case, he told the Millers it would require additional funds for an investigator and other medical experts. Additional money would also be needed for the defense attorney to continue to advise Miller on legal matters. Those matters included him being a suspect in the disappearances of Martha Sue Young, Wendy Bush, and Kristine Stuart, in addition to being a suspect in the murder of Marita Choquette. The Millers didn't have the money for Bengston to continue beyond the preliminary examination.

On the morning of the circuit court arraignment, Don Miller, now without legal counsel, stood alone before the judge in the circuit courtroom before the Honorable Judge Richard Robinson.

Hocking knew Bengston had withdrawn. He asked the judge if he was going to appoint counsel for the defendant.

"Mr. Miller, you are not represented by an attorney?" Judge Richard Robinson asked.

"Not at the time, no, sir," Don Miller replied.[73]

---

73. People v Don G. Miller, Transcript of appointment of attorney, November 30, 1978, 2

Robinson began asking where he worked, if had any money or assets, or if anyone owed him money. Miller told him he had no property, and didn't even have a car anymore. All he had were books and clothes.

Confident that Miller couldn't afford to hire an attorney, the judge appointed the law firm of Zimmer and Dietrick to represent him, and entered a plea of not guilty on his behalf, at least for the time being.

Don Zimmer and Bob Dietrick were both well-known local attorneys. At one point, Miller had spoken with Tom Bengston about his new court-appointed attorneys, and Bengston had told him they were top-notch lawyers.

Dietrick spent two weeks preparing for the case by interviewing Don Miller at the jail. By the time of Miller's formal arraignment on December 14, the Millers weren't satisfied, and they re-hired Bengston to represent their son.

On December 14, Mike Hocking had another matter and couldn't attend the arraignment, so Assistant Prosecuting Attorney Ray Buffmeyer stood in for him. Buffmeyer and Hocking had gone to law school together.

Bengston and Buffmeyer had already discussed what was about to happen.

In the formal proceeding, the defense attorney told the judge that his client was waiving the circuit court arraignment and standing mute to all four charges.

Judge Robinson set a pretrial conference for two weeks later, and Bengston addressed the Court again, asking for the Court to delay the pretrial conference. Robinson already knew Bengston was going to file some motions. Robinson set the conference for January 11, 1979, but told Bengston to have his motions filed by December 28.

The judge cautioned the defense attorney, asking, "Mr. Bengston, you are aware of my policy against accepting pleas to other than the original charge after the pretrial date, I believe?"

"Yes, I am," Bengston said.[74]

By December 28, Don Miller's attorney had several motions he intended to make before the Court, and on January 5, 1979, he appeared in front of Judge Robinson.

Bengston was concerned his client might not get a fair trial and relayed this by presenting his motions to the Court.

He explained the first of seven motions before Judge Robinson, with Prosecuting Attorney Paul Berger representing the People. Bengston wanted Miller brought to his office in the Michigan National Tower Building in downtown Lansing so he could confer with both his client and his client's family over their legal strategy.

Berger wasn't aware of any case law allowing or not allowing it, and his only objection was that it could set a precedent for other prisoners at the jail. He suggested that a conference room be made available at the courthouse rather than transporting Miller to Lansing, and the judge agreed. He told both attorneys that he felt it would impose an undue burden on the sheriff's department in terms of security. He asked that Bengston coordinate with the prosecutor's office on some dates, and then have the prosecutor coordinate with the sheriff's department for security in the conference room.

Bengston's next motion was for a change of venue, and Paul Berger had no objections. The defense attorney was concerned about the pretrial publicity in the rape case, and even more concerned with his client being the lone suspect in the disappearances of four women in neighboring Ingham County.

While he spoke to the judge, Bengston said his client's name had been associated with the four missing women in Ingham County, and there was also a grand jury looking at the missing person cases. He was certain that prospective

---

74. People v. Don G. Miller, Transcript of circuit court arraignment, December 14, 1978, 4

jurors wouldn't be able to put that aside and give his client a fair trial.

Berger felt it was at the discretion of the Court and pointed out in other case law that it was the burden of the party seeking the change of venue to show that potential jurors had been influenced by pretrial publicity. He said existing case law stated that mere exposure to pretrial publicity didn't constitute sufficient grounds to grant a change of venue.

Judge Robinson had always followed the guidelines that Berger had referred to about a change of venue. But he was just as concerned about a fair trial for Miller. He had seen the news reports. He had followed the headlines. Bengston wasn't telling him anything that he didn't already know. With that in mind, the judge told both attorneys that he didn't believe it was possible to pick a jury of twelve people who hadn't heard of the cases or who would be able to put aside what they might have heard through the media. He granted the motion for a change in venue.

Judge Robinson quickly moved to the next motion by Bengston. Bengston wanted the breaking and entering charge against Miller dismissed.

The defense attorney argued that an element of breaking and entering was to have the intent to commit a felony, and there was nothing in the testimony of Lisa Gilbert that showed Miller's intent to commit a crime when he entered the house. Bengston said it was only after he re-entered the house behind Lisa that he committed the assault, and he suggested the only crime committed at that point was the misdemeanor charge of entry without permission.

Paul Berger had anticipated Bengston's motion. He said that a person's intent could be inferred by his actions. Lisa Gilbert hadn't invited him into the house when she first saw him inside, and when she re-entered the house, his intent was manifested. The prosecutor asked the Court to bind Miller over on the breaking and entering charge.

Rather than make a decision at that point, the judge asked both attorney's for written briefs explaining their positions.

Bengston stood up again. This time, he was asking to have the attempted murder charges dismissed. He explained that if his client wanted to commit murder, there was nothing to stop him from doing it, and added the court record failed to show his client's conduct was aimed at taking a life.

The judge was familiar with the preliminary examination transcript. He asked Bengston which element of the offense was lacking.

Bengston said it was the lack of dialogue between Don Miller and his two victims. His argument centered on the fact that Miller hadn't said he was going to kill anyone, or anything comparable to that. He agreed that there was probably enough information to bind over his client on assault with intent to do great bodily harm less than murder, but added that the district court judge had erred by not considering the lesser charge.

Bengston mentioned the choking and the stabbing, but said that those, in and of themselves, didn't constitute an assault with intent to commit murder.

Paul Berger calmly asked the judge to review the entire preliminary exam transcript again. He described how Lisa had testified she was choked with a belt first, and then with the defendant's bare hands, and only survived because Miller was distracted by Randy coming into the house. He also described Randy's stab wounds, and finished by saying he didn't believe that Judge Hansen had abused his discretion.

Judge Robinson was quick to say he didn't need any briefs on the motions. He denied them.

Bengston stood again, this time asking the judge to throw out the visual identification of Miller by James Regan. He said he would probably have to call two or three witnesses, so Robinson set aside the day before Don Miller's preliminary exam for Bengston to call his witnesses.

On the morning of January 10, at 8:51 a.m., the prosecution's first witness, Detective Norm Kelley, took the stand.

After Kelley had described how he had come into contact with James Regan on the day of the assault on Lisa and Randy Gilbert, Mike Hocking asked if he had shown any photographs to Regan. When Kelley said he had, Hocking asked him where he had gotten them.

Kelley said he picked them up from an East Lansing police officer.

The detective had brought the photos to court with him in a three-ring binder, and told Hocking there were four photographs on one side and a large photo on the back of the page. He added that the large photo was never shown to the witness.

Kelley said they were shown to James Regan at the Delta Township fire station in the squad room. "The group of four photographs, three of which were covered up with my hand. The upper left photograph was the only one shown to Mr. Regan. I asked him to carefully observe the photograph and see if he recognized the subject in the photograph as being the same one that he observed leaving the house on Canal Road."

"And what did he reply, if anything?"

"He stated immediately, without hesitation, that that definitely was the same individual exiting the Gilbert residence at 902 South Canal," Kelley said.[75] He said the time of the identification was at 4:40 p.m., and afterward, he took the taped statement from Regan.

When asked if had ever told James Regan the name of the suspect, Kelley said he hadn't. Regan had given him a

75. People v Don G. Miller. Defendant's motion to suppress visual identification. January 10, 1979, 5

description of the suspect before he was ever shown any photos.

To close his direct examination of Kelley, Hocking had him identify Don Miller in the courtroom.

When the assistant prosecutor was finished questioning Kelley, Bengston asked the detective how many photographs he had initially shown to Regan. Kelley told him one.

"And then you say he immediately made identification of this particular male person in the photograph, is that correct?"

"That's correct."

Bengston continued, "And there is, in fact, only one male in the photograph?"

"That's correct."[76]

Bengston had made his point. Miller was the only male standing with four women in the picture.

Kelley said that once he finished with the upper left-hand photograph and was satisfied Regan had time to look at it and make an identification, he had him look at the rest of them. Regan kept looking back at the one in the upper left that was more clear. Regan had positively identified Miller in one other photograph, but wasn't sure about the other two.

"Was there an attorney present in behalf of Mr. Miller or anyone else?" Bengston asked.

"No, there was not."[77]

When Kelley was asked about the license plate number of the car Regan had seen, he said Regan told him he wrote it down, but he couldn't recall it when he was being interviewed by the detective.

The defense attorney was trying to illustrate that law enforcement had focused on Don Miller as a suspect before Kelley had ever shown the photos to Regan, and Kelley

76. People v Don G. Miller, January 10, 1979, 11
77. People v Don G. Miller, January 10, 1979, 13

admitted he had, but that it was based on information from the license plate number.

"Other than the license number, was there anything else which prompted you to conclude that this was the person responsible for the conduct on Canal Road?"

"Not at that time, no," Kelley said.[78]

Hocking stood and asked if Don Miller had been arrested before Kelley had shown the photos to Regan. He hadn't.

Mike Hocking called his next witness.

On the stand, Rick Westgate told the prosecutor how he'd become involved in the case and the eventual arrest of Miller. He had called into the East Lansing police dispatch at 4:47 p.m. because he had seen Miller's car approaching the apartment complex in East Lansing, and one minute later, Don Miller was in custody.

Bengston's only concern was if Westgate had known Miller's license plate number before he was arrested. Westgate told him he did, but he arrested Miller based solely on the radio transmissions from the Eaton County Sheriff's Department.

Mike Hocking's final witness was the man who had confronted Don Miller as he came out of the Gilbert home, but he didn't want Miller in the courtroom when Regan testified about the identification. He didn't think it was fair to Don Miller to sit and listen to Regan's testimony about what he saw that day. The assistant prosecutor thought if Miller was in the courtroom, the hearing would be tainted.

Bengston spoke with Miller privately, and together they decided he shouldn't be in the courtroom when direct testimony was taken, but asked that he be brought back in when Bengston cross-examined Regan.

Detective Kelley escorted Miller from the courtroom, and as Hocking called James Regan to the stand, he began

---

78. People v Don G. Miller, January 10, 1979, 14

by asking him about his background, then moved directly to the day of the assault.

Regan described what he had seen that day when he said, "The young lady ran out of the house and ran down the road toward me, screaming for help. She was totally naked, except for a necktie around her neck, and her hands were behind her back, and she was screaming hysterical."

He pulled into the drive on South Canal and came into contact with a man coming out of the house. He described the man, how close they were to each other, and the conversation he had with the suspect. After the brief discussion, the man had run by him trying to escape.

Before beginning his cross-examination, Tom Bengston asked that his client not be brought into the courtroom just yet. He asked Regan if he had been struck by the suspect's vehicle as he fled. Regan said he had grabbed the door handle, and as the car lurched forward, he was pulled down to one knee.

Bengston asked Regan if he could identify the suspect if he were able to put aside the photographs he had been shown by Kelley. Regan was confident he could. "Yes, sir. I had a conversation with the man, and it was quite a traumatic experience, and I was standing in front of him, talking to him at the time."[79]

Bengston asked for Don Miller to be brought back into the courtroom. Norm Kelley left the courtroom and returned with the defendant. As Miller took a seat back at the defense table, Bengston asked Regan to look at him, and asked if he'd seen him before.

Regan replied he had, that he'd seen him coming out the front door of the house on Canal. There was no reason to have Miller speak because he saw Miller face to face. "I know what he looks like, I know who he is."[80]

79. People v Don G. Miller, January 10, 1979, 46
80. People v Don G. Miller, January 10, 1979, 47

Bengston had nothing else to offer.

At the conclusion of testimony, the judge instructed both attorneys to incorporate their closing arguments in the form of briefs. Bengston was required to present his brief to the Court the following day, while Hocking was asked to have his ready by January 19.

The following day, Don Miller's defense attorney presented his brief. In the written document, he cited two cases that had been decided by the Michigan Supreme Court. One of those case required counsel to be present at a photographic lineup when a defendant was in custody, while the second stated the same rule should be applied where the defendant was not in custody but was still the focus of an investigation. Bengston wrote that it was clear his client was the focus of Kelley and Westgate's investigations.

A week after Tom Bengston filed his brief, he notified the Court he would be using the insanity defense. When Mike Hocking found out, he knew Bengston had no other defense to offer. Hocking also knew he had never seen a case where the insanity defense had been successful.

Mike Hocking submitted his brief to the Court on January 19 on Bengston's motion to exclude the identification of his client and didn't deny that the lineup might have been tainted.

Citing the same case Bengston had referred to in his brief, the assistant prosecutor wrote that the issue was whether there was an independent basis for Regan's in-court identification of Don Miller. He argued that through the testimony of James Regan and Norm Kelley, a near-perfect record had been established for the in-court identification.

He identified the same points Bengston had referred to in his brief, and he outlined the testimony of Regan and Kelley to support each point.

In closing, Hocking wrote:

The People submit that it would be burdensome to conceive of a set of circumstances better suited to demonstrate the ideal "independent basis" and further, that the ends of justice require that James Regan be permitted to testify as to his very personal three-dimensional confrontation with the defendant.[81]

Four days after Hocking filed his brief, Judge Robinson ruled on Tom Bengston's motion. The judge agreed that Don Miller should have been represented by counsel when Regan was shown the photographs, and he agreed that the photographic identification of Miller was suggestive and amounted to a denial of due process for the defendant. Ultimately, though, Judge Robinson agreed with Hocking in opining that there was, in fact, an independent basis for Regan's in-court identification, and the motion was denied.

———————

Three days after his motion was denied, the defense attorney stood before Judge Robinson again with a motion to have his client obtain an independent psychiatric evaluation at Miller's own expense. Bengston had retained Dr. Arthur Hughett, a doctor of psychiatry at Wyandotte General Hospital near Detroit, to evaluate his client. He told the Court the evaluation would include two days of testing, examination, and observation regarding Miller's sanity at the time of the assault. Bengston was simply asking for judicial authority to have the sheriff's department transport Miller to Wyandotte, which the judge granted.

A few days after granting Bengston's most recent motion, Robinson responded to his request for a change of venue by

81. People v Don G. Miller. Plaintiff's brief in opposition to Defendant's motion to suppress identification. January 19, 1979, 5

moving the trial location to Berrien County in southwest Michigan.

The judge also issued two orders denying the defense's request to dismiss the attempted murder charges for the assaults on Lisa and Randy.

At eleven a.m., with sixteen mile-per-hour winds, a high temperature of twenty-three degrees had just been reached in Ann Arbor. It was February 6, and Don Miller was sitting down with two doctors for another evaluation at the Center for Forensic Psychiatry.

Both Dr. Blunt and Dr. Stock were interviewing Miller again and explained to him that their purpose was to evaluate his criminal responsibility about the events on August 16, 1978.

When the interview began, Miller told both doctors he couldn't recall the events leading to his arrest. As he got to the point where he said he was alleged to have broken into the house and raped and assaulted a teen, he said he'd been a Christian since he was eight-years-old. He had even been a youth minister.

The doctors asked him why he couldn't recall the events, and Miller said he had bumped his head, and it seemed like he gone into some stores and a gas station. It was the same scenario he had described months earlier when he had been evaluated before being found competent to take part in his preliminary exam.

He said the only thing in his memory was a furious gripping of the steering wheel.

Miller said he spent the night at his girlfriend's house, headed to work, and felt badly for his girlfriend's two kids because they were with their father, who had a violent temper. He said he didn't care for his job "because seventy-five percent of people treat you like a watchdog."

Don Miller began talking about his own life. His father had a temper and would sometimes lash out at his mother or his sister and sometimes him. He recalled a time when his father had broken a stick over his sister's legs because she wasn't at school when she was supposed to be. He said that after he turned eight years old, his father had become a Christian, and his temper gradually subsided.

Miller began talking about his job as a store detective and said he dressed so people wouldn't notice him. He would watch people and wait until they got out of the store, follow them, and when he finally approached them, he would show them his badge. He said if they didn't cooperate, he would try to get their license number but wouldn't ever try to stop them. "I don't believe in that stuff and you could get hurt," he said.

To the doctors, it appeared Don Miller always tried to express the Christian aspect of life. He felt that people who stole things were usually dependent on being poor or were stealing on a dare.

Miller said he made $2.65 per hour, and although he'd been promised an increase to three dollars per hour, he still hadn't seen it.

On the day of the assault, he recalled bumping his head as he stood up from his car and having a fuzzy, dream-like sensation. After changing his clothes, he saw someone in the parking lot at Meijer Thrifty Acres who he had met once during a meeting with an occult group. As he had watched Regan testify in court, Regan reminded him of the man he had met in the occult group. His next memory was going to his girlfriend's apartment and being arrested.

Miller said the occult group was called The Way, and he admitted to being associated with the group for about six months, but eventually left.

There was doubt in the minds of the two doctors about Miller's ability to recall events during the time of the assault. They asked him to consider the use of hypnosis, or having the doctors administer a dose of amytal, then continue the interview. Miller said he couldn't allow that because of his religious beliefs. "You shouldn't put yourself in anyone's hands but Jesus'."[82] Miller claimed he didn't believe in drugs or hypnosis, and the only drug he would take was a cough syrup for a cold.

Both doctors tried to explain that hypnosis or amytal could help resolve some of the doubt in his mind about what led to the charges against him. Miller told them that as a Methodist, the use of medication wasn't forbidden. Even if Miller's own minister told him it was okay to use medication in his religion, he would disagree with him.

The doctors tried to counter his argument by telling him he was doing other things that were against his religion, pointing out his sexual relations outside of marriage and living with a divorced woman he had planned to marry.

Miller said he was depressed about that, and couldn't reconcile why he would do one thing against his religion, yet not submit to a amytal interview or hypnosis.

He switched to talking about his childhood, and said he had become depressed about his parents. It was the way they treated each other that bothered him, and he even considered running away. He also said he had injured a bird after he had hit it with something, and it eventually died. The doctors asked if there were times when he killed other animals, and he said he hadn't because he always respected life.

While Miller knew what his father's occupation was, he didn't really know what his father did. He said he considered himself to be close with his parents, but recalled

---

82. Lynn Blunt to Paul Berger and Thomas Bengston, February 16, 1979

an incident before he started kindergarten when he had wet the bed. As punishment, his father had made him sleep on the cold linoleum floor, and added that at least once a day, his father would become upset over something.

Curious now, the doctors asked about Miller's anger. He said he kept it to himself when he was depressed or angry, and talked with God about it, but his parents didn't understand, and that upset him.

Miller weighed everything he said very carefully. He emphasized very strong religious beliefs dating back to the age of eight, while he overemphasized his dislike for violence and aggression, and he used religion when it seemed to fit his purpose.

As a result of the interview, the doctors couldn't find any evidence of a thinking disorder, and Miller had denied having any auditory hallucinations or having periods where he had done things and not remembered them.

The doctors quickly picked up on Miller's claim that he couldn't recall specific events leading to his arrest, yet in September of 1978 when he was being evaluated, he said he recalled everything he did that day and had given a detailed narrative.

The doctors felt it would be impossible to fully evaluate him because he was withholding information about himself. He refused to cooperate with the idea of using amytal or hypnosis. He'd also been told not to discuss certain things by his attorney.

In their report to both Tom Bengston and Paul Berger, the doctors wrote:

> The general withholding quality of his personality may well be indirect expressions of considerable underlying anger and resentment which he very much wants to deny. It appears that he tends very much to put himself in a good light and obviously changes circumstances or uses his religiosity in order

to accomplish his purposes. This was particularly seen in the fact that he has given different accounts of the time of the crime in two interviews, claiming they were both true. It appears that the Defendant is covering up considerable underlying character psychopathology.[83]

The doctors also wrote that mental illness is defined as: *a substantial disorder of thought or mood which significantly impairs judgement, behavior, capacity to recognize reality or ability to cope with the ordinary demands of life.*

Both doctors agreed that Miller wasn't suffering from any thought or mood disorders on August 16, 1978, and the bump on his head was unlikely to have anything to do with his claim of lacking memory.

Given the different stories Miller offered on two separate evaluations, they thought he was withholding information about his ability to remember the events leading to his arrest, and they also came to the joint conclusion that given the events of August 16, 1978, if it were proven that Miller was indeed involved, he would have known what was going on at the time and that it was wrong. They summarized a report, writing that the person involved acted in a deliberate fashion, was prepared, responded to someone entering the house, and fled the scene after a violent attack to protect himself. They closed the report by saying Miller was criminally responsible for the charges against him.

The following day, two doctors working on behalf of Tom Bengston had their opportunity to interview Don Miller. Their observations of him were much the same as Dr. Stock and Dr. Blunt, noting that Miller's responses to questions were guarded and vague as he weighed each question carefully before answering. It was difficult for

---

83. Lynn Blunt to Paul Berger and Thomas Bengston, February 16, 1979

Miller to answer a question directly, and to them, he seemed to ramble.

Miller still claimed that even though there was incontrovertible evidence of his involvement in the assaults on Lisa and Randy Gilbert, he was perplexed at how that could be. He said he couldn't intertwine the facts with his memory, or with his own character and how he saw himself.

Miller described himself to the doctors as a Christian whose life was dedicated to "doing good works unto others." He couldn't understand being accused of a crime of violence. It was inconsistent with the values he held so dear. Aggression and hostility were not something that were part of his life, and he saw himself as an intellectual— rational and controlled in his own way of thinking.

In their evaluation, the doctors felt Miller was an angry person, and he could only deal with the anger by keeping it repressed to a point where he had no awareness of it. They discovered that other than his engagement to Martha Sue Young, his current fiancée Janet, and his close relationship with his immediate family, he really had no other types of relationships with anyone. The relationships with Martha and Janet were based on religious foundation rather than personal commitments.

They believed there was evidence of psychosis, based on his living in an over-intellectualized world, and agreed that he had no capacity to be involved on a personal basis. The doctors felt he was withdrawn and incapable of feelings or emotion, and he was extraordinarily angry. When Miller experienced deep rage, he could not accept nor allow any conscious experience of it. He relied heavily on rigid, obsessive thinking, and he was over-ideational about religion. His conscious life was dominated by religion, and he saw himself as the personification of good. It was in sharp contrast to the feelings that formed the foundation of his personality structure, which he felt were satanic and demonic.

The two defense experts were sure Don Miller was schizophrenic, but with a psychotic multiple personality. Those traits, under certain conditions, could cause him to become emotional and violent.

They needed more evidence of Miller's condition, and decided the use of sodium amytal could be used to get through his defenses. He never objected.

After being given a dose of the sodium amytal, Miller slowly began to describe the day the rape occurred. On August 16, 1978, he was angry while he was working as a store detective. His anger stemmed from the way he felt he'd been harassed over the disappearance of Martha. He was also angry at his work supervisor. He felt he was being spied on by her and other employees, and he was upset about the quality of the books in the store because he felt evil books outnumbered the religious books.

His anger continued to build until he left work at two p.m., and he bumped his head while getting a comb from his glovebox. That intensified his anger. According to the doctors, that was when he began to spiral out of control. He needed to seek out and rescue good people like himself from evil occult groups. He felt he should find the occult house where he'd gone to meetings with The Way. As he went in search of the house, he noticed a young girl, and he was sure she was associated with the occult group. Stopping his car, he went into the house and started to look for other good people. When the occult girl returned to the house, he was sure she was going to attack him, so in a confused manner, he tied her, gagged her, and tried to question her about other people he thought might have been in the house. As this was going on, he said he heard demonic laughter and went in search of it. He came face to face with a demonic boy. He thought the boy was going to attack him, and in the process of trying to take the boy to another room to get him out of the way, the boy resisted. This only increased Miller's belief that he was being attacked, so he struck out at the boy with a knife he had found in the kitchen.

As he began to leave, he encountered another demon, and he quickly fled in his car.

Miller said that the entire time he was in the house and fleeing in his car, he felt there was someone near him. He believed it was his other self. While he was fleeing, the two of them merged together and he began to recover to his more usual, controlled personality.

The doctors had one concern: was Don Miller making it all up? In their report, they wrote:

> The consistency of the test material both within each specific test and among all the tests administered, as well as his clinical behavior and his behavior under sodium amytal, are such as to be virtually impossible to reproduce even if you were working with a script produced by experts and coached through extensive theatrical rehearsal.[84]

Their final conclusion was that Don Miller was insane when he committed the crime, unable to appreciate that what he was doing was wrong, and couldn't conform his conduct to the law. They felt he was suffering from a thought or mood disorder that significantly impaired his judgement, behavior, and ability to recognize reality. They wrote, "He meets every definition of legal insanity under current Michigan law and is not culpable for the crime which he stands accused."[85]

---

84. Arthur Hughett and Gerald Briskin to Thomas Bengston, April 3, 1979

85. Arthur Hughett and Gerald Briskin to Thomas Bengston, April 3, 1979

On February 15, Judge Robinson met in his chambers with Paul Berger, Mike Hocking, Tom Bengston, and the defendant.

The trial was set to begin on February 20, but Bengston was asking the Court to adjourn the trial date. He needed more time. Progress was being made on his client's psychiatric evaluation, and the doctors had told him they would need about four more months. Bengston was also asking for a bench trial before Judge Robinson instead of a jury trial.

Berger and Hocking had no objection, but asked that either Bengston, or Miller himself, to put it on the record.

Judge Robinson also vacated the change of venue.

While Don Miller's defense attorney had been filing motions with the Court over the previous months and arranging for his own psychological examination, a seventeen-member Ingham County grand jury had been working quietly behind the scenes taking testimony from various people about the disappearances of Martha Sue Young and Kristine Stuart.

One of the seven people to testify before the grand jury was Nancy Daniels. After her hypnosis session when she recalled seeing Miller struggling with Kristine Stuart and then stabbing her, she was terrified and had become fearful for her own life. Her identify was kept secret for six months until she could testify.

On February 22, 1979, the grand jury indicted Don Miller on two counts of second-degree murder in the deaths of Martha Sue Young and Kristine Stuart. Miller wasn't charged in Marita Choquette's homicide because investigators still hadn't linked him to her death.

With the two indictments, Peter Houk said, "We have two cases without bodies. This provides a difficult standard to prove what it takes to be first-degree murder."[86]

Researching homicide cases where there were charges without a body, Houk learned of only four cases in the entire world where a person was convicted. While none of the four cases were in Michigan, he was confident of the indictments and had every intention of prosecuting Don Miller. He was asked why Miller wasn't charged with first-degree murder, and he said that charge involved premeditation. "That's a significant element to prove. We didn't feel we could sustain it."[87]

Miller had to be arraigned in East Lansing District Court on the two new charges.

Gene and Elaine Miller were there to support their son and sat quietly in the front row as he was led into the courtroom. Standing before Ingham County Circuit Judge Michael Harrison, who had presided over the grand jury, Miller stood mute to both murder charges. After entering a not guilty plea on his behalf, Judge Harrison didn't set bond because Miller was already in custody.

As word of the indictments against Don Miller spread, Kristine's husband Ernie Stuart said he still had hope, and he would maintain that hope until his wife was found.

Tom Bengston was strategizing now. With two new murder charges hanging over his client's head, he conferred with Miller and his family about withdrawing his waiver for a jury trial and reinstating the change of venue.

86. Mark Nixon, "DONALD MILLER INDICTED IN MURDER OF TWO WOMEN," *State Journal*, February 22, 1979
87. Mark Nixon, February 22, 1979

On March 22, Tom Bengston stood before the Court again at a hearing regarding his motion. The defense attorney made it clear to Judge Robinson that they were not appearing in court to challenge the previous waiver or its compliance with the law.

Mike Hocking told the Court that he wasn't arguing either for or against Bengston's motion, but was simply making the Court aware that a waiver of jury trial had to be done in open court, and since the original waiver had been done in the judge's chambers, he didn't believe it would be accepted as open court.

Judge Robinson disagreed, and he paid an indirect compliment to Bengston when he suggested that if anyone else had made the request to withdraw the previous motion, he would have suspected they were playing games with the Court.

The judge knew they were starting from square one again, but he granted Bengston's motion. He told both attorneys the trial would be scheduled in May. His concern was that Miller get a fair trial.

12

Don Miller's trial was moved back to Berrien County for a second time. On April 2, Judge Robinson issued the order changing the venue and setting the trial date for April 30.

On the same day, Tom Bengston had other concerns. With Miller having been indicted by a grand jury for the murders of Martha Sue Young and Kristine Stuart, his preliminary examination was set for the same day in East Lansing in front of East Lansing's District Court Judge Daniel Tschirhart.

Assistant prosecutors Lee Atkinson and Mike Woodworth had been preparing for the exam since the indictments had been handed down. They knew it would be tough without having the bodies of the victims, but both of them, along with their boss Peter Houk, were confident Miller could be convicted.

At 9:54 a.m. on April 2, Judge Tschirhart called the court to order.

Asked if he was ready to proceed, Tom Bengston said he had a preliminary motion he wanted to bring before the Court. He'd been provided transcripts of the grand jury testimony, and knew about Nancy Daniels hypnosis session where she had seen the murder of Kristine Stuart.

Bengston was concerned. Speaking of both Nancy Daniels and Harold Duncan, he said it was going to be difficult to figure out what came before the hypnosis and what came after.

Citing an *Ohio State Law Review* article titled "ADMISSIBILITY OF HYPNOTIC STATEMENTS: IS THE LAW OF EVIDENCE SUSCEPTIBLE," Bengston read from the article,

"The subsequent opportunity for cross-examination at the trial is virtually ineffective as a means of assuring that no false suggestions have been implanted."

The concern he had was that Nancy Daniels' identification of Miller might be tainted. He knew the hypnosis sessions with her and Harold Duncan had been videotaped, and he asked the Court to be able to view the video tapes before proceeding. He was trying to tie the hypnosis session into whether or not she was competent to testify. He had to be certain there were no suggestions made to her or Duncan during the hypnosis.

As Atkinson stood to respond, he said Bengston had the transcript of the testimony, it was specifically mentioned that no photos were shown to Nancy Daniels and she had described the killer while a composite sketch was being done by a police artist. Bengston also had Dr. Rossi's testimony outlining the procedure he went through for the hypnotic interview.

He argued it would unnecessarily delay the preliminary exam and that most courts had said the cross-examination of a witness was more than sufficient to allow defense counsel to explore a witnesses testimony.

Responding to the prosecutor, Bengston said Michigan law was unclear about what impact a hypnotic interview had on a particular witness.

As the two attorneys finished their arguments, the judge granted Bengston's motion. He said the exam would continue after the defense was allowed to have a separate record regarding the hypnosis session. The judge added, "Now, the Court does wish to place on the record two things: Mr. Bengston, the attorney for the defendant, was the chairman of my campaign in 1974, and from that time and since that time, Mr. Bengston and I have remained personal friends. Mr. Atkinson, I believe you're aware of that. Do you have any objections to this Court sitting as the examining judge in this matter?"

"Of course not, Your Honor."

"Mr. Bengston?"

"No, Your Honor."[88]

Dean Tucker and Rick Westgate were sitting in the courtroom while the motion had been made. As the separate record was about to begin, Tom Bengston asked that any potential witnesses be sequestered. Atkinson didn't have any problem with the request, but asked that Tucker and Westgate, as the investigating officers, be allowed to remain, and the judge granted his request.

Dr. Donald Rossi, the department psychologist for the state police, was called to the witness stand at 11:10 a.m.

Lee Atkinson questioned the doctor about his qualifications as a psychologist and as an expert in hypnosis.

Bengston objected, saying he wasn't arguing Rossi's qualifications in psychology, but in the field of hypnosis. Tschirhart overruled the objection.

Dr. Rossi began his testimony explaining the difference between forensic hypnosis and clinical hypnosis. He said the purpose of the forensic hypnosis was to assist a person in recalling what was in their memory. By doing it properly, the hypnotist avoids giving the person any additional information.

The doctor described the procedures used, including a simple interview beforehand and the induction procedure, or how he had the subject relax. There were certain characteristics a person would exhibit while under hypnosis, including movement of the eyelids, dryness of a person's throat, mouth, and lips, and some slowing of a person's speech.

Rossi said as he hypnotized Nancy Daniels, she was in a reclined position in his office, with Tucker and the police sketch artist present in the same room.

---

88. People v Don G. Miller, Transcript of preliminary examination, April 2, 1979, 16

He said there was a point when she made reference to seeing a black book. Rossi knew about the black book because he'd been told she was hypnotized by a person before she had been brought to his office. The information about the black book had come to light during that session.

Dr. Rossi said he asked her about the black book, and she became quite emotional. He noticed her tears first, and as she told him about it, she realized it wasn't a black book she had seen, but a knife.

The chief assistant prosecutor was curious. Had the earlier hypnosis session had any effect on his session with her? Rossie told him no, and it actually had made her feel more comfortable. He said he hadn't seen any evidence of any previous suggestions made to her.

When the prosecutor was finished questioning Dr. Rossi, the court recessed for lunch so video equipment could be set up in the courtroom.

After the lunch break, the videotape of Nancy Daniels' hypnosis session with Dr. Rossi was played. There were four tapes, and by the time they had finished playing the first three, it was late in the day, and court was adjourned until the following morning.

The last video tape was viewed the following morning, and afterward, Lee Atkinson continued his questioning of Dr. Rossi.

He asked if Nancy Daniels had been able to recall the license plate on the car she saw, and Dr. Rossi said she hadn't. It was very difficult for people to recall numbers under hypnosis, and she may not have paid attention to it.

While Rossi described the process of using forensic hypnosis to do a composite sketch, he said he hadn't shown any photos to Mrs. Daniels. To avoid any suggestion in the process, it was preferred that no photos of eye styles, face shapes, or hairstyles be shown to the witness. The artist had to be skillful in drawing strictly from a verbal description given by the witness.

Atkinson glanced at his notes as he thanked Rossi.

When Bengston asked the doctor if he had reviewed a list of nine open homicide cases, including Kristine Stuart's case, or if he had compiled it himself, Rossi said he didn't, but it did exist. He only reviewed it after his session with Nancy Daniels.

The only thing Rossi knew about Daniels was that she had seen a situation near her home, it involved a man and woman by a car, and he knew the date and time of day. He said his primary purpose was to help the police get a composite sketch of the suspect. The other things that came to light were additional things that weren't part of his original consultation with the police.

The doctor explained there was a lunch break during the session, and everyone had gone to the restaurant next to his office. He said Nancy Daniels had gone to lunch with them, but had sat and talked with the woman who was running the video equipment during the interview, and there was no attempt to discuss the case during lunch.

Bengston asked if anything had developed with the witness during the lunch break.

The assistant prosecutor was on his feet to object. He told the judge that anything that happened when she wasn't hypnotized wasn't relevant.

The judge agreed and sustained the objection.

Bengston moved to having Dr. Rossi describe the three stages of hypnosis, and he asked why he had Mrs. Daniels in the second, or medium, stage.

Rossi said it was the preferred stage for that particular type of work.

Dr. Rossi said the black book appeared during his session with Mrs. Daniels, and as he focused on it, she described it as knife with a black handle. As her session progressed and she started to describe a knife with a black handle, he asked her about the black book. She said the black book was gone.

Rossi also said that as the police artist was drawing the sketch, it was shown to Mrs. Daniels four separate times. Each time, the artist would change a feature after being directed by Mrs. Daniels, and the end result was one composite rendering.

The judge asked Lee Atkinson if he had any additional witnesses, and he called Damon Reinbold to the stand.

Reinbold wasn't a doctor. He told the Court he was a professional hypnotist and most of the work he had done was in weight control and helping people to stop smoking. He sometimes helped with memory recollections too.

Reinbold described the induction technique he used to hypnotize both Harold Duncan and Nancy Daniels. He called it progressive relaxation.

The only thing he had been told was that Duncan had seen Kristine Stuart; no other details had been given to him, and he hadn't given Duncan any post-hypnotic suggestions either.

Atkinson moved to the session with Nancy Daniels.

Like he had done when he talked about Harold Duncan's session, Reinbold described the signs he observed indicating Nancy Daniels was in a hypnotic state.

He said the only information he had about what she had seen was an approximate time and that she had been driving along a street.

He summarized her session by saying she hadn't needed any questioning at all.

Atkinson had two more questions. He wanted to know if Reinbold had any type of composite drawing done based on her session or if he had shown Nancy Daniels any photographs.

Reinhold hadn't.

Bengston's questioning was quick when he asked about any post-hypnotic suggestions, and why he had been notified in the first place. After a brief objection, the witness was allowed to answer. He'd been asked by Dean Tucker to assist them with the witnesses' memory recall.

After the lunch break, Lee Atkinson stood to address the Court. He said Bengston's purpose of the separate record was to see if there had been any intentional suggestions made about Daniels and Duncan's future testimony. He didn't feel he needed to call any witnesses.

Bengston stood. His concern was the memory of Nancy Daniels between August 14, the date of Kristine Stuart's disappearance, and when she was hypnotized. He wanted to call her as a witness to see what her recollection was prior to the hypnosis session. He also wanted to call Tucker to the stand so he could question him about what discussions he had with Nancy Daniels. Lastly, he wanted to call the police composite artist because he wanted to know if the artist had any prior contact with Don Miller.

After a sweeping argument by Atkinson against extending Bengston's separate record regarding witness credibility, Judge Tschirhart denied the request to call three additional witnesses.

Tom Bengston still wanted to address the Court regarding his motion, but Tschirhart shut him down.

On April 3, 1979, Don Miller, facing charges of attempted murder and sexual assault, now sat in the district court in East Lansing for his preliminary examination on second-degree murder.

Tom Bengston's separate record regarding hypnosis was done, and the assistant prosecuting attorney called Harold Duncan as his first witness.

Duncan had been a contractor for approximately thirty years, and he worked for Ernie Stuart when Kristine disappeared. He'd been introduced to Kristine the previous summer when he was building a deck on the back of their house.

Atkinson focused his attention to the day of the disappearance, and Harold Duncan described what he was doing that morning. While working on a house on Fairoaks, he needed some more materials, so he got in his pickup to go to Erb Lumber. Approaching the intersection, he saw Kristine walking as she rounded the corner. He stopped for a moment and joked with her about Ernie taking the car away from her, then turned his truck southbound to head to the lumber company.

Atkinson showed a picture of Kristine to the contractor, and Duncan suddenly became very emotional when asked what it was.

"It's a picture of Kris."

"Mr. Duncan, would you like a glass of water, or do you want to take a break or something?" the prosecutor asked.

"No."[89]

Judge Tschirhart quietly interrupted, saying, "Let him take a minute."

While Harold Duncan regained his composure, Atkinson moved to have the photo entered as an exhibit. He had one last question. "Mr. Duncan, could you describe, to the best of your ability, what Kris Stuart's mood seemed to be at the time when you talked to her?"

"Well, she was smiling at me, laughing, you know. When she told about the car, I mean, as far as I could tell, there was nothing wrong."[90]

Tom Bengston began by asking if Duncan could recall what Kristine was wearing, but he couldn't. Pressing for details, Bengston asked what time it was when he saw Kristine, and Duncan guessed it was between nine and 9:30 a.m. He's spoken with her as he sat at the stop sign

89. People v Don G. Miller, April 3, 1979, 137
90. People v Don G. Miller, April 3, 1979, 139

and he hadn't seen any other vehicles on Fairoaks or any pedestrians.

Lee Atkinson's next witness was Nancy Daniels.

Nancy began describing where she lived, and how she had come to leave the house on August 14. She was going to meet her husband so she could pick up his check and take it to the bank, but she was running late. She had started her car, turned on the air conditioning, then ran over to her neighbors for a moment to ask her to keep an eye on her daughter while she ran to the bank, because her daughter was still sleeping.

Daniels said she had gotten to the intersection near her house, then turned right. As she approached Fairoaks, she saw two people outside a car. They were arguing and wrestling.

She told the prosecutor a car turned in front of her, and she had to slam her brakes to keep from hitting it. After stopping, she turned to watch the man and woman she had just seen.

Nancy Daniels described the woman as having reddish auburn hair, with a light complexion, and very slim. She also gave a description of the woman's clothing, including her brown sandals.

Nancy knew she would be able to identify the woman if she saw her again, and Atkinson showed her the picture of Kristine. She identified her by name; although she hadn't known Kristine prior to that day, she learned her name later.

She also described the man she had seen. He was healthy looking. She added that he wasn't too skinny and wasn't too fat. His hair was brown, he looked clean-cut, and she was able to describe his clothing too.

When Atkinson asked her to look around the courtroom to see if could find him, she said, "I do."

Asked to describe what he was wearing in court, she said, "A tan jacket, light pants, and tie, and a white shirt."[91]

Bengston had reservations about her identification. He wanted more clarification on her identification of Miller in the courtroom.

Atkinson interrupted. "I think she's already done that, on the record."

Bengston shot back, "Clarify it."

Judge Tschirhart interrupted both men. He overruled Bengston's objection and let Nancy Daniels' identification of both Miller and Kristine Stuart stand.

As Atkinson continued, he asked if the car door was open.

It was, and the man had a knife. She saw him push the woman backwards into the car. She couldn't see the woman too well at that point, and the man had his arm on the back of the seat, but then his arm went down to hold her down. She could see the man leaning forward as he stabbed at her several times, and as he raised up, he looked straight at her. He stared at her, and she stared right back at him.

Atkinson asked if he had stabbed at the woman.

"Yes." She described the knife, and the assistant prosecutor asked how many times Miller had stabbed her. "I think three."

Asked if she had noticed anything different about the knife after he began the stabbing motion, she said, "Yes, it had blood on it."[92]

Nancy Daniels described what the woman was doing as she was being stabbed. "Her legs and arms came up, and her left hand came up and grabbed his hair, and then her arm fell."[93] As she and the man stared at each other, she

---

91. People v Don G. Miller, April 3, 1979, 155
92. People v Don G. Miller, April 3, 1979, 158
93. People v Don G. Miller, April 3, 1979, 158

closed her eyes, turned her head, and drove away as fast as she could.

The prosecutor asked if she remembered anything about the car.

After describing tinted windows, she said the car had two decals on the righthand lower front of the window. One was a map of Michigan and one had stars on it.

He showed her a photo of Don Miller's car, and Nancy Daniels said it was the car she had seen. He also showed her pictures of the windshield, and she identified the decals located on the lower right corner.

Atkinson moved to the composite sketch, and he asked Nancy if it accurately depicted the man she had seen on August 14, 1978.

"Yes, sir, only his hair was messed when I saw him."[94]

As the prosecutor offered the sketch as a proposed exhibit, Bengston wanted to question her about it. He asked what the circumstances were when she first saw the drawing.

Nancy said she'd been in an office and had been hypnotized.

She thought she had been shown the sketch approximately five times. She was talking as the artist was drawing, and he would show her the sketch to see if any changes needed to be made to make it look more like man she had seen.

Bengston asked the Court for a continuing objection to Nancy Daniels testifying.

As Lee Atkinson began his re-direct, he moved to her identification of Don Miller in a lineup at the sheriff's office.

Before asking her specifics about Miller, Atkinson clarified for the Court the parameters for the lineup, asking if they were all the same race, the same sex, and if their height was similar. He asked if she recognized anyone; she said, "Yes, I did."

94. People v Don G. Miller, April 3, 1979, 164

"And who did you recognize that person to be?"

"Donald Miller."[95]

When Lee Atkinson asked her if she had ever seen Don Miller before that, she said she had seen him on August 14, 1978, on Coolidge.

"It's the person sitting in the center of the table on the righthand side with the tan jacket on, pants are dark. I think they're brown. He has a tie on and white shirt."

"Any objection to that, Mr. Bengston?" Tschirhart asked.

"Not that one, Your Honor."[96]

Tom Bengston began his cross-examination after a short break.

Nancy Daniels said she had driven to meet her husband and could tell he was in a real hurry when she pulled up. She told her husband that she had almost been in an accident, and he told her they would talk about it later when he got home. She said the next person she told about it was police. She said she called at two a.m. on August 15, and she had no idea there was a woman named Kristine Stuart who was missing when she made the call.

As Bengston continued to press her about the details of what she'd seen, she was honest with him when she said she didn't recall something. As he asked her about the struggle between the man and woman on the side of the road, she said the man had a hold of at least one of the woman's arms, and she was backed up against the open door. She saw the knife, and it was in his right hand. She thought he grabbed it from dash because that's where he reached to, and at first, she thought it was a book because she was too frightened to remember. It was only during her hypnosis session when she realized it was a knife.

---

95. People v Don G. Miller, April 3, 1979, 169

96. People v Don G. Miller, April 3, 1979, 171

Bengston repeated some questions and Nancy was getting confused. He told her he wasn't trying to confuse her and that maybe he was confusing himself.

She described the stabbing again.

"Stabbed at her?" he asked.

"Sir, I couldn't see all of her then."

She said the man must have realized somebody was there, and he raised up backwards out of the car. He stood there and stared at her.

"Okay, and then you stared back at him?"

"Yes, sir. He still had the knife in his hand," she said confidently.

"And was there anything on the knife?"

"Yes, there was blood on the knife."[97] She said the man had stabbed the woman three times because she saw his arm go up and down.

As Bengston finished his questioning about the knife, he asked Nancy if she had heard of Martha Sue Young, and if she had read anything about the case prior to August 14, 1978.

She thought she might have seen one news report about her disappearance, but hadn't paid attention to it.

Tom Bengston also wanted to know when she was able to associate Don Miller's face with his name; he wanted to know if it was before she had done the sketch in Dr. Rossi's office.

"When the artist sketched it, sir, and then that night, his picture was in the paper that night."

"All right, and that would have been the 24th, then?" Bengston asked.

"That's right."[98] She'd never seen a photo of Miller before that.

97. People v Don G. Miller, April 3, 1979, 206
98. People v Don G. Miller, April 3, 1979, 218

The following day, Don Miller's preliminary examination continued with Mike Woodworth calling the prosecution's next witness. Ernest Stuart was called to the stand.

The testimony would be difficult for Stuart. He began by saying he and Kristine had been married for eight years, and at Woodworth's request, he described her physically.

Woodworth moved to the date of August 14, 1978, and had Stuart describe his day; he told the Court that as he got ready for work at 5:30 a.m., Kristine was still in bed.

Stuart said his wife had appeared healthy that morning, and there were no problems. He knew his wife was going to take her car to be repaired, and she was going to clean their motorhome that day.

When he got home at around six or 6:30 p.m., he noticed there were some things she had started to do that morning. There was a load of wash in the washing machine, and the dishwasher had been run, but she hadn't come home.

None of her clothing had been removed from any of the hangers in the closet, and none of her luggage was missing. None of her personal items, such as her driver's license and credit cards, could be found, and he said the credit cards had not been used since her disappearance. There hadn't been any activity in their joint checking account either.

Asked if his wife owned brown sandals, Ernie said she did, but he hadn't been able to account for them since August 14.

She was healthy, and her only physical problem was allergies, but she took an allergy shot once a week, and those shots had stopped after August 14.

Mike Woodworth turned to Kristine's state of mind, asking if she had any psychological problems.

"No."

Kristine Stuart's husband said his wife had worn contact lenses in the past but had recently gotten a new pair of glasses. He had found her contact lenses and her old glasses at the house after August 14, but he wasn't able to find her new glasses.

As the prosecutor showed Stuart a pre-marked exhibit and asked him what was inside, Stuart very quietly said his wife's glasses were inside.

Judge Tschirhart reminded him he would have to speak up and asked him to repeat his answer.

"Yes, they appear to be my wife's."

"Those were not in the home after August 14?"

"No."[99]

Ernie Stuart said his wife's driver's license was restricted because she needed her glasses to drive. He said she couldn't see the clock on the dresser without her glasses unless she was very close to it, and her maximum distance for seeing something clearly was six to eight feet. She wouldn't go anywhere without her glasses or contact lenses.

Woodworth wanted to know the nature of her employment.

"She was a teacher at Gardner Junior High."[100] She had both a bachelor's degree and a master's. As a teacher, Kristine had enjoyed working at Gardner and planned on staying there. She was teaching summer school until the week before her disappearance.

The last weekend they had together had been spent on a canoe trip, and there was nothing bothering her while they were on the trip.

"Sir, apart from the disputes which ordinarily arise in a marriage, would you characterize your marriage as a relatively tranquil one or as a peaceful one? What was your relationship with your wife, sir?"

"We were very close. My wife was as much a good friend of mine, and my best friend, as she was my wife. We

99. People v Don G. Miller, April 4, 1979, 244
100. People v Don G. Miller, April 4, 1979, 245

had not had any major arguments."[(101)] They had never been apart for any length of time.

Stuart said Kristine was involved in the design of their home and helped with the planning and layout. She had decorated it and picked out the furniture too.

"To your knowledge, sir, has your wife seen her parents or any member of her family since August 14, 1978?"

"No, sir."[(102)]

He and Kristine had plans to go to an amusement park, and to the west side of the state. Kristine had made the reservations for both trips.

Ernie Stuart told the prosecutor that he had taken part in searching for his wife. He outlined the searches that he had participated in. Some were as small as a few family members, while others were as large as two hundred people. "We searched probably about four weeks straight, and we had a couple organized searches on weekends."

"Was she wearing her wedding ring, to the best of your knowledge, on the morning that you saw her, August 14, 1978?" Woodworth asked.

"Yes."

"Have you ever seen the wedding ring again?"

"No, I have not."[(103)]

He described some of her personal items at home. She had a watch she had received from some of her students, and it was still at their house on August 14.

Mike Woodworth was nearing the end of his questioning when he asked about health insurance and if there had been any activity on their account. There hadn't been.

"Sir, I would ask you to think just a moment. Are you aware of any reason why, since August 14, 1978, your wife

101. People v Don G. Miller, April 4, 1979, 247

102. People v Don G. Miller, April 4, 1979, 249

103. People v Don G. Miller, April 4, 1979, 253

has not contacted you to give you an idea of where she might be?"

"No, sir."

"Sir, to your knowledge, was there any event, any humiliation, any embarrassment, any psychological trauma, physical injury, that would account for your wife's absence since August 14, 1978, short of death?"

"No, sir."[104]

Tom Bengston had been taking notes. He stood and began by asking about Kristine's plans to take the car to Herm's Body Shop and how she had intended on returning. Ernie had simply assumed a neighbor was going to bring her back, as had happened in the past.

"Your recollection is, Mr. Stuart, that you returned home that evening of August 14, about six or 6:30?"

"Yes, sir."[105]

Stuart described the doors to the house, and said when he got home, all of the doors were locked.

He said after the police had left, Kris's parents arrived, and they were checking with some neighbors to see if anybody had seen her. He spoke with Harold Duncan, and that's when he found out he had seen her the previous morning.

On redirect, Mike Woodworth asked if there were any signs of forced entry into the Stuart home, or any signs of a struggle inside, and Ernie Stuart told him there wasn't. They had a dog, and when he got home that evening, the dog was much more hyper than normal. To him, it indicated the dog had been left alone all day.

Both attorneys had finished, and the prosecution moved to Sgt. James Kelley as their next witness.

Kelley recounted his part in finding Kristine Stuart's glasses and identified them to the Court by the mark he had

---

104. People v Don G. Miller, April 4, 1979, 256
105. People v Don G. Miller, April 4, 1979, 260

placed on the inside of the frame. Woodworth was done almost as quickly as he had started.

Bengston began his cross-exam by going through Kelley's activities on the morning of Kristine's disappearance. Kelley described the scene where the glasses were found and said there was no blood found on them. The glasses were checked for fingerprints but none were located.

The defense attorney asked Kelley about a Bass shoe that had been found in a nearby backyard. Kelley said he had found it, and it was eventually turned over to Detective Fitzgerald from Ingham County. Kelley briefly described the shoe before he was excused, and Dean Tucker was called to the stand.

Tucker had worked the case tirelessly for several months. He had followed up on investigative leads, issued press releases, organized and participated in numerous searches, followed tips, and he assigned officers to follow up on leads. He had checked the hospitals in the area to see if Kristine was injured in some way, and he checked the public transportation system to see if she had used that on August 14. He also checked with the airlines and bus terminals but had come up empty handed.

As Tucker continued describing everything had been done, he told Woodworth about the foot searches in the area and the utilization of helicopters to search the tri-county area. They checked river banks from the air and sent in officers on foot to check areas and abandoned buildings they couldn't see from the air. He described it as a continuous four-week operation.

They still had no indication where Kristine Stuart was.

They had taken steps to monitor phone communications at the Stuart home and all incoming phone calls were recorded with the permission of Ernie Stuart.

Lee Atkinson asked Tucker if he was familiar with Don Miller and his car; he was and gave a description to the Court, describing a sticker on the passenger side of the windshield and the license plate of GMV-588. He also said the windshield had a Michigan State Park sticker in the lower corner, and a large crack.

Atkinson asked Tucker how many missing person cases he had investigated in his career, and the detective estimated forty to fifty cases, both major and minor. He said he hadn't found anything to suggest that Kristine had left home voluntarily.

On cross-examination, Bengston focused on Nancy Daniels' contact with Tucker, wanting to know when he first had contact with her. Tucker told him that he picked her up at her home and drove her to Dr. Rossi's office. Tucker had never met her before that.

Wanting to make sure the Court understood exactly what happened, Tucker said he had not shown any photos to Nancy Daniels, and they hadn't discussed the case on the way to her hypnosis session.

Tucker said he had been contacted on August 25 by Nancy, and she had been upset because she had seen Don Miller's photo in the *Town Currier* newspaper. She was certain the police had released her sketch of the suspect to the media.

Bengston tried summarizing Tucker's contact with Daniels by saying she had not really given him any information of value but Dean Tucker disagreed.

"Well, I felt that there was something that she gave to me, yes, sir."

"And what was that?"

"Her observing the photograph in the *Town Currier* and her thinking that I had released the photograph of the composite to the *Town Currier.* I felt that was something," Tucker responded.[106]

Tucker said he had Westgate take Nancy Daniels to see Damon Reinbold because they were having trouble getting

---

106. People v Don G. Miller, April 4, 1979, 310

an accurate description of the clothing that Kristine was wearing on August 14, so he asked Westgate to take her to see if she could give them a better idea. He also knew of her witnessing the struggle on Coolidge and thought she might be able to recall a license plate number.

"When did the focus of your investigation isolate Miller, defendant Miller?"

"Probably around—his name had come up prior to that, but around August 16th."[107]

When Atkinson took back over questioning Tucker, he recalled heavy rains during the evening on the first night she was gone, and that would account for lack of information found at the scene on Fairoaks. There was no direct evidence that pointed to Miller being involved in the disappearance of Kristine Stuart at that point, and no reason to arrest him either.

Atkinson moved to the lineup with Don Miller. "And it would be fair to say, would it not, that you withheld any attempts to suggest material to Nancy Daniels until after she had an opportunity to herself describe to an artist what she had seen?"

"That's correct," Tucker said.

"Now, would it be fair to say, sir, that once Nancy Daniels had, from her memory, assisted you in the construction of a composite of the person you had seen, that at the point, you began to have stronger suspicions about Donald Miller's involvement?"

"Correct."[108]

Tucker said it was after August 24 when the lineup was set up.

Lee Atkinson had made his point, but Bengston still wasn't giving in.

---

107. People v Don G. Miller, April 4, 1979, 317
108. People v Don G. Miller, April 4, 1979, 325

The exam was nearing an end when Bengston asked two more questions of Tucker. He asked about Tucker's probable cause to arrest Miller, and Tucker said it was after the grand jury's indictment.

With that, both attorneys had finished their proofs.

Mike Woodworth stood to address the Court, asking that Miller be bound over to the circuit court on a charge of second-degree murder.

Tom Bengston argued the prosecution had only shown an assault of some sort, and there was not any evidence of a homicide. He said Tucker had testified that on at least one missing person case he had handled, it was resolved six months later. He said it was even possible that Kristine Stuart could show up later that day, or even the following day.

"I don't think the proofs are sufficient to establish the requisite homicide, which is obviously one of the elements in the corpus delicti in the charge of murder in the second degree."[109]

Finally, he argued that while he still disagreed with the testimony of Nancy Daniels, he said, "I think the Court could find probable cause but the corpus delicti, I think, comes short." He asked the Court to consider binding Don Miller over on a lesser assault charge.

Woodworth began his final argument, saying that for the charge of second-degree murder, he had to establish the intentional killing of Kristine Stuart, and that it was committed by the defendant Don Miller. He said there were two aspects to look at, and the first was that the People hadn't established the death of Kristine. He said Bengston had suggested that she could appear at any time. It could have been that day, or even the following day, but there was nothing founded in reason. Woodworth said there was

109. People v Don G. Miller, April 4, 1979, 331

nothing to suggest she would be found alive now or in the future.

The assistant prosecutor said there was a great deal of interest in the case because there was no body, yet Kristine Stuart's death had been established better than any death could have ever been. Her death could be established by circumstantial evidence, absent the body.

As the young prosecutor continued, he said that with Kristine's satisfaction with life, absent any reason to leave voluntarily, and Nancy Daniels witnessing the stabbing, all pointed to the conclusion that she was murdered.

Woodworth cited Bengston's questioning of Tucker and working a missing person's case for six months before discovering where the person was. He argued that the only thing Bengston had shown in that argument was that Tucker had solved that disappearance by checking with State of Michigan to see if that particular missing person had sought a new driver's license. When he checked with those same sources regarding Kristine Stuart, it wasn't productive.

He assured the Court that all of the elements of the crime were there, saying both circumstantial and direct evidence had been established. Adding that the People had the defendant and had his identity as the perpetrator of the crime, he asked that Miller be bound over to circuit court on the second-degree murder charge.

Judge Tschirhart agreed and denied Bengston's motion.

13

On Thursday, April 5, Tom Bengston arrived at the district court in East Lansing for Don Miller's second preliminary examination.

His only motion before starting was to have the witnesses sequestered.

Sue Young sat nervously in the courtroom. When the assistant prosecutor called her name, she stood and approached the witness stand.

Sue began her testimony by describing where she lived, adding that she was divorced and lived with her two daughters. She told how Martha was born in Corpus Christi, Texas, and began school while living in Pakistan with her family. Her daughter was a very good student who was in the honors program in Dallas, and had made the Dean's List at Southwestern. Martha had never run away, and she'd never been disciplined while she was in school. Sue added, "Well, she loved school; she was there every time that classes met except when she was ill."[110]

She added that her family had strong religious ties, and Martha participated in all the church activities with her mother.

When she was asked if Martha would come home from Southwestern University in Texas to visit, Sue said Martha came home every chance she had.

Sue Young said her daughter was a good letter writer and she wrote volumes. In turn, she wrote to her daughter often and they talked on the telephone a lot. She said she would

---

110. People v Don G. Miller. April 5, 1979, 6

receive a letter and phone call at least once every week from Martha while she was away at school in Texas.

The assistant prosecutor moved to when Martha transferred from Texas to Michigan State University.

Sue explained Martha was considering a French program that MSU had. She was hoping to go overseas and spend some time in France and become fluent in the language. Her daughter was thinking about ways she could use the language in a career like in foreign service. She was also considering the possibility of being a French teacher.

Atkinson moved to Martha's relationships, asking if she was seeing anyone.

"Donald Miller," she answered.[111]

Sue Young said Miller was a member of the same church they attended and thought she had known him for about five years, adding he had attended East Lansing High School.

When Atkinson asked how frequently Martha and Don dated, Sue said it was constantly and he was over at their house quite frequently, and the two of them went mostly to bible study together.

When Sue Young was asked about her daughter's health, she said Martha was very healthy.

"During the time that you raised Martha Sue, did she ever at any time see a psychologist or psychiatrist?"

"No."

"Are you aware of her ever having any severe or emotional trauma or problem that you are aware of?"[112]

Sue said that while Martha was at Southwestern University, she had talked to a minister because she was upset about some letters and phone calls from Don.

Tom Bengston stood, interposing an objection to the testimony. He told the judge that the court rule required Sue

---

111. People v Don G. Miller. April 5, 1979, 9
112. People v Don G. Miller, April 5, 1979, 12

Young to actually state what Martha had said. He didn't think it had been done yet.

Lee Atkinson was prepared for the objection as he stood before the Court. He had filed a memorandum of law and explained that in cases where the defendant has been successful in disposing of a body, there is a necessity and a permissibility of showing the existing mental state of both the victim and the defendant before and leading up to the time of the disappearance. He said it allowed the Court to have an idea of what was going on and to know the facts surrounding the relationship.

He added the testimony was essential because of the manner in which Martha disappeared.

Tschirhart overruled Bengston's objection.

Lee Atkinson continued by asking Sue if her daughter had ever sought counseling, or had any psychological or emotional problems.

"No."

Sue talked about Martha's engagement and said Don had come over one morning with Martha and asked her permission to marry Martha, and she described the plans her daughter was making for the wedding.

The assistant prosecutor asked if Martha had spoken in December about the upcoming wedding plans.

Sue said that Martha was concerned about being smothered in her relationship with Don. She said they never did anything with any other people, and Don didn't seem to have any friends. Martha didn't want to be isolated or to give up her own friends. Her daughter also had concerns about Don not making any financial preparations for the marriage.

Lee Atkinson had a specific order he wanted to progress through in Sue Young's testimony; he moved to Christmas of 1976, asking if she and her daughters had done anything special, and she told him they had gone to Pennsylvania. They had arrived at their friend's home a few days prior to

Christmas, but she couldn't recall the exact date they had left.

After they returned from Pennsylvania, they had dropped Kay off at the airport, and she had a chance to speak with Martha alone about her engagement. Martha had told her she was going to give the ring back to Don and break the engagement, but she was going to wait because they had a date that evening, and she didn't want to do it then.

Sue said Martha had come home that evening and told her that she had gone ahead and talked with Don about it. She had told Don she didn't want to be engaged and wanted to give the ring back, but Don had told Martha the ring was a gift and she could keep it because he wanted to remain friends with her.

Bengston was on his feet again and he objected, arguing the statements didn't fall within the hearsay rule.

"Mr. Atkinson?" Tschirhart asked.

The assistant prosecutor said the statements indicated Martha's intentions and mental feelings, and that no one was claiming Miller had said that; it was simply what Martha had told her mother.

"I'll take the answer," the judge said.[113]

Atkinson continued, focusing on the evening of Martha's disappearance, asking if Sue had seen her daughter at any time during the evening of December 31, 1976.

She said she had come into the kitchen to tell her goodbye before she went to babysit for some friends. Martha had told her about babysitting and Don was going along to keep her company. Originally, they had planned to go dancing, but they couldn't get reservations, so she took the babysitting job. Martha said she'd be in early.

Sue Young described everything that she knew Martha had on when she left the house and gave the Court Martha's physical description too. She had been wearing the

---

113. People v Don G. Miller, April 5, 1979, 22

engagement ring when she left, and also had on a watch and her glasses.

As she recounted her own activities on New Year's Eve, Sue said she had gone to a late supper with some friends, and she had stayed until around 1:30 a.m., coming straight home and using the garage door opener to enter the garage at her home. She said it was very cold; she was able to hear the crunching of the snow under tires as cars drove by her house.

Her testimony was becoming difficult as she talked about arriving home to an empty house. She said Martha wasn't home and her bed was still made. She sat down on her own bed around two a.m. and was becoming increasingly concerned that Martha hadn't arrived home yet. She thought of calling the Miller home to see if Martha was over there, but decided against it, thinking that it was New Year's Eve, and Martha might simply be out with some friends.

She heard nothing all night to indicate her daughter had arrived home.

The most difficult part of her testimony was about to begin as she described waking up and realizing Martha hadn't come home. She had gone to Martha's room, but her bed hadn't been slept in, then went to the basement to see if she might be asleep in one of the beds down there, but Martha wasn't there. Coming back upstairs in a panic, she called the Millers.

"Since January 1, 1977, have you had any contact with your daughter?" Atkinson asked.

"No."

"Have you ever seen her again?"

"No."

"Have you received any telephone calls or letters from her?"

"No."[114]

---

114. People v Don G. Miller, April 5, 1979, 30

Sue said her daughter had registered for her MSU classes by that time and paid the tuition for her classes and books. Martha had a part-time job lined up back at a bank where she used to work.

Martha also had plans to attend a party on January 1 during the evening with some friends other than Don and planned on spending the entire day with her mother.

Sue Young described the one hundred twenty-five dollars she had gotten for Martha by cashing a check and leaving the cash for Martha in her bedroom. It was still in her dresser on January 1. She also described Martha's purse and what she would typically have in it.

As the questioning progressed, Atkinson had a very difficult job. He had to have Sue identify the clothing that had been found in October 1977.

She was determined yet emotional as she went through each piece of clothing shown to her. She identified her daughter's jacket and her scarf.

"Would you like a drink of water?" Atkinson asked, taking a moment to pause.

"No, thank you."[115]

As the prosecutor produced another piece of evidence, she identified them as the slacks Martha had been wearing when she left the house on New Year's Eve. She also identified Martha's shoes, her purse, and her watch.

As Sue Young identified items in her daughter's purse, she pointed out a small Bible that Martha always carried. She had gotten the Bible as a child when her family lived in Texas.

When Tom Bengston began questioning Sue Young, he asked if she had actually seen the engagement ring on Martha's hand before she left the house on New Year's Eve. She had.

---

115. People v Don G. Miller, April 5, 1979, 40

Again, Sue went through the entire sequence of events on the morning she discovered her daughter missing, then calling the Millers. She said Elaine, Gene, and Don all came over.

Bengston asked if she was aware that her daughter and Don often just drove around on a date.

"I hadn't been aware that they spent a great deal of time just driving around."

"You hadn't been aware of that? Yes or no, please," Bengston told her.

"No."

Sue spoke of the drive she had taken after Martha's disappearance, with Gene Miller driving and Don in the passenger seat. She and her ex-husband were in the backseat, and they had driven around the same Lansing area Don had said he and Martha had driven around on New Year's Eve. They were trying to re-trace the route where Don had driven for over two hours on the morning of January 1.

The defense attorney wanted a chance to review the exhibits that Atkinson was going to offer to the Court, but Sue Young had an important engagement, so she was excused as a witness for a few hours.

Mike Woodworth stood and asked that William McCracken be called to the stand. Martha babysat for the McCrackens on the last night she was seen.

After touching on how he had come to know Martha, McCracken said she had come over with Don Miller to babysit.

He and his wife were counselors for the youth group when Martha was in high school, and they often talked to her.

Each time Woodworth asked if Martha suffered from any impairments or suffered from any psychiatric problems, McCracken said no. She appeared healthy.

He said Martha was very close to her family and she loved them very much.

When William McCracken talked about the last night Martha was seen alive, he said she had agreed to come over to babysit because she wanted to help them out. She asked if it was okay for Don to come with her because they were planning on watching a movie on television. If they could come over together, they could watch the first part of the movie, and McCracken agreed.

Mr. and Mrs. McCracken returned home around 8:30 p.m., and he saw Martha and Don, and both appeared to be happy. He said in the entire time he had known Martha, she was responsible and dependable, and he never had any problems with her.

Nearing the end of his questioning, Woodworth asked if there was any reason he could think of that would have kept Martha from contacting her family for the previous two years.

"No, I can't." He said it would be out of character for Martha to voluntarily go missing.

Tom Bengston's first question on his cross-examination of William McCracken was if the television was on when he and his wife had arrived back home.

McCracken said Martha and Don had planned on watching *it's a Mad, Mad, Mad, Mad World* that evening, and it was on when he and his wife had gotten home.

As Bengston was finishing, Woodworth was looking over his witness list.

"Call your next witness, Mr. Woodworth," Judge Tschirhart said.

"Yes, Your Honor. At this time, the People would call Karen Miller."[116]

---

116. Name has been changed.

As Don Miller's sister began her testimony, she said she lived with her parents in their house, and her sister lived there too, but she was currently studying in Europe.

"Anyone else currently residing in the home?" Woodworth asked.

"Don, except for right now."

"You are, in fact, the sister of the defendant in this case, are you not?"

"Yes."[117]

He directed her attention to the December 31, 1976, and asked her if she had seen her brother that day. She didn't think she had. She asked if that was right before New Year's Eve.

"Yes, ma'am."

She said it was just an ordinary day, and she saw her brother every day.

"You're basing your testimony that you saw your brother based upon the fact that this was an ordinary day, like any other day, so you must have seen him; is that you're saying?"

"Yes."[118]

She had no specific recollection of seeing her brother that day.

The assistant prosecutor wanted to get directly to the testimony she had given before the grand jury in January. He asked if she had told her mother that she would be going to the Trinity Church that night.

"Yes."

"Now, ma'am, you testified before the grand jury in this case?"

She knew where Woodworth was going with her testimony, and she said she was wrong during her testimony. She had corrected herself.

---

117. People v Don G. Miller, April 5, 1979, 80
118. People v Don G. Miller, April 5, 1979, 80

The assistant prosecutor followed up, asking her if she had testified that she never told her mother she was going to the Trinity Church.

"No, I told her I did."

Woodworth persisted, asking, "The question was, ma'am, did you testify before the grand jury on January 19, 1979, that you gave your mother no reason to believe you were going to the Trinity Church on that evening?"

"No reason to believe that I was going?"

"That you did not tell your mother that you were going to the Trinity Church."

Karen Miller tried to explain by saying her mom thought she was going to the church.

"Did she think you were going to the Trinity Church because of anything you told her, or did she gather that impression from somewhere else?"

"No, from me."

"You told her?" Woodworth asked.

"Yes."

Mike Woodworth wanted her to be clear, and he showed her a copy of her testimony to the grand jury.

"Have you had the opportunity to read that testimony?"[119]

She had.

He asked if that's what she had said. When Karen Miller said yes, Woodworth continued, "At that time, did you not testify before the grand jury that if your mother believed you were going to the Trinity Church, it was nothing you told her that would have given her that impression?"

"I can't remember if I told her or not, but she believed that I was going to go to the church, and she asked my brother to come and pick me up. He went there, but I wasn't there. I was at the party, and I never asked my bother to come and pick me up."

---

119. People v Don G. Miller, April 5, 1979, 87

Woodworth wouldn't let go. "Is your memory and recollection of the events of what happened on the evening of December 31, 1976, would you say it was clearer last January, or do you believe it's clearer now?"

"It was clearer then because it happened then, you know."[120]

"In fact, at that time, after reviewing your testimony, did you testify that there was nothing you told your mother to give her the impression that you would be at the Trinity Church, yes or no?"

"I didn't give her any impression."

"Thank you. Now, ma'am, in fact, you didn't go to the Trinity Church that night?" the prosecutor asked.

"No, I didn't," she said.[121]

Judge Tschirhart interrupted. He asked her if what she had just testified to was a mistake.

She said it probably was.

The judge continued, "Your testimony is then that you did not give her any impression that you were going to the Trinity Church on the evening of December 31, 1976?"

"Right."

Woodworth then asked, "In fact, the place where you did go was where?"

Karen said she had gone to an MSU coach's house with friends for the evening. She had stayed out late, but she couldn't recall until what time. She was able to say it was past midnight, and that a friend's parents had driven her home.

Woodworth asked her if anyone had been awake when she got home, and she told him no.

Her family was home. Their car was there, and that usually meant they were sleeping in the bedroom, but she didn't actually look to see if they were there. Her parents'

120. People v Don G. Miller, April 5, 1979, 87
121. People v Don G. Miller, April 5, 1979, 88

door was cracked open as she walked by, and it appeared they were sleeping. She added her sister was asleep in the room they shared together, but she didn't know if Don was home because his door was closed. She just assumed he was home, but didn't really know for sure.

"Did you see him?"

"No, I didn't. His door was closed."[122]

Woodworth was confirming a key point when he asked her if she had seen him in the kitchen or the living room.

"No."

She said when she got up on January 1, there was a lot of confusion in the house, and she thought she saw Don there. The only thing she knew was that Mrs. Young had called, and Don left with her mom and dad. When they got back, she found out Martha was missing.

"Did you have any reason to believe, based upon your contact with Martha Sue Young, that she had any psychological or psychiatric problems?"

"No."[123]

Woodworth had made a key point, and he knew it. So did Bengston.

When the defense attorney began his questioning, Karen said she had told her brother she was going to the Trinity Church on New Year's Eve. She said he knew what her plans were, and any time she was doing something with the church, she would tell him. She said Don even came to some of the events. Her intent was to go to the Trinity Church first, then go to the coach's house.

As Bengston finished his last question, the prosecutor had taken notes in anticipation of re-direct.

Woodworth asked her exactly what function she was going to attend at the church.

"Services."

---

122. People v Don G. Miller, April 5, 1979, 92
123. People v Don G. Miller, April 5, 1979, 95

"A service. How is it that you came to know that this particular service would be occurring on the night of December 31, 1976?"

She said she had found out through her friend, and it was a regularly scheduled service.

"Your testimony has been that, in fact, you told your brother Don of your plans to go to the Trinity Church that evening?"

"Yes," she answered.[124]

Woodworth produced the grand jury transcript again and confronted her with her own testimony. "Isn't it true that during that proceeding, the following questions were asked of you; Question: And you hadn't had any discussion with Don about picking you up at the church that night. Isn't it true that that question was asked?"

"For picking me up, yes."

"And isn't it true that your answer was 'no'?"

"Yes."

Woodworth pressed her further. "You made a distinction in your testimony. You emphasized the word 'picking you up.'"

"I didn't ask Don to pick me up at Trinity Church, but I did discuss that I was going to go there, but we were late and so we didn't go."[125]

Woodworth had made his point.

Lee Atkinson took back over questioning and called his next witness, Elaine Miller.

As he began to progress through his questioning of Mrs. Miller, he asked if she had seen Martha Young on New Year's Eve. Mrs. Miller she had been at home, and she had first seen Martha at around 9:30 p.m. when she and Don came back to the house.

---

124. People v Don G. Miller, April 5, 1979, 100
125. People v Don G. Miller, April 5, 1979, 101

When Atkinson asked where Karen was, Mrs. Miller said, "She left to—or was at—she was going to go to Trinity Church." She said she thought Karen was going over to her friend's house first.

She said that when Don and Martha returned to the house, they went to the basement to finish watching *It's a Mad, Mad, Mad, Mad World.* She said they left the house at around 11:30, because she had looked at the clock when they left. Mrs. Miller testified that when they left, she had asked them to go to the Trinity Church to see about picking up Karen because she was supposed to be at a service, and they were supposed to bring her home.

She thought the time Don returned home was at two a.m. on January 1. She was on the couch in the living room, and her husband was sleeping. She said she began to talk to Don and tell him that Karen had gotten home at 1:30 in the morning, and Karen hadn't called to let her know a friend was bringing her home.

Mrs. Miller said when Karen came in, they had a discussion about her not seeing Don, and Don not seeing her. She said her daughter had been at a party, and the two of them missed each other.

"I see. Did you know at that time that Don hadn't seen her?" Atkinson asked.

"She said she hadn't seen him."[126] She said Karen went to bed after they finished talking.

The prosecutor moved to the point where Don Miller arrived home on January 1, asking what he'd done when he first entered the house.

Mrs. Miller said he'd taken off his coat and put it on a chair, and the only light on was a small light over the stove.

"Was that the only light that was on when your daughter Karen came home?"

---

126. People v Don G. Miller, April 5, 1979, 108

"Yes."[127]

Mrs. Miller said they went into the kitchen, and Don sat in a chair by the phone as they talked while she made him a sandwich. They talked about missing Karen at the church, and Don didn't say too much. She asked him what he and Martha had done between 11:30 p.m. and two a.m., and if they had a good time. Don had told her he left Martha sitting on the porch. She questioned him about it because she thought it was strange, but he said Martha does that once in a while as he drives away, and he was going to call her the next morning.

"Mrs. Miller, did you and Don talk at all that morning about why he didn't come in until two?"

"No, why should I?" she asked.

"Well, as I understand your testimony, Mrs. Miller, and correct me if I'm wrong, you have testified that Don left at 11:30 to pick up Karen, is that correct?"

"Yes," she answered.[128]

After having Mrs. Miller look at a map to identify where the Trinity Church was located in relation to the Miller home, Lee Atkinson asked, "And, ma'am, it's your recollection that you did not have any conversation with Don about what he was doing the other two hours that he was gone?"

"He said they went to see the lights, and I thought I had mentioned when they went to pick up Karen that maybe they would like to get in on the New Year's service, because that's at twelve."

Atkinson asked if he had gone to the service.

"I didn't ask him."

"Did he make any mention that he had, in fact, gone?"

"No."[129]

---

127. People v Don G. Miller, April 5, 1979, 109
128. People v Don G. Miller, April 5, 1979, 111
129. People v Don G. Miller, April 5, 1979, 114

With Elaine Miller's testimony done, it was mid-afternoon, and Sue Young had returned.

During the completion of her testimony, Bengston asked her if Martha had been wearing the watch she had previously identified.

"Yes."

The defense attorney was trying to determine if Sue had a specific recollection of it being worn, or if Martha had it in her purse, as she sometimes did. She admitted she didn't have a distinct recollection of it actually being worn.

When Bengston asked Sue if the divorce had an impact on her daughter, she said divorce always has an impact. She felt Martha got the brunt of some of the arguments between her and Le, and Martha would defend her and be on the receiving end of her father's anger.

Sue Young said one of her concerns about Martha was that she didn't participate in extra-curricular activities on campus. She said Don took her to a Bible study prayer group, but that was it.

"Let me address your attention, if I may, Mrs. Young, to the month of December 1976. Were you made aware as to whether your daughter, Martha Sue Young, had any, had a menstrual cycle that month?" Bengston asked.[130]

Sue said that when they went to Pennsylvania, Martha and Kay had stayed in the basement apartment of a friend's house with their four daughters. Martha and her best friend were discussing the fact that they were menstruating, and the other four girls weren't. She thought it was just before Christmas.

When he shifted his questioning to how many times Martha and Don Miller had gone out together, Sue said she really didn't know, because Don was there all the time; he would even make up excuses to come over and bring her things.

---

130. People v Don G. Miller, April 5, 1979, 120

He asked if she had ever seen the two quarrel, and she said she didn't think so.

As the defense neared the end of his questions, he asked if she had a hearing problem. She admitted she did in her left ear. She had normal hearing in her right ear.

Atkinson picked up on Bengston's questions about her hearing and quickly focused on her two dogs as he began his re-direct questioning.

He asked Sue Miller if both of her dogs were in the house on the evening of December 31, 1976.

"Yes, they were."

Sue said if the dogs were familiar with a person, they didn't necessarily bark. If it was someone they didn't like, they would bark.

The prosecutor asked if the dogs had gotten excited at any time in the early morning hours of January 1, 1977.

"No, they didn't."

Lee Atkinson and Tom Bengston had both finished questioning Martha Sue Young's mom and it was getting late in the day. Court was recessed until Friday morning.

Friday, April 6, 1979, began like any other day in East Lansing District Court as the preliminary examination for Don Miller continued at 9:30 a.m.

Sergeant John Boggs, a towering man who had been with the Michigan State Police for over twelve years, was sworn in before his testimony began.

Boggs testified that he had been called to the Potter Lake area in Bath Township on October 20, 1977, because of some clothing that had been found. He described the location as a half to three-quarters of a mile north of State Road on Center Road. Being more specific, he described the location of the clothing as being approximately twenty-five yards off the road in a boggy area that had high weeds and bushes, and extensively overgrown.

Boggs described having flown over the area later in an effort to get an idea of how the entire area was laid out so additional searches could be done. He described photographs taken from the air to show where the location of the clothing was.

Tom Bengston was allowed to question Boggs after the photos were introduced. He asked about the clothing being in a pile, and Boggs said that the clothing was in that position when he arrived.

To establish the chain of evidence, Lee Atkinson had Boggs describe how he collected the clothing and what he had done with it after leaving the scene. Boggs had taken it to the state police post, hung it in the property room to dry, and later transferred it the crime lab.

Describing the clothing, he mentioned how some of the clothing was inside other pieces of clothing. Inside the legs of the pants were a pair of off-white tights or pantyhose and inside the pantyhose was a pair of white cotton underwear. He described two sweaters: a blue turtleneck and a greyish-colored crew cut. The grey sweater was on the inside and the dark blue on the outside, and the sleeves of both were inside of the clothing.

The bra was unclasped and not broken, and both shoes were at the scene too. A sapling was growing through the scarf that lay with the clothes.

Lee Atkinson began going through each piece of clothing recovered from the Potter Lake area. Boggs identified each piece, and the prosecutor had him place some of the clothing inside the other pieces as they had been found in the pile when he got to the scene.

Atkinson moved to the purse and had Boggs identify it.

Beyond the clothing, Boggs talked about the search done after the discovery of the clothing, including the one by the Community Radio Watch Volunteers and the Michigan National Guard.

Atkinson concluded his questions, and Bengston began. "Sergeant Boggs, with respect to your placement of the underpants and the pantyhose within the pants that you found, as you found them on October 20, is it a fair description to say that it appeared as if the lady who had been wearing those garments and had simply slipped out, is that correct?"

"That's exactly what it looked like, sir."

"It would then be accurate to say that the pantyhose was not simply cuffed into the pants; but rather the pantyhose had extended itself all the way down through the pants, is that right?"

"That's right, sir," Boggs answered.[131]

Bengston asked about the sweaters, and Boggs said it appeared that they were inside out; that the blue sweater would have originally been underneath the other one. He said the brush was so thick, a person would have to almost step on the clothing before seeing it.

Boggs said there were no measurements taken to precisely indicate where the clothing was because the vegetation was too thick and the investigators couldn't stretch a measuring tape through the underbrush.

Bengston asked if any glasses were located.

"No, sir."

He asked if any rings were found.

"None."

Now curious if a weapon had been found, he asked Boggs about any rope.

"No, sir."

Bengston's last question was whether a knife or gun had been found, and Boggs told him no.

---

131. People v Don G. Miller, April 6, 1979, 148

As the prosecution moved through their list of witnesses, Lee Atkinson called Martha's ophthalmologist to the stand.

The doctor said that Martha had both contact lenses and glasses available to her.

The prosecutor moved to her health, and the doctor told him he didn't know of any physical problems or conditions that Martha had. He added that he didn't know of any psychological problems either.

Atkinson called Gerald Butler to the stand next. Butler had been one of the two hunters who had discovered Martha Sue Young's clothing on October 20, 1977.

Butler said he and his hunting partner were pheasant hunting near Potter Lake, and his partner called him over because he had found something. He said he never touched the clothing, but had looked through the purse and found Martha Young's identification while his partner, John McCafferty, had picked up the clothing and put it in a pile.

Butler also told the prosecutor that McCafferty had taken the purse and put it in his hunting vest, and they continued the hunt until late in the afternoon, then drove to Spagnuolo's Party Store in Bath to notify the state police about what they had found.

As Butler was handed the purse by Mike Woodworth, he described it as being the purse they had found while out hunting.

Woodworth asked him if he recalled how the clothing had been laid out before McCafferty had stacked it into a pile. When Butler said he did, the prosecutor asked him to carefully lay it out in the courtroom just as it had been found. Butler admitted that McCafferty had moved the coat before he got over to him, but he did the best he could. Using the coat, scarf, pants, and shoes, he laid them out as if they were in the area where they had been found. Butler didn't think the clothes had simply been thrown there.

When Bengston had his chance to ask questions of Butler, he touched briefly on the position of the clothes, and he asked if there were any rings found.

"No, sir."

"You don't recall observing any ring inside the purse?"

"Not to my knowledge," he said.

"Any glasses, please?

"No, sir."[132]

Bengston drew his cross-examination to a close, and Mike Woodworth called Earl McCafferty to the stand.

McCafferty's testimony was the same as Butler's, other than saying that he was the first to discover the clothing laid out, and he had called his hunting partner over to see it.

Like Butler, he had looked at each piece of evidence shown to him by Woodworth and identified each piece as looking like the clothing he had discovered on October 20, 1977.

McCafferty also said that he was the one who had put the clothes into a pile before they continued on their hunt.

Much like Butler's questioning, Tom Bengston was brief.

As the witness identified where the clothing had been found, he said he hadn't found any glasses or any rings of any kind, and there were no knives, guns, or rope at the scene either.

On re-direct, Mike Woodworth asked McCafferty if, because of the way they were laid out, it appeared that someone was laying in the clothing, even though there wasn't anyone.

"Yeah," McCafferty responded.[133]

Officer Ken Ouellette took the stand as McCafferty stepped down.

---

132. People v Don G. Miller, April 6, 1979, 176

133. People v Don G. Miller, April 6, 1979, 194

Officer Ouellette described the early morning phone call he had received on New Year's Day 1977, telling Lee Atkinson he had done a brief interview over the phone, and because of some of things that had been said, he felt the need to go to the house to get some more information.

Ouellette said that as he asked questions inside the Youngs' home, they weren't directed at anyone in particular. He described it more as a meeting, but felt something was suspicious. The officer described the cold, blowing snow as he tried looking for evidence outside the home. By that time, Ouellette had started to look outside and been joined by Officer Austreng, but they didn't find anything significant. Ouellette continued, describing how he and a colleague had gone to the Miller home on Gainsborough and asked to look in Don Miller's car.

When Atkinson began to ask if the officer had found anything inside the car, Bengston was on his feet.

Tom Bengston was waiting for this point in Ouellette's testimony as he objected. He was questioning the validity of the consent to search Miller's Cutlass.

Judge Tschirhart told Lee Atkinson he would allow him to lay more foundation.

Atkinson was sure he could build on it, saying, "Now, sir, let me ask you this. You indicated that when you arrived in the morning, you had conversation with the people in the house, is that correct?"

"Correct."

"At that time, did you have any idea of what had actually happened to Martha Sue Young?"

"No, sir."[134] He didn't have any reason to believe anything criminal had happened when he first got to the Youngs' house, and he didn't have any reason to believe Don Miller was a suspect in anything. Miller wasn't in custody when he was there, and he had answered all of the

134. People v Don G. Miller, April 6, 1979, 200

officer's questions. "Basically, we had no reason to have anybody at the house be suspect at that point," Ouellette said.[135]

Ouellette said he had a conversation with Don Miller at his home on Gainsborough after he had left the Young home. He was trying to explore every possibility of where Martha could be, and he asked if he could look in Miller's car to see if Martha might have dropped her house key. He thought it could explain why she might not be at home.

Atkinson asked Ouellette what some of the other possibilities were about where Martha might be, and he said that she may have gone for a walk or gone to a friend's house, but the one that seemed the most logical was the possibility of her dropping her house key in Don's car.

He told the prosecutor that Don had been very cooperative throughout the morning and even agreed that there was a possibility that Martha had dropped her house key inside the car.

Ouellette said that when he asked Don if he could look inside his car, Miller had said, "Sure."

The officer said as he and his colleague began to look in the car, he noticed a dark brown stain on the front seat.

Tom Bengston interrupted the officer's testimony saying that he thought he was going to be able to cross-examine Ouellette regarding his client's consent, and Atkinson agreed.

Bengston stood and asked Ouellette what time it was when he had a desire to search Don Miller's car, and the officer told him he thought it was around two p.m.

Ouellette said he had conversations with Miller several times, and Don Miller had come to the police department at around two p.m. when they had asked him to. Ouellette said he had asked him to come in for an interview that afternoon, and he had met him at the front desk.

---

135. People v Don G. Miller, April 6, 1979, 201

Miller had been interviewed in an office across from the front desk by himself, Officer Austreng, and Officer King.

As the interview began, there were two or three initial questions, then Officer King read Miller his rights. The search of the vehicle didn't come up until later in the interview.

Ouellette said they were becoming a little suspicious of the nature of the investigation. They decided to play it safe. He said that after the interview with Miller, he and his partner had gone back to the Young residence to speak with Sue Young, then returned to the Miller home a few blocks away. Officer Ouellette and his partner were invited into the Miller home, and he said there was a brief discussion. "We just asked Don Miller if we could look inside the car for the key. He cooperated and indicated there was no problem with that."[136]

Ouellette said that both Gene and Elaine Miller were present when Don had given them permission.

After the two officers spoke with Miller inside the house, the two went outside to the car and found it was unlocked. As they started looking inside, Don and his father came out.

Ouellette said he had opened the driver's door, and his partner had opened the passenger door. After they noticed the stain on the front seat, they got an evidence envelope so they could collect a sample.

The officer continued, saying they had asked Miller what the stain was on the front seat, and he said he'd had a nosebleed a few weeks prior.

"Did you find the key?", Bengston asked.

"No, we didn't."[137]

Bengston sat down as Judge Tschirhart told Atkinson he could continue with his direct examination of Officer Ouellette.

---

136. People v Don G. Miller, April 6, 1979, 211
137. People v Don G. Miller, April 6, 1979, 216

As the prosecutor began to summarize Ouellette's testimony, he went over each of the points that the officer had made, including the rights read to Miller. As he began going over the search of the car, he asked if either Don Miller or his father had asked him to stop searching the car.

Ouellette said no.

"When you came back with the evidence envelopes and Don's father talked to you about what you were going to do, did he at that time tell you could not do anything?" the prosecutor asked.

"No, sir."

"Did Don Miller at any time say, 'Stop, I don't want you to take that from the car'?"

"No, sir."[138]

Ouellette said that when he asked Miller about the stain in his car, Miller had to think about it before he answered and he never expressed a desire to speak with a lawyer.

Atkinson moved to the point when Ouellette and his partner had taken Don to try to retrace his route from the previous evening.

The officer said the purpose of their trip was to see if Miller could account for the time between when he had left his home and the point when arrived back at two a.m.

Ouellette said they had explained the purpose of the trip to Miller, and Miller was very cooperative and open-minded about it, adding that he was willing to help the officers out. The officer said Miller had been read his Miranda rights again before the trip had started, and again, never said anything about not wanting to go along, or wanting to speak with a lawyer.

Lee Atkinson turned toward Judge Tschirhart to close out his questioning. He asked the Court to rule that the search of Don Miller's car was consensual, and the statements made to Ouellette and his colleague were admissible. He said

---

138. People v Don G. Miller, April 6, 1979, 218

that Miller wasn't in custody, the officers had continually advised him of his rights and never restricted any of his movements.

Atkinson said that Don Miller was completely cooperative with the officers, and seemed concerned about providing information concerning the whereabouts, or perhaps the disappearance, of his fiancée. Lastly, Atkinson said all of it was done without any coercion or any violation of Don Miller's rights.

"Mr. Bengston?" Judge Tschirhart said.

Tom Bengston began by agreeing with Atkinson. He knew Miranda rights weren't required to be given, but he suggested there was coercion, and it was based on the officers' prior contact with Don Miller at two p.m. while he was at the police department in East Lansing.

As defense counsel made his argument, he said that at best, when Don Miller agreed to allow Ouellette and his partner to search his car, it was a limited search. Bengston said at the point the stain was discovered, the officers should have re-secured a general consent to search, or even gone so far as to get a search warrant.

Bengston also wanted to see the Miranda rights form that Don Miller had signed that day, and added that until the elements of a crime could be shown, any statements made by his client were inadmissible.

Atkinson had his chance to rebut Bengston's statement. Citing *Michigan Rules of Evidence*, he said a statement isn't hearsay if it's offered against a party and is his own statement.

The prosecutor cited another previous Michigan case; in that case, the Court pointed out that in order to construct a case of circumstantial evidence in a reasonable manner, it might be necessary to intertwine the statements made by a suspect with other evidence to be introduced. Citing a third Michigan case, he told the Court the corpus delicti rule is "aliunde." He continued his argument and reference to it by saying, "Some people think that rule means 'without,' however, or excuse me, 'before,' but in fact it means 'without.' It means that at the conclusion of the People's proofs, we must have, independent of the statements of the defendant or his admissions or confessions to the police, have produced sufficient evidence of the corpus delicti.

"To simply stand for the proposition that a witness's testimony concerning the statements of the defendant should not be considered by the fact finder unless all of the other evidence independent of it establishes corpus delicti," he added.[139]

Judge Tschirhart reminded Atkinson that Bengston had objected to the consent of the search of the car as it not being a general consent search, but limited in scope to the discovery of a key that might belong to Martha Sue Young. He asked the prosecutor if he wanted to respond to that.

Atkinson told the Court that once Miller had allowed the police to look in his car, he consented properly and lawfully regarding his car. If, while the police were searching for a key, they came across evidence that was in their plain view, they were in a place where they had the lawful right to be, and anything they discovered at that point could be seized. He said it could be seized even without a search warrant because the police were faced with exigent circumstances when they found blood inside the car. He said that Gene and Don Miller both asked what the officers were doing, and they in no way made any attempt to withdraw their consent or asked them to stop. The prosecutor ended by saying the officer's activities were reasonable and done with Don Miller's consent.

The judge quickly overruled Tom Bengston's original objection. He said Don Miller did give consent to the police to search the car, and it was not limited to a search for a key, even though it was originally. He also said the officers were

139. People v Don G. Miller, April 6, 1979, 225

there legally inside the vehicle, and they were allowed to seize any evidence that fell into their plain view while they were searching.

While it wasn't the ruling Tom Bengston wanted, he told the judge that his other objection was that he simply was asking to see the form that was read to Miller.

Tschirhart told Lee Atkinson that before he would rule on it, he would allow him to lay some additional foundation.

Officer Ouellette was still on the stand when Atkinson asked if he had been at the East Lansing Police Department at two p.m. on January 1 when Don Miller came in. Ouellette said he was, adding that Austreng and King were also there. Ouellette also said that Miller had also been given his Miranda rights.

When asked what was said, Ouellette responded, "That he had the right to remain silent, had a right to an attorney, and so on; that's contained in the statement, verbatim, which was read to him." He said that Miller had said he understood each of them, and never said anything about exercising his rights.[140]

As Bengston began to speak, Judge Tschirhart told him he was sustaining his objection and told Atkinson he would have to lay more foundation regarding Don Miller's advisement of rights.

Atkinson was prepared, asking for a recess so the audio tape of the interview could be produced.

While the audio tape with Don Miller's interview was being retrieved from evidence, Lee Atkinson asked to excuse Officer Ouellette and be allowed to continue with the next witness.

Richard Bisbing was a lab technician from the Michigan State Police, and he had another court engagement set for later in the day. Tom Bengston agreed to allow his testimony to be taken.

---

140. People v Don G. Miller, April 6, 1979, 228

Officer Ouellette stepped down from the stand and was told he would be recalled once the audio tape was brought to the court.

14

Richard Bisbing was assigned to the Bridgeport Laboratory, one of several MSP crime labs around the state. He'd been with the state police as a laboratory specialist for six years, and prior to that he had been with the Michigan Department of Public Health's crime lab in Lansing.

Bisbing's primary specialty in the crime laboratory was in serology, which involved the identification of bodily fluids, mainly blood and semen.

He had examined the car with officers from the police department after Don Miller had agreed to it being searched a second time. The search of the car took place at the East Lansing City Garage.

Bisbing had removed more of the stain from the front seat and from the passenger door panel inside the car and just below the door handle. He'd been given original samples by Officer Ouellette the day before and had received information about various blood types of people involved in the investigation.

Officer Westgate had told him that Martha Sue Young's blood type was Group AB. Bisbing was also provided information about the blood type of both Don Miller and his other sister, Lori.[141] Their blood type was Group A.

After performing chemical tests, he found the presence of blood on at least one of the samples submitted to him on January 2. He said the sample was small and he couldn't do any additional tests on it.

---

141. Name has been changed.

When asked if he had done any tests on the samples he had collected himself on January 3, he said that he did. He found that both samples he had taken, both from the seat cushion and the passenger door, contained human blood. It was blood type B. He said he couldn't conclusively determine whether or not there was also Group A.

Because of the small amount he had been able to collect, he said he could only do one test, one examination, and one time.

Lee Atkinson asked him to explain the ABO Factor System.

Bisbing said he was referring to the major, or international, blood groups, and he added there were four: Group A, Group B, Group O, and Group AB. Group A contained only the blood factor A. The Blood Group B contained only the blood factor B. He said Blood Group O contained neither of the blood factors A or B, and the Group AB contains both the blood factors A and factor B.

Atkinson asked about the probability of someone with Blood Group A being responsible for the blood stains in the car.

"A person with Blood Group A could not have deposited those blood stains because it demonstrated the factor B, which would not be in a person with Blood Group A."

"Could a person with Blood Group O have been responsible for these stains in the car?"

"No, they could not."

"As I understand your testimony then, this stain would have had to come from a person who had either Blood Group B or Blood Group AB?"

"That's correct."

Atkinson asked if it was possible the blood belonged to Martha Sue Young.

"Martha Sue Young could have deposited the blood stain, yes."[142]

Atkinson had gotten what he wanted from the laboratory specialist.

Bengston had all of the lab reports, and he had known what Bisbing was going to say. He asked if anyone with AB blood or B blood could have deposited the blood, and Bisbing said yes.

Bisbing said there were tests available to determine whether blood was menstrual, and those tests would include identifying blood group substances other than blood types. He said they would require a much larger sample, and that none were done in this case.

When asked exactly where it was on the seat cushion, Bisbing said it was in the front seat, on the passenger side. "I believe it's about seventeen inches or so from the right edge of the front seat, the passenger's edge or the passenger's door side, and eight or nine inches from the front of the seat. So, it's essentially on the top of the seat cushion on the right side."[143]

Bengston asked him if the location was consistent with where a woman would be seated who might be having her menstrual cycle.

"It's a little bit more to the left, maybe towards the left leg area and up further than the vagina would be normally."[144]

Bisbing described the blood smear on the door as just below the handle and visible to the naked eye if someone looked close enough with a good light. He said he also found a number of light brown pubic hairs on both the front and back seat.

Explaining about subcategories to each blood group, Bisbing said every person's blood contains numerous other

---

142. People v Don G. Miller, April 6, 1979, 237
143. People v Don G. Miller, April 6, 1979, 239
144. People v Don G. Miller, April 6, 1979, 240

blood groups, or genetic markers, that could be used if the stains had been sufficient.

The defense attorney hypothesized that if there were two AB blood samples in different locations, could they be distinguished by being subcategorized?

Bisbing told him that if the two samples had originated from two different people with different subgroups, they could be, and there were several thousand different subgroups.

On the prosecution's re-direct, Bisbing said there was no blood or semen found on any of Martha's clothing.

Officer Ouellette was called back to the stand after Bisbing had finished testifying, and the jury listened to the first recorded interview with Don Miller after Martha Sue Young's disappearance.

Ouellette identified the voices as Officer King, Officer Austreng, Don Miller, and himself, adding that Miller was not under arrest at the time of the interview.

"If Mr. Miller had asked to leave the room, would he have been allowed to, sir?" Atkinson asked.

"Certainly."

"Did you restrain his comings and goings in any way?"

"No, we did not."[145]

Lee Atkinson followed up by asking if Don Miller had wished to exercise any of the rights that Officer King had read to him on tape, and Ouellette confirmed he hadn't.

Atkinson turned to address Judge Tschirhart and stated that based on the tape they had just listened to, Don Miller's Miranda rights had been read to him, and the statement made by Miller should be allowed.

In opposition, Bengston said there was nothing on the tape to indicate a court appointed attorney would be available if Miller couldn't afford one, and it was clear the focus of the investigation had shifted to his client because they had

---

145. People v Don G. Miller, April 6, 1979, 252

asked him to come to the police station for an interview, read him Miranda, and taped the interview. Quoting several cases, he argued that statements, admissions, or confessions couldn't be used to establish a crime.

Lee Atkinson was quick to respond. He said the evidence on the record supported the conclusion that Martha Sue Young was dead. Testimony about her character and habits, her state of mind, her health, and the circumstances surrounding her disappearance all suggested that she disappeared due to unnatural or unusual circumstances.

He outlined the fact that her personal effects were found in an unusual manner, in addition to some of her things that were still missing. "We would suggest that death, and criminal agency as its cause, has already been established on this record and that because of that, the Court could accept the admissions of the defendant on the grounds that the corpus delicti has already been established."[146]

Judge Tschirhart responded to both attorneys saying he would allow the statement, and he overruled Bengston's.

Atkinson had completed his questioning of the East Lansing officer by that point, and Bengston had his chance at cross-examination.

Tom Bengston began walking Ouellette through the steps of his initial contact at the Young residence on January 1, 1977.

Ouellette said his initial inquiry at the Young home was a missing person, and he estimated he had been at the house for thirty to forty-five minutes. He'd then gone back to the police department to continue the investigation after he left the Young home, adding that they had looked for footprints outside the home but the blowing snow had made it nearly impossible to find any.

As the two attorneys finished questioning Officer Ouellette, he was excused, and Rick Westgate was called.

---

146. People v Don G. Miller, April 6, 1979, 258

Westgate testified that had accompanied Sue Young and her ex-husband Le around the Lansing area in an effort to trace Don Miller's route on New Year's Eve, and Atkinson asked where he'd gotten the information about the different blood types.

Both attorneys had already agreed to stipulate that the blood types were, in fact, the blood types of both Don Miller and his sister.

The questioning of Westgate turned over to Bengston, but he had nothing at that point, and he asked the Court if he could recall Officer Westgate on Monday.

Lieutenant Maynard Markham was called to the stand after Westgate, and he described how had interviewed Don Miller on January 2, 1977, at the police department. The prosecutor was quick to point out that Miller wasn't under arrest or in custody at the time of the interview, and he could have left at any time if he'd have wanted to. Those questions led into Markham describing how he had read Miller's Miranda rights to him before the interview, and how Don Miller had said he understood each of his rights and would go ahead and answer some questions.

Markham said that Miller had told him what he and Martha Sue had done on New Year's Eve. Miller told him they had done some babysitting and afterward, they had gone back to his house, watched television, ate pizza, and drank 7 Up until 11:30. He and Martha had then gone to the Trinity Church to look for his sister, and when they didn't find her, they went to look at Christmas lights. Miller also told Markham that he and Martha had parked a few times during their drive.

The lieutenant then told the Court how Miller described dropping her off at home and how he had watched her wave goodbye as she sat on the porch.

Lee Atkinson moved to the interview Lt. Markham had done with Miller on January 11. Markham said that Dean Tucker had sat in on the interview. The officer described reading Don Miller's Miranda rights again before they started the interview and how Miller had waived his rights.

Markham said that during the second interview, Miller had changed his story. Miller said that he and Martha had a fight, and she had wanted to get out of the car to pray. Miller told Markham he wouldn't allow her to do that. He went into more detail about the Trinity Church by saying both he and Martha had gone into the church looking for his sister.

Markham continued by saying that Miller had told him that when they went into the church, the congregation or group of people that were there at the New Year's Eve service were standing and singing but Miller hadn't seen his sister so they left. Miller had added that they had entered the main worship area of the church, and they had gone through the main entrance. Miller couldn't remember if he had to go up any stairs to the main worship area, but it was about twenty-five feet from the entrance.

Markham had asked about the blood on the front seat of his car and if it turned out the blood found in his car belonged to Martha Young, how it could have gotten there. Miller told him that he and Martha had engaged in sexual foreplay. Miller said she could have been having her period at the time, and one of them might have had blood on their hands. He was trying to explain how blood could have gotten on the door.

Miller told the lieutenant that he had checked his hands for blood that night, but he didn't see any. He said it was his normal practice to eat something when he got home from a date, and he always washed his hands before eating. That said it could account for him not seeing any blood on his hands. He told the lieutenant that he specifically remembered going home and eating a sandwich after washing his hands.

"Had Mr. Miller told you about this foreplay prior to the eleventh of January, 1977?" Atkinson asked.

"No, sir, he did not."[147]

When the prosecutor asked Markham if there was any discussion about the blood during the interview on January 2, Markham said Miller told him about a nosebleed, then later in the same interview said the blood could have been from his sister menstruating.

Markham had also asked Don Miller if Martha had tried to break up with him and give the engagement ring back. Miller told him no and said their fight consisted of her being upset with her family. He said he was not actually fighting with her, but she was extremely upset.

Tom Bengston stood to address the witness for cross-examination, and he asked Lieutenant Markham if he had recorded the interview January 11. Markham hadn't.

Bengston had a copy of a report by Markham, but he hadn't had a chance to review it. He asked the Court if he could recall Markham on Monday and for the time being, allow Atkinson to do his re-direct questioning.

As Atkinson began, he asked if Markham had interviewed Don Miller on February 7.

Markham had, and he said Tom Bengston and Officer Westgate were both there during the interview. It was the interview that was done with written questions, and he said he was able to ask Miller about his answers while Bengston was present at the interview. Markham went over three specific points in Miller's interview. He made sure of Miller's answers about going to the Trinity Church, what was going on when he got there, and where the service was being conducted.

The second point Markham had covered with Miller was asking if Martha had wanted to break their engagement and had offered to give the ring back. Markham said Miller claimed she had never offered the engagement ring back to him nor offered to break the engagement.

---

147. People v Don G. Miller, April 6, 1979, 288

The corporal continued into the third area he had asked Miller about. It had to do with whether or not he had ever lived with anyone else. Markham added that he wasn't interested in the question after realizing what the answer was. When Don Miller had answered yes to the written question about that, he had been referring to living on Mackinac Island during the summer of 1976.

After his testimony, Lt. Markham was asked to return on Monday.

The following Monday, recounting his testimony from the previous Friday, Markham described Miller's second interview with him on January 11, 1977.

"So, there is no ambiguity or confusion on this record, if you used the word 'fight' on Friday regarding conversation on January 11 between Don Miller and Martha Sue Young, that, in fact, was not the word Don Miller used, is that right?"

"I would say that's not the word he used, correct," Markham said.[148]

Lieutenant Markham expanded his explanation by saying that on January 2, Miller told him that he and Martha Sue had discussed her family during their drive, but on January 11, he described it as a rather heated discussion.

When Bengston asked him which interview it was when Miller had tried to explain the blood in the car was the result of a nosebleed, Markham said it was the second interview. He added that it was a later interview when he said his sister was menstruating, and then on January 11, he had said the blood could have come from his sexual foreplay with Martha.

Markham had forgotten that he had also spoken with Don Miller on January 5, so Bengston clarified the exact dates as January 2, January 5, and January 11. Asked about the interview he had forgotten about, Markham said there

148. People v Don G. Miller, April 6, 1979, 298

was virtually no change in the statement from January 2 to January 5.

Markham said that on January 2, both he and Tucker had talked to Gene and Elaine Miller, and they had volunteered to speak with their son about Martha's disappearance.

Both attorneys had finished, and Lt. Markham stepped down from the witness just as Mike Woodworth stood to call Willard Michael, the pastor from Trinity Church.

Pastor Michael said there was a combination of a social event and an informal, sort of watchnight service on December 31, and it all took place in the Fellowship Hall in the basement of the church. He said the rest of the building was locked and there were no lights on in the main worship area.

The pastor said that as midnight approached, everyone lit candles, and they were all gathered in the Fellowship Hall.

When Bengston began his cross-examination of Pastor Michael, he asked if the pastor was acquainted with Don Miller and if he would have recognized him had he come into the church on December 31.

The pastor said there weren't any young people at the gathering, so if Miller had come in, he would have noticed him.

"But your attention was not addressed entirely as to who was coming and who was going, is that accurate to say?"

"No, that's not accurate to say. I was aware of the people who were at the situation. It is unlikely that anyone would have entered and participated in what was going on. It was a small gathering, Mr. Bengston, and it was very unlikely that anyone would have gathered with us and participated without me knowing it."[149]

The pastor said the singing began at around 11:30-11:40 p.m., and it was informal. After, there was a short devotional

---

149. People v Don G. Miller, April 6, 1979, 311

by candlelight. Communion took place around 11:50 p.m., and after that, the event would have ended.

When Bengston asked what sort of festivities were going on for young people at the church, the pastor said there wasn't anything for young people that evening. He said there was a gathering at the home of assistant coach Marvin Braden, a Michigan State football coach.

Bengston sat down and scribbled some notes as Mike Woodworth stood for re-direct.

"Sir, could you tell the Court, if someone were in your church standing either in the main worship area or looking on to the main worship area, would they also be able to look into the Fellowship Hall where this particular meeting took place that evening?"

"Absolutely not…that would not be possible."[150]

Woodworth, already knowing the answer, asked how the Fellowship Hall differed from the main worship area of the church.

The pastor said there was no way the two could be confused. The Fellowship Hall had concrete block walls, a tile floor, and ordinary windows. The sanctuary had pews, a slanted floor with carpeting, a semi-circle configuration, and was very church-like.

Lee Atkinson had narrowed his witness list. His next witness was Lieutenant Richard Simmers from ELPD, whose testimony was brief.

Simmers had been with Officer Ouellette on January 3 at the Miller home when they asked for permission to search Don Miller's car by taking it to the East Lansing City Garage.

Woodworth asked if there were any concerns expressed by the Millers about the search of the car, and Simmers said there was nothing but complete cooperation. He said Don Miller had signed a Consent to Search form.

---

150. People v Don G. Miller, April 6, 1979, 317

Simmers had taken some clothing, and Miller had told him it was the clothing he had been wearing on the night Martha disappeared.

Simmer's testimony ended very quickly, and Lee Atkinson called his next witness. It was Ernest Boillard, the inmate who had heard Don Miller make incriminating statements at the Eaton County Jail after he was arrested for the rape and attempted murders of the Gilbert children.

Boillard quietly took the stand. He repeated the same story he had told Detective Norm Kelley first and then Lt. Tucker about what he had heard Don Miller say at the Eaton County Jail after Miller's arrest.

"Yes, I said to him, I asked him how he got caught, and that's when he stated that he went to his girlfriend's house. He also indicated to me that he should have done away with the boy and girl like he got rid of his girlfriend."[151]

When Atkinson asked if Miller had given any reason for doing away with his girlfriend, Boillard said that she aggravated him.

After Lee Atkinson's brief examination, Tom Bengston began his cross-examination, and he touched on why Boillard was at the Eaton County Jail in the first place.

Bengston asked how loudly Miller had been talking when he made the statement.

Boillard was referring to another cellmate when he said, "Loud enough for Mr. Force to say, 'I told you he did it.'"[152]

Still trying to attack the witness's credibility, the defense attorney pressed him about a phone call he had made to the *State Journal*, and Boillard admitted he had made a call, yet each time Tom Bengston tried to attack his credibility, Boillard calmly described what had happened.

---

151. People v Don G. Miller, April 6, 1979, 329
152. People v Don G. Miller, April 6, 1979, 346

Bengston also asked about the discussion he had had with Gene Miller in front of the Eaton County Jail. He wanted to know exactly what was said.

"Yes, he was kind of upset when he was saying it to me. He said, 'friggin' head.'"

"'Friggin',' or did he say something else, sir?"

"Well, I mean I am under oath, but there's a lot of ladies in the room here and I wouldn't like to use the four-letter word that is what he indicated to me."

Bengston turned to the judge, saying, "Your Honor, I'd ask the witness be instructed to tell exactly what this person told him."

Judge Tschirhart turned toward the gallery of spectators in the back of the courtroom and said, "Ladies, if you don't want to hear some vulgarity, you may leave the courtroom." He turned back to the witness, saying, "I am going to instruct the witness to answer the statement that was made to you at that time, as exactly as you can recall it."

"Okay, he said, 'I'll bust your fucking head.'"[153] Boillard told the Court that he knew Gene Miller was talking about him.

As Boillard left the courtroom, Mike Woodworth stood and called Martha Sue Young's gynecologist to the stand next.

The doctor testified that he had examined Martha in July of 1976 and it was a routine exam. He said there was nothing in Martha's history to suggest a life-endangering illness or any psychological or emotional problems.

When Tom Bengston took over questioning the doctor, the doctor said the examination was strictly a physiological exam and not a psychological exam.

Woodworth called a second doctor who testified that he had seen Martha Sue Young as a patient in October of 1976 for her college physical exam, and he said he hadn't

---

153. People v Don G. Miller, April 6, 1979, 358

found any disease, injury, or abnormalities that would cause Martha to have died in the near future. He added that emotionally, he considered her stable.

Once again, under cross-examination, Tom Bengston touched on whether or not the exam had touched on any psychological testing and the doctor told him there hadn't been any.

The preliminary examination for Martha's murder mirrored the previous exam for Kristine's murder. As it continued into the early afternoon, the first witness called was Lt. Dean Tucker.

Like Tucker had done in the previous exam for the Kristine Stuart case, he outlined everything he could think of in his investigation regarding the disappearance of Martha Young, and had helped secure her clothing when it had been found.

"Other than that occasion sir, have you come across any other information that would indicate the present whereabouts of Martha Sue Young if she were alive?" the prosecutor asked.

"No, sir."

"Have you come across any information which would lead you to believe she is alive at the present time?"

"No, sir."[154]

Tucker outlined the search areas that had been made around the tri-county area over the previous two years. He said during the initial searches, extreme snow conditions had made it difficult.

Tom Bengston knew the preliminary exam for his client was nearing the end. As Lee Atkinson finished his direct examination of the witness, Bengston began his cross-examination.

He asked Tucker if contact had been made with any airlines to check for Martha Sue, and the lieutenant

---

154. People v Don G. Miller, April 6, 1979, 370

explained that he had personally taken a photo of her to the Capital City Airport in Lansing to check and had phoned Detroit Metro to check her name through their system.

He also checked with the Amtrak station to see if anyone had used the name of Martha Sue Young, and he was told that information was actually kept in Washington, DC. They had eventually contacted Tucker and told him that no one named Martha Sue Young had used the Amtrak.

"Further proofs, Mr. Atkinson?" Judge Tschirhart asked.

Atkinson was done. He didn't have any additional witnesses.

"Mr. Bengston, does the defense intend to offer any proofs at the preliminary examination?" the judge asked.

Bengston said that he intended to briefly recall Officer Westgate.

The defense attorney asked Westgate if, during his investigation, he had determined whether or not Martha had purchased shoes at the Jacobson's store, and if so, if had ever been able to locate those. The officer couldn't recall.

Asked about whether or not he was able to find out if Martha Sue had worn earrings on December 31, 1976, he also said he couldn't recall.

The cross-examination was over as quickly as it had started.

Lee Atkinson stood to address the Court. His closing argument was brief. He moved to have Don Miller bound over to the circuit court for second-degree murder in the death of Martha Sue Young.

"Mr. Bengston?" the judge asked.

Tom Bengston's said he wasn't going to recap the entire testimony offered by the prosecution witnesses. "I think some of the salient aspects of this case are that one Martha Sue Young disappears on January 1 of 1977. Subsequently, on October 20 of '77, clothing was located by several hunters in the Township of Bath. Significantly, no glasses were ever located of Martha Sue Young." He understood the prosecutor's theory as "There is a disappearance, therefore there is a death, therefore a homicide, therefore a wrongful homicide, therefore a murder in the second degree."[155]

Bengston disagreed. He said Martha had difficulties with her family, and he suggested the testimony supported his observation. He also said she wasn't married, wasn't leaving a husband, and was of college age.

Asking the Court to consider the discovery of her clothing, Bengston said there was absolutely no testimony indicating a finding of blood or semen on any of the clothing. He said there was no finding of a knife, gun, rope, or weapon of any kind to support the prosecuting attorney's theory.

The defense attorney moved his argument to the blood discovered in Don Miller's car. He suggested that the blood was hardly supportive of a second-degree murder, and the prosecutor was simply trying to prove she was dead by convicting his client.

"I suggest to this Court that that's unadulterated conjecture," he said.[156]

As Bengston made his argument, knowing it was his only chance, he addressed the corpus delicti in the context of the admissibility of statements or admissions by Don Miller. Citing a court of appeals case, and referring to Ernest Boillard, he quoted, "The corpus delicti rule reflects an uneasy feeling, based on experience, that persons who attribute statements to the accused person are often not trustworthy witnesses." Going further, he cited eight separate cases that indicated a crime couldn't be proven by a defendant's statements alone.

Reading from *The American Jurisprudence*, an encyclopedia of United States law, Bengston said, "In every homicide prosecution, the evidence must be

---

155. People v Don G. Miller, April 6, 1979, 384
156. People v Don G. Miller, April 6, 1979, 385

sufficient to prove the corpus delicti, that is, the actual offense committed. The proof must show first, that the life of a human being has been taken; and second, that the death was occasioned by the criminal act or agency of another person."

Continuing with the title *Evidence*, he read, "The circumstantial proof of the corpus delicti must be acted on with caution; especially one where the public anxiety for the detection of a great crime creates an unusual tendency to exaggerate fact and draw rash inferences."[157]

Bengston outlined the definition of second-degree murder, adding that Malice of Forethought was an element. Citing another case, he said, "In pertinent part, the Court observed that the law does not imply malice where a deadly weapon is used. Michigan has long ago considered malice a permissible inference to be drawn by the jury rather than a presumption of law."[158] He suggested the prosecutor's theory didn't find that any weapon was ever used against Martha Sue Young.

Lee Atkinson, Mike Woodworth, and Judge Tschirhart listened intently to Bengston's argument when he said it was the prosecutor's burden to make out a prima facie case of second-degree murder. His position was that Atkinson and Woodworth hadn't done that because there wasn't a homicide.

Bengston also made a point to tell the judge that Martha's clothing was found in a neighboring county and not in Ingham County.

Closing his argument, he asked the Court to consider dismissing the charges against Don Miller. His last statement was that the evidence was insufficient and the jurisdiction was misplaced.

---

157. People v Don G. Miller, April 6, 1979, 386
158. People v Don G. Miller, April 6, 1979, 388

The burden of proof was on Lee Atkinson. He was given his chance at rebuttal. In preparation, the prosecution had a courtroom display to demonstrate their case against Don Miller.

The prosecutor began by addressing a statement made by the defense in his closing argument about Martha having difficulty with her family. He said the only evidence of that came from Don Miller when he said it to the police, and it didn't come from Martha's mother, friends, or other family members. He said it was a justification from Miller himself.

Atkinson continued his attack on Bengston's closing argument when he said there was no other reasonable explanation for the disappearance of Martha Sue Young.

Addressing the defense's position that the blood discovered was equivocal, Lee Atkinson said it might be doubtful in the context that it hadn't been proven to be Martha's blood. He said that when a person disappeared under the circumstance which surrounded Martha's disappearance, and blood was found in the very automobile where she had been, then it wasn't equivocal at all.

Atkinson said the most difficult matter in the case was that Martha's body had not been found. Citing the case of *People v Manson,* he said the issue was squarely confronted by the California Court of Appeals. "Here, Manson places great emphasis on the fact that Shea's body was never recovered. The fact that Shea's body was never recovered would justify an inference by the jury that death was caused by a criminal agency.

"Legally justifiable inference, Your Honor. It goes on to say, 'It is highly unlikely that a person who dies from natural causes will successfully dispose of his own body.' The Manson Court goes on to suggest the highly unlikelihood that a person who dies a natural death would in fact successfully dispose of their own body points to one conclusion for the disappearance of that body under the circumstances involved there, and that is a criminal agency."[159]

Moving to the courtroom display, Lee Atkinson said that Martha Sue Young's disappearance could be broken down into three major categories. The first, as he explained, was that there was a death. The second was that the death was caused by a criminal agency or act. Finally, that the prosecution had identified the perpetrator.

He asked the Court to consider what led to the conclusion that Martha was dead, then suggested the Court look at her habits.

Atkinson recapped the testimony of Martha's relationship with her family, and how she wrote to her mother on a continual basis. She often phoned her mother. She had moved back to East Lansing so she could go to school closer to her family and be a part of the community she had grown up in.

The record reflected a person who was so disposed by character and habit that they were not likely to disappear voluntarily. Martha was not a young woman who was involved with some strange element or had brushes with the law. She wasn't someone who had in some way established a pattern of erratic behavior. On the contrary, this was a young woman who was so characteristically stable in her habits that her disappearance was irrefutable proof that she did not go missing voluntarily.

The Court had heard much about Martha's state of mind, and Atkinson added that her state of mind reflected her intent of staying in the community. He said, "One does not make employment appointments; one does not pay tuition; one does not set up one's courses; one does not make plans to spend New Year's Day with their mother if they are, in fact, intending to, at that time, voluntarily disappear."[160]

---

159. People v Don G. Miller, April 6, 1979, 394
160. People v Don G. Miller, April 6, 1979, 396

As he moved on, he told the Court the there was nothing in Martha Sue's health history that would lead anyone to believe she would die suddenly of natural causes, and nothing in any of the testimony that would lead anyone to believe her mental health was at issue.

He said the blood found in Miller's car was a salient fact, adding that finding human blood in Miller's car under those circumstances, regardless if there was enough to type, should have been evidence enough to conclude that Martha was dead.

Continuing his closing, he reminded the Court that all of her personal belongings were still at her home on the night she disappeared. None of her mementos, none of her luggage, none of her additional clothing was taken. Moreover, she didn't take any money out of the bank, or the one hundred twenty-five dollars left in her dresser at home. "It's untraceable, it's livable, one could eat off of it, one could clothe oneself off of it, one could get shelter off of it. The money is left behind. We would suggest the circumstances surrounding the personal effects left behind in the home are strong indications that Martha Sue Young did not voluntarily absent herself from her community."[161]

Atkinson asked the Court who the last person was to see Martha alive. Surprisingly enough, it was Don Miller and his mother. He said from 11:30 to two a.m., no one knew anything about her movements except what Don Miller had told the police. "She disappeared. She disappears totally from the face of the earth under circumstances where she is last seen and only known to be with Donald Miller."

Moving to the third column in his courtroom display, Lee Atkinson mentioned criminal agency. "The first item of evidence which strongly points to criminal agency is the lack of a body, as we have indicated already to the Court." Mentioning the blood found in Don Miller's car again,

---

161. People v Don G. Miller, April 6, 1979, 397

Atkinson said, "When we go from the issue of death over to the issue of criminal agency, the blood, I think, speaks even more strongly than does the blood serve the issue of death. Again, that single concrete evidentiary fact is an item from which two separate factors and conclusions can be inferred."

The prosecutor pointed out the peculiar fashion in which Martha's clothing was laid out when it was found. He said the clothing wasn't laid out in the manner of a natural death or an accidental death. He said it was an intentional placement in a patterned manner, and the only two things missing were the engagement ring and her glasses. He reminded the Court that the engagement ring was the same ring she was trying to give back to Miller, and the same ring Miller suggested he never received back.

To address the theory that Martha Sue Young had disappeared voluntarily, Lee Atkinson said, "To that, I respond, you may leave behind your identification, you may even leave behind your personal Bible, but if that is your purpose, to disappear, why leave behind your underwear? Where is Martha Sue Young going to go without a bra, without panties, without pantyhose?" He continued, "I suggest the finding of those items in that field, in that manner indicates one and one thing only; and that is, that Martha Sue Young had no further need, ever, for such items."[162]

He moved to motive when he said that Don Miller had the opportunity, and he had the motive. Miller told the police that Martha was upset that night. He added there was evidence on the record from which her reason could be inferred. Her attitude towards her relationship with Don was unsatisfactory, and she had been expressing that continually. Moreover, there was clear evidence of Miller's

---

162. People v Don G. Miller, April 6, 1979, 400

motive; his statement to Ernest Boillard that she aggravated him.

The prosecutor was leaving no stone unturned. He said it was the consciousness of Miller's own guilt that pointed to his identity as the killer.

Atkinson began to highlight the different versions of events offered by the Millers.

"Mr. Miller said he leaves the home at about 11:30. He returns to the residence at two. There is only one witness who has verified his story, and that is his mother. She verified it. She said, 'Yes, he arrived home at two.' She says yes, that happened, it happened this way, we talked, he did not wash his hands, he went straight to the kitchen from dropping his coat off without a stop. 'I fixed him a sandwich...He mentioned leaving Martha sitting on the stoop, and I thought that was peculiar.'"[163]

Atkinson said that before believing Elaine Miller and her son's version of events, it had to be considered with Karen Miller's statement about the events in the early morning hours of January 1, 1977.

Both Karen and Elaine Miller could not both be correct. Either Karen came home at some point after New Year's Eve and found the house dark with everyone in bed, then went to bed herself, or she came home at approximately 1:40, had a confrontation with her mother about missing Don, and then went to bed. He said she couldn't have it both ways; and neither could Elaine Miller; and neither could Don. There was nothing, other than Don Miller's say so, to indicate that he got home at two a.m.

Reminding the Court about Miller's changing stories, he said Miller initially indicated that the blood in his car was from a nosebleed. Later, he came up with circumstances surrounding sexual foreplay with Martha. He didn't relate

---

163. People v Don G. Miller, April 6, 1979, 403

the story at the beginning. He waited until he was asked, "What if it's not?"

Lee Atkinson said that as Miller began to work on his story, another interesting thing came out. It was the details of his supposed visit to Trinity Church. Atkinson pointed out Pastor Michaels' testimony, saying it refuted Miller's version of events, and that Don Miller did not go into the Trinity Church or into the sanctuary area, nor did he see people in the sanctuary and search for his sister. He lied about it, and Atkinson said it was evidence of his consciousness.

Finally, the prosecutor said that the People had established that the crime had been committed. He asked the Court to consider the testimony of Ernest Boillard. He said Boillard never once attempted to feign the circumstances surrounding his story, nor, under heavy cross-examination, did he contradict himself concerning the essential details of that statement. He said Boillard was simple and straightforward and had admitted to his own past. The prosecutor pointed out that Boillard was a convicted criminal who was familiar with prison jargon and was con-wise, but added there was no evidence on the record that he wasn't telling the truth. Atkinson suggested to the contrary, saying that based upon his demeanor, and the coherence and consistency of his statement, that he caught Don Miller in what might have been a moment of his defenses being down. He said Miller's statement was a clear indication of what happened to Martha.

Atkinson knew it wasn't the type of confession he wanted to bring into court, but he said that when it was added to the other irrefutable evidence, the Court could come to only one conclusion; that Martha Sue Young was dead, that her death was the result of a criminal agency, and that criminal agency was Don Miller.

As he neared his closing rebuttal, Atkinson pointed to the box of evidence on the table. "That, Your Honor, in that box is all that is left of Martha Sue Young. We would suggest that merely because Donald Miller was successful in hiding the body of Martha Sue Young, that that does not preclude the Prosecution from establishing that he, in fact, murdered her. Because if in fact he caused her death, and in fact he successfully disposed of her body, then there can be no doubt, I suggest in this Court's mind, considering the requirements which it must apply in deciding the Bind Over Motion, that in fact that death was second-degree murder. For his to have been responsible for her death under these circumstances could be nothing else but second-degree murder."

As in Miller's preliminary exam for the murder of Kristine Stuart, Judge Tschirhart had no hesitation. He said there was reasonable cause to believe the crime had been committed, and reasonable cause to believe that Don Miller had committed it. He bound Miller over to the circuit court and set the arraignment for April 18.

Tom Bengston knew he had his hands full. His client was going to stand trial for two counts of second-degree murder, and he was also facing a trial in less than a month for rape and two counts of attempted murder.

15

As the trial date quickly approached for the assaults on the Gilbert children, one last pretrial conference was held on April 24 in front of Eaton County's Judge Robinson.

Both Assistant Prosecutor Mike Hocking and Don Miller's defense attorney told the magistrate they were ready to begin the trial.

As the judge read through Hocking's pretrial statement, he noted several witnesses that both he and Bengston had agreed to remove from the trial. Judge Robinson also highlighted each piece of evidence that Mike Hocking intended to produce at the trial. As he read on, he asked Hocking, "Motion to strike Count IV. What is that count?"

Hocking told him it was the breaking and entering, and he hadn't made the formal motion yet. He'd discussed it with Bengston and decided not to proceed with the count.

Mike Hocking was experienced enough to know the first three counts were serious felonies, and he couldn't conceive a jury returning a guilty verdict for the breaking and entering, and not the criminal sexual assault and both counts of attempted murder. It was a tactical move. Even with a life sentence conviction, Miller would still be eligible for parole in ten years. Hocking didn't want Miller eligible for parole in ten years. He wanted a conviction on each count, and he wanted a thirty to fifty-year sentence.

"Are you moving at this time to strike Count IV?" the judge asked.

"Yes, Your Honor."[164]

Tom Bengston had no objection to Hocking's motion.

Robinson reminded both attorneys that they had agreed the entire jury panel would be kept out of the courtroom while the questioning was going on.

Tom Bengston brought up the issue of the insanity defense, saying there was some confusion in the law. The defense attorney briefly mentioned the competency evaluation that was done on his client for purposes of the preliminary examination by two of the State's experts. He knew they were going to be called at trial to testify about insanity. His concern was they would be using some of the information they learned from Miller regarding his competency and bring it up in the trial. He knew that Hocking would try to do that by using historical data they had obtained at the competency evaluation. The defense had no problem with the prosecution using historical data as long as it hadn't been obtained at the competency hearing.

Hocking said the best way to deal with it was to avoid the issue of competency and proceed on the basis that it was an examination over Miller's state of mind.

The prosecutor wasn't prepared to argue whether the law allowed the use of a competency exam for the basis to show the defendant was sane.

Robinson threw the ball to Bengston when he said, "Seems to me, Mr. Bengston, that you are addressing a question more of credibility of witness rather than you are a legal question as to the admissibility of that testimony, because I can conceive that a person could be interviewing a person for one purpose, and in the course of it, pick up information that could be used for another purpose."[165]

---

164. People v Don G. Miller. Transcript of pretrial conference. April 24, 1979, 8

165. People v Don G. Miller, April 24, 1979, 11

Tom Bengston had done his homework. He had researched the law regarding that very question. He was certain the statute said competency couldn't be used except under two specific sections of law that relate to "competency and restoration of competency after having been found incompetent."

Judge Robinson didn't quite agree with Bengston's interpretation. "I'll agree that you can't get in the issue of competency to stand trial unless somebody raised it, and that can be raised at any time, although he has had one competency hearing, but to say he can't use all of the information he got in the interview, seems to me you are trying to accomplish the impossible, Mr. Bengston."

The defense attorney wasn't giving up. "Well, Your Honor, I would understand that the rationale behind it is, if a particular defendant is going to invoke the defense of insanity, he may be disinclined to submit himself regarding competency. I mean, if the Forensic Center is going to be able to take the data they got on the competency and bring it over to the insanity, and that's what I think the prosecutor is going to do, it's unfair to the defendant."[166]

The judge said that the matter of competency wasn't necessarily a matter of the defendant consenting to it and pointed out it could be done without his consent. He turned to Hocking and asked if it presented any problems to him.

"Well, the only problem I can see, Your Honor, is from Mr. Bengston's point if the prejudicial effect of the mentioning the word 'competency' in front of the jury."

Robinson agreed.

Hocking continued, "I think the two physicians, and they happen to be the same two physicians in the case, make an examination as to insanity, I don't think they should have to black out of their minds something they learned from the defendant in some other examination."

---

166. People v Don G. Miller, April 24, 1979, 12

Bengston countered Hocking's argument by saying that Miller had been remanded to the Forensic Center for the limited purpose of a competency examination in the district court. It wasn't for the purpose of a Not Guilty by Reason of Insanity defense. That defense hadn't even been raised at that point. He continued to tell the Court that when he did raise that defense, Miller was remanded again to the Forensic Center for evaluation. Bengston didn't think it was fair to have Miller remanded for competency and then have the experts say they also examined him for the insanity defense.

Robinson told both attorneys to bring briefs to the trial regarding the matter.

On a final note, Judge Richard Robinson told Hocking and Bengston that he intended to use the entire first day of the trial to pick a jury, and the trial would start each day at ten a.m.

—————————

Mike Hocking had a hard time believing that Miller had simply "snapped" and started killing women. His impression of Miller was that he was bright enough that he thought he could fool the judicial system. He knew Bengston's client had a problem, but he also knew that he would never admit it.

—————————

Located in the southeast corner of Michigan in the state's fruit belt, the huge, five-story Berrien County Courthouse sat on the St. Joseph River three blocks from Lake Michigan. It was one hundred six miles from Charlotte. The judge, prosecutor, defense attorney, and the witnesses would have to make the drive each day for Don Miller's trial.

On April 30, the seventeen mile-an-hour wind blowing in off Lake Michigan made the forty-six-degree temperature seem much colder.

In the Berrien County Circuit Court, Judge Richard Robinson began jury selection at 9:45 a.m. He explained to the pool of jurors that fourteen would be chosen to hear the testimony at trial, and at the end of the trial, two jurors would be dismissed before deliberations. The extra two jurors were used in case a couple of other jurors fell ill during the trial.

As the jury selection began, each potential juror was asked general questions by Judge Robinson, with specific questions by both Hocking and Bengston to follow. Several of the prospective jurors were dismissed by the attorneys during the questioning, and no reason had to be given.

By 11:15, Judge Robinson ordered a recess, and by 11:30, court was called back to order, and questioning of the potential jurors continued. The same questions were asked again and again of each potential juror, and oftentimes the answers given by the prospective jurors were exactly the same.

By 11:50, all of the prospective jurors in the first panel had been questioned.

Jury selection continued for another three hours. All of the candidates seemed to answer the questions the same, but one potential juror was excused on a challenge by Mike Hocking. He told the Court he would give the testimony of a juvenile less weight than that of an adult. Bengston agreed to the challenge and removal of the potential juror.

By 3:30 p.m., both Mike Hocking and Tom Bengston were satisfied with the fourteen Berrien County residents who would sit as jurors in the trial of Don Miller. After a long day of sitting, waiting, and listening to question after question, the judge declared a recess until the following morning.

When the attorneys arrived in the courtroom, Mike Hocking and Paul Berger sat on one side of the courtroom, while Tom Bengston, his assistant Jonathan White, and Don Miller sat on the opposite side of the courtroom at the defense table.

At 9:30 a.m., Hocking stood, buttoning his suit, and began his opening statement. The assistant prosecutor emphasized to the panel of jurors how important their role was in the system of government and told them his opening statement would serve as an outline of what he expected to show them in the trial.

Carefully and methodically, the assistant prosecutor described the charges against Tom Bengston's client and began to tell the jury where the crimes occurred by describing where Delta Township was located in Eaton County.

Hocking moved into a description of how the events of August 16, 1978, had transpired by telling how Lisa had left the house to call for Randy in the backyard, then encountering a man in the kitchen of the house as she came back into the garage. He described the brief conversation between the two and told how the man pulled a knife, then told Lisa not to say anything.

The assistant prosecutor told the jurors that lab personnel from the Michigan State Police would testify about what they found at the crime scene, and they would describe finding the defendant's fingerprint from his left hand inside the house on the front door.

Hocking outlined the vivid details of the assault on Lisa and told the jurors he would prove it occurred not only from the testimony of Lisa, but with the testimony of doctors who examined her at the hospital.

After describing the rape to the jury, he detailed the strangulation by Miller on the fourteen-year-old girl and said that Miller pulled the belt so hard, that the entire whites of Lisa's eyes were blood red due to the hemorrhages. He said Don Miller pulled that belt so hard that it broke, and when it broke, the next best weapon for strangling Lisa was Don Miller's hands. He said Miller strangled Lisa Gilbert until she heard the door slam from the kitchen to the garage, because during that time, Randy Gilbert was on the way to the house.

Hocking continued his narrative to the jury, moving to describe the assault on Randy Gilbert. He said the testimony would show that Miller took the knife and started to slit Randy's throat, until Randy grabbed the knife and threw it under the bed.

"He's fighting for his life," he said.[167] Hocking continued, telling the panel how Miller took his hands and strangled Randy Gilbert. He told the jury that Miller strangled Randy so hard that he started to gasp, couldn't breathe, started to get dizzy, and all of the capillaries in the whites of his eyes broke.

Mike Hocking wasn't done. He continued to describe Randy's actions after waking up and discovering he was covered in blood. The assistant prosecutor described James Regan confronting Don Miller in front of the house. He told them about the brief conversation between the two, and he described Miller jumping into his car, locking the door, and fleeing southbound away from the house.

As Mike Hocking closed his statement, he told the jury that after all of the proofs were shown, he would come back and ask them to find Don Miller guilty on all counts.

As the assistant prosecutor sat down, Tom Bengston stood for his opening statement.

Bengston said it was the prosecuting attorney's responsibility to prove his case beyond a reasonable doubt. He said the events of August 16, 1978, were a human tragedy. He told the jury that he was not denying his client

---

167. People v Don G. Miller, Transcript of jury trial, May 1, 1979, 159

was at the residence on that day, and he told them that he was not there to deny that Lisa and Randy were assaulted.

Bengston said he would concede the nature of the assaults, but it would be up to them to decide if the assaults were an attempt to commit murder, as Hocking had suggested.

Bengston also told the members of the jury that he would not concede as to the nature of the sexual assault, and he moved into the crux of his defense by saying the pivotal issue of the case was going to be whether or not Don Miller was criminally responsible for his conduct. He said that in his closing arguments, his proofs would show Don Miller was insane on August 16, 1978.

As Tom Bengston went into more detail about the upcoming testimony of the four doctors he would have testify about his client's sanity, he said the constant theme that would run through their testimony was that Miller lived with an angel and a devil inside, coexisting, but frequently not aware of the other's existence.

Ending his opening statement to the jury, the defense attorney sat down, and it was Judge Robinson's turn to speak. With the defense of insanity being raised in Miller's case, it was up to the judge to instruct the jury on two notes regarding mental defects in the state of Michigan. Under Michigan law, legal insanity and mental illness were not equivalent. A mentally ill person was not necessarily insane, because the law recognized a distinction between legal insanity and mental illness, in addition to providing different consequences for acts committed under those states of mind.

As the judge finished his explanation, he defined both, explaining that mental illness meant a substantial disorder of thought or mood which significantly impaired judgement, behavior, and capacity to recognize reality or a person's ability to cope with the ordinary demands of life. A person was legally insane if, as a result of mental illness, that person lacked substantial capacity, either to appreciate the wrongfulness of his conduct, or to perform his conduct to the requirement of the law.

With that, the judge had Mike Hocking call his first witness.

Lisa and Randy Gilbert's dad approached the witness stand and took a seat. After having the witness sworn in, Hocking began his questioning much like he had at the preliminary examination, asking how long Doug Gilbert had lived in his home prior to August 16, 1978. Gilbert told the assistant prosecutor he had only been living in the house for forty-five days prior to the attack.

Hocking showed Mr. Gilbert a diagram of the house, and he had him describe every detail in the floor plan.

As Mike Hocking showed ten photographs from inside the house, he asked Doug Gilbert to identify what each photo depicted and where each was taken. He was trying to acclimate the jury to the layout of the home.

When Hocking asked if anything appeared to be missing after his return from the hospital late that night. Gilbert told the assistant prosecutor a couple of ties were missing.

Doug Gilbert also told Hocking there was fingerprint powder all over the walls, and there was a large pool of blood on the carpet in Randy's room. In his own bedroom, he described a small amount of blood on the carpet.

The assistant prosecutor showed him two separate ties that had been recovered from the scene, and Doug Gilbert identified them as his.

Mike Hocking had a difficult question to ask Mr. Gilbert, and it was because the MSP lab technicians had recovered semen from the carpet at the foot of his bed. "At the foot of your bed, sir, on the carpet, in the forty-five days that you lived there, did you ever have sexual intercourse in that location?" he asked.

"No, sir, I never did."[168]

In his testimony, Gilbert said he didn't know the defendant, and he had never given him permission to enter his house.

Hocking steered his questioning to Lisa and Randy's appearances after they returned from the hospital, asking if there was anything unusual about them.

"The bruises. Of course, they were bruised about the throat and head, and Randall had the wounds on his chest and on his neck. And their eyes were extremely bloodshot," he told the assistant prosecutor, adding that it took about ten days before the bruising started to subside.

Tom Bengston stood to cross-examine the witness.

Bengston asked if any clothing was in disarray at the house when Doug Gilbert had returned that evening, then asked if there was a pond behind the house. After telling Bengston how far the pond was from the house, the cross-examination was over very quickly.

Lisa was the next witness for the prosecution, and she was just as apprehensive as she had been during the preliminary examination.

A myriad of feelings overwhelmed Lisa as she took a seat on the witness stand, and like before, she spoke very softly. The assistant prosecutor gently asked her to speak up as she began to answer questions, and the bailiff helped the eighth-grade student by moving her chair closer to the microphone.

As he had done in the preliminary examination, Mike Hocking began leading Lisa through the events of August 16, 1978.

Lisa described listening to the radio all day, and as 3 p.m. approached, she had gone to the lagoon in the back yard to call for Randy because they had to call their step-mom.

---

168. People v Don G. Miller, May 1, 1979, 188

Her voice was still just above a whisper when the judge asked her to speak up again.

Lisa described the path she took to get to the lagoon, and then calling for her brother.

"When you returned, Lisa, did you see any vehicles in the driveway?" Hocking asked.

"Yes." Asked to describe it, she told him it was brown car, and he showed her a photo of Miller's car. "That was the car in the driveway," she said.

Mike Hocking showed Lisa another photo. "Can you tell the People, the jury, what's in the picture?"

"It's my belt in the driveway."[169]

Lisa described to the jury how she had first seen the car in the drive and had gone back out in back of the house to see if anyone was out there. When she found no one, she went back into the garage, and she described seeing Miller standing inside the house.

Slowly, she told the jury what Miller was wearing when she first saw him.

Hocking asked the young witness if she would recognize the man again if she saw him, and she said she would. She described Miller sitting at the defense table. "He has a light tan coat on, with a white shirt, with a blue and tan color in his tie."[170]

Lisa told the jury about the initial conversation with Don Miller when she first encountered him, and how she had gone back into the house to get a piece of paper to write her dad's phone number on.

Hocking asked if she had ever invited him into the home.

"No."

The prosecutor asked her if she knew where he was when she entered the house.

---

169. People v Don G. Miller, May 1, 1979, 197
170. People v Don G. Miller, May 1, 1979, 202

"He was right behind me."[171]

As Hocking directed her attention to the point where Miller became aggressive, her voice seemed to shrink, and he had to remind her to speak up.

As Mike Hocking continued to question her, Lisa quietly described how Don Miller had raped her. She told the jury how he had restrained her with her hands tied behind her back, and how he had gagged her with a nylon so she couldn't scream. She described the rape in vivid detail and told the jury how Miller had tied her legs together afterward. Hocking gently asked her to speak up.

As Lisa described Miller rubbing her back afterward, Hocking asked if he had done anything else.

She said he got her belt and began to choke her. She described the strangulation in graphic detail, saying her eyes were "bugging out," and she had trouble breathing, then described the belt breaking. Miller started to choke her with his bare hands, and as her vision began to blur, she heard the door open. She knew it was her brother coming into the house.

She could hear her brother screaming as she frantically tried to hide in the bathroom and then decided to get out of the house. She told the jury her hands were still tied behind her, and part of a binding was still around her foot as she ran nude through the dirt and toward the road.

The judge could see Lisa becoming more emotional and softly interrupted her to tell the jurors it would be a good time for a recess.

When the jury returned at 1:30 p.m., Judge Robinson immediately told them about a news article that had appeared in the local paper. He urged them to ignore any publicity about the trial in hopes that when they went into deliberation, their decision would be based solely on the

---

171. People v Don G. Miller, May 1, 1979, 204

evidence they heard presented to them. He asked if any of them had read the article, and no one had.

With that issue set aside, Mike Hocking recalled Lisa to the stand.

As an eighth grader, Lisa's life had been turned upside down. During her morning testimony, she would occasionally smile or chuckle when asked a question, and it was purely out of nervousness. The assistant prosecutor didn't want the jury to get the wrong impression of Lisa, so he asked her about it.

"And can I ask what you have in your hands?" he asked her.

"Pictures."

"What are those pictures of?"

"My friends," she said.

"And why do you have those? To keep you company?"

"Yes."[172]

With that, Mike Hocking resumed his questioning about the day of the assault.

To be certain the jury hadn't lost track, Hocking highlighted her testimony about running from the house nude with her hands tightly bound behind her back, and he had her describe how a truck had stopped to help her.

Lisa described a second car stopping and how she got in, still sobbing.

She also told the jury about getting into Barb Krapf's car and how the Krapfs had offered her some clothes to put on.

When the prosecutor asked how she got to the hospital, she said she was taken by ambulance, and her brother, along with Mrs. Krapf's daughter, was also in the ambulance.

Hocking handed a piece of evidence to Lisa on the stand. It was a green shirt.

Lisa said it was the shirt Miller was wearing on the day he attacked her.

---

172. People v Don G. Miller, May 1, 1979, 232

Hocking began going through the evidence and having Lisa identify each piece, including the top she had been wearing when she was attacked and the pants Miller had been wearing.

When Hocking produced the belt Lisa had been choked with, he asked her if it was the same belt. She told him she was wearing it that day, and she knew he had choked her with it because she saw the white of the belt as he wrapped it around her neck.

Each time Mike Hocking showed Lisa an exhibit, there was no objection by Tom Bengston.

"Are you absolutely sure that the defendant is the one who performed the attack that you described today?" he asked Lisa.

"Yes."[173]

Mike Hocking's questioning of Lisa was complete, at least for the moment.

The defense attorney began his questions by asking Lisa to describe the time frame from when she left the house to the point where she encountered his client, and she said she thought it was three or four minutes.

Bengston asked the young witness how long Miller had rubbed her back, and she said only a few seconds.

Lisa couldn't describe the length of the knife when the defense attorney asked her about it, but through Lisa's answers to his questions, Bengston made sure the jury knew that she was never stabbed, and the knife never touched her skin.

He asked Lisa if she had ever said anything to the man. When she said no, he asked if she had screamed, and she said no, and he asked if she had ever physically resisted the assault.

Again, Lisa said no.

---

173. People v Don G. Miller, May 1, 1979, 247

Bengston also asked her if the man had ever hit her with his hand or a fist.

"No."

"Did this person ever kiss you or any part of your body?"

"No."[174]

As Don Miller's attorney was nearing the end of his cross-examination, he had her describe how she escaped through the front door.

When he finished, Mike Hocking stood and said he had a few more questions for Lisa.

"Mr. Bengston asked you, Lisa, if you offered any resistance throughout this event. What resistance could you offer when you were bound and gagged? Was there anything at that time you think that you could have done?"

"No."

"From the time, Lisa, that you were confronted by the defendant with the weapon, the knife, and the time that you ran out of the house, were you in fear of your life?"

"Yes."[175]

With that, Mike Hocking had finished.

Lisa quietly stepped down, and at 2:20 p.m., the assistant prosecutor called her brother Randy to the stand.

Randy, just a year younger than Lisa, began his testimony much like his sister had. He described the afternoon and how he had been fishing in the lagoon behind the house. He described the neighborhood where he lived and told Mike Hocking the closest neighbor was about five hundred yards away.

Randy was asked about coming around the front of the garage with his fishing gear, and he described a car in the driveway, even noting a crack in the windshield on the passenger side.

---

174. People v Don G. Miller, May 1, 1979, 253

175. People v Don G. Miller, May 1, 1979, 258

Randy said that when he saw a man in the house, he thought it was a contractor coming to do some repairs.

The teen began to describe how the assault had occurred, and he said he hadn't seen the knife, but could feel it pressed against his neck.

As Hocking presented photos for Randy to look at, the teen described each point in the photos where he had stood when he was confronted by Miller.

"What happened inside the bedroom?" Hocking asked.[176]

Randy said Miller began trying to slit his throat with the knife. He was yelling as it was happening and was somehow able to grab the knife with his right hand and throw it under the bed.

The jury was paying close attention to Randy's description of the attack, but it was time for a break. When the judge and attorneys returned to the courtroom, before the jury was brought back in, Tom Bengston renewed an earlier motion to have the jury sequestered, basing his request on the news article published that morning that had been mentioned earlier by Judge Robinson. The article had mentioned Don Miller being charged in two other homicide cases. Bengston told the judge he was satisfied thus far that the jury hadn't seen or read the article, but he was trying to anticipate any problems that might arise down the road.

Hocking responded to Bengston's request by telling the judge he was satisfied the jury hadn't seen the article, and he was confident they would take their charge by the Court very seriously, yet he deferred to Judge Robinson for the final decision on sequestration.

Bengston's motion was denied.

After the jury was brought back into the courtroom, Randy walked back up to the witness stand, and Mike Hocking renewed his questioning.

---

176. People v Don G. Miller, May 1, 1979, 271

The assistant prosecutor had Randy look at photos from his bedroom and describe which bed he had thrown the knife under and where he was lying as Miller sat on his back.

"What did the defendant do to you, Randy, after you threw the knife away?"[177]

The young teen began to describe how Miller had started to choke him with his bare hands. He was having a hard time breathing and quickly passed out.

"What is the first thing you remember when you woke up?"[178]

When he woke up, he had two stab wounds in his chest. He tried to use the phone, then made his way downstairs as he was bleeding from the stab wounds and started for the open front door.

"I saw a car taking off out of the yard, and I saw a pickup truck in the driveway with a man. He was out there."[179]

It was the same car he had seen in the drive.

Hocking moved to the point where James Regan had found Randy near the front door and asked if he had said anything to Randy.

"Yes. He told me to sit there, you know, just lay down and relax, and he was saying some kind of numbers... I think they were license plate numbers."[180]

The judge knew it was getting late as Hocking finished his questioning of Randy.

Tom Bengston began his cross-examination at 3:20 p.m. by asking the boy about his fishing gear and having him describe it. He asked briefly about the conversation Randy had with Miller when he first saw him in the house, then confirmed that Miller wasn't wearing any gloves. When

177. People v Don G. Miller, May 1, 1979, 280
178. People v Don G. Miller, May 1, 1979, 281
179. People v Don G. Miller, May 1, 1979, 283
180. People v Don G. Miller, May 1, 1979, 284

asked if Miller was wearing anything across his face, Randy said no.

After Randy's questioning was done, Mike Hocking called Delta Township's Fire Chief Ken Dorin to the stand.

Chief Dorin said he had been driving northbound on Canal Road on the day of the assault, and he described his car with the Motorola fire department radio in it.

The chief was very precise as he described how he had seen a young female run from a drive on the west side of the road as he came across the highway overpass. He could see she was nude, and he saw a green pickup coming from the opposite direction stop to help her.

Dorin said that as the pickup was pulling into the drive at the house where the girl had run from, the driver yelled at him to pick up the girl, which he did. She was bound with her hands behind her.

He told the jury about Lisa's frantic cries and how she had pleaded for him to help her because she had been raped. As she started to calm down, she told him there was man in the house stabbing her brother, and then looked over her shoulder and saw him in the front yard of the house.

Hocking showed the green shirt to Dorin. He identified it as the shirt Miller had on the day of the assault. He also identified Miller in the courtroom as the same man he had seen on the day of the assaults.

Dorin described Miller's car, identified the necktie that had been around Lisa's neck when she ran from the house, and identified the second tie she was bound with. He was given the license plate number by James Regan and said he had written it down as Regan told him the numbers. The box he'd written the license plate number down on was turned over to police as evidence, and Dorin read the numbers out loud for the jury.

Dorin had also helped Randy as he lay near the front door and told the jury how serious he felt the stab wounds were to the teen.

Bengston passed on any questions for the chief.

James Regan was called next, and Hocking led him through his contact with Lisa on August 16, 1978.

As he got to the point where Regan actually encountered her for the first time, he asked, "Can you describe what she looked like at this time?"

"She was naked. She had a necktie around her neck. She ran out the front door and there were some bushes in front of the house. She ran in front of the bushes and out in the street and down the road, into my truck. She was completely naked with the exception of a necktie around her neck, and her hands were tied behind her, and she was hysterical, screaming."[181]

Regan didn't know how old she was, only that she was a young girl.

Regan continued, "She had blood on the corners of her mouth, and there was blood down the front of her body, but I didn't notice any cuts on her. But she did have blood coming from her mouth."

Regan pulled into the driveway to block Miller's car in after he had yelled to Chief Dorin to grab Lisa.

The witness told the jury about the very brief conversation he had with Miller and how Miller had run by him to get to the car, then locked the door and made his escape.

Regan said he had written down the license plate number and had kept repeating it out loud at the scene so he wouldn't forget it.

Hocking's last question to Regan was if there was any doubt in his mind that the man in the courtroom was the same man he had seen that day, and Regan said he was certain.

As Tom Bengston stood at the defense table, he asked James Regan to describe the encounter with Miller, and if he would characterize the man as soft-spoken.

---

181. People v Don G. Miller, May 1, 1979, 307

Regan agreed, and he said Miller never cursed at him, and he hadn't seen any type of a weapon.

Much like the previous witnesses, Bengston's cross-examination was brief.

At 10:05 the following morning, with attorneys at both tables and Don Miller in the courtroom, witness testimony continued with Cheryl Krapf, the young friend of Lisa whose mother had been driving by the house when Lisa fled.

Cheryl described what she had seen that day and the condition Lisa was in when they first saw her, then described both James Regan and Don Miller standing in the driveway. At fourteen, Cheryl was the same age as Lisa and just as hesitant about testifying.

Hocking asked Cheryl how it was that Lisa got into their car, and she said they had turned around because they were the only females there to help her.

Cheryl said that Lisa didn't have any clothes on, she still had a necktie knotted around her neck, and her hands were still bound behind her back with pantyhose that were tied in small knots. She said Lisa was crying and telling them that "he" had tried to kill her, and she kept asking if Randy was okay.

"Did you talk to either Lisa or Randy inside the ambulance?" Hocking asked.

"I talked with Lisa, and Lisa talked to Randy. But I never talked to him. She just asked me if I would come with her to the hospital."[182]

Mike Hocking looked down at the legal pad on the table with his scribbled notes.

When Bengston began asking Cheryl questions, he wanted to know if Lisa Gilbert had told her that the man who had done this to them had used a kitchen knife from their house.

---

182. People v Don G. Miller, May 2, 1979, 327

Cheryl remembered a conversation with Lisa about Randy getting stabbed, but nothing about a kitchen knife.

Bengston showed her the statement she had written on August 16, 1978. As she looked it over, he asked her, "And in part, does your statement at page two provide, quoting, 'When Lisa talked to me, she said she just came in the house, and he used one of their knives to stab Randy.' Is that your statement of August 16, 1978?"[183]

She said it was.

Bengston was trying to impeach her testimony. It was the last question he had asked her. When Hocking began his re-direct, he simply asked if she had made reference to the bindings on Lisa's hands in her statement, and Hocking had her describe them again.

Cheryl's mom, Barb Krapf, testified right after her daughter, and she too described coming across Lisa running down the road nude. She said Lisa's face was bloody, and she was running and screaming for help.

Just as Cheryl had, she described the events exactly as everyone else and the very brief exchange with the killer.

Hocking redirected his questioning to Lisa's condition when she got in the Krapf car.

"The little girl had nothing on whatsoever. She just was tied up."

Mrs. Krapf said she tried desperately tried to untie the knots to free Lisa's hands, but someone else had to do it, and then she was able to get some clothes for her.

"I just talked to her and tried to comfort her because she kept crying for Randy, her brother. And so I just tried to comfort her, and I tried to find something to cover her body."[184]

---

183. People v Don G. Miller, May 2, 1979, 331
184. People v Don G. Miller, May 2, 1979, 339

James Regan had given her the license plate number, and she wrote it down on a picture packet. She identified it when Hocking showed it to her.

As Tom Bengston cross-examined Mrs. Krapf, she said Lisa hadn't spoken to her about what happened inside the house.

Bengston's point was to confirm that Lisa had told her about Miller using a knife from the kitchen to stab Randy. Like he had done with her daughter, Bengston had Barb Krapf refresh her memory by reading a statement she had given to a detective on the evening of the assault.

Hocking's next witness was the woman who had seen Lisa run from the house and realized she was in trouble. She could see Lisa was nude.

"How do you know she was in trouble?" Hocking asked.[185]

She described a horror-struck look on the teen's face.

As she passed Lisa, she began to slow down and looked in her rearview mirror to see James Regan stopping to help her, so she figured Lisa was in good hands and continued driving south over the highway. Several minutes later, a car passed her. "It was a two-lane road, and the car was passing me so, going against traffic on the other side of the road and going very fast, and not pulling in between the cars, just zipping down the wrong side of the road. And it occurred to me he might have had something to do with the girl."[186]

She wrote down the license plate on the car, and she recited Don Miller's license plate in the courtroom from memory, in addition to describing the car. She also looked at the photo of Miller's car and identified the car along with the license plate as the same car she had seen.

After Hocking's questions, Bengston asked her to describe the speed of the car that passed her. She said she

185. People v Don G. Miller, May 2, 1979, 348
186. People v Don G. Miller, May 2, 1979, 350

was traveling at forty-five or fifty miles per hour and the car that passed her was going at seventy or eighty.

It was almost eleven a.m. when Deputy Dave Bankhead was called to the stand.

Bankhead described everything he had seen and done, including searching the house for more victims and a possible weapon. He told the Court about being given the license plate number and checking the registration.

Deputy Bankhead also described going to the hospital three days after the assault to photograph the kids' injuries.

One by one, Hocking continued to call the police officers who were on the scene and having them recount what they had done. Together, they pieced together each small segment. As part of his questioning, Hocking accounted for each piece of evidence and how it was collected, tagged, stored, and eventually sent to the crime lab.

As the third day of trial continued, the emergency room doctor who had treated Lisa was called as a witness.

The doctor described the hemorrhages he saw on Lisa, saying, "Well, from the neck up, her face, head, ears, were totally covered with what we call petechial hemorrhages."[187] He looked directly at the jurors, describing small surface hemorrhages on Lisa's face. He said they were so thick they gave her a darker complexion from the neck up. He added that the blood vessels in the whites of Lisa's eyes were ruptured too.

The jury was listening intently when the doctor said there were areas of linear bruising around Lisa's neck, in addition to more petechial hemorrhages and lineal markings around each breast. He also found there was bruising around her wrists and slight bruising around each ankle.

"Sir, can you explain the possible causes of these petechial hemorrhages about the face that you noticed?" Hocking asked.

---

187. People v Don G. Miller, May 2, 1979, 391

"Well, petechial hemorrhages of that nature are due to increased back pressure to the blood vessels, plus the loss of oxygen, and blood seeps into the tissues. And I would say in the area they were located, together with the markings found on the neck, indicated to me that she had been choked."[188]

That wasn't good enough. Hocking wanted the jury to know how serious the strangulation of Lisa had been. He asked how much pressure it would take to cause those types of injuries to Lisa.

The doctor said it would take a great deal of pressure, adding, "I would say the choking would be a very serious attempt to either subjecting her to unconsciousness, or even killing." Then explaining the injury pattern to Lisa's ankles and wrists, he said it appeared she had been bound because of the linear bruising around those areas.

Hocking showed him a photo of Lisa taken three days after the assault while she was still in the hospital and asked the doctor about her eye.

He said her left eye was the one particularly affected by the hemorrhages in her eye. "There were so many of them that the white of the eye was totally red with hemorrhage."[189]

As the prosecutor wrapped up his questioning, he had the doctor describe the other injuries to Lisa that indicated she had been raped.

The doctor said the injuries Lisa sustained from being raped hadn't been caused by some other medical condition, and they weren't caused from her menstrual cycle.

The second ER doctor also testified.

Asked to describe the wound he observed on Randy Gilbert, the doctor said he had found three knife wounds.

188. People v Don G. Miller, May 2, 1979, 392
189. People v Don G. Miller, May 2, 1979, 394

Two of the stab wounds were located over his heart and one was at the base of his neck.

"And, sir, was there a way for you to gauge the depth of these chest wounds?" Hocking asked.[190]

The doctor hadn't been able to probe the stab wounds on Randy without introducing air into them, and Randy had already been suffering from a ten percent collapse of his lung. Hocking wanted the jury to understand how serious the stab wounds were.

"But the wounds were deep enough to pierce the space, to get into the space of air between the lung itself and the chest material?"

"Yes, that's my judgement."[191]

The doctor described how low Randy's hemoglobin level was when he was brought into the emergency room and said it was caused by a large loss of blood, and the knife wound on Randy's neck was very similar to the two in his chest.

Mike Hocking moved his questioning to Randy's face, and like the doctor who had just testified about the petechia caused to Lisa's face, he described the same thing. He added, "These spots conform to or are consistent with the history Randy gave to me about being choked to unconsciousness."

When Hocking asked about the amount of pressure it took to cause Randy's condition, the doctor said it was severe. The development of hemorrhage in his eyes had continued for several days, and by the third day after being admitted, the whites of his eyes were almost completely replaced by collections of blood.

The doctor had also found petechiae in the ear canal, and to him, that indicated severe strangulation. They were also in Randy's scalp, on the face, the cheeks, and on his neck.

---

190. People v Don G. Miller, May 2, 1979, 404
191. People v Don G. Miller, May 2, 1979, 406

Norm Kelley had been sitting with Hocking throughout the trial as the investigating officer. He stood and walked toward the witness stand as his name was called as the prosecution's next witness.

Kelley began his testimony by accounting for each piece of evidence he had brought to court, then he described Miller's car and the tire marks left at the Gilbert home caused by Miller as he fled.

Mike Hocking had several pieces of evidence introduced as exhibits through this process, but his questioning of Kelley was done.

Surprisingly, Tom Bengston didn't ask the detective anything.

The next witness was Don Miller's supervisor from the bookstore where he worked as the store detective.

Miller's supervisor said he had been hired by Intercept Security and the company scheduled him at the store.

When Hocking asked if she had seen him on August 16, 1978, she said that particular day was the only day she had spoken to him about watching a specific area in the store because some things had come up missing during the lunch hour. She told Hocking she had talked to him between eleven and noon. At the time, he was wearing a dark green shirt and dark colored pants with dress shoes. He never wore blue jeans.

She went on to identify the shirt that had been entered as an exhibit as the shirt Miller had been wearing on the day of the assault.

Like many of the other witnesses presented by Mike Hocking, Tom Bengston had nothing to ask her.

Mike Hocking had slowly and methodically built his case against Don Miller. He watched Miller as each person testified against him. Miller never made eye contact with Hocking, and as each witness was questioned, Hocking would look back at Miller's hands. He couldn't help but wonder what else those hands had done, and to whom.

The assistant prosecutor called Officer Rick Westgate to the stand.

Westgate described Miller's arrest, step by step, and described what he'd been wearing when he was arrested.

Bengston only wanted to know if his client had offered any resistance when he was arrested, or if he'd made any spontaneous statement, and Westgate said no.

It was late in the third day, after the jury had left the courtroom, when Judge Robinson asked Tom Bengston if he wanted to put something on the record.

Bengston had asked the Court not to make reference to the jury about mental retardation as part of their insanity defense. "It was our judgment to give the instruction of mental retardation would be unduly made, and that's what prompted us to make the request to the Court."

Judge Robinson replied, "I agree with you, and I take it you have no objection, Mr. Hocking?"

"No. That's correct, Your Honor."[192]

With that, the forensic testimony would begin the following day.

---

192. People v Don G. Miller, May 2, 1979, 445

16

It was Thursday, May 3, at ten when the trial of Don Miller resumed.

Mike Hocking began with presenting testimony by the lab specialists from the MSP crime lab.

The first to testify said he'd taken photos and tire impressions at the Gilbert house on the day of the rape, and he also took impressions from the tires on Miller's car. When he compared them, the tread design, pattern design, and the tire characteristics were all consistent with each tire on the car.

Hocking showed him the green shirt that had been admitted as an exhibit and asked him where he had found it. It was found it in the trunk and he had turned it over to the Serology Unit to be analyzed for body fluids. He also identified the pants found in the trunk and said those had been turned over to the unit also.

Tom Bengston didn't challenge any of his testimony.

Hocking called a second lab specialist who had been at the house and asked him what he had taken as evidence. He described searching the master bedroom where Lisa had been assaulted, and he described the clothing he had collected. He also told the jury he had collected a portion of the blue and white belt that Lisa had been wearing.

The emergency room doctor who had taken samples from Miller on the night he was arrested testified very briefly, and he said he had taken blood, saliva, and hair from Miller.

When Bengston started his cross-examination, he asked if the doctor had located any blood on the inside of Miller's thighs or on his penis, and the doctor said he hadn't.

Bengston also asked if the doctor had found evidence in the pubic area, and again, the answer was no.

Mike Hocking was moving through his witnesses pretty quickly. Another lab specialist from the state police was called to the stand.

He said he'd been sent to the Gilbert home to help process the crime scene, as he was in the Microchemical Unit. He was sent to the master bedroom to look for the possibility of seminal stains on the floor, and he used a black light to search the carpet for possible stains.

"We found one big stain which we determined was not a seminal stain at the time, and we found several smaller ones that indicated they might be semen," he said.[193] He tested smaller areas of stains and collected them to take them back to the laboratory. They were found near the foot of the bed in the master bedroom. In a photo, he identified the area in the master bedroom where they were collected and identified the court exhibits as the actual samples that he had collected.

The lab technician told the jury that he'd been directed to go to the Delta Township Fire Station early in the evening on August 16 to process Don Miller's hands. He said he had taken fingernail scrapings from his hands and described swabbing Miller's hands with cotton swabs.

When Hocking asked him what effect washing hands would have on the validity of any eventual tests, he said any evidence would likely be washed away.

Bengston took a quick turn at the witness by asking the purpose of taking fingernail scrapings.

The tech explained how scrapings are used to try to place a defendant back at the scene of the crime.

Bengston asked him if it was possible that they might not see something using a microscope that is actually there, and the lab technician admitted it was a possibility.

---

193. People v Don G. Miller, May 3, 1979, 463

Most of the evidence retrieved by the lab specialists from the Gilbert home had been turned over to the Serology Unit. The lab specialist from serology was the next witness to testify and had an impressive resume.

At the start of his testimony, Hocking needed the jury to understand what serology meant.

"Serology, in itself, deals with the analysis of serum, which is present in blood. Serology, in general, is the analysis of blood and its different components. Forensic serology deals along the same lines, although modifying methods for the interpretation of blood staining."[194] It could deal with the examination of other bodily and physiological fluids.

When Hocking asked about the fingernail scrapings he had analyzed, he said he had found nothing significant in them. He said he also found nothing when asked about the swabs from Miller's hands. The tests were dependent on what time they were taken with relation to what they were looking for, and any hand washing would interfere with the analysis.

Mike Hocking knew the lab specialist had examined the evidence taken from Lisa at the hospital and hadn't found any semen or public hairs.

"Your lack of finding these, your lack of finding, seeing in the vaginal area, does that rule out sexual intercourse?" Hocking asked.

"No, not necessarily."[195]

Tests had been done on the carpet taken from the master bedroom and there was a screening test done for semen.

He said human semen has a uniquely high concentration of acid phosphate, and the mere fact that the test came up positive was indicative of the presence of semen.

---

194. People v Don G. Miller, May 3, 1979, 471
195. People v Don G. Miller, May 3, 1979, 475

"After I conclusively identified the presence of semen, the samples were submitted to trying studies, mainly in the ABO blood group. And unknown portions of the carpeting were also tested."[196] The tests had been inconclusive, but he was able to positively identify semen.

When the specialist was handed a pair of men's white undershorts, he explained he had examined them at the lab and had found blood mixed with semen on the inside of them, but hadn't found any hairs or fibers. He tried to do secretion studies but they came back inconclusive. He added that it was a very light smear. "That might account for not coming up with the blood type, but also one has to take into account the presence of the mixture of semen and blood which could interfere with any blood typing results."[197]

Tom Bengston wanted to know if any tests were conducted on the shirts that Hocking had introduced as exhibits, so on cross-examination he asked the lab specialist if he had done any tests on them. The specialist had tested two small white stains on the green shirt, but the tests indicated they weren't semen stains.

Bengston was already building his closing argument. He scribbled notes with each answer.

Roger Bolhouse was Hocking's next witness. Bolhouse worked in the Latent Print Unit of the crime lab and identified a latent fingerprint he had compared with the inked fingerprints of Don Miller after his arrest. Hocking left it at that and called his next witness, Lieutenant Lewis Wilson.

The lieutenant told the jury that a fingerprint is simply a reproduction of the ridge structure that appears on the underside of the finger on a smooth surface.

---

196. People v Don G. Miller, May 3, 1979, 476
197. People v Don G. Miller, May 3, 1979, 479

Explaining how an identification was made, Lieutenant Wilson said it was made with a small magnifying glass under laboratory conditions. Wilson had looked for certain conditions in the fingerprint patterns and compared those conditions with both unknown latent prints and with known inked impressions. When enough of the characteristics match, an identification was made. Wilson identified the five characteristics he looked for in a fingerprint, describing them as a ridge ending, a bifurcation, a short ridge structure, a ridge dent, and an enclosure.

Hocking produced an item he intended to introduce as an exhibit, and Wilson identified it as the print he had lifted from the front door of the Gilbert house. "This particular lift came from the inside of the front door of the residence. Not the storm door, but the main front door of the residence on the inside portion, three inches above the knob."[198] Wilson had lifted the fingerprint from the door and preserved it.

Hocking asked if had an opinion about the comparison he'd made with Don Miller's inked impressions after his arrest.

Wilson said the print was made by the same finger that made the left ringer finger of the inked impressions he had. There were eighteen points of comparison between the two, and there was an unwritten policy at MSP that at least eight points of comparison were required for an identification. His identification had far exceeded their unwritten rule.

Showing Wilson the next two proposed exhibits, Hocking asked him to identify them, and Wilson said they were photographic enlargements of the fingerprint on the door at the Gilbert house and the number 9 digit from the inked impressions he compared it to, and he explained each point of identification for the jury.

Tom Bengston already knew his client's fingerprint had been found inside the house, and that's why he had switched

198. People v Don G. Miller, May 3, 1979, 490

to the insanity defense. He knew it was his only option. The defense attorney had nothing for Wilson.

"Call your next witness, Mr. Hocking," Judge Robinson said.

"Your Honor, the People rest."[199]

Judge Robinson, along with the attorneys, had anticipated using the entire day to finish the testimony of the prosecution witnesses, but it had gone much quicker than they expected. Bengston's witnesses would start the next morning.

As Judge Robinson entered the courtroom on Friday, May 4, he knew the defense attorney's next motion would be for a directed verdict.

Asked if he had anything for the Court, Don Miller's defense attorney stood with a legal pad in hand and said he was asking the judge for a directed verdict on all three counts. He said a case hadn't been made against his client, and asked the judge to reduce the charges of attempted murder on Lisa and Randy. He also asked that the judge reduce the charge of sexual assault from first-degree to second-degree.

Hocking argued there was ample evidence that Miller had assaulted Lisa. From Lisa's testimony, it was clear she was choked with the belt, and when it broke, Miller tried to strangle her with his hands. He reminded the Court of the doctor's testimony about her injuries and how she was bound and gagged. "I think the area of the throat is a factor, and when an attack takes place manually, or with a weapon such as a belt, I don't know any better area to attack another person if one wants to commit the crime of murder."[200]

199. People v Don G. Miller, May 3, 1979, 498
200. People v Don G. Miller, May 4, 1979, 501

Mike Hocking moved to the assault on Randy by describing how he had been choked, and then stabbed. "I think the intent is clear Don Miller intended on the killing of Randall Gilbert."[201]

As Hocking argued against Bengston's motion about Lisa's rape, he highlighted that she was threatened with a knife, and while no knife was found, it was corroborated by Randy's testimony that he was threatened with a knife and then stabbed. He described Lisa's testimony, how she was raped, and he mentioned the doctor's testimony about her condition at the hospital when she was examined.

At the conclusion of his argument, he asked the judge to deny the defense attorney's motion for a directed verdict.

Bengston's motion was denied. The judge also knew there was another matter that the defense wanted to bring before the Court. With that, Bengston's colleague, Jonathan White, stood to address the Court.

White said that Don Miller had been subjected to interviews using sodium amytal; however, the defense and prosecution had agreed that the defense experts would not be allowed to testify about the opinions they arrived at from using the sodium amytal.

Judge Robinson said he would allow the experts to testify, based on their opinion, as to what they learned from the sodium amytal interview without disclosing the specific questions and answers. "I'm satisfied that the so-called truth serum tests have not reached the level of accuracy that the Michigan Courts are letting them into evidence, and I'm satisfied too, if they do allow them into evidence, there would be the strong risk that the jury would see their responses for their own purposes, that is to decide substantive matters in the case." The Judge continued, "The fact that truth serum was administered, I believe is admissible to establish a basis for the doctor's opinion as to

201. People v Don G. Miller, May 4, 1979, 502

the defendant's sanity or lack thereof, but not to establish the truth of the matters served therein."[202]

Hocking asked the judge to instruct the witnesses not to refer to sodium amytal as truth serum because it hadn't been found to be reliable when eliciting the exact truth from someone.

With everyone in agreement, the jury was led into the courtroom, and each juror took their seat for day five of Don Miller's trial. This would be Bengston's one chance to show the jury that his client was insane on August 16, 1978.

Bengston called Dr. Rudolph Bachman to the stand. Bachman was the president and co-owner of Metro-West Psychological Associates in Garden City, Michigan. As a certified consulting psychologist, Bachman was involved in testing both individual and group psychotherapy.

As the defense attorney finished going through Bachman's qualifications as an expert witness, Mike Hocking had the chance to question him.

"Sir, can you give us a definition of forensic psychology?" he asked.

"I would say forensic psychology deals with psychology of human behavior as it applies to legal issues and criminality."[203] He had examined about a dozen people regarding legal responsibility, and one-third of those weren't legally responsible.

"Is one-third of all the people that you've seen that you've come to the conclusion they are not legally responsible, have you seen any studies on the statistics of criminal population at large?"

"No."

"So, you don't know whether your one-third is consistent with the general population of alleged persons charged with crimes?"

---

202. People v Don G. Miller, May 4, 1979, 506
203. People v Don G. Miller, May 4, 1979, 512

"I don't know that, no," Bachman answered.[204]

When the prosecution was finished, Tom Bengston began his direct examination of Bachman by asking if he had seen Don Miller on January 15, 1979, at Bengston's own request.

Bachman had examined Miller at the Eaton County Jail and had done a clinical interview, in addition to three psychological tests: Bender-Gestault, the Rorschach, and the Thematic Apperception tests.

The Bender-Gestault test was a series of nine geometric designs. The person interviewed was asked to look at shapes and draw what he sees on a piece of paper. The test had two purposes. It was a screening for organic brain damage, but even more important was the question of personality and the question of organization, judgement, ability to see and to duplicate the figures.

When describing Miller's specific responses to the test, his renditions were meticulous, drawn with great care and with great diligence. Bachman said the renditions were constructed tight, and all of the figures were on the top half of the page. To Bachman, that indicated a kind of constriction. It was more than what one would normally expect to see.

On the back of the paper, almost all of Miller's figures showed through, which meant more than normal pressure was applied, and it coincided with issues of anger and what's done with anger.

Bachman felt Miller had both underlying anger and rage, and compared him to a coiled spring. On its surface, the spring looked compact and tight, but he felt there was a potential for sudden release with consequences.

"Its tremendous energy is ingested in containing the control, but even with that, with all that energy, it's not

204. People v Don G. Miller, May 4, 1979, 512

completed, indicating periods of loss of control and errors of judgement and errors of reproduction."[205]

Moving to the Rorschach test, it was both objective and projective. The objective test was clearly structured and looked for right and wrong answers. While the objective test might be a question such as "What is four dollars and five dollars?", the projective test was designed to be purposely ambiguous. The ambiguity allowed the subject to try to make sense out of them. The test used a series of ten inkblots.

When Don Miller was shown the first inkblot, it reminded him of a movie. He rotated the card several times. Bachman felt he was trying to structure the situation by asking how much time he had to answer. Miller's response was longer than average, and he finally described the inkblot as a beetle. He told Bachman there were wings, and at the bottom and sides were leaves under the trees. Miller felt the beetle was crawling around. When Miller asked the doctor a question about how the test was devised, Bachman said it showed suspicion and paranoid ideation.

When shown the second inkblot, Miller said it looked like a rocket ship saying, "And right here, the bottom, red, is an exhaust, and it's just traveling."

Bachman felt that Miller had identified motion in both inkblots, and that indicated an issue of control and losing control.

"Now the significant response is the rocket exploding. It reflects the explosions internally, specifically associated with rage."[206]

Miller described the third card as two people dancing to disco music as he laughed anxiously. Miller said, "Two bodies, two arms, legs, and looks like a disco place."[207]

---

205. People v Don G. Miller, May 4, 1979, 517
206. People v Don G. Miller, May 4, 1979, 522
207. People v Don G. Miller, May 4, 1979, 523

The doctor thought that because Miller was putting his own kinetics in the inkblot by saying that he knew a lot of dance moves; in a sense, he was losing the task.

Card four, the Father Card, was supposed to generate responses about Miller's relationship with his dad.

There was a long delay in Miller's response. The doctor's interpretation was guardedness and tightness. Miller thought it looked like petrified wood.

Bachman looked at the jury. "Can you imagine seeing someone that you've been involved with all your life as a petrified piece of wood or rock? The absence of feeling, the absence of relationship, the distance, the closed off quality to that?"[208]

Don Miller had looked at card five with a forty-five second delay and said it looked like a butterfly. He also asked Bachman what he thought it looked like. The analysis of Miller's response was that he was putting it off on someone else to decide what it was. Bachman said that indicated Miller was uptight.

When Miller described the next card as a nuclear explosion, Bachman told the Court, "Here's a man who outwardly is presenting a picture of control, of order, or stability, of an absence of feeling, an absence of kind of stoic intellectual view, and again, we get the explosion. It's an extremely rare response in card six."[209]

Bachman said that as Don Miller looked at inkblot seven, he again took a long time to answer and finally told Bachman it looked like an old horseshoe in terrible shape. It was supposed to be the Mother Card. Miller said it looked as if it had been exposed to the elements and was decayed.

The doctor said that the card not only represented a relationship with his mother, but also a relationship with women. But to Bachman, the response meant that women

208. People v Don G. Miller, May 4, 1979, 524
209. People v Don G. Miller, May 4, 1979, 525

are decayed, defective, and decomposed. There was a noticeable absence of any warmth in Miller's response.

Miller studied the eighth card for sixty seconds. "I guess I'm supposed to say something. I'm trying to analyze different things they might be and the question of the test and what it's all about."[210] Miller was trying to get back in control and told him, "This is the worst one of the whole bunch. Looks like something I've seen in an art museum. Nothing complicated about it. Some drawing, some painting. It sure isn't realism."[211]

Both card eight and card nine were purposefully in color, and that was to gauge Miller's response. Miller said, "The color, the green, pink, autumnally. I don't know if the word is in the dictionary. Autumn colors. Some are better than this."

To the doctor, there was a sort of criticism and negativism. He told the jury, "The anger seeps through, but again, he's thrown by the color."[212]

The last card was symmetrical, and Miller picked up on it immediately. "Symmetrical. School life. Symmetrical is very programmed, very laid out, programmed."[213]

Bachman said Miller was programmed. "He had a lifelong program of nice things, good things, religion in terms of goodness of the Word and rightness, and on the surface a very articulate, thoughtful, bright, seemingly kind individual." He added, "But underneath this, the explosions, the loss of control, the rage that's in this man, that's buried."[214] Dr. Bachman said that when the test was over, he asked Miller about getting angry.

"I never get angry."

---

210. People v Don G. Miller, May 4, 1979, 527

211. People v Don G. Miller, May 4, 1979, 527

212. People v Don G. Miller, May 4, 1979, 528

213. People v Don G. Miller, May 4, 1979, 528

214. People v Don G. Miller, May 4, 1979, 530

"Never?"

"Oh yes, I got angry once at my father, but it was only because I loved him. It was only out of love."[215]

Bachman told the jury that Miller had one other issue; he wasn't consciously aware of certain things. "There are parts in him that he has hidden from himself as well. There's a split. There's a good part, there's the angel, the good guy. And then there's the ugly, explosive, dangerous, painful part, the devil, the ugly part. That has to be separate."[216]

Dr. Bachman arrived at two diagnoses. Miller was psychotic and had a split personality. There were two sides. There were parts that were excluded from the other. He added, "As long as there's no rage, as long as there's no stimulus, as long as there's no triggering, he's quietly subdued...crazy." He added, "The other side is he's crazy, but not quiet and subdued, violent, explosive, like a railroad train trying to put on the brakes that you can't."[217]

Bengston finally asked if Miller was suffering from mental illness.

"Yes... The mental illness is not new. It's longstanding. It's been there for many years."[218]

Mike Hocking doubted the doctor's evaluation. He knew Don Miller wasn't insane, and he knew that as an assistant prosecutor, he had a huge responsibility. He had to tear down the doctor's testimony in order to prove there was no insanity. In the back of his mind, Hocking knew there was at least one woman who had been murdered, three others were still missing, and Miller was the man responsible.

When the assistant prosecutor began his cross-examination of Dr. Bachman, he asked if there would be an effect of some sort on his opinions and conclusions based

215. People v Don G. Miller, May 4, 1979, 531
216. People v Don G. Miller, May 4, 1979, 532
217. People v Don G. Miller, May 4, 1979, 536
218. People v Don G. Miller, May 4, 1979, 537

on the fact that Don Miller had been incarcerated for several months. Bachman believed the effect would be minimal.

Miller had been interviewed by Dr. Bachman behind bars in the old, dimly lit, two story Eaton County Jail, and Hocking asked if an office would have been more suitable for the interview.

"In terms of test responses themselves, no."[219]

Hocking moved to the test itself and wanted to know if Bachman had the accuracy of his diagnosis verified by anyone else. He asked if the doctor had any information about mental illness in the Miller family.

He didn't, and the prosecutor asked if the Miller family had relayed any behavioral problems they had had seen of Miller that might have verified his diagnosis.

"They described him pretty much as one half of the personality surface, being quiet, involved in religion, studious."[220]

As Mike Hocking moved into questioning Bachman about the inkblot tests, the doctor handed him a copy of Miller's drawings.

"Sir, what is there about the way the figures were copied that caused you to come to the conclusion, I believe, that he was overly controlled or compulsive, and was bunching the figures?" Hocking asked.

To the doctor, because the figures drawn by Miller were smaller, there was constriction to Miller's behavior.

"Let me stop you there, sir. How much bigger were the figures on the cards than they appear there?"[221]

"Oh, maybe a quarter." Bachman had told Miller to draw the figures as they were, but he had tightened them up.

219. People v Don G. Miller, May 4, 1979, 539
220. People v Don G. Miller, May 4, 1979, 540
221. People v Don G. Miller, May 4, 1979, 542

Hocking pointed out that there were no right or wrong answers to the test given to Miller, and asked if the examiner could inject his own personality into each card.

"No, not with me," Bachman answered.

"Isn't it true you have to, in fact, take your own training and experience and some of your own expressions to determine whether one is giving an unusual response?" Hocking asked.

"I'm interested in the normal level of responses, the location of the responses, determining the responses, and these things go into a trend that's developed and based on my understanding and experience with various personality types and clinical situations, diagnostic impressions made."[222]

Hocking moved to the cards shown to Don Miller by Dr. Bachman. Asking the doctor about the first card Miller had looked at, he said, "How do you know it didn't remind him of a movie?"

"Well, it did apparently, but not in any detail until you talk about the card itself," Bachman answered.

"What does that card look like to you, Doctor?" Hocking asked.

Bachman said the inkblot looked like a bat with a person in the center.

"Does everybody respond that way?"[223]

It was a common answer.

The assistant prosecutor wanted to know what it was about Miller's response to that specific card that led Bachman to conclusion that Miller had a paranoid ideation, and the doctor said it was because of Miller's delay in his response that suggested his difficulty with thoughts.

---

222. People v Don G. Miller, May 4, 1979, 545
223. People v Don G. Miller, May 4, 1979, 546

"Isn't it true that you asked him, instructed him to take his time?"[224]

Bachman admitted that each person is told to take their time, but in general, most people take between five to fifteen seconds to answer.

Hocking wasn't buying it.

"Doesn't the person's life history and life situations and experiences and hobbies, don't these things go into how quickly they might respond to a given form in response to something they've seen in the past?"

"You suggest he looks back over his life in terms of his hobbies before he responds?" Bachman asked Hocking.

The assistant prosecutor's voice boomed when he replied, "I'm not asking the question, Doctor. I'm asking for an answer. How can a person say the card looks like anything unless he's seen something similar in his past life?"[225]

Mike Hocking decided to ask the same question in a different way. "To say it looks like some leaves and looks like a beetle with wings, he would have had to have seen a beetle with wings or leaves from the past."

"Well, I've heard people call it a Martian, and I don't think they've seen a Martian."

Hocking was getting impatient. "All right, what is the answer to my question?"

"In general, that's true."[226]

Hocking asked if basic human intelligence had anything to do with the test, and the doctor wouldn't commit to a definitive answer.

The prosecutor moved to the next card, which was the one Miller had said looked like a rocket ship taking off, and

224. People v Don G. Miller, May 4, 1979, 547
225. People v Don G. Miller, May 4, 1979, 549
226. People v Don G. Miller, May 4, 1979, 550

he asked Bachman if the defendant had said the rocket was taking off or that it was in flight.

"He just said it looked like a rocket ship."

Hocking thought it sort of resembled a rocket ship too.

"That's one way of looking at it," Bachman answered.[227]

Mike Hocking still didn't believe the doctor's analysis. Why would a person seeing movement in the card indicate a lack of control?

The doctor said that most movement responses reflected human movement, though he clarified the amount of movement Miller was seeing was unusual.

As Hocking moved on to the father-figure card, Bachman said the normal response he gets from an evaluation would be a giant or even a monster.

The assistant prosecutor knew Miller's response was that it reminded him of petrified wood. He asked if the doctor ever inquired whether or not Miller was a collector of petrified wood.

"He mentioned that he associated to collecting some rocks."

"So that, in fact, he could have been comparing it to something he had seen in the past?"

"He did at that moment, yes."[228]

Asked if Miller's petrified wood response was less appropriate than a monster, Bachman said it was a distant response of what was considered a common response.

The assistant prosecutor thought Don Miller was faking many of his responses, so he asked the doctor if he knew what malingering meant.

Bachman said it meant faking, and there was a quick follow-up asking how the doctor would verify if someone was faking or lying.

"You can't fake it," Backman said.

---

227. People v Don G. Miller, May 4, 1979, 552
228. People v Don G. Miller, May 4, 1979, 554

"How do you know that, sir?"

"Because the individual doesn't know what's expected," he answered.[229]

Mike Hocking moved to the card that Miller said looked like a butterfly, and he asked Bachman if, to him, it looked like a butterfly.

"The point isn't what it looks like to me, okay? That happens to be a common response. However, people come up with a myriad of responses."[230]

As Mike Hocking continued moving through Don Miller's responses, he asked Bachman if he had ever asked Miller about reading materials available at the Eaton County Jail, and if any of those could have influenced Miller's answers.

"Only very remotely."

As Mike Hocking began asking Bachman about the Mother Card, he said, he wanted to know how the doctor had come to the conclusion that men are petrified rocks and women are defective and decomposed.

"All right, on card four, for example, he sees petrified wood and then associates rocks. It's an absence of feeling. It's a concrete, cold, inanimate sort of thing, and in contrast, for example, to a monster that someone might see, there's an element of fear perhaps. There's an element of awe."[231]

The prosecutor asked if Bachman had any historical data about Miller.

"Not at the time, but later."

Bachman said Miller was suspicious and hesitant during the evaluation. He knew Miller was concerned about any conclusion he might come up with after examining him, even though Bengston had asked him to be evaluated, and it

---

229. People v Don G. Miller, May 4, 1979, 554

230. People v Don G. Miller, May 4, 1979, 556

231. People v Don G. Miller, May 4, 1979, 558

wasn't an adversarial situation. He described Miller's state of mind as conscious, subconscious, and preconscious.

"But the fact that he didn't know of the other half would be predicated on your consideration that there is one, isn't that correct?"

"There is one," Bachman said.

"That's your opinion?"

"That's right."[232]

Bachman said multiple personality is a splitting of personality into separate components. The most popular example was that of *Sybil,* in which there were sixteen distinct personalities, some of which were aware of each other.

Mike Hocking knew the study of Sybil Dorset was a landmark case in psychiatry and psychology by establishing multiple personalities. He knew it was a long, drawn out process for a doctor to come to a diagnosis like that.

Hocking finally asked Bachman how many people he had diagnosed with multiple personalities.

The doctor said three, and was still treating a woman who had seventy-two personalities. He said Don Miller could have more than two personalities, but he didn't believe that either one was aware of the other. He added that multiple personality wasn't a psychosis, and the best term for it was neurotic.

Bachman described Miller's personalities and said one was good, upstanding, studious, religious, a model son and student, and was a good boy. He said the other personality was filled with rage and fury with little regard for relationships and people. That particular personality was angry with women, and he believed Miller experienced a devil in the other personality. With the first personality, he felt it was more of a Christ-like identification. All people

---

232. People v Don G. Miller, May 4, 1979, 561

have impulses, anger, and thoughts of various kinds, but people normally don't put a good and evil label on it.

The doctor felt Miller would become violent, though still trying to control it. He said it was a battle of good and bad, adding that once it was triggered, the bad would carry on until it was spent. He said that on August 16, 1978, he believed the rage in Don Miller was running. The rage had built slowly, and there was a period of intensity that peaked in a gradual decrease that resulted in a switch over to the good Don Miller.

When Hocking asked if Miller had ever had periods where he couldn't recall something, Bachman told him no, except for the incident for which he was being evaluated.

Mike Hocking moved to a state of mind called *dissociative reaction*, in which an individual disassociates himself from a particular experience, and he asked if Miller had ever mentioned periods he couldn't account for.

The only thing Miller had said was he didn't understand why he was being charged with rape and assault, and he didn't recall anything that would implicate him in those charges.

Bachman's first diagnosis was psychosis, and the multiple personality was incidental to that. The multiple personality wasn't his dominant diagnosis. Miller had never experienced any hallucinations, and there wasn't any evidence of any organic brain dysfunction.

Hocking felt he had gotten the answers he needed. As he sat down, Bengston's questions were brief.

Asked about neurosis, Bachman said it wasn't a mental illness, but it was characterized by feelings of guilt, anxiety, and tension.

"Did you offer any hesitancy in offering the opinion that you've already tendered to the jury that he's mentally ill and was not otherwise criminally responsible on August 16?"

"No."[233]

After the lunch recess, Judge Robinson kept the trial on track, and at 1:35 p.m., Tom Bengston called Dr. Dennis Koson to the stand. Dr. Koson was a psychiatrist from Ann Arbor who had also been asked to evaluate Don Miller, much like Bachman had.

Dr. Koson described his visit with Don Miller as a clinical interview done at the Eaton County Jail.

As he interviewed Miller, he had talked with him about his personal background. He asked Miller about his family, his parents, his own personal background in terms of school, upbringing, and the kind of family life he had.

Miller was mildly depressed during the interview; he looked withdrawn and kind of apathetic, much like he did in the courtroom. Koson said that, except for the day of the offense, his memory was generally good, and Miller appeared to be fairly bright and intelligent. At one point in the interview, Miller had become almost tearful, but never actually cried.

Tom Bengston asked his expert witness about Miller's emotional part of the interview, and Koson said the discussion had to do with the charge against him, being locked up in jail and not being with his family. The whole situation depressed him.

Miller had some disjointed recollections about the day of the offense, and he couldn't put them in order. He didn't have any memory of what happened during the time frame, and the rest of his recollections were vague. Koson said they were impressionistic. There were hints of illusions to him meeting someone he thought was a demon, but he couldn't tell Koson anything more than that.

Diagnostically, Koson felt Miller was fairly ill, and was schizophrenic. He said schizophrenia was a major mental

---

233. People v Don G. Miller, May 4, 1979, 576

illness, and he based his diagnosis on the history Miller had given him and Miller's personality.

The doctor had listened to Miller's sodium amytal interview, and felt he was suffering from mental illness, and he wasn't criminally responsible for what he had done. "I think, at the time, he was operating under delusion—a false, very outlandish belief that he was a product of his own sickness and his own psychology."[234] Koson said, "He must have told me ten times during the interview, 'I wouldn't do something like this, I'm a good Christian. I'm a youth minister. I don't lie.'"[235]

The doctor didn't believe Miller was lying. He believed he was covertly psychotic, meaning that someone only sees Miller when he's under stress, disturbed, or distressed. He said that otherwise, he's extremely polite, self-conscious, and shy. Miller's responses weren't unusual for someone who had been incarcerated.

When he was asked about how had come to his opinion about Miller based on his own interview and listening to the sodium amytal interview, Koson gave an example of someone walking up on the street who suddenly begins talking about demons and cults. "You don't have to be a psychiatrist to know that the guy is crazy," he said.

"Who conveyed these thoughts to you, sir?"

"Thoughts of demons?" Koson asked.

"Yes."

"He did."

"Don Miller?" Hocking asked the doctor.

"Yes."[236]

Hocking paused. He was more than skeptical now.

234. People v Don G. Miller, May 4, 1979, 588
235. People v Don G. Miller, May 4, 1979, 589
236. People v Don G. Miller, May 4, 1979, 599

Koson felt it was possible that Miller's incarceration, and the seriousness of the charges against him, could certainly be an excuse for him lying and bringing forth the demons.

"Do you have any control over any verification, Doctor, that you can explain to the jury that assures you that the demon defense, so to speak, is a result of mental illness and not an attempt to excuse his conduct and lay it on something such as a demon?"

"I wouldn't call the notion of demons or the like a defense. He was most reluctant to talk about it. Indeed, that's why we had to go so far as to have amytal."[237]

Mike Hocking was quick to ask what motivated Don Miller to have sexual intercourse with a demon.

"He wouldn't touch that with a ten-foot rosary, if I may use the term."[238]

Hocking turned toward the jury as he was speaking to Dr. Koson. He said the only information to validate Miller's story was that he was the one who had told the story, and Miller had told it to someone else under the influence of a barbiturate.

He turned back to face the doctor and asked if there were things at the scene that could show Miller's ability to conform to normal rules and regulations in society. As an example, he asked the doctor to suppose that someone was about to have sexual intercourse in a bedroom, and before the penetration, the person got up and closed the curtains.

"You seem to be saying that if someone shuts the drapes, that can only mean that they know they are doing something wrong. Is that what you are saying?"[239]

He was asking if the doctor had an opinion as to whether that might be a factor someone could consider, and Koson admitted it was a possibility.

---

237. People v Don G. Miller, May 4, 1979, 600
238. People v Don G. Miller, May 4, 1979, 601
239. People v Don G. Miller, May 4, 1979, 607

The prosecutor asked if another factor to consider would be a person who quickly fled the scene after committing a criminal act, and knew what he had done was wrong.

"It's a possibility, sure."

Assuming the person fled the scene and sometime within the next couple of hours, he changed his clothes for no apparent reason? He asked if that would be a factor someone would consider in trying to establish whether, at the time of the crime, that person knew that the conduct he was performing was wrong.

"Sure. You have to look at all of these," Koson said.[240]

Hocking's last hypothetical was if a person retrieved and disposed of a weapon involved in an offense, would it be another factor for someone to consider in trying to determine whether the defendant, or a patient, knew what he was doing was wrong.

"Again, you've got an apparent there. It's another factor, just as all the other questions you raised about all of the things that he did, sure."[241]

When Koson was asked about a person lying under sodium amytal, he said it was possible.

Hocking knew he had the doctor right where he wanted him. "Correct me if I'm wrong, isn't sodium amytal, if properly administered, similar to four or five shots of whiskey?"

"I would say it's closer to peppermint schnapps, but it's something in this area in terms of depressing effect."

Hocking asked if a person under the influence of peppermint schnapps was able to make up stories.

"I know five hundred people who can tell fish stories under peppermint schnapps. I go fishing with half of

---

240. People v Don G. Miller, May 4, 1979, 608
241. People v Don G. Miller, May 4, 1979, 608

them."[242] Again, he agreed with the prosecutor that people could tell lies even under the influence of sodium amytal.

Miller had understood that the purpose of the interview was to establish if he was legally responsible for the crimes he was charged with, and Koson agreed that it could have some effect on whether or not Miller was lying.

When Tom Bengston stood and began asking questions under re-direct, Koson told him he had an associate interview the Miller family for several hours to corroborate what he'd been told. He said that most people who are mentally ill don't have a history of mental illness in their family.

If a person looked strictly at the facts in the four hypothetical situations mentioned by Hocking, that person would say Miller knew what he was doing. But after his own interview with Miller, Koson said the root of the entire matter was Don Miller's crazy thinking.

Hocking had one last chance. He asked why there was no assault when Miller came face to face with James Regan.

Koson said Regan could have been the demon Miller was referring to, and Miller was afraid of him because he was a man and not a younger person.

"There are those types of distinctions, older demons and younger demons?"

Koson admitted that he really didn't know.

"Thank you."[243]

On Monday morning, Tom Bengston had two other psychiatric experts on his list of witnesses. Dr. Gerald Briskin was his first witness.

---

242. People v Don G. Miller, May 4, 1979, 609
243. People v Don G. Miller, May 4, 1979, 615

Dr. Briskin was the Director of the Department of Clinical Psychology at Wyandotte General Hospital in Wyandotte. Like the other two doctors, he had interviewed Miller at the request of Tom Bengston.

Briskin said Miller had no emotion in his answers during the interview. He found Miller to be a young man who was choirboy type. He had been religious since the age of eight, and had been raised in a family with strict moral values. Miller had never been encouraged to show feelings or emotions. He was devoid of feelings. He added that Miller didn't get angry, and the only thing he did to show enthusiasm was a slight smile. Briskin thought he was extremely intellectual, and very rational.

Miller had told the doctor that for his entire life, he had tried to do good, and no one had ever recognized it. He felt insignificant, and Briskin saw this as a departure from reality.

The doctor felt that Miller could be absolutely furious inside, yet still maintain that he never gets mad, and if he began to experience anger, he would go to bed and sleep for twenty-four hours.

"I thought I detected signs of a serious thinking disorder, schizophrenic in proportion with a lot of paranoid overtones."[244] He felt Miller was extraordinarily angry and paranoid and had a very significant mental disturbance.

Briskin learned in the interview that Miller accidentally killed a bird when he was five or six, and even to the point of the interview, he felt remorseful about it.

The doctor gave Miller two of the same tests that Bachman had given him, the Bender-Gestault and the Rorschach tests.

Miller began by describing the rocket taking off that he had described to Dr. Bachman. As he described the second card, Miller had said, "I guess you would say this is the

---

244. People v Don G. Miller, May 7, 1979, 630

ground, the black stuff, and this red stuff could be oil. The white is a cavity, either by drilling or natural, and the red stuff is oil going up, and there's some red stuff in the back that must have got in there somehow."

Briskin wondered why he didn't simply describe it as an oil well. He viewed Miller's description as blood spurting, and the cavity as filling a sharp object, or stabbing. He felt Miller was unconsciously releasing details of the crimes he was charged with. He felt it wasn't available to Don Miller in his conscious state, but it leaked out when he responded to the red shape on the card.

As Briskin described Don Miller's response to each card, he had an explanation for each of the responses. He finished with his analysis of the answers, and Bengston asked for his opinion.

"At that point, I was convinced that we were dealing with a very seriously disturbed young man who had a major psychiatric illness, but I wanted to know some more."[245]

Briskin said Miller had no recollection of the events on August 16, 1978, and he was perplexed when he was told about what had done. To the doctor, it meant Miller was repressing the events and suffering from amnesia.

Because of Briskin's belief that Miller was repressing the events, he thought of using sodium amytal for an interview. He thought it would reduce his conscious control and free the underlying repressive memories.

After the sodium amytal interview, Briskin felt that on the day of the rape, Miller had decompensated into a psychotic state, and he was so out of control that he was able to act out of impulses because his reality was distorted. The rage and anger Miller had been storing had ultimately broken loose.

Bengston moved toward the doctor's final opinion of what caused Don Miller to snap. He asked the doctor to

---

245. People v Don G. Miller, May 7, 1979, 657

take into account his opinion and the historical data he'd been provided by the family.

Briskin said Don Miller saw himself as a good force seeking out evil. He was seeking out evil places to rescue poor souls that were going to be gravely influenced by Satan. Based on everything he knew about Don Miller, he believed that his perception of the people he encountered on August 16, 1978, were evil demons, and he was frightened of them. Miller's impression was that those people were going to harm him, and he reacted.

"He was out of control," Briskin said. He emphasized that when Don Miller was out of control, he didn't look that much different from Don Miller in control.[246]

Briskin described Miller by associating him with a popular TV show. "Now it wasn't the question of Don decompensating into a raging incredible hulk, kind of dichotomy from the mild-mannered, I think it's Dr. David Banner, into this kind of terrible incredible hulk. Don would look very much the same."[247]

Briskin considered the possibility that Miller was lying during his interview, but he didn't feel that Miller had the ability to lie in the tests. "I think if he were coached, directed by a drama director, he couldn't have produced what we saw. It might just be impossible for him to be malingering and produce that kind of record."

"Having in mind the definition I previously addressed to you on mental illness, on August 16, 1978, was Don Miller, in fact, suffering from a mental illness?" Bengston asked.

"He was, indeed."[248]

As Hocking began his cross-examination, he asked Briskin if, in his report, he had written that Miller weighed each question very carefully during the interview.

246. People v Don G. Miller, May 7, 1979, 663
247. People v Don G. Miller, May 7, 1979, 664
248. People v Don G. Miller, May 7, 1979, 669

He had, and it was indicative of Miller's compulsive, careful, deliberate structure. He was very suspicious and paranoid, and he didn't like to reveal things about himself. When he did, he would respond in a tortuous way. The doctor said it was very difficult to follow what Miller was going through.

When Hocking asked if rage was more consistent with innocence, rather than guilt, Dr. Briskin said, "He had no knowledge of guilt."[249]

"Yes, but my question is, if he had knowledge of guilt, isn't the sublime attitude that he exhibited more consistent with knowledge of guilt than being enraged over something he knew didn't deserve being enraged about?"[250]

Briskin had seen many people who had knowledge of their guilt, yet their enraged sense of innocence was perfectly disguised.

"What if that's all he's got? What if the demon is all the excuse he has for his conduct?" Hocking asked.

"Under these circumstances, he's still psychotic. His anger, which he cannot accept, is projected to someone else, seeing them as trying to harm him. That's psychotic."[251]

Briskin said that during the sodium amytal interview, Miller's conscious and subconscious were both present at different times. Miller's use of religion substituted for his ability to relate.

When Dr. Briskin began describing his amnesia diagnosis, he said Miller was amnestic because, at that point, he was crazy.

"And that's a conclusion, isn't it, Doctor?"

"That's what it was all about, sir," Briskin answered.[252]

---

249. People v Don G. Miller, May 7, 1979, 675
250. People v Don G. Miller, May 7, 1979, 676
251. People v Don G. Miller, May 7, 1979, 677
252. People v Don G. Miller, May 7, 1979, 697

Moving back to the amytal interview, the doctor said a person has the ability to make up stories while under the influence of the drug. The drug puts someone to sleep much faster than five or six shots of whiskey, and there's no control. He described the process of administering it, saying it had to be injected in small increments to the point where Miller was drowsy and not quite conscious.

"Doctor, can you answer specific questions as to sexual intercourse with a supposed demon which he was to do away with? How does that compare?"[253]

Briskin's explanation was hard to believe, and the jury quickly picked up on it. Miller felt Lisa was trying to seduce him. He said those were Miller's own sexual feelings projected onto her in his psychotic state. Miller had seen Lisa as seductive and frightening, and it frightened him so much that he had to cover her head with the shirt she was wearing.

"Isn't it just as consistent, or even more consistent, that to cover one's face is so the person cannot see your face, or the actor's face, in this case, Don Miller's face?"[254]

The doctor said Lisa Gilbert had already seen Miller's face, and it was crazy to cover it. He didn't know what purpose it would serve.

The prosecutor pressed the doctor for an answer, saying, "My original question was, what was the purpose of having sexual intercourse with a demon, if that is in fact true?"

"Part of a crazy acting out."

"Is it your opinion that when he saw Lisa Gilbert, he thought she was demon?"[255]

Briskin said yes, but didn't have an explanation why Miller hadn't attacked her when he first saw her.

---

253. People v Don G. Miller, May 7, 1979, 701
254. People v Don G. Miller, May 7, 1979, 701
255. People v Don G. Miller, May 7, 1979, 702

Mike Hocking moved back to Miller's actions after the assault by asking the doctor if he could explain the motivation in changing clothes before going home, and Briskin explained it by saying that Miller, a very ostensibly neat person, suddenly found his clothes had gotten dirty.

As Hocking moved toward the end of his cross-examination, he asked if the doctor was aware that the test of insanity in Michigan was not just mere mental illness or distorted thought or mood, and he agreed.

"There's a substantial capacity to recognize the one's wrongfulness?" Hocking asked.[256]

Briskin agreed again, and he said the jury would have to weigh the professional evidence to decide if Don Miller had realized the wrongfulness of what he'd done.

Tom Bengston stood as Hocking sat down, and he asked what type of conduct would be expected if Miller had delusions of satanic beings in the Gilbert home.

Don Miller would behave much like he would normally. He said Miller saw Lisa Gilbert as threatening and dangerous to him. Miller was only trying get her to tell him where the cult people were in the house. He said Miller heard demonic laughter, and he saw Randy coming into the house. Seeing Randy as threatening and dangerous, he attacked him.

Briskin didn't believe Don Miller went in that house with the intent to kill Lisa. While he had ample opportunity to do it, he said the acts were irrational, and they didn't make sense.

After an afternoon break, Tom Bengston called his last witness, Dr. Arthur Hughett.

Dr. Hughett agreed with Dr. Briskin in the sense that he felt Don Miller was a paranoid schizophrenic.

Like the other doctors, Dr. Hughett maintained Miller was withdrawn and kept very much to himself. Other than

---

256. People v Don G. Miller, May 7, 1979, 713

the people he might relate to through his religion, Don Miller didn't have any close friends. He was strangely rigid, circumstantial, very guarded, and Hughett felt Miller was terribly intellectual. He said Miller weighed and measured every single word that he said, and he was terribly overcontrolled.

Dr. Hughett had made his diagnosis within the first fifteen minutes of the interview.

Dr. Hughett felt Miller was psychotic on that day and wasn't in any emotional condition to have been responsible. He said Miller's awareness of reality was grossly distorted and he lacked the capacity to appreciate the wrongfulness of his acts.

Asked if there were symptoms to help him conclude Miller was paranoid schizophrenic, Dr. Hughett told the jury he had a tremendous amount of anger. Though Miller was full of rage, he had no perception of it, and he was using a defense structure to imprison himself from being aware of it.

Hocking began his cross-examination later in the day, and he tried to make a point to the jury when he asked if Hughett was familiar with the term sociopath, and if he would consider that a mental illness.

Hughett told him that sociopathy was generally not considered a mental illness, and he agreed with Hocking that some people might use their religion as a blanket-type alibi for antisocial behavior.

Hughett said that Miller was trying to answer the questions too appropriately.

Mike Hocking moved to the possibility of Miller lying during the interview with Dr. Hughett. He asked about Miller's actions of checking to see when Lisa's father would be home, shutting the drapes, and gagging his victim, but Hughett didn't think it would take Miller out of his delusion.

As the day's proceedings wound down, Mike Hocking had rebuttal witnesses he intended to call, but it would have to wait until the following day.

The jury was in place by 8:30 the following morning, and Mike Hocking called Dr. Lynn Blunt as his first rebuttal witness.

Blunt hadn't seen any sign of mental illness in Miller when he was interviewed. He said Miller used his religion inconsistently as a convenience, and he would invoke a tremendous amount of religiosity whenever it served his purpose, but would violate other areas of it when it didn't.

Don Miller was adamant in his dislike of violence, and he kept anger bottled up inside him. Blunt felt Miller was an extremely angry person who didn't openly show it. He was certain Miller's underlying rage could cause a psychotic break and could result in an outburst of his temper, loss of control, or even aggressive impulses.

The doctor said Miller wasn't confused when he was interviewed, but was guarded and very careful about any information he offered. He weighed his responses in terms of what would be good and what wouldn't be good. He said it wasn't a case of not being able to answer a question, but a case of choosing not to answer in a couple of situations.

When the prosecutor asked if he'd seen any evidence of Miller lying, Blunt said there was historical data about Miller, and both he and the other doctor had picked up some falsehoods in the interview. Miller claimed he couldn't recall certain details, but in general, he had recalled several things that had gone on that day.

Blunt felt any substantial gaps in Miller's memory were on the basis of his withholding information or choosing not to talk about it.

Miller never mentioned any demons to Blunt. That information came in the form of a letter. He said Miller's letter was about a dream he had had about demons and how he'd been in pursuit of them on August 16.

Hocking needed to make a point to the jury. "Doctor, did you ever suggest, as an aid in accessing Mr. Miller, that he submit to an examination under the influence of sodium amytal?"

"Yes, we did."[257]

Dr. Blunt told the jury he had suggested either sodium amytal or hypnosis, and Miller had replied he couldn't because it was against his religion. He added that Miller said he was not to take any drugs.

The doctor was certain Miller was using religion whenever it served his purpose; he was also certain that Miller wasn't suffering from multiple personalities.

Hocking knew that Dr. Blunt had extensive experience with sodium amytal, so he asked for an explanation. Blunt said it was an intravenous barbiturate, and it brought the person under the control of anesthetic. He described it as the pre-anesthetic one might get prior to an operation. Sodium amytal lowered a person's resistance and put them in a twilight phase. To make his point, he said it was like giving someone eight ounces of alcohol. The result would be a lowering of the person's resistance and they would talk more.

Blunt said he'd used it about twenty-five times in forensic psychiatry, but because people were able to control themselves under sodium amytal, they were able to make things up.

Mike Hocking had Blunt read the definition of mental illness in the state of Michigan, and he asked him if he felt, after his interview with Don Miller, if Miller was suffering

---

257. People v Don G. Miller, May 8, 1979, 765

from any substantial or significant problem or disorder with his thoughts.

"No, I did not." Miller didn't have anything that affected his capacity to recognize reality.[258]

Dr. Blunt said the person who committed the crimes against the Gilbert children was aware of reality and what was going on at the time. He said the person was prepared and organized, and he responded when Lisa's brother came into the house by attacking him, and then he left.

Blunt had watched the sodium amytal interview with Miller, and it only strengthened his opinion.

"And what is your opinion, Doctor, as to Mr. Miller's criminal responsibility as to the events which allegedly occurred on the 16th of August of last year?" Hocking asked.[259]

Blunt said that if Miller was found guilty, he was criminally responsible under Michigan law for his behavior.

"Thank you, Doctor."

Hocking had only taken thirty minutes to question Dr. Blunt, and now it was Tom Bengston's chance for cross-examination.

As Bengston began, he had Blunt describe the interview where he and Dr. Stock talked with Miller, and followed up by asking if it was correct that his client had never mentioned demons, or anything satanic, and Blunt said he couldn't recall any reference to either of those things.

By the end of the interview with Miller, he had formed his opinion, but testing was a way to confirm it.

He felt Don Miller was suffering from a personality disorder. It was a mixed type with passive and aggressive features. He explained by saying a person that tends to withhold anger may be prone to temper outbursts and anti-social characteristics. The doctor added, "And in addition,

---

258. People v Don G. Miller, May 8, 1979, 770
259. People v Don G. Miller, May 8, 1979, 771

I made a diagnosis of probable sexual deviation, rape and sadism. Rape being clear, and sadism being he gets pleasure out of inflicting pain."

Blunt said that if Miller hadn't seen Lisa, he would have gone by and looked for some place where he could find a young girl.

"So, it's your testimony that Don Miller was looking for a female person on that occasion?"

"I would think so, yes," Blunt replied.[260]

Hocking stood and asked the doctor why he had wanted to use sodium amytal in the interview. Blunt said he actually hadn't been that interested in using it, but he wanted to see what Don Miller's reaction would be to suggesting it as a tool that might offer more insight into his guarded position.

As the doctor's testimony closed, the jury took a quick recess, and by 10:04 a.m., Mike Hocking was calling his last witness.

Dr. Harley Stock took the stand.

Describing Don Miller, Stock said Miller had appeared to be evasive and guarded. It was difficult to get a straight answer from Miller about anything, and through the entire interview, he didn't see any sign of mental illness. The behavior he saw was not the result of a mental illness, but was a conscious choice on Don Miller's part to not answer questions.

Miller had made it clear that he considered himself a Christian, and he had moral and religious values that he held very highly. Dr. Stock felt Miller was hiding behind the religious theme. He told the jury he didn't think Miller was trying to fake mental illness. He felt Miller was simply a person who weighed everything he said very carefully, and he didn't see any evidence of multiple personalities.

Hocking moved to the different tests that Dr. Stock had given to Miller. The first test was the Multiphasic Personality

---

260. People v Don G. Miller, May 8, 1979, 779

Inventory, which consisted of 399 true or false questions. In evaluating the test, Stock said Miller was very defensive. He said that in the evaluation of Miller's test, he saw the defendant as uptight, somewhat depressed, and introverted. Miller was a person who kept emotions to himself, and he saw Miller as angry and hostile, but not crazy.

"Is a psychopathic personality, is that considered a mental illness?"

"No, it's a personality disorder," Stock said.[261]

Asked about the second test, Dr. Stock said he administered the Bender-Gestault test to Don Miller.

As he described how he had administered the test, he said that Miller had only used the top portion of the paper when he was drawing the figures, and said that it showed Miller was constricted, emotionally isolated, and withdrawn. But he added that could be normal behavior for Miller.

Dr. Stock described the third test given as the Draw Person. It was a projective test, and he asked Miller to draw a person. Most males will draw a male first. Stock said that if a male draws a female first, a doctor questions why he's identifying with that. He said Miller drew a female first, and he pointed out the hands were hidden. The interpretation was that Miller was a person who was covering up, who wasn't reaching out in his environment. By holding his hands behind him, though he was afraid, the aggression that the hands represented would be out of control.

Stock said Miller's second drawing was also a female, and the hands were behind the back again.

Dr. Stock said that after the first two people were drawn, he told Miller to draw whatever he wanted, and he drew a house, a river, a canoe, and some trees. When Stock asked him about the drawing, Miller told him the canoe was going upstream. That typified how Miller approached life.

---

261. People v Don G. Miller, May 8, 1979, 801

When Miller drew his family, both his mother and father had their hands at their sides while everyone else had their hands behind them. Miller had separated his parents from the children in the drawing, and Stock saw that as his parents having hostility toward the children. He felt there was no family bond.

The prosecutor asked if there were criteria used to indicate criminal responsibility, meaning that the defendant wasn't mentally ill and recognized the wrongfulness of his actions.

Stock said he would look first at how bizarre the crime is, and whether or not it was unusual. The second thing he would look for was how the crime was carried out, and what the interactions were between the perpetrator and the victim.

The doctor was impressed by the fact that victim was approached and asked straightforward questions by the perpetrator. To him, it showed the perpetrator was able to look at the situation and plan out how he was going to carry out the crime.

Stock said the use of neckties was indicative of someone who wanted to restrain the victim, and choking showed the intent of killing the person. Stabbing someone with a knife showed an intent of doing great bodily harm and perhaps killing them. He concluded the acts committed in the crime were well thought out, coordinated, and systematically carried out.

The doctor said when Miller came out of the Gilbert home and was confronted by a witness, he calmly conversed with the witness by saying he didn't know what was going on inside the house. Stock said that Miller didn't come out and say, "You are a demon, and I must kill you."[262]

Mike Hocking asked if there was any significance in someone taking the time, and thought, to get up, close the

262. People v Don G. Miller, May 8, 1979, 809

drapes and commit a sexual act with regard to criminal responsibility.

"I think common sense dictates he's trying to make sure nobody saw what was going on."[263]

Hocking also asked if there was any evidence that Don Miller held views, or opposing views, of God on the one hand and the Devil on the other.

Stock said Miller gave the impression that he was very religious, and there was some kind of cult he was familiar with that had some kind of connection with a satanic organization, but he didn't think it influenced Miller's perception of the world.

By the time Dr. Stock had seen the sodium amytal interview, he had already formed his opinion. He thought the interview was a replay of the letter Miller had written to Tom Bengston. To the doctor, the letter had served as the script for the interview and Miller was saying what he wanted to say to get his point across.

"Thank you, Doctor."

Bengston asked if the doctor had written his diagnosis in a letter he co-authored with Dr. Blunt.

When the doctor said he hadn't, Bengston asked what his opinion was.

Stock said Don Miller suffered from personality disorder, which meant anti-social personality with a passive aggressive feature. He felt it was a lifelong disorder, and he said that anti-social personality meant a person usually goes against society norms. With passive aggressive, although a person has all kinds of passive aggressions, they're not acted out when he talks with somebody else.

Dr. Stock said that Miller had absolutely no feelings of guilt because he had already told them he couldn't remember what had happened. He added that he felt Miller was faking his memory loss.

263. People v Don G. Miller, May 8, 1979, 810

As the prosecutor began his final questions after Bengston, Dr. Stock said that once a person was in an overtly psychotic stage, and when that person lost touch with reality, they would be out of control and unable to deal with their behavior.

"The People have no further rebuttal witnesses, your Honor."

Assistant Prosecuting Attorney Mike Hocking began his closing argument by thanking the jury for their patience over the previous seven days of testimony. Trying to come up with a way to summarize the case, the idea came to him when one of the witnesses had described the look of horror on Lisa Gilbert's face.

Hocking asked the jury to discover whether or not there's guilt regarding any of the counts. He suggested that if they found guilty on a specific count, to look and see if there was evidence of mental illness.

As the assistant prosecutor continued, he began going over the evidence regarding each count starting with the rape. He highlighted the testimony of Lisa Gilbert and told the jury that they would have to judge her credibility. He asked that as they did that, to keep in mind the testimony of the witness who described the look of horror on her face, in addition to the testimony of James Regan and Ken Dorin.

Mike Hocking described Don Miller's own actions as he entered the Gilbert home. He described what Lisa had seen and heard as the assault was occurring, and he described how she had been bound.

Hocking also asked the jury how they might corroborate the testimony of Lisa, and he suggested they consider the testimony of the doctor who treated her in the emergency room.

His reminded the jury about the semen stain found in the bedroom of the Gilbert home where the rape occurred, and the blood and semen mixture in Don Miller's underwear.

As he highlighted each detail, he described Lisa's statement to Ken Dorin about being raped.

"Did she make that up? As to that, ladies and gentlemen, he had the means; penis and fingers. He had the motive; his quest for lust. And above all, he had ample opportunity: she was bound; she was gagged."[264]

Hocking reminded the jury that Miller was armed at the time, and told them that both Lisa and Randy had described a knife in his hand. He also reminded them that Randy had been stabbed.

Describing Randy's stab wounds, he told the jury that the doctor had testified Randy probably wouldn't have died from them, and added, "But that's not the test. The test is, what was the defendant's intent. Look at the circumstances in which he assaulted Randall Gilbert, and determine his intent."[265]

Hocking went over the elements of the attempted murder of Lisa as he graphically described her being bound and gagged. "The defendant takes this leather belt with stitching in it, wraps it around her neck and begins to pull on it until it breaks. He pulled until the belt broke around her neck." He asked, "What other area of the body is more susceptible to that type of manipulation than the neck?"[266]

The prosecutor refocused on the assault on Randy. He said Miller had started to cut Randy's throat, and when the boy was able to wrestle the knife way, Miller had used his hands to strangle him until he was unconscious. He graphically described how Miller rolled Randy over,

---

264. People v Don G. Miller, May 8, 1979, 829
265. People v Don G. Miller, May 8, 1979, 831
266. People v Don G. Miller, May 8, 1979, 831

grabbed the knife from under the bed, and stabbed him twice in the chest.

"Is there any set of facts, ladies and gentlemen, that shows intent to murder more vividly than that?"[267]

Mike Hocking was passionate now. He told the jury that the attack on Randy demonstrated the intent to murder Lisa, and conversely, the attack on Lisa demonstrated Miller's intent when she was raped.

Hocking said Randy had caught Don Miller in the act, and Miller had no choice but to save himself. His only choice was to get rid of both witnesses.

He moved to the proofs identifying Don Miller as the person who was at the Gilbert home. He described Miller's car and how it had been shown that it was registered to him.

Hocking said he anticipated the defense arguing that it was not an attempted murder, and he suggested that anything less than that would be ridiculous.

The prosecutor moved to Don Miller's defense. He said Don Miller must somehow be different because he viewed himself as a great Christian, yet two doctors said that Miller used Christianity any way that he saw fit.

Wanting the jury to understand his argument, Mike Hocking turned to the four experts who had testified for the defense. He said all four doctors' testimony was inconsistent, and he pointed out each of the inconsistencies.

Highlighting each of the defense experts' testimony, he asked the jury, "How does Hughett correlate the sex activities with the demon theory? Lisa is an evil seductress, obviously. Based upon that, your common sense, does that make it a convenient way to fit the facts into the hypothesis?"[268]

The rebuttal witnesses for the prosecution, Dr. Blunt and Dr. Stock, were mentioned, and Hocking recalled Blunt's

267. People v Don G. Miller, May 8, 1979, 833
268. People v Don G. Miller, May 8, 1979, 840

statement that Miller had told him he was getting some pills from his glovebox and had bumped his head and got dizzy. Hocking argued that that was the seed from where the demon theory evolved. From there came the dream letter.

"I had a dream that when I went to the residence, went into that area, there were demons," he said.[269] Hocking said that from that point on, the demon theory evolved.

Judge Robinson reminded Mike Hocking that he had five minutes left in his closing argument.

"Evil acts of man are judged by how they are performed." He said the demon theory was just that; a theory. It was the only thing Don Miller had to cling to. The prosecutor said that Lisa and Randy Gilbert had found themselves in a nightmare, and to allow their nightmare to end was in the pursuance of justice.

As Hocking finished, he reminded the jury that the demon theory was ridiculous. He asked the jury to find Don G. Miller guilty, and echo the verdict through the entire expanse of the courtroom.

Tom Bengston stood from the defense table. He began his closing argument by reminding the jury of the process they had undergone at the before the trial had even begun, reminding them that they had promised to return the correct verdict if the prosecution, or the defense, hadn't proven their case. Asserting that the prosecution hadn't proven their case, and based on all of the testimony, he said their verdict should be one of not guilty by reason of insanity, or not guilty.

Bengston said there was agreement between the prosecutor and himself that there had been a human tragedy that occurred on August 16, 1978. He reminded them that the case wasn't one of emotion, but one of common sense in evaluating all of the testimony.

---

269. People v Don G. Miller, May 8, 1979, 841

As Tom Bengston began to recap the assault on Lisa, he didn't want the jury to think that she wasn't a credible witness, but suggested that she was mistaken about any sort of penetration during the sexual assault, and he used the testimony of the lab technicians from the MSP to further his position by saying they never found any semen on Lisa, nor any blood on Miller himself. He suggested there was no evidence of penetration, and therefore, at best, there was only an attempt at the sexual assault.

As the defense attorney moved to the attempted murder charges, he told the jury the assaults were more consistent with the crime of assault with intent to do great bodily harm less than murder, or assault with a dangerous weapon. If Don Miller had the intent to kill Randy and Lisa, he certainly had the opportunity.

Bengston recounted Don Miller's actions as he tried to strangle Lisa, coming from behind her and choking her back, then mentioned the belt breaking. He said that by Miller trying to choke her from behind, it was satanic and ritualistic, and he never had the intent to murder Lisa.

Highlighting each aspect of the events on August 16, the defense continued to suggest to the jury that everything happened on a busy street, in the middle of the day, and near a second busy intersection. Miller hadn't concealed his license plate and didn't wear any disguise. He said Miller wasn't armed when he went into the house and suggested that he had taken a knife from the kitchen. Describing how Don Miller had tied Lisa up, Bengston said to the jury that it was bizarre behavior. He asked that the jury look at the bindings that were recovered from Lisa.

Bengston criticized the testimony of the prosecution's rebuttal witnesses by saying their testimony was inaccurate and wrong, yet he praised his own witnesses.

The defense attorney said his witnesses were professionals, and they were risking their reputations when they offered to testify.

Highlighting each expert witness, both prosecution and defense, Bengston finished his closing argument by cautioning the jury. He said, "I want you to be fair to the Prosecutor's witnesses, I want you to be fair to our witnesses, but just keep in mind, if you would put it on your level, not the level of our experts, but use your good common sense, and I suggest to you if you do use your good common sense, that the appropriate verdict, bearing in mind the Prosecuting Attorney has to prove criminal responsibility, not the Defense, that your verdict should be one of not guilty by reason of insanity. Thank you, ladies and gentlemen."[270]

Mike Hocking knew he had the burden of proof. He stood for the rebuttal argument to Bengston's closing. It was his last chance to put Don Miller in prison.

The rebuttal began by reminding the jury to use common sense when they viewed the facts of the case.

"There's a doctrine which is applied to the civil law in some states, the *Doctrine of Res ipsa loquitur* means, 'The thing speaks for itself.'"[271]

He reminded the jury that Bengston wanted them to conclude the crime speaks for itself, or speaks of the crime of criminal responsibility. He asked if the more serious crime gets the greater likelihood that a person is not criminally responsible, how could people have order? If that were the case, lives couldn't exist.

Hocking told the jury that because Miller hadn't performed the perfect crime and made some mistakes, he must have been insane.

He pointed out that the demon defense didn't begin during his first initial forensic interview, but had started the following day.

270. People v Don G. Miller, May 8, 1979, 876
271. People v Don G. Miller, May 8, 1979, 876

He closed his final argument by asking the jury to look at the seriousness of the offense, look at the way it was acted out, and use common sense.

Judge Robinson took a brief recess. Twenty minutes later, as the jury took their seats in the courtroom, it was the judge's role to instruct the jury, and how they had to consider the testimony of all the witnesses. He told them that after their deliberations, they had to be satisfied beyond a reasonable doubt that Don Miller was guilty, and they had to begin with the presumption Miller was innocent.

As Robinson outlined the charges against Don Miller, he told the jury specific instructions that had been agreed upon by both attorneys.

Judge Robinson addressed the issue of legal insanity. He said that legal insanity and mental illness were not the same. He added that a mentally ill person is not necessarily legally insane, and the law recognized a distinction between legal insanity and mental illness.

The jury began deliberations at 4:15 p.m. Forty minutes later, Judge Robinson had them re-enter the courtroom and let them know they were excused for the evening.

On Wednesday, May 9, the jury reconvened for deliberations, and by 10:15 a.m., they had reached their verdict.

Mike Hocking and Paul Berger both stood, as did Tom Bengston and Miller.

The jury foreman read the verdict. Don G. Miller was found guilty on all three charges.

His bond was immediately revoked, and Judge Richard Robinson set his sentencing for May 31.

Ingham County Assistant Prosecuting Attorney Mike Woodworth had come to Berrien County to watch the trial of Miller with great interest, knowing he was still facing two counts of second-degree murder for the deaths of Martha Sue Young and Kristine Stuart. He couldn't help but chuckle at some of the testimony from the defense experts and their diagnosis of Miller having multiple personalities.

Faithful to their son, Gene and Elaine Miller had attended the trial every day. Like everyone else involved, they drove from their home in East Lansing to the Berrien County Courthouse, and each day they would sit quietly toward the back of the courtroom. If anyone knew who they were, it was never mentioned. The Millers sat behind the press, and they were appalled at some of the things said about their son by the media. At one point, comments from the media upset them so much, they became physically ill.

On May 31, before a crowded courtroom back in Charlotte, Judge Richard Robinson called the sentencing hearing to order. After addressing the pre-sentence investigative report, he looked directly at the defendant.

"Would you like to say anything, Mr. Miller, before sentence is imposed? Don Miller addressed the Court, saying, "Your Honor, I really can't account for August 16, and I'm deeply sorry for it."

Judge Robinson responded, saying everyone was sorry for what had happened. He said there was sorrow for Miller himself, for the victims, their families, and for the Miller family. He told Don Miller that he had some serious problems, and he felt that if fate had not intervened, he would have killed both Lisa and Randy. Robinson said he felt Miller would repeat the crimes, and that's what worried him the most. With that, Don G. Miller was sentenced to thirty to fifty years in prison.

He was led from the courtroom and driven back from the courthouse to the Eaton County Jail.

17

Detectives Norm Kelley and Kent Reusch already knew they would be taking Miller to Jackson Prison, and there was no delay. Don Miller was shackled with belly chains and ankle chains at the jail. The large metal door made a loud clunking sound as the automatic lock was released. The door was pulled open, and Miller shuffled out onto the landing and down the three steps to the waiting unmarked detective car. The ankle chains kept him from taking full strides as he walked. He slid into the back seat.

As the detective car backed out of the sally port at the jail, Kelley turned from the jail onto and headed south through the small city. When he reached the intersection of M-50 on the south end of town, he turned to the east as he headed toward Jackson. The total time for the trip would be less than an hour.

Don Miller was quiet as he sat in the back seat. Kelley and Reusch began to talk about Miller's religious convictions, beliefs, and his family, knowing full well that there were still three women missing in the Lansing area, and their passenger was going to stand trial for two of those deaths, even though their bodies hadn't been found.

As the three passed through the small town of Eaton Rapids, both detectives mentioned that it would only be proper that the families of the missing women have some sort of closure and proper burials.

Don Miller remained silent. He shrunk down in the back seat as best he could while trying to shut everything out.

Miller's attorney had weighed the possibility of an appeal to his conviction. He had had an agreement with Judge Robinson and the prosecutor about refraining from certain jury instructions, and they had agreed to not mention certain areas of those instructions. Bengston was sure he had a legitimate appeal, but the risk was that his client would ultimately be sentenced to more than he had already received, so the decision was made to not appeal the conviction.

———————

Arriving at the prison, the convicted rapist was placed in segregation by the superintendent of the reception and guidance center for his own safety.

The following day, an administrative hearing was held to explain his segregation status, and during the hearing, Dr. John Prelesnik noticed that Miller was suffering from depression and psychosis.

Tom Bengston knew his client had been placed in segregation, and he called Dr. Prelesnik to find out why. He asked about treatment programs that might be available for Miller. As the doctor explained the options available, Bengston asked what type of experience the prison staff had in dealing with people who had the same problems his client suffered from. Bengston also asked for a personal meeting with the doctor.

At that meeting, the same treatment programs discussed over the phone were presented a second time to Tom Bengston and his assistant, and after, the defense attorney had developed a trust in Dr. Prelesnik.

Tom Bengston called the doctor a second time to see if he would be willing to meet with Gene and Elaine Miller to discuss his client's progress at the prison, and he agreed.

Don Miller's parents, Bengston, his assistant, a prison psychologist, and Dr. Prelesnik all met at the prison.

While trying to help his client, Tom Bengston's goal was to resolve the disappearances of Martha Sue Young and Kristine Stuart.

At a third meeting with Prelesnik, Tom Bengston and his assistant, along with Ingham County Prosecutor Peter Houk and his chief assistant Lee Atkinson attended. The discussion centered around an informal hypnosis session with Miller, and Peter Houk had the same concerns that Bengston had had in the earlier conversations with Prelesnik. The doctor explained that individuals with symptoms as severe as Miller's became mentally unbalanced, homicidal, and eventually suicidal. Dr. Prelesnik explained the process of projection, which helps the inmate go through the process. He said there was a degree of art involved in keeping the patient from slipping too deeply into psychosis as the repressed material rose.

Don Miller had already been interviewed by the prison psychologist and was aware of the options being discussed.

After the meeting, Bengston asked Peter Houk if he would agree to have Dr. Prelesnik do whatever it took to try to get the truth out of Miller. Bengston and Houk both were hopeful they might be able to get more information to resolve all of the cases.

Tom Bengston's motive behind unlocking Don Miller's memory was to give the families of the victims something, knowing they needed closure. He knew they should be told about what happened to their daughters. He also knew it would take some work. In return, knowing his client was still facing two counts of second-degree murder in the deaths of Martha Sue Young and Kristine Stuart, he wanted some sort of a plea agreement.

The idea of the plea deal was Tom Bengston's. Knowing that Houk had banned plea bargaining on armed robbery and murder cases six months after taking office, it would a tough sell.

When he was confronted with the idea, Peter Houk knew he had a tough decision. Should he adhere to his rigid policy of no plea agreements in murder cases, or should he make a humane exception? He knew the answer, and he made the decision with the support of the Young family and the Stuart family.

With Houk agreeing, next was to approach Judge Robert Bell about the possibility of a plea and have him agree to it. Judge Bell was on board as well.

Bengston made a call to Prelesnik at the prison, asking for an immediate meeting. Bengston, Houk, and his chief assistant all met with the doctor in his office. Bengston said that Miller had agreed to the procedure, and he asked that both Prelesnik and the prison psychologist who had interviewed him be present.

Peter Houk told Prelesnik that he also wanted his help. Houk told him that he had discussed it with Judge Bell, who would be the potential sentencing judge in the second-degree murder trials, and with Judge Richard Robinson, as well as both victims' families, and everyone had agreed to try to find the remains of the missing women.

Dr. Prelesnik knew that one of the stipulations in the plea agreement was that the bodies had to be located within a week, or Peter Houk would continue the prosecution for the murders.

Prelesnik and the prison psychologist met with Don Miller for the hypnosis session. It lasted several hours, and they were successful. Don Miller had recalled the murders of Martha Sue Young and Kristine Stuart, and he agreed to take the police to where he had hidden the bodies.

After the session, the doctor met privately with Tom Bengston, and afterward, Bengston met with Miller privately.

There was no delay. Bengston and Houk contacted Prelesnik and told the doctor they would have a writ drawn up by a judge so they could take Don Miller from the prison the following morning to find the bodies.

Another session was arranged to be done at Wyandotte General Hospital. The hope was to resolve the murder of Marita Choquette and the disappearance of Wendy Bush.

After the three bodies were found, the plea agreement was typed.

The agreement stated that Miller had been charged by a citizen grand jury with second-degree murder in the deaths of Kristine Stuart and Martha Sue Young. Marita Choquette's murder was noted and so was the disappearance of Wendy Bush.

The document read that Miller had admitted to the murders of Kristine Stuart and Martha Sue Young and had led authorities to their bodies. Because the two bodies had been identified as Stuart and Young, a second count of voluntary manslaughter would be added to the original indictment, and Miller would be allowed to plead guilty but mentally ill to the Stuart murder. He would also be allowed to plead guilty to voluntary manslaughter in the Young murder. If the two pleas were made, the original two counts of second-degree murder would not be prosecuted, but if he backed out and decided not to plead guilty, the two counts of second-degree murder would continue. Lastly, the plea agreement stated that Miller had admitted to murdering Marita Choquette and Wendy Bush, and had led investigators to Wendy's body. Because he had agreed to do that, there would be no prosecution for either of those murders.

Peter Houk took a lot of criticism for his decision to plea bargain with a killer in exchange for the bodies.

On September 2, 1979, he published an editorial in the Lansing paper to explain his reasoning.

The best thing that came out of his decision was something that he considered a "heightened citizen awareness of certain critical issues" that faced the criminal justice system.

Beyond that, personal attacks on the prosecutor's office suggested the undermining of law enforcement and that Houk had not kept his promise to do away with plea bargaining in murder cases. In the editorial, he explained that he had made that promise without knowing that the Lansing area would be "plagued by a bizarre set of murders unequaled in this state's history for missing bodies and no evidence."[272]

The prosecutor outlined the fact that there was absolutely no evidence found linking Don Miller to the deaths of Martha Sue Young and Kristine Stuart despite an investigation that spanned over two years. He wrote that the only witness to Kristine's murder had to have her memory refreshed by hypnosis.

Houk explained there was only one reported prosecution for homicide where no body had been found. He added that in an appellate decision in the Michigan courts, there was not a single decision "combining and resolving both the 'no body' and the hypnosis issues" that were presented in Don Miller's case.

In other words, there were no guarantees in taking Miller to trial on second-degree murder.

Without the concern expressed by both the Young family and the Stuart family, Don Miller's offer to accept a plea of manslaughter would never have been accepted.

---

272. Peter Houk. "Miller Case Handled Right Way." *State Journal*, September 3, 1979

The possibility that the bodies of Martha Sue Young and Kristine Stuart would have been found after two years was remote.

Houk wrote that even the State's own psychologists and psychiatrists said that Miller would never have revealed where the bodies were.

"What disturbs most citizens about the Miller case is the possibility that he may someday walk the streets of this state again, despite his admission to being a killer and his psychiatrist's statement that Donald Miller is seriously mentally ill."[273]

Houk wrote that neither he, nor anyone in the criminal justice system, could have guaranteed Miller's removal from society, and while the second-degree murder conviction carried the possibility of a life sentence, the sentence wasn't mandatory. Even with a conviction for second-degree murder, Don Miller would still be eligible for parole after ten years.

Trying to detail Miller's parole eligibility, Houk said that any sentence for second-degree murder, on top of the thirty to fifty year sentence he had already received in Eaton County, would be served concurrently, or at the same time. Therefore, second-degree murder convictions may not have increased the actual time he would spend in prison.

Wanting to make his point clear, Houk wrote that if Don Miller had been tried and acquitted of second-degree murder, he would still be eligible for parole after thirteen years from the convictions in Eaton County, and none of those charges involved a death. It was hardly an accurate portrait of Don Miller.

"I made a humane exception in favor of the families of Miller's victims. I, too, wish a harsher penalty could be imposed on Miller. However, the fact and law do not provide a likely way to do that. I made a hard decision

273. Peter Houk, September 3, 1979

in the Donald Miller case. I remain convinced that it was the right one - for the families of Miller's victims and the community in which I and my family live."[274]

---

274. Peter Houk, September 3, 1979

18

With the murders of four women now solved and a sense of closure for the four families of the victims, Don Miller pled guilty to two counts of voluntary manslaughter for the murders of Martha Sue Young and Kristine Stuart.

By June 1980, only a year after his plea, Miller had taken himself out of the group psychotherapy counseling he had been a part of since his arrival at the prison. His participation in the group had waned after a female co-therapist joined the group. The prison staff felt he was running away from his problems, and he had offered very little insight into his crimes.

Eventually, Miller rejoined the group, and the prison newspaper's editor recommended him for a job.

In the fall of 1987, Don Miller was transferred from Jackson Prison to Kinross Prison in Michigan's Upper Peninsula, quickly adjusting to his new surroundings.

Within a year after his arrival, Miller was assaulted at Kinross. Twice propositioned for sex with another inmate, Miller refused, and the inmate began to drag him toward an office. Miller fought to escape and was able to wrestle himself free.

Don Miller had his first chance at parole in September 1989 after serving in excess of nine years for the deaths of Martha and Kristine, but according to the parole board, because of his history in group therapy, the board noted he was making poor progress. His parole was denied.

Sex offender therapy had begun for Miller in April 1989. His primary interest in participating was to show the corrections administration the strides he'd made in the previous ten years.

Keeping much to himself by the August sessions, he was confronted by the others in the group because of the nature of his crimes, and at one point he wanted to return to individual therapy, but he stuck it out. He would discuss his feelings, emotions, and behaviors in abstract terms to disassociate himself from his crimes. His answers were carefully thought out and repeated, and the prison staff felt it was a way for him to exercise self-control over himself and others in the group.

By January 1990, Miller had become much more comfortable with others in the sex offender therapy group, and he was able to handle confrontation from the other members much better than when he had first started. His answers to questions were still vague, and many of the inmates in the group considered him less than honest when it came to answering questions. Prison officials felt he still had genuine difficulty in coming to terms with his crimes.

In a June report, prison officials noted that while he attempted to help others in the group by offering feedback, his religious convictions seemed to distance other members within the group.

Officials thought Miller would make gains in the program if he explored his anger toward women.

By May, one of the therapists believed the crimes he committed were related to his tendency to store up his anger until it exploded. Miller admitted the first person to suffer from his anger was Martha Young, and eventually the other women. He referred to the second, third, and fourth murders, and the final attempted murder as re-enactments of his first murder. He admitted that some of his crimes involved rape, with some prior to the death, and some after death. In his group discussion, he said the sexual aspect of his crimes was an attempt to regain the love he had invested in his relationship with Martha Young. He described her as having "off and on" commitments, and that was a trigger for him. He also described his desire for sex as a conflict with his religious beliefs. Don Miller was certain that his religious faith had taught him to love and forgive, ridding him of the anger and hurt that led to his crimes.

Miller had made great strides by 1992 in discussing the details of his rape and murder cases. Before that, he had always left out the relationship with his sister when he was much younger and how that had played a part in the sexual assaults.

By mid-'93, Miller spoke of the assault on a younger sister when he was an adolescent and how his sister finally refused, and his mother intervened. He finally admitted responsibility for the crimes he had committed, and he developed his own relapse prevention plan for himself. His prevention plan incorporated risk factors, cues, and coping responses. Prison experts felt his coping responses were limited. He insisted on turning control over his life to God, and a heavy reliance on prayer to rid himself of the deviant thoughts, added with abstinence, seemed unrealistic.

Prison officials felt that he needed to reconcile his deeper conflict with women and his own sexuality.

Don Miller had reached the maximum benefits of the sex offender therapy, and after his July session, he was terminated from the group.

Prison life for Don Miller became routine over the years as he worked for *The Link*, a prison newspaper, but it hadn't come without minor prison violations and tickets issued to him for violations of prison policy. He'd been given tickets for being out of his area or in someplace that he shouldn't be at various times during his fifteen years behind bars, and he hated female corrections officers.

The Kinross Correctional Facility in Michigan's Upper Peninsula opened in 1977 and was home to Don Miller in 1994. He was housed in Unit B-3, and he shared a twelve foot by seventeen foot room with three other inmates while still working for the prison paper.

On October 15, Miller asked permission from a corrections officer to go see another inmate in another room. A short time later, the officer saw Don Miller standing in the hall outside the inmate's room, and he was leaning into the room with his left foot inside the door. Miller was issued a ticket for "unauthorized occupation of a cell or room." When he was confronted with the violation, he told the officer he thought both feet had to be in for a violation. He said he leaned in to look at a picture album, and that he wasn't looking for trouble.

As a result of the violation, Miller received another ticket, and he pled not guilty. A hearing was scheduled for November 2, and he was found guilty. His punishment was a loss of privileges for two days.

———————

Michigan Corrections Officer Leo Schwesinger had been with Corrections Division for ten years. On November 4, 1994, two days after Don Miller had been found guilty in the administrative hearing, Schwesinger was assigned as a custody officer, and his job was to provide relief for some of the officers at chow time. Another officer, Jim Couling, had asked for relief so he could go to the chow hall, and Schwesinger took his position. Couling was the resident unit officer responsible for overseeing the seventy-two inmates on the third floor of the unit.

While Schwesinger was waiting for the other officer to return from break, he decided to do a shakedown of an inmate's room while they were working in the kitchen area. Miller was in the room when Schwesinger arrived, and the three inmates were told to leave, so they went to a dayroom. Required by the prison to do a certain number of shakedowns, the officer searched through an inmate's property looking for contraband.

Schwesinger didn't want that one inmate to think he was being targeted, so as he finished searching the first inmate's area, he decided to shakedown Don Miller's area in the same cell. As he opened up Miller's wall locker, he noticed the footlocker inside. The corrections officer thought it was unusual for the footlocker to be inside the wall locker because most footlockers were kept under an inmate's bed.

Schwesinger removed the footlocker and unlocked it with a master key. Inside the locker, he saw a small cardboard box with a rubber band around it. Removing the rubber band and opening the box, he saw a piece of pleated velvet. To the officer, the way the velvet was folded reminded him of casket. As he pulled the folded velvet open, he discovered a long shoestring tied together at both ends, as if to shorten it, and wooden barrel buttons threaded onto the lace at both ends. To the officer, they appeared to be handles.

Schwesinger, who had been in the room for five to ten minutes, stepped into the hall and saw the other officer had returned from break. He called to Couling. The corrections officer knew Don Miller was in prison for strangling women, and he knew what a garrote looked like. He'd had specific training on the identification of different types of weapons commonly found inside a prison.

When Couling saw what the custody officer was holding, he asked, "Is this straight?" Officer Couling had had a confrontation with Schwesinger in the past over a ticket issued to an inmate. Couling didn't agree with the ticket, and he told Schwesinger he wouldn't lie for him. As the two officers stood together and looked at the garrote, Leo Schwesinger assured Couling it was legitimate.

The two officers notified their sergeant and showed him what had been found in Don Miller's footlocker. Miller was quickly located, and the sergeant had him handcuffed and taken to segregation.

Schwesinger notified the supervisor on duty, and took several photos of the garrote.

Schwesinger and Couling both knew that Don Miller was dangerous. Schwesinger knew Miller had problems with female corrections officers and also knew that at least one female corrections officer was fearful of Miller. There was concern by the prison staff that the garrote was going to be used on the female corrections officer recently assigned to his unit.

Miller had spoken to Officer Couling on at least one occasion when he came to Couling's desk and told him that he had had a dream about Martha Young. He said that she was in heaven, she had forgiven him for the murder, and she was smiling. Officer Couling asked him if the other three victims had forgiven him, and Miller never showed any remorse. He just stood there.

Couling had also spoken to one of Miller's prison roommates, and the roommate told him that Miller couldn't tolerate anything that was feminine. He said that if Miller was watching television and saw a commercial about women's bras, he would turn his head. The roommate felt that Don Miller was very angry and focused, and considered him to be extremely dangerous.

Miller vehemently denied possessing a garrote, and he said it was a drawstring used to tighten up the waist on his aging prison coat. In a typed statement, he wrote that he was contesting the report because a shoelace wasn't considered dangerous contraband. He had bought it from the prison store when tokens were used to make a purchase. The two wooden pieces on the shoelace were from an old coat and were used as a drawstring on his coat. He also wrote that he kept it in case he found another use for it.

Despite Miller's insistence that he had purchased the six-foot shoestring from the prison store, he was found to be in possession of a dangerous weapon at an administrative hearing, and by the end of the month, he was transferred back to Jackson.

Before the garrote was found in his footlocker, Don Miller had been the topic of conversation among the inmates at Kinross because he was nearing his release date from prison. Because of the mandatory good time he received, the maximum time he could spend in prison, even with the thirty to fifty year sentence, was only nineteen years. After the loss of his good time for the garrote, he was scheduled for release in 1999.

In the late nineties, as Don Miller was approaching his release date from the Michigan Department of Corrections, he had plans to go back and live with his parents in East Lansing.

At the same time, the Committee for Community Awareness and Protection was being formed. The group was quietly organized in the Lansing area to explore legal options that might be available to prevent the serial killer's release, with the help of internationally known psychiatrist Dr. Frank Ochberg. The group consisted of representatives from three police agencies, prosecutors, judges, state representatives, Miller's surviving victims, family members of the women he killed, and corrections officers.

Eaton County Prosecuting Attorney Jeff Sauter invited Ingham County's newest prosecutor to attend the meetings. There were no politics involved with the group, and each member was able to share their thoughts about strategies to keep Miller behind bars. The group slowly grew as members with a vested interest in the Miller case would join.

One of the members of C-CAP was with the Michigan Attorney General's Office, and he was closely following an appeal by the United States Supreme Court. The case had originated in Kansas and the Supreme Court had upheld the right of the state to confine a serial sex offender to a mental hospital after his sentence in prison. It was a close decision, but there were a few other states having similar laws.

Sue Young saw the Supreme Court ruling as a fighting chance and championed the cause in the hope of having legislation drafted in Michigan that would mirror the Kansas legislation. Hoping that the best way to keep Don Miller in prison was through legislation, the Senate Serial Killer Bill 649 was drafted. There were four provisions in the bill, and they included a requirement that the Department of Corrections notify the attorney general when a killer was scheduled to be released from prison, and the attorney general would refer the matter to a judge if they deemed there was sufficient cause. Beyond that, the judge would call for a psychiatric evaluation through the Center for Forensic Psychiatry, and if a civil commitment was recommended, a trial would be conducted.

The bill passed through the Michigan Senate, but never made it to the floor of the House.

By 1997, C-CAP still didn't have any answers, and Miller's release was only eighteen months away.

At one of the meetings, Peter Houk told the Committee that the best way to find out about an inmate was to research prison records.

As Jeff Sauter reviewed the records he had gotten from the Michigan Department of Corrections, he discovered the garrote case at the Kinross Facility. Miller hadn't been charged criminally in that case. He'd only had an administrative hearing. Sauter knew it wouldn't be case of double jeopardy under Michigan law, and he knew the statute of limitations hadn't run out yet.

The members of C-CAP discussed the possibility of Miller being charged criminally for possessing the garrote, and Sauter ultimately contacted Chippewa County's Prosecuting Attorney Patrick Shannon to see if he might consider charging Miller. The Eaton County prosecutor assured Shannon that he would do all of the work on the case.

Shannon was in agreement. He contacted Sergeant Robin Sexton at the MSP Post in St. Ignace and asked him to investigate the case. Sexton began his investigation in March 1997, two and a half years after the incident.

Sexton contacted the Kinross Facility and asked for copies of Don Miller's disciplinary records at the prison. With those records, he also obtained Miller's written statement and the findings of the hearing officer. The hearing officer, as part of his own investigation, had contacted the storekeeper at the prison to ask about shoelaces being sold there. The storekeeper remembered that at one time, the prison store did sell white shoelaces, but he couldn't recall when that was. Included with the files that Sexton received was a copy of the photograph taken of the garrote found in Miller's room.

Two days after Sexton's initial report, the Chippewa County prosecutor asked him to see if he could locate Corrections Officer Leo Schwesinger for an interview. Sexton also interviewed Corrections Officer Couling. Couling told Sexton that he believed Don Miller was an extremely dangerous person. He said that he felt he knew Miller better than any other member of the Michigan Department of Corrections, and Miller was a very complex person.

When interviewed, Schwesinger told Sexton he was speaking with Miller's roommate, who was the original focus of the shakedown, and that inmate had told him that

Don Miller had made up the shoelace with the wooden handles the night before it was found. The inmate continued telling Schwesinger that Miller was mad because he'd been written up by a female corrections officer, and the fact that she was a female was very offensive to Miller.

When Sexton was able to track down the inmate who had told Schwesinger about the garrote being made up the night before it was found, the inmate said he wasn't surprised that he was there, but he didn't want to get involved. He didn't believe in talking about the other inmates' business.

As Sexton continued the interview, the inmate told him he'd been a roommate of Miller's for several months, and he denied ever having made the statement about the shoelace, or that he'd seen Miller making it up the night before it was found. He said that he had seen Miller with the shoelace previously, and he thought Miller wore it as tie for his hood, or maybe around the waist of his coat.

Just as Officer Couling had said, Miller's former roommate said he believed Don Miller was a dangerous person.

On June 12, 1997, Sexton finally sat down with Don Miller for a taped interview. The interview was done at the Robert G. Cotton Facility in Jackson.

After Miller was read his Miranda rights, a casual conversation took place as Sexton wanted to find out about Miller's past. As the interview progressed, Sexton informed Miller why he was there. He told him it was regarding the garrote found in his room in 1994.

Cautious, Miller quietly replied, "Alleged."

As they two talked, Miller, in his characteristically low and deliberate voice, told the sergeant that he'd gladly speak about his past incidents with Tom Bengston present, and maybe they could set up a time in the future when the three of them could sit down and talk. Sexton changed the course of the interview by talking with Miller about who his past roommates were, and who some of the corrections staff were in his unit in 1994. He asked Miller if he had any problems with them, and Miller said a couple times he was written tickets for violations. He added that Schwesinger had written him a ticket for loitering in his own office where he worked for the prison paper. Miller chuckled as he told the detective about it.

Jeff Sauter, working from Eaton County, received the reports from Chippewa County, and assigned two of his own investigators to begin working on the case. Jim Kus and Bob Dutcher, retired police officers from the Lansing area, were both seasoned investigators.

By mid-May, Patrick Shannon, who realized the importance of the case, charged Don Miller with possessing the garrote in prison, and while there was a valid warrant for Miller when Sexton had interviewed him, the sergeant never mentioned it.

On July 27, Don Miller stood alone before the district court judge in the 91st District Court of Chippewa County for his arraignment.

The judge asked the forty-two-year-old inmate if he understood the charge against him.

Miller said he understood the charge, and he asked for a preliminary examination.

After filing his notice with the Court that he would be representing Miller, Bengston waived the fourteen-day requirement for the preliminary exam. He began to file motions to have the case dismissed before the preliminary exam even took place. In September, he stood before the district court judge, saying that he had filed a request for discovery in the case in August. He said Miller had only been provided with a black-and-white duplicate photo of the shoestring and nothing else.

Bengston's concern was that his client's right to due process, and a speedy trial, had been compromised, and that equated to prejudice against his client.

In addition, Bengston said that all of the evidence had been destroyed. There was no shoelace, no buttons, and no photographs. Miller's coat had also been destroyed. He argued that Miller's rights had been jeopardized because there was no evidence to prove his innocence.

Bengston thought that his client being charged administratively with possessing a garrote three years earlier had been a complete sham. He was certain someone was hunting for a way to keep his client in prison, and whoever it was had little concern for Don Miller's rights. Tom Bengston had deep seated feelings about his client. He knew the prison system had failed his client, and anything Don Miller had done in prison to better himself had been done on his own.

Before Patrick Shannon would have a chance to respond to Bengston's motion, the defense attorney told the Court that the warrant had been authorized for Miller in mid-May, yet Sergeant Sexton hadn't interviewed him until June. He also wanted to know why Miller hadn't been told by Sexton that there was a warrant for him when he was interviewed.

As Patrick Shannon stood to address the Court, he said that he had received the request and that it asked for the shoelace, buttons, the footlocker, the contents of the footlocker, the entire cell area, and any other items related to the subject's shakedown. Shannon argued to the judge that he couldn't present the entire inside of a prison cell to the Court.

The judge asked Shannon if the only thing he had in the way of evidence was some photographs, and when Shannon said yes, the judge then confirmed with him that they didn't exist.

Shannon told him he was correct.

After a brief recess, the judge returned and told both attorneys that the People would make photos of the garrote itself available, along with the footlocker. He also told Bengston that he could tour the room where Don Miller had resided at the time. The judge added that all reports from MSP, or any other investigators, as well as all physical or demonstrative evidence that the prosecutor might be in possession of, would be made available.

On November 25, 1997, now three years after the garrote had been found in Don Miller's footlocker, and six months after he'd been charged, his preliminary examination was set to begin in Sault Ste. Marie, Michigan.

The first witness called was Corrections Officer Leo Schwesinger. Wearing his gray uniform shirt with black pants, he took a seat at the witness stand.

The officer began his testimony by describing for the Court how he went into the room Don Miller shared with two other inmates so he could do a shakedown. He was looking for any contraband or other prohibited items in the room.

Schwesinger described the garrote, saying it was a heavy shoelace that was doubled and tied in a knot. There were two wooden toggles that served as handles and would fit nicely in someone's hand, and they were attached at both ends. He also said there was a knot in the center of the shoelace.

Shannon asked why he had taken it.

Schwesinger said it didn't appear to be a shoelace, and from the way it was made, it appeared to be a weapon.

The shoelace was seventy-two inches long. The two wooden handles had holes through them, and the shoelace was run through both of the handles and brought back around, doubled, and knotted so they were securely attached.

As Shannon tied up his questioning, Bengston began his cross-examination by asking if the shakedowns were recorded, and Schwesinger told him the housing unit officer made a notation of each one. The defense attorney also wanted to know how Schwesinger could be sure the locker or footlocker were Miller's.

Schwesinger knew it was Miller's locker because it was in Miller's area of control.

Tom Bengston went through the procedures for a shakedown and asked if Schwesinger had seen a cross in the box where the garrote was found.

Schwesinger said he had seen a small cross inside the box, and velvet was on top of the box. He had taken ten photos of the garrote after it was found, and it was tied a couple times with a large knot, but he never untied it.

Schwesinger told Bengston that shoelaces were sold in the prison store, in addition to electrical wires and extension cords.

When Bengston asked if they sold cables for televisions, the officer said they did. The attorney knew shoelaces had been sold at the prison store, but he was trying to point out other, similar items sold there that could be used as weapons, yet inmates could still purchase them.

When he asked the corrections officer what time he had written the report on the incident, he said it was 2:50 p.m., and Bengston asked why there was a two-hour delay from the time of the incident to when the report was written.

Schwesinger said that the garrote had been shown to several people, and the supervisors were trying to determine if it was a weapon.

Tom Bengston went over each photo that Schwesinger had taken on November 4, 1994, and when he finished his questioning, the judge began to ask the corrections officer a series of questions. He, like Patrick Shannon and Tom Bengston, took the officer through every step he had taken that afternoon. As he finished, the judge asked either attorney if they had any additional questions. When they didn't, the judge asked for closing motions.

Patrick Shannon simply asked the Court to bind Miller over to the circuit court to stand trial on the charge.

Bengston moved for a dismissal of the charges based on his earlier motion to the Court regarding the evidence being destroyed. He reiterated his motion for dismissal based on the delay in processing the case, and asked the motion to have Miller bound over be denied because the prosecution hadn't proven their case. He read verbatim the law that his client was charged under and added that if Miller was allowed to purchase the shoelace from the prison store, then he was authorized to possess it. He said even if there were buttons attached to the ends, Miller still didn't lose his authority to possess it.

Shannon asked to address the Court about the authorization issue Bengston had just mentioned. He said the store sells quite a few things at the prison, but it's the reconfiguration of the items that was important. He pointed out that a lock alone is not a problem, or a sock. But a lock in a sock, or a bar of soap in a sock, made them weapons. It didn't matter if the items were sold and authorized for possession, but when they were reconfigured into something like a garrote, then there was a problem.

On December 18, Don Miller's preliminary examination reconvened in Sault Ste. Marie for the judge's decision.

The district judge began with wanting everyone to understand the difference between evidence which was credible and evidence which was relevant. He said not all relevant evidence was credible.

The judge was trying to address Tom Bengston's motion for dismissal when he explained that the more remote in time a prosecution was from the events that led up to it, the more questionable or less credible the evidence is. He was skeptical of the case against Miller when he heard the evidence had been destroyed.

He looked directly at Don Miller and told him it wasn't his prerogative to question the prosecuting attorney's motives. He knew what their motive was, and that was law enforcement.

"The distance in the law between the responsibilities of a presiding magistrate in a preliminary hearing and guilt beyond a reasonable doubt are just as great as the distance measured in light years between here and the closest star, in my opinion."[275]

The judge recapped the testimony of Corrections Officer Leo Schwesinger and addressed the fact that no one had shown what happened to the garrote after the officer had turned it over to a supervisor. He likened the shoelace used for the garrote as a commodity the government provided for the inmates, much like soap or socks. The one differentiating factor was that the configuration in which it was found was not the same configuration in which it was purchased from the prison store.

Addressing both attorneys and the defendant, the judge said that it was for those reasons he was binding Miller over to the circuit court.

Bengston was puzzled. He asked if the judge had received his ten-page written motion. The judge said he thought the issue was one of credibility, rather than admissibility or lack of evidence. He added that the photo was demonstrative proof that the item was found. The question was whether it was believable. That was why he felt there was sufficient evidence, but he didn't know how credible it was going to be as proof beyond a reasonable doubt.

Bengston seemed satisfied with the judge's explanation.

Jeff Sauter, who had brought the Ingham County prosecutor into the case by now, knew it was their one and only shot at keeping the serial killer behind bars. Both Sauter and his colleague would work with Patrick Shannon. They would be sworn in as assistant prosecutors and participate in the trial.

Both sides began their preparations. The prosecution would maintain that the shoelace with attached buttons was a garrote. The defense would maintain that Miller was

---

275. People v Don Miller, Transcript of Motion to Bind Over and Motion to Dismiss, December 18, 1997, 5

allowed to have both the shoelace and the buttons inside the prison.

One of the first motions made by the prosecutor, prior to the trial, was to allow Don Miller's past record to be introduced at his trial. That would include the manslaughter convictions, and the assaults and attempted murders of the Gilbert children.

Knowing the prosecution's case involved a garrote, a device fashioned to strangle someone, Chippewa County Circuit Judge Lambros said that if he heard Miller had strangled a thirteen year old with a belt, and the garrote found in his cell was fashioned to strangle someone, he would convict Miller in a second. He added that fact far outweighed the admissible fact, and it would prejudice the jury.

After a lengthy discussion, Judge Lambros ruled that the jury would not be allowed to hear about Miller's past. It was a blow to the prosecution's case, but it wasn't the end.

Tom Bengston had also filed numerous motions to have the charges dismissed. One of his first was to quash Miller's bind-over to circuit court because the evidence presented at the preliminary examination didn't support it. The judge denied his motion.

Bengston also filed a motion to quash because the evidence hadn't been preserved. In his argument, he said the shoelace had been destroyed ninety-five days after it had been discovered, and Miller had been administratively disciplined.

In response to the motion, the Ingham County prosecutor, now sworn in as a temporary assistant Chippewa County prosecutor, told Judge Lambros that the police hadn't destroyed the evidence, but the Department of Corrections had and that was their policy. Had Miller chosen to appeal the administrative hearing, it surely would have been kept but he didn't. Judge Lambros denied Bengston's motion.

In all, there were eleven motions filed by the defense, and they ranged from a change of venue to what Miller would be allowed to wear during the court proceedings.

Built in 1877, the Chippewa County Courthouse in Sault Ste. Marie was located just a few blocks from the Soo Locks. The red cut-stone exterior walls were two feet thick with a large clock tower over the center of the building. With large, arched windows on the second floor of the ornate structure, and no air conditioning, the windows were often open to catch the afternoon breeze. With large freighters traveling through the locks during the summer, trials often slowed because testimony would have to stop as the ships would sound their loud horns as they approached.

On August 25, 1998, Judge Nicholas Lambros called Court to order. Jury selection took until noon, and when the jurors came back after lunch, there some minor matters discussed among the attorneys and the judge. By mid-afternoon, Patrick Shannon made his opening statement to the jury.

As the prosecutor outlined his case and described what had been found in Miller's locker, he said that bootlaces and buttons were not dangerous, but when they were configured or combined into an implement that could be used as a weapon, or could be used to help someone to escape, then the items became prohibited inside the prison and were illegal.

Tom Bengston, having the opportunity to waive his opening statement, chose to go ahead and familiarize the jury with the defense position. He would not contest the fact that Don Miller was in custody at Kinross on November 4, 1994. When he outlined the discovery of the shoelace with the buttons attached that was found in the footlocker, he said it was authorized by the prison for Miller to possess the shoelace. The question was whether Miller's right to possess it was revoked when he added two buttons to it. The other question was whether or not the item was actually a weapon of some sort.

After both attorneys had made their opening statements, Sergeant Robin Sexton was called to the stand.

Sergeant Sexton told the Court how he had become involved in the case and how he had been with two other investigators, Jim Kus and Bob Dutcher, when photos were taken of Don Miller's footlocker at the prison in 1998. He said he had contacted the Kinross Facility when the investigation first began and discovered the evidence had been destroyed. He said that MSP never had possession of the item.

Tom Bengston began his cross-examination by asking if Sexton had ever learned that the Kinross Facility had sold shoelaces to inmates, and the detective said he had received a memo that they once did, and the length of the laces sold was seventy-two inches.

Patrick Shannon began his re-direct and asked if the prison had their own investigators who investigated violations within the prison. Sexton explained that the investigator within the prison would handle inmate problems, deal with staff problems, and hold an administrative function, but when a crime was involved, they would contact MSP.

Shannon was starting to build his case when he asked about the prison store selling seventy-two-inch shoelaces, and asked what other things they sold. Sexton informed him the store sold soap, deodorant, pencils, pens, safety razors, and various other things. He added that it included locks and socks.

The prosecutor left it at that for the time being.

· After some additional brief questioning by Bengston, the prosecutor asked Sexton if he had ever investigated other combination types of permissible things that could be purchased inside the prison that were converted to weapons.

When Sexton said he had, he was asked for examples. The most popular was a lock on the end of a belt, while a padlock inside of a sock was used as a club. Going a step further, he described toothbrushes with razor blades stuck in them that were used to slash people. Inmates would use anything sharp to fashion into weapons.

Shannon asked why the case wasn't turned over in 1994. Sexton explained that while narcotics found within the prison are immediately turned over to MSP, there were so many weapons found that many times, the prison handled the cases administratively.

Bengston had only a few questions for his cross-examination.

"When the prison does refer cases to you for criminal investigation, do they typically provide you the actual physical evidence at or about the same time?"

"Yes, sir."

"And you never received the shoelace in this case?"

"No, sir, I did not."[276]

After Sexton was excused from the witness stand, there was brief testimony from a records clerk at the prison who testified that Don Miller was in fact assigned to room 48 on the third floor of B-unit on November 4, 1994.

On the second day of Don Miller's trial, as the three prosecutors sat on one side of the courtroom with Sergeant Sexton, Tom Bengston sat on the other side with co-counsel and his client.

The first witness to be called was Corrections Officer Leo Schwesinger.

Schwesinger testified just as he had at the preliminary examination. He described his assignment for the day, what

---

276. People v Don Miller, Transcript of Jury Trial, August 26, 1998, 161

he was doing, and how he had gone to do a shakedown in an inmate's room that he shared with two others.

Shannon had the corrections officer describe how had found Don Miller's footlocker inside his wall locker, and how the footlocker was padlocked, and Schwesinger also described what he had found inside.

Shannon listened intently as the officer described finding several small items, including a cross, and the plastic package with the garrote in it.

Schwesinger admitted that he had seen shoelaces sold in the prisoner store, but he couldn't be sure they were exactly the same as the one he found. However, he knew immediately that it was a weapon.

When the Shannon asked how many corrections officers were assigned to inmates, Schwesinger said there was one officer per seventy-three inmates.

Shannon wrapped up his questioning by having Schwesinger identify Miller in the courtroom, and then Tom Bengston began his cross-examination.

Bengston asked the officer if he had reviewed the transcript of his testimony from the preliminary examination, and he asked the officer if he had met with anyone prior to his appearance in court for the trial.

Schwesinger said he had met with three attorneys, including Patrick Shannon, and several other corrections staff in the same room, including the prison warden.

Much of Bengston's questioning mirrored the preliminary exam. He became very specific about how the items were positioned inside the box found within Miller's footlocker. He wanted to know if the shoelace were tied, would it be unauthorized?

The officer said that because the shoelace was in an altered state, it was no longer considered a shoelace.

Bengston wanted to know if Miller was a packrat. When Schwesinger said he felt that he was, Bengston asked for his definition of a packrat.

Schwesinger felt it was a person who kept anything and everything.

Going through the entire process again, Leo Schwesinger described exactly how he had performed the shakedown that day, how he had the ruler brought to him to use in the photos as a reference, how he had gotten the camera, and how he had taken the photos.

Bengston went back over the same questions he had asked in the preliminary examination about other things available to an inmate at the inmate store such as extension cords, cable television cables, belts, and shoelaces, knowing he would make the argument that those, like the shoelace and buttons found in Miller's locker, were all authorized and sold to inmates.

The defense attorney pointed to different things in the box that had been found in Don Miller's footlocker as he asked the corrections officer if he recalled what each item was.

The questioning circled back to the garrote when Schwesinger was asked if he had tried to move the buttons on the shoelace after it was found.

He hadn't, and he hadn't seen anyone else trying to move them either.

Tom Bengston cut right to the chase when he asked if Don Miller was a target of the correctional officers because he was getting short on time.

Schwesinger said no, and he didn't make targets of any prisoner.

Bengston even questioned Schwesinger about his nickname at the prison, and the officer told him the nickname was Cowboy.

Schwesinger had been on the stand all morning. It was nearing the lunch break as Patrick Shannon stood to ask a few more questions.

Shannon asked the officer if he'd seen any other weapons that had been altered or seized as contraband, but in and of themselves separately would be innocuous and authorized for an inmate to possess.

Schwesinger said he'd seen a heater vent that had been taken from a cell and altered into a shank or knife. He'd also seen ink pens with heavy needles melted into them to use as a stabbing device, in addition to razors melted into pens.

Shannon asked the officer if he wore boots at work, and if they were commonly known as cowboy boots, and Schwesinger said they were. Shannon had made his point.

The Chippewa County prosecutor asked the judge if could he have the right to recall Schwesinger in the future if it was needed, and Judge Lambros agreed. Shannon told the judge that another colleague would be handling the questioning of the next witness, and the Ingham County prosecutor stood to call Dr. Stephen Cohle, a forensic pathologist from Spectrum Health East Medical Center in Grand Rapids.

As a forensic pathologist, Cohle described himself as a physician who specialized in the investigation of sudden and unexpected death, and step by step, the prosecutor questioned him to outline his qualifications with the intention of having him qualified as an expert witness.

As part of his profession, he'd been called upon to describe certain injuries and how they would affect the human body, adding that he'd also been asked in his profession to determine whether certain items were consistent with certain injuries.

"Yes. That's a frequent question that I have to answer," the doctor said.

"Somewhat of a death detective?"

"Yes."[277]

As Dr. Cohle explained how a forensic pathologist investigated a death caused by ligature strangulation, he

---

277. People v Don Miller, August 26, 1998, 245

also might investigate an unknown death by looking for patterns of injury that might indicate that a ligature was used.

After some very brief questions by Tom Bengston, Judge Lambros allowed Dr. Cohle to testify as an expert.

The prosecutor began his examination by asking the doctor to describe ligature strangulation to the jury.

Cohle told the jury that a ligature was any item that could be used as weapon, which would be wrapped around the neck of a victim and pulled tight so that one of several things occurs. If it's extremely tight, it could shut off a person's airway.

Dr. Cohle identified two mechanisms of injury involved in ligature strangulation. The first was a person's inability to inhale, and the second was the lack of oxygenated blood in the carotid artery to the brain. He said there was no way to monitor what the mechanism of the death was; meaning whether the person was dying from their air being cut off or their blood being cut off.

Cohle said he had discussed the possibility of using a facsimile of the garrote found in Don Miller's cell during the trial. He had taken a seventy-two-inch shoelace and fashioned a similar one as a demonstration to the jury. He asked the prosecutor to come up and face the jury while he demonstrated the device.

Cohle twisted both ends of the device. He walked up behind Jeff Sauter and looped the shoestring around his neck. He showed a second technique to the jury by looping around Sauter's neck again and crossing his hands to pull even tighter.

Dr. Cohle described additional movements that a perpetrator might use to effect the strangulation, showing the jury how he could get a better grip if he wrapped it around his fingers and then pulled.

Asked about how long it would take a person to pass out or die, a victim would pass out in under two minutes if there was continual pressure, and death would occur somewhere in the three minute range with continual pressure applied and absolutely no oxygen getting to the brain.

"So, would it be fair to say that the handles significantly increase the effectiveness of the weapon?" the prosecutor asked.

"Yes, I think that's fair to say. I agree with that."[278]

Tom Bengston was ready for his cross-examination. He asked how the doctor had been contacted initially for an opinion, and was then asked if his opinion was elicited over the phone.

Cohle said he was given a description by phone of what was found and asked, in a general sense, if it was possible that the contraband could have been a ligature. After a meeting with the prosecutors, he formed his opinion.

Bengston asked Cohle if neckties, a belt, or even a shirt sleeve could be used as a ligature, and Cohle said yes.

During re-direct questioning, Cohle explained how the knot in the shoelace would increase the efficiency of the ligature, and demonstrated it to the jury by explaining where a person's carotid artery was. If the assailant was the same size as, or even larger than, the victim, a ligature could be very effective.

The assistant prosecutor had finished, but Bengston had one more question for the doctor.

"In summary, with or without handles on this item, either way, it can be used to strangle someone; is that right?"

"Yes, sir."[279]

After a lunch break, the jury returned to the courtroom and Patrick Shannon called Sergeant Al McClean to the stand. Sergeant McClean was a shift supervisor at the Kinross Facility on the day the garrote was found. He was shown the device and suspected it was a weapon. He

---

278. People v Don Miller, August 26, 1998, 262
279. People v Don Miller, August 26, 1998, 270

described it as a shoestring with two wooden handles on the ends, and he added that in the configuration it was found, it was not authorized to be possessed inside the prison.

Tom Bengston had a few questions for his cross-examination. He started with what the sergeant's role was the day when he got to Miller's room, and then had him describe minute details about Miller's room, many of which the sergeant couldn't recall.

Warden Arthur Tessmer testified after the sergeant, and he described some of the items that were available to inmates in the prison store such as socks and locks. He said inmates were allowed to possess them because they were available in the store.

Asked about putting a lock inside a sock and whether a prisoner could still possess them at that point, the warden said no. He said in that particular configuration, the item would be considered a weapon, and it would be serious offense for an inmate to possess it inside the prison.

The prison had a strict policy on dangerous contraband, and Tessmer described how the items were destroyed after a period of time if there was no appeal by the inmate.

When Tom Bengston had his chance to question the warden, he asked a hypothetical question about prison staff finding a loaded pistol in a footlocker. Bengston wanted to know if MSP would be notified, and Tessmer said yes.

The defense attorney was trying to make a point that in the hypothetical, it didn't matter if the pistol was in a footlocker, or if an inmate had it in his possession, and Tessmer agreed.

Bengston tried to suggest that Don Miller was profiled by prison staff but quickly dropped his line of questioning.

Shannon began questioning Tessmer again.

Tessmer told Shannon that the retention period for items confiscated was ninety days, and it was an internal policy of the prison. It wasn't unusual that the garrote wasn't turned over to MSP immediately after it was found. Tessmer's opinion was that only a small amount of contraband was turned over to MSP.

The prosecutor wanted to clear up one last thing with the warden. He showed the warden a ticket written to Don Miller in 1994, and asked which officer had written the ticket.

Tessmer said the name on the ticket was Officer Peltier. Schwesinger wasn't even assigned to the unit where Miller was housed in 1994. He would have only been there to fill in for chow.

Shannon had made his point to the jury. He wanted to dispel any belief that the corrections officer was targeting Don Miller.

The prosecution rested their case.

The following day, as the trial continued, Don Miller's defense attorney made a standard motion for a directed verdict to dismiss the case, saying the prosecution had not proven it. It was quickly denied by Judge Lambros, who said that based on the testimony from Dr. Cohle, Warden Tessmer, and the corrections officers involved, a jury could conclude that Don Miller had possessed a dangerous weapon within the prison.

Tom Bengston had one shot with one witness. He called David Balash to the stand, and he intended to offer him as an expert.

Balash was a former state trooper who had retired in 1992 after twenty-five years with the department. Assigned first to the Niles Post, he was transferred to the Sandusky Post in 1972 and eventually was assigned to the State Police Forensic Science Division, working in firearms, tool marks, and the bomb and explosives unit in both the Plymouth and Northville laboratories for over twenty years.

Bengston asked his expert witness how many times he had visited a crime scene over his career where a strangulation death had occurred, and Balash estimated there were approximately eighteen. He said the majority of times when he was qualified as an expert, his testimony would involve firearms, tool mark examinations, explosives, blood spatter analysis, and crime scene reconstruction.

As the visiting assistant prosecutor was allowed to question the defense expert, he asked if Balash had ever testified as an expert in a ligature strangulation death.

Balash hadn't.

When asked if he had ever attended any workshops that dealt with strangulation by ligature, Balash hadn't.

All of his experience with strangulation was related to the eighteen or less crime scenes he had attended over his career.

After an objection by the prosecutor about Balash being offered as an expert witness in the area of ligature strangulation, Bengston clarified he was offering the former trooper as a weapons expert.

The prosecutor continued his questioning, asking who would make a determination about a cause of death, and the defense expert said the cause of death would be determined by a forensic pathologist.

"Would it be safe to say that the determination as to whether or not a particular implement was the implement used to create or cause the ligature strangulation, is the determination also made by the forensic pathologist?" the prosecutor asked.

"No, I don't believe it would be, sir."

"You don't believe that would be?"

"Normally, an implement that would be utilized would probably be submitted to the laboratory for analysis."

"Have you ever analyzed such an implement?"

"No, sir, I have not," Balash said. "One had never been submitted."[280]

The prosecutor renewed his objection.

---

280. People v Don Miller, August 26, 1998, 330

Because of his skill, expertise, training, and education, Judge Lambros felt that could help the jury understand the facts, and he allowed Balash as the defense's expert to continue.

Bengston handed his witness the two photos of the garrote found in Don Miller's room and asked if it was weapon.

Balash said it wasn't a weapon, and it wasn't a garrote, adding that it wasn't a strangulation device either. He said a garrote is a device specifically designed to strangle someone. Speaking specifically about the item found in Miller's cell, he said it was too long. He added that if it was a garrote, it would have to be made from a rounded cord, rather than a shoelace, and the knot should be at one end, rather than in the middle. The purpose of a garrote would be a surprise attack from the rear, and the intention would be to strangle or incapacitate someone as quickly as possible. Because the item in Miller's cell was so long, it would be difficult to wrap it around someone's neck a second time because the element of surprise would be lost.

Balash finished by saying a shoestring without buttons attached would be more viable to strangle a person.

The prosecutor wrote notes as Balash gave his testimony, and when Bengston had finished with his witness, took over. He highlighted Sergeant McClean's testimony from the previous day by describing the shoelace used as a heavy bootlace.

The prosecutor asked several questions, and slowly, Balash began to agree with the scenarios described.

The defense expert admitted he had only been involved in two investigations inside a prison, and both had involved explosives. He agreed that if a person was in prison, that person would only have a certain number of items available to fashion a garrote, but reiterated that the item found in Miller's cell wasn't a weapon. When asked why, he simply said it didn't appear to be a weapon.

The prosecutor quickly reminded him of his previous testimony, saying, "Well, you said that one could, if one was inclined, absolutely use this to commit ligature strangulation."

"That is correct, sir."

"Well, then why is it not a weapon?"[281]

Balash said he'd seen several homicides where screwdrivers or hammers were used to murder people, but those tools weren't identified as weapons if they were simply sitting in a static position. If they were used to commit a murder, then they would be classified as a weapon.

The prosecutor quickly realized what Balash was saying. "Well, so, oh, once I use this to strangle somebody, then it's a weapon?" he said.

"It has turned into a weapon, that is correct, sir."[282]

Balash was asked if the item found in Miller's cell could be used to injure or kill another person, and Balash admitted it could. He also agreed it could be used by someone who was making an escape from prison.

The prosecutor had gotten exactly what he wanted from the defense expert.

Asked by Tom Bengston about the buttons on the end, Balash said they could interfere with the intended purpose. He said they served no purpose.

When Tom Bengston finished his last question, the prosecutor's final questions for the witness were brief.

Balash admitted that during his career, he'd seen occasions where criminals had used less than optimal means to accomplish a crime, and because criminals didn't always have the necessary knowledge to achieve their intent, they would use less effective means.

Referring back to the photographs, the prosecution wanted it to be clear. "Okay, and once again, one can

---

281. People v Don Miller, August 26, 1998, 346
282. People v Don Miller, August 26, 1998, 346

absolutely use what's in the photographs to perpetrate ligature strangulation, correct, if one were so inclined?"

"If one were so inclined, one could use that to strangle someone," Balash answered.[283]

As David Balash stepped down from the witness stand, Tom Bengston, having represented Don Miller since 1977, said, "At this time, the defense rests."

Patrick Shannon stood to address the jury with his closing argument.

The key thing for the jury to remember was whether Don Miller had possessed a weapon in his cell on November 4, 1994. He reminded them that he was referring to a law that applied within a state prison.

Patrick Shannon recounted each witness the prosecution had presented and told the jury how each witness had become involved in the case. He highlighted Schwesinger's testimony about how he had discovered the garrote in Don Miller's area of control and how it was packaged in a small box. "And the officer, at that time, felt that it looked like a casket, meticulously pleated at the corners," he said, describing the material found covering the garrote.

He moved to Sergeant McClean's testimony and how the sergeant believed it was contraband. He reminded the jury that the question still remained: could the item have been used as a weapon?

As Shannon described Dr. Cohle's testimony, he said the doctor was an expert in ligature strangulation and had testified because of the way the item was prepared, it could have been used to strangle someone.

Nearing the end of his closing statement, the only thing Patrick Shannon was asking was for the jury to agree with him. There was no legal justification to possess a weapon in a prison, and it was clear that Don Miller did possess a weapon in his area of control within the prison.

---

283. People v Don Miller, August 26, 1998, 358

Next it was Tom Bengston's chance to make his final argument to the jury. Hoping to convince them of Don Miller's innocence, the accomplished attorney began, as Patrick Shannon had, thanking the jury for sitting through three days of trial.

Bengston told the jury there was no question about Don Miller possessing the item. It was in his area of control and in his footlocker.

However, they would have to consider whether or not the item was authorized, and they would have to make that decision themselves, in addition to having to decide whether or not it was a weapon.

Bengston moved to Officer Schwesinger's testimony and his statement that he didn't target Don Miller, yet testified that he checked the board first and saw another inmate's name, who he decided to do a shakedown on. Bengston also highlighted Schwesinger's testimony about taking ten photos and keeping them in his possession until they were turned over to the prison administration, yet only two photos still existed.

To Bengston, Dr. Cohle was above his own expertise because the case wasn't an autopsy. It was a weapons case.

"If you would, from the defendant's perspective, what we would like to suggest is this prosecution, this trial, is unfounded. It's contrived. And based on all the testimony, it should not receive your approval or your sanction with a verdict of guilty."[284]

Highlighting the prison's directive of turning criminal cases over the state police, Bengston suggested to the jury that by the Kinross Facility failing to notify the state police when the item was found in 1994, they rejected the claim of Officer Schwesinger that it was a garrote. Bringing in Dr. Cohle was an effort to make something out of nothing.

---

284. People v Don Miller, August 26, 1998, 390

Bengston asked the jury to consider why the case had been brought against his client. He said the entire case was existent in 1994 and wanted to know why it had been resurrected.

With the burden of proof on the Chippewa County prosecutor, Patrick Shannon began his rebuttal.

He began by moving directly to the policy directives mentioned by the defense only moments earlier when he said, "It says also prohibited are sport coats, suit coats and neckties. Well, we can't even have neckties in prison. I wonder why?"[285]

When the prosecutor spoke of how the defense had attacked every witness, he mentioned there still hadn't been one piece of information allowing Don Miller to possess the item found in his footlocker.

In the case against Don Miller, common sense ruled, and that's what the entire case was about. Shannon asked the jury to look at the photographs, listen to the testimony, and use common sense in their decision.

Judge Nicholas Lambros excused the jury for their lunch break, and at 2:15 p.m., he began his instructions to the group of twelve after they returned. Fifteen minutes later, they left the courtroom and began their deliberations.

Two and a half hours later, the bailiff told Judge Lambros that the jury had reached a verdict. As the jurors re-entered the courtroom, everyone else remained standing until the jury sat down.

Addressing the jurors, the judge said, "Okay. Members of the jury, have you agreed upon a verdict, and if so, who will speak for you?"

There was a palpable anxiousness in the courtroom. It was as if everyone was holding their breath.

The jury foreman spoke up saying, "Our verdict is…"

"Please stand," the judge said.

---

285. People v Don Miller, August 26, 1998, 398

"We, the jury, find him guilty."
Don Miller sat emotionless in his chair.

19

Before Don Miller's sentencing, both the prosecution and defense prepared sentencing briefs outlining their arguments. Tom Bengston's would be on the low end, and Jeff Sauter's would be just the opposite.

In an overview, Tom Bengston wrote that his client had engaged in out of control conduct twenty years prior that had resulted in the deaths of four women. His client had been sentenced to a long-term prison incarceration. While in prison, Miller had conducted his affairs in an exemplary manner and had even been described by a prison chaplain as a model prisoner. He had tutored inmates, taught himself sign language to help hearing-impaired inmates, and had been very active in religious organizations.

Bengston took aim at the Committee for Community Awareness and Protection in Lansing, and he said they had been formed with the sole purpose of keeping his client in prison forever. He described C-CAP as having lobbied the Michigan legislature to enact a civil commitment statute to warehouse his client if and when he was ever released from prison.

Bengston wrote that if his client was convicted, his release date would automatically be extended to December of 2008, and it was only then that he would begin to serve whatever sentence he would receive in the garrote case.

In the written brief, Tom Bengston began making his argument that as of February 1995, the incident involving the garrote at the Kinross Facility was a closed matter, and the shoelace with the two buttons strung on it had been deliberately destroyed.

He said the efforts by the Lansing area prosecutors had one unmistakable purpose, and it was to extend Don Miller's maximum prison release date beyond February 14, 1999.

Citing the Pre-Sentence Investigation Report, Bengston said that his client had worked as a volunteer tutor, served as an assistant editor to the Kinross prison newspaper, *The Link,* and had even received a letter of commendation for his work there.

Citing his participation in Group Psychotherapy for Sex Offenders, Don Miller had participated between 1989 and 1993. In a written summary of his participation, the prison staff noted, "Mr. Miller also acknowledges anger and confusion over the conflict he felt between his desire for sexual relations and his religious belief that sex outside the marriage is sinful."[286] In a second summary, another staff employee wrote, "Mr. Miller is able to identify the thoughts, feelings, and activities which constitute risk for relapse. He seems to understand intellectually his sexual assaultive pattern. Mr. Miller developed a relapse prevention plan for himself incorporating risk factors, cues, and coping response. However, his coping responses are limited. He needs to reconcile his deeper conflict with women and his sexuality."[287]

Don Miller's attorney knew he needed to include his client's family support network in the brief, and after describing the continued support he received from his parents and his two sisters, Bengston wrote, "Not unlike the families of Don's victims, this family has also been irreversibly devastated by his out-of-control conduct of twenty years ago. Notwithstanding their best efforts, they cannot undo what he has done. As he has caused great

---

286. People v Don G. Miller, Defendant's Pre-sentence Brief, October 5, 1998, 9

287. People v Don G. Miller, October 5, 1998, 10

sorrow for these other families, he has also turned upside down the lives and dreams of his family members."[288]

Tom Bengston knew he had done the best he could. Knowing that his client's release date would be moved up by eleven years and that he wouldn't begin serving his time for the offense he was just convicted of until he reached that eleven years, Bengston closed his sentencing brief by asking the Court to impose a sentence of two to five years for the garrote conviction.

Special Chippewa County Prosecutor Jeff Sauter was handling the sentencing phase of the Miller case. On the title page, he quoted President Theodore Roosevelt by writing, "No man is above the law and no man is below it; nor do we ask any man's permission when we require him to obey it. Obedience to the law is demanded as a right, not asked as a favor."

Jeff Sauter had a special interest in this case. As he opened his brief, he urged the court to consider four factors in imposing a sentence on Don Miller: the need for punishment, the need to protect society from the defendant, the potential for reforming the defendant, and the deference of others.

Because Don Miller had been convicted in the garrote case, as a habitual offender, sentencing guidelines didn't apply. Citing a property crime case, *People v Hansford*, Jeff Sauter wrote, "Certainly, if Hansford's history of property crimes lawfully supported a severe sentence as a habitual offender, Don Miller's possession of a strangulation weapon, within the context of his past offenses of sexual assault, strangulation and murder, compels a sentence that will protect society from the possibility of his release from prison."

Prior to citing Don Miller's criminal history, Sauter noted that under the current framework of indeterminate

---

288. People v Don G. Miller, October 5, 1998, 11

sentencing, sentences were based more on an assessment of the offender than the offense, therefore, it would be appropriate for the judge to consider the defendant's extensive criminal history and his potential for rehabilitation.

Jeff Sauter began to describe the missing person cases in the Lansing area beginning on January 1, 1977, when Miller's girlfriend, Martha Sue Young, was reported missing. Sauter briefly detailed each case, including Marita Choquette, Wendy Bush, Kristine Stuart, and Lisa and Randy Gilbert.

After a brief description of the circumstances surrounding each case, he wrote that Sgt. James Kelley of the East Lansing Police Department had written a letter to the Michigan Parole Board regarding the search of Don Miller's car after his apprehension and what was found in the trunk. Kelley had said that a number of disposable lab coats, disposable rubber gloves, chains and heavy wire that was made into loops similar to something that would fit over a person's hands and feet were all found.

"If review of this sentence is merely for abuse of discretion, one must ask, 'If the maximum sentence is not appropriate for Don Miller, who are we saving it for?'"[289]

Sauter noted that while Miller had not been convicted in two other killings, he admitted to murdering both Marita Choquette and Wendy Bush.

He asked that the Court consider Miller's admission that all of his crimes involved rape, some before the murder and some afterward, and his admission that he strangled three of the four murder victims to death. He added that Miller also tried to strangle both Lisa and Randy Gilbert to death. He said Miller strangled Lisa, pulling so hard that the belt broke, and he then used his hands to squeeze her throat.

---

289. People v Don G. Miller, People's Sentencing Brief, October 7, 1998, 8

After stabbing Randy, Miller also strangled Randy with his bare hands, rendering the young boy unconscious.

Sauter wrote that Miller had, by now, admitted to the ongoing sexual assault of his younger sister beginning when he was about fifteen years of age.

Describing the garrote case, Sauter wrote of Miller's conflicting statements when it was discovered.

When Sauter described Don Miller taking risks to commit crimes, Miller had shown he would take the risk of getting caught and punished for crimes much greater than weapon possession. He boldly attacked women in broad daylight, sexually assaulted them, and killed them. He committed the offenses in spite of his college degree in criminal justice, and in a chilling admission to his therapist, Miller admitted that as time went on, he became less concerned about secluded places and took less precautions.

Citing that Miller hadn't been cured yet, Sauter wrote about his family frequently claiming he had been rehabilitated; however, he mentioned an earlier pre-sentence report, quoting Elaine Miller, saying they never had any problems with him yet she was aware of the incestuous attacks.

Next, Jeff Sauter mentioned Miller's insanity defense at his trial for the crimes against Lisa and Randy Gilbert. Since that time, Miller had admitted he made up the story of the demons for his own benefit. In the face of Miller's admission that he fabricated his earlier insanity defense, there was no reliable psychological history to consider Miller's assertion of rehabilitation.

"The fact of the murders suggest that they were not committed in an emotional rage, but rather that they were extremely well-planned events, with considerable thought going into the locations for disposition of the young women's bodies. The other murders and the attack on Lisa

Gilbert suggest calculated and predatory acts, not a re-enactment of emotional rage."[290]

In the final conclusion to the sentencing brief, Jeff Sauter wrote:

There is no fact which would justify reduction or mitigation of the sentence. Don Miller is a strangulation murderer and possessed a strangulation device in an environment where weapons cannot be tolerated. Given the nature of his prior crimes, his possession and concealment of this weapon put both guards and other inmates at risk. His weapon was purely offensive, requiring only stealth or surprise to launch a deadly attack, and only a minute or two to complete it. The guards, both male and female, work virtually alone and are outnumbered seventy to one. These men and women who serve in our prisons are at immense personal risk, and the Court's sentence needs to have a deterrent effect, to discourage other inmates from possessing and concealing dangerous weapons. Most disturbingly, Don Miller's possession and concealment of a strangling device shows that his homicidal tendencies are still at the surface, despite two decades of imprisonment and the Defendant's claim of rehabilitation. The Defendant postures himself before the Court as meek and mild, suggesting that he poses no danger to other inmates or guards. His persona is a disguise…the same disguise that he used before, both to get closer to his victims and to deny culpability. Miller's crimes identify him as a human predator and there is no reliable basis to conclude that he has changed.[291]

290. People v Don G. Miller, October 7, 1998, 15
291. People v Don G. Miller, October 7, 1998, 16

Sauter asked the Court to impose a sentence of at least forty to sixty years.

With both written briefs filed with the Court on October 1, Don Miller's sentencing was a week away.

On October 7, the Circuit Court of Chippewa County, Michigan, was called to order at 2:12 p.m. Judge Nicholas Lambros took his seat on the bench.

Tom Bengston knew this was his last chance. He made a motion to have the habitual offender charge dismissed.

Bengston addressed Judge Lambros, saying if a person is an inmate and is in possession of a weapon while in prison, that conviction shouldn't be used as a means of enhancing the sentence by the habitual statute.

Bengston reminded the judge of his client's two manslaughter convictions, and said that at the time of the offense on November 4, 1994, he had already been released from the manslaughter charges because he had served his time. He wasn't in prison for those two offenses.

"So, Judge, what we are saying, he's going to be punished this afternoon when the Court imposes sentence for his conviction. He's already been disciplined by the Department of Corrections with more to come with regard to special good time. He should not then, on top of that, be subjected to the enhanced sentencing powers of the court by the habitual statue."[292]

In response to Tom Bengston's motion, Jeff Sauter said that if Miller was still serving the two manslaughter offenses when he was caught with this weapon, would he then be protected from the underlying convictions? Would he then be protected virtually from the legislatively intended enhancement effects of a habitual offender's act? Sauter said that wasn't a persuasive argument.

---

292. People v Don G. Miller, Motion to Dismiss Habitual Offender and Sentencing, October 17, 1998, 6

Judge Lambros denied the defense attorney's motion and moved to sentencing.

The judge asked if Jeff Sauter wanted to address the Court, and while he did, he said Bengston asked to address the Court first.

Bengston stood at the podium, and as he began his statement, he told the judge he wanted to bifurcate. He would address the sentencing brief written by Jeff Sauter first, and then highlight some of the points he'd made in his own brief.

As Don Miller's attorney started, he drew the Court's attention to page ten of Sauter's brief. The prosecutor had noted the belief that incidents with female prison guards were connected to Miller's possession of the garrote. Bengston told Judge Lambros that Sauter's statement was simply conjecture and speculation and there was nothing to support it.

Addressing the rumor that his client had threatened a member of the parole board, Tom Bengston told the Court that the pre-sentence investigator had proven that rumor was false.

Bengston also told the judge that the prosecution had asserted there was no witness who could confirm Miller's claim that the garrote was a drawstring for his coat. Bengston cited Miller's roommate at the prison who had told Detective Sexton he recalled it being used by Miller, but he simply couldn't recall if it was for his hood or around the waist.

The defense attorney moved on by saying his client's possession of the shoelace, or garrote, demonstrated that his client still had homicidal tendencies. He began arguing that the shoelace was authorized by the prison. He added that Miller had worn a belt in prison for the previous twenty years. It could be used to strangle someone, but it certainly wasn't indicative of homicidal tendencies.

Referring to the murders his client had committed, Tom Bengston said that none of those cases involved a garrote.

"Moreover, Judge, my client does not stand convicted of any assaultive conduct as he appears before the Court this afternoon. He was determined by the jury to have possession of a weapon while he was an inmate. But the jury never determined that he was intending to use this article as a weapon," Bengston said.[293] His client failed to appreciate that a shoelace with buttons might be construed to be a weapon, but from his perspective, it was no more a weapon than the prison-authorized shoelace that he had possessed. The attorney continued, "His was an innocent mistake in having these two buttons as construed now by the jury. Mr. Miller's possession of this article does not demonstrate his inability to conform his conduct to the laws of society or to the rules of the prison."

Moving to the psychiatric exams in the late seventies, Bengston said the only serious question resulting from those interviews was whether Don Miller was lying to the doctors. He cited the doctor's reports, saying they determined Miller was not malingering during the interviews.

Addressing his client's claim of demons in his defense during his trial in the Eaton County case, the experts felt he was mentally ill at the time, and anything he had told them wasn't reliable.

"My client's prison record, Your Honor, is exemplary," Bengston continued. He highlighted his client's accomplishments in the prison system over the previous twenty years and mentioned the Group Therapy for Sexual Offenders and how helpful Don Miller was to others in the group.

Miller continued to have the loyal support of his mother and father. Gene and Elaine Miller had sat quietly in the back of the courtroom. His two adult sisters continued to

---

293. People v Don G. Miller, October 17, 1998, 15

support their brother, and when the time came for Don's release, the family had resolved to participate further with regard to a psychologist who might be able to help Miller as he made the adjustment back to society.

Bengston was pointed as he began to criticize the prosecution's call for a stiff sentence, saying he had a sense they were asking the Court to make up for the sentence Don Miller received in Eaton County Circuit Court when he got thirty to fifty years for his conduct.

Bengston said the prosecution was ignoring the "super job" Miller had done for the previous twenty years.

"He's, I believe he's forty, forty-three years of age right now. And he has done a very nice job in prison. He's taken advantage of the group therapy, sexual offenders' program, and in order to right the situation the best he could, he's done a very nice job. And I urge the Court to take that into account."[294] Thanking the judge, Tom Bengston had made his final appeal for Don Miller, and sat down.

"Mr. Sauter?" Judge Lambros asked.

Jeff Sauter, Eaton County's Prosecuting Attorney and Special Prosecutor for Chippewa County, began his statement to the Court saying the sentencing was not about a shoelace, and it wasn't about a weapon in prison. It was about a strangulation murderer who devised a strangulation weapon and concealed it in his prison cell. In Don Miller's hands, it was a very dangerous weapon. Using recent historical events, he said that farmers use fertilizer and chemicals every day, and no one thinks about it. But if those same fertilizers and chemicals were put into the hands of Timothy McVeigh, it would make everyone pause and reflect on the danger.

Miller had killed before. He had admitted strangling three women to death, stabbed a fourth, and then almost killed Lisa and Randy Gilbert using the same method.

---

294. People v Don G. Miller, October 17, 1998, 28

Sauter said when Miller made his weapon in prison, it was purely offensive, and it was designed to kill.

Reminding the Court of Miller's protest that the item was merely a homemade drawstring, Sauter said that every officer who looked at it made the determination that it was a weapon, and that included a jury of twelve people from Chippewa County.

Sauter also reminded the Court that Miller had first said he didn't destroy it because he thought he might find another use for it, yet Tom Bengston asserted that his client was going to repair a coat and put it back in the waist or hem of the coat. The bottom line was that Miller was inconsistent in his statements, and not a single person ever saw Miller use it as a drawstring.

Jeff Sauter was hitting his stride. He said that if Don Miller wasn't a predator, what should they call a man who coldly extinguished the lives of four young women?

"He took their dignity as women, raping them before and after he killed them. He took their dignity as persons. He left their bodies to decompose in remote fields. He also extinguished the hope and security of thousands of women who feared they would or could be next."[295]

Describing the helplessness, despair, and rage felt by those who had lost a daughter, a sister, or a wife, he said their pain hadn't faded simply because two decades had passed.

He had told the parole board that any discussion of Don Miller's early release was an absurd position.

The prosecutor read a letter from both Lisa Gilbert and Sue Young, mentioning Lisa's constant fear, and the irreversible toll Martha's death had taken on Sue Young.

Sauter moved to Tom Bengston's stance that his client's prosecution in the garrote case was contrived and unfounded. When he learned of the case, and the fact that

---

295. People v Don G. Miller, October 17, 1998, 32

a strangulation device had been found, it bothered him. He said it was disingenuous for Bengston to suggest that the Department of Corrections hadn't considered the garrote as a weapon, because they had disciplined Miller for it.

Jeff Sauter looked at the judge and said he would not apologize for bringing the resources of his office to push when he was doing the right thing.

"So was it contrived? Yes, if the definition that I read in Webster's says... 'it is the result of forethought and planning, not spontaneous.' Yes, this prosecution was contrived, planned; but it was not unfounded. It is a valid exercise of prosecutorial charging authority."[296]

Sauter believed Sue Young when she said she really believed that if Don Miller got out, she would have to move and leave her home in Michigan. And he believed Lisa Gilbert when she said if Miller got out, he would come after her again.

Moving to Wendy Bush's murder, he said that Wendy's brother, Russell, said that he would authorize his sister's body to be exhumed if Sauter thought he could initiate a murder prosecution. There were no illusions about how dangerous Don Miller was.

As Jeff Sauter moved into Don Miller's life in prison, he said that Miller was active in his religion when he killed Martha, so his work with the prison chaplain wasn't compelling. Miller was a student of law when he cut off the hands of Marita Choquette to recover his handcuffs, so his exemplary behavior in prison didn't persuade anyone. He said that Miller was gainfully employed when he killed Kristine Stuart and attacked Lisa and Randy Gilbert, so his work on the prison newspaper meant nothing about his ability to kill again.

Don Miller would have the Court believe he was successful in sex offender therapy. What was actually

---

296. People v Don G. Miller, October 17, 1998, 39

said was that he had reached the maximum benefits in the program, and Sauter said it was significant that it was omitted from the quote.

Don Miller's coping responses were limited. His insistence on turning his life over to God, his heavy reliance on prayer to rid himself of deviant thoughts and feelings, and his plans for sexual abstinence were unrealistic. He was described by one parole board member as a volcano ready to explode.

As he neared the end of his statement, Jeff Sauter was passionate. He said that if the maximum sentence wasn't appropriate for Don Miller, who were they saving it for?

After asking the Court for a forty to sixty-year sentence, Sauter concluded by saying, "You reach a point where a democratic society should be able to say enough is enough. And when a strangulation murderer prepares and conceals a strangulation weapon, endangering the lives of the men and women who staff our correctional facilities, we have reached that point. Enough is enough."[297]

Jeff Sauter returned to his chair as Judge Lambros turned to Bengston and asked if he wished to make a final statement.

"No. I appreciate the offer. I have had my opportunity. Thank you."

Judge Lambros turned to Don Miller and asked if wished to make a statement.

Don Miller quietly said, "Yes, Your Honor."

Miller admitted that what he'd done twenty years before was horrendous, and he wished he could undo it. He apologized to his victims' families, and he apologized to his surviving victims. He knew this was his only chance, and as he continued speaking, he apologized to his parents.

He went into detail about the things found in his trunk when his car had been searched twenty years earlier,

---

297. People v Don G. Miller, October 17, 1998, 44

describing most of what had been found as things he used to fix his muffler, and he denied having rubber gloves in his trunk. He admitted being a packrat and said he was going to fix a coat with the drawstring found in his locker, but then decided to wait and keep it for something else.

His statement to the judge seemed confusing and disjointed as he said, "Now the prosecutor has raised part of the limited response. It did say that my coping mechanisms as far as my plan of action to not recommit was quote, unquote, limited response. Limited response is not dysfunctional response. I do have room for growth. But room for response is not dysfunctional response."[298] He maintained an almost monotone voice with no inflection. "In a way, I wish we could have talked about this side of my story about the winter coat. Maybe it could have made a difference with the jury.

"With my education in criminal justice, I would not place something dangerous in my own footlocker. I never knew it would be construed as a weapon. If I did, I would never have put it there. Never knew that could be construed as a weapon and never intended for it to be used as such.

"Before I close, once again, I hope all these comments are taken to heart and parameters and boundaries of time and effort. And I thank you, Your Honor."[299]

Judge Lambros called a recess so he could consider the remarks.

Twenty minutes had passed, and Judge Nicholas Lambros re-entered the courtroom. After some brief remarks about the media and their ability to speak with Miller after the sentencing was concluded, he turned his attention to Miller.

As he spoke, the judge reminded Don Miller of his felony convictions, and that allowed the Court to sentence him as a fourth habitual offender. He added that the state

---

298. People v Don G. Miller, October 17, 1998, 48
299. People v Don G. Miller, October 17, 1998, 49

statute allowed for imprisonment for a term of any number of years, up to life in prison.

"In imposing sentence, the Court does not wipe a clean slate," the judge said. "In this regard, it is the obligation of the sentencing Court to consider among other criteria: First, the need for punishment; second, the need to protect society from the defendant; and potential for reforming the defendant; and deference of others."[300]

Judge Lambros continued the sentencing as he reiterated why Miller was in prison in the first place, reminding him of his assaultive crimes, criminal sexual conduct, and assault with intent to commit murder.

Lambros said it was troubling that after twenty years of incarceration, he had now been convicted of possessing a dangerous weapon, and he'd been unable to modify his earlier behavior. "Lingering doubts must be resolved in favor of public safety, particularly in the case of such grievous human suffering," he said.[301]

The judge was very succinct as he moved to his next point saying there was nothing in the pre-sentence report to allow him to conclude that Don Miller had re-examined his course of successful rehabilitation. "A garrote is a weapon of ultimate violence. It is assaultive. Not defensive. It demonstrates a mindset which is at once threatening and uncompromising. It appears to this Court, to this day, that the defendant retains an attitude antisocial at best, even dangerous at worst."[302]

The judge was looking directly at Don Miller and said a decision of separation and segregation for a long period of time weren't lightly imposed. "Your victims do carry their own scars, and no amount of time will restore their loss of innocence or sense of security.

---

300. People v Don G. Miller, October 17, 1998, 54
301. People v Don G. Miller, October 17, 1998, 55
302. People v Don G. Miller, October 17, 1998, 56

"There is nothing in your history, Mr. Miller, which gives this Court any confidence to expect you are truly reformed and the public has no more to fear from you. Indeed, there lies a conviction which compels the opposite conclusion."[303]

With that, Don Miller was sentenced to an additional twenty to forty years in prison. His discharge date is May 1, 2031.

---

303. People v Don G. Miller, Motion to Dismiss Habitual Offender and Sentencing, October 17, 1998, 57

PHOTOS AND MAPS

Martha Sue Young (Lansing State Journal)

Marita Choquette (Lansing State Journal)

Wendy Bush (Lansing State Journal)

Kristine Stuart (Lansing State Journal)

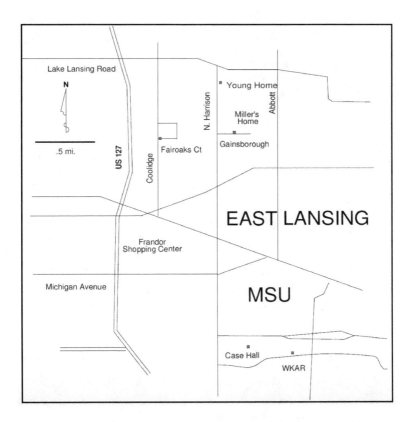

East Lansing area showing the close proximity of Don Miller's house to Martha Sue Young's home and the locations where the other victims were last seen.

Lisa Gilbert's clothing and a part of the belt used
to strangle her. (Crime scene photo, courtesy
of the Eaton County Sheriff's Office)

Blood identifies the location where Randy Gilbert
was strangled, then stabbed. (Crime scene photo,
courtesy of the Eaton County Sheriff's Office)

Investigators examine tire tracks from Miller's car where he made his escape. (Crime scene photo, courtesy of the Eaton County Sheriff's Office)

Open garage door where Lisa Gilbert first encountered Don Miller. (Crime scene photo, courtesy of the Eaton County Sheriff's Office)

Police photo of tire mark from Miller's car (Crime scene photo, courtesy of the Eaton County Sheriff's Office)

Don G. Miller after his arrest by the East Lansing Police

Composite drawing by a witness and
one of Miller's booking photos

Don Miller's car being processed by crime
lab technicians after his arrest (Courtesy of
the Eaton County Sheriff's Office)

Damage to Miller's car from striking Kristine
Stuart (Eaton County Sheriff's Office)

Miller (second from left) is taken into the Eaton County
Courthouse for a hearing (Lansing State Journal)

Miller faces manslaughter

By JOHN SCHNEIDER
Staff Writer

Donald Gene Miller will be charged with manslaughter in the deaths of two East Lansing women after having led police to two sites in Clinton County where they found their skeletal remains.

The remains were those of Martha Sue Young and Kristine Rose Stuart.

On Saturday, Ingham County Prosecutor Peter Houk said the skeletons were "virtually intact." He said Miller, a criminal justice graduate of Michigan State University, will be allowed to plead guilty to two charges of manslaughter in the deaths in exchange for having led police to the sites.

HOUK SAID the primary motive in allowing Miller to plea bargain was to end the "lingering uncertainty" suffered by the families of the two young women.

Induced by Southern Michigan Prison psychologists, Miller confessed to the murders of the two women late last Thursday night.

On Friday, the 24-year-old zealously religious East Lansing man led local police to two different sites.

The remains of Miss Young, the 19-year-old former fiancee of Miller, who disappeared Jan. 1, 1977, were found in a thicket in Priggooris Park, off Drumheller Road, northeast of Lansing. In October 1977, Miss Young's clothing was found about two miles northwest of that spot.

THE BODY of Mrs. Stuart, the 30-year-old Lansing junior high school teacher, who vanished last Aug. 14, was recovered from a deep drainage ditch in a farm field near Jason Road and US 27.

At a press conference Saturday afternoon, East Lansing Police Lt. Dean Tucker said air and ground searches had been conducted in both areas but that the bodies were concealed by heavy brush.

During autopsies performed Saturday, dental

Concluded on page A-21

Staff photo by BRIAN BURD

Miller's attorney Bengtson and Prosecutor Houk hold conference

Tom Bengston (L) and Peter Houk (R) announce the plea agreement at a press conference (Lansing State Journal)

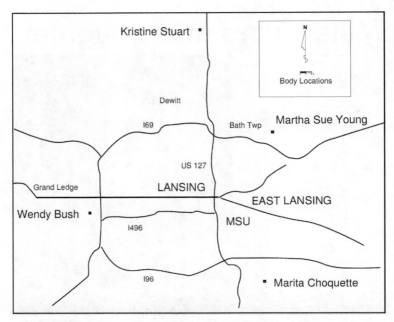

Locations where the bodies of Martha Sue Young, Marita Choquette, Wendy Bush, and Kristine Stuart were found

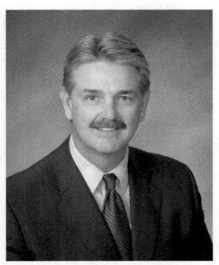

Assistant Eaton County Prosecutor G. Michael Hocking

The garrote found in Miller's prison dorm
(Michigan Dept. of Corrections)

Eaton County Prosecutor Jeffrey Sauter

POSTSCRIPT

On May 4, 2019, the author received the following letter from Don Miller. With Don Miller's permission, it's reproduced here in its entirety.

I (Don Miller) am ashamed and grieved over my sins 1977-78 that led me to being incarcerated. I write the following hoping it will give insight and help people to deal with (cope) with themselves or others. Certain factors (elements) taken together will give insight and help:

Prior to my engagement to Martha Young, we dated for over a year. Said dating was bipolar; either very up (good) or very down (heart wrenching).

The "down" moments consisted of Martha blaming me for something, but then going silent, and not wanting to communicate and work through it. This silence and non-communication hurt me deeply… especially with my flaw to "repress" these hurts (with its anger/frustration); thus, I was "stuffing it" and subsequently stock piling the anger frustration.

Another factor (element) that went with my flaw of "repression"…see above… was to think that "love" between a couple, can "conquer all" and "prevail." I let this immaturity of mine lead me to ignore my "repression" and what it was doing to me week after week.

After a year of such dating, I proposed marriage to Martha Young and she said yes. For the next two weeks, approximately, things were wonderful. Yet in retrospect, I see the factors of her and my behavior (already mentioned) had not been dealt with; Martha continued to periodically get upset, go silent (1 to 4 days) and "not want to communicate and work through these issues"… while I continued to "repress" such hurts (with anger frustration) and my unrealistic concept of "just put up with it in love" (which fueled my repression and stockpiling corresponding anger inside of me).

Untreated, I could (like a blocked steam pipe) only stockpile so much anger frustration and over 2-3 years accumilation [sic] via repression, I exploded (like a blocked steam pipe) on Martha Young and wrongfully took her life…while at the same time, crying out, "The pain must stop."

Note: My God, I wish I could undo all this. People reading this, please deal with "repression" issues you or others may have. Plus, any related unrealistic concept of love. "Repressing" such issues with is frustration and anger eats away at your personality and "repressing" has its accumilation [sic] unto an eventual behavior explosion (remember examples given).

Subsequent crimes by me between 1977-78 were based on me "replaying" mental tapes "within" of my, one time, unresolved issues (noted earlier in this statement) with Martha Young, re-living noted cycle of "repression", "accumilation [sic] of frustration with anger" unto an eventual explosion "discussed in this statement", coming apart at the seams, and at this "cycle explosion" I took three other lives between 1977-78.

My historical flow statement (above) is not meant to be a complete autobiography. It is a statement to give useful insights and such insights can help. Such knowledge and understanding can help others.

A bonus perspective, for those who have ears to hear, is recorded in Proverbs 3:5-6.[304]

304. Don Miller to Rod Sadler, April 30, 2019

BIBLIOGRAPHY

Flowers, Barry. *Terror in East Lansing*. Amherst, NY: Prometheus, 2014

James, Earl. *Catching Serial Killers*. Lansing, MI: International Forensic Service, 1991

Young, Sue. *Lethal Friendship*. Self-published: iUniverse, 2005

Perry, Tekla and Nowack, Nancy. *Thou Shalt Not Kill, Lansing Magazine*, 1979, 23

Eaton County Sheriff's Department. Original Report. Attempted Murder. 78-2654-C, August 16, 1978

East Lansing Police Department. Original Report. Attempt Murder-Assist. Officer Rick Westgate. 2390-C-78, August 16, 1978

East Lansing Police Department. Original Report. Missing Person. 6-C-77, January 1, 1977

East Lansing Police Department, Original Police Report, Missing Person, 3268-C-78, August 14, 1978

Michigan State University Department of Public Safety, Original Report, Missing Person, 2568-78, June 18, 1978

Ingham County Sheriff's Department, Original Report, Homicide Investigation, 8279-78, June 27, 1978

Grand Ledge Police Department, Original Report, Missing Person, 192-C-78, June 15, 1978

Michigan State Police. Original Report, Assist, 11-5892-77, October 22, 1977

Michigan State Police, Original Report, Possession of Dangerous Weapon in Prison, 083-000497-97, March 25, 1997

Letter from Dean Tucker to Thomas Bengston, March 30, 1977

Letter from Dr. Lynn Blunt and Dr. Harley Stock to Paul Berger and Thomas Bengston, February 16, 1979

Letter from William Meyer and Dr. Lynn Blunt to The Honorable Kenneth Hansen, October 20, 1978

Letter from Don G. Miller to Rod Sadler, April 30, 2019

Michigan Dept. of Corrections, Major Misconduct Report, October 15, 1994

Albright, John. "No New Evidence of Coed Found at Search Scene." *State Journal*, October 22, 1978

Bausa, Margarita. "Families Plead to Keep Miller Locked Up." *State Journal*, March 15, 1997

Christoff, Chris. "Bills Would Extend Lockups For Some Killers." *Detroit Free Press*, June 16, 1998

Clegg, Helen. "Donald Miller Allowed Independent Psychiatric Exam." *State Journal*, February 2, 1979

Clegg, Helen. "Miller Asks Trial by Judge For Rape, Attempted Murder." *State Journal*, February 21, 1979

Clegg, Helen. "Miller Now Wants a Jury After All." *State Journal*, March 21, 1979

Clegg, Helen. "Miller Says He Will Appeal." *State Journal*, July 26, 1979

Clegg, Helen. "Miller Costs Eaton $3258." *State Journal*, August 19, 1979

DiFrencesca-Heberlein, Mimi. "Keep Community Safe From Confessed Killer." Editorial, *State Journal*, June 6, 1998

Douglas, Karen. "Twenty Years Later, The Pain Doesn't Go Away." *State Journal*, April 2, 1998

Douglas, Karen. "Cosmetics, Car on Road to New Life." *State Journal*, October 12, 1982

Drumond, Dee. "Predators Ignite Parent's Anger." *State Journal*, April 3, 1998

Durbin, Dee-Ann. "Civil Commitment Law Advances." *State Journal*, April 29, 1999

Frazier, Dick. "Missing Woman Hunted Lansing State Journal." *State Journal*, June 21, 1978

Frazier, Dick. "Area Police Huddling to Name Female Body." *State Journal*, June 29, 1978

Frazier, Dick. "Body Identified, Police Search for Slayer." *State Journal*, June 30, 1978

Frazier, Dick. "Choquette Witness Sought." *State Journal*, July 14, 1978

Frazier, Dick and Nixon, Mark, "Ex-Boyfriend of Missing Coed Faces Assault, Rape Charges." *State Journal*, August 17, 1978

Frazier, Dick, "Police Silent, Build Case Against Miller." *State Journal*, August 18, 1978

Frazier, Dick. "Miller going to Ypsilanti for Psychiatric Exam." *State Journal*, August 19, 1978

Frazier, Dick. "Rape Suspect Declared to be Mentally Competent." *State Journal*, October 24, 1978

Frazier, Dick, "Miller Ruled Competent." *State Journal*, November 4, 1978

Frazier, Dick, "Innocent Please Entered for Donald Miller." *State Journal*, November 30, 1978

Frazier, Dick. "Miller Back in Court, re-Enters Innocent Plea." *State Journal*, December 14, 1978

Frazier, Dick. "Donald Miller Case File Reveals Little That is Unknown." *State Journal*, December 15, 1978

Frazier, Dick. "Ask Venue Change in Miller's Trial." *State Journal*, December 19, 1978

Frazier, Dick. "Ask Venue Change in Miller's Trial." *State Journal*, December 29, 1978

Frazier, Dick. "Miller Won't Be Tried in Eaton." *State Journal*, January 9, 1979

Guest, Greta. "House Panel Oks Sex Predator Controls." *State Journal* May 28, 1998

Guidi, Gene. "Purse is Clue to Missing MSU Coed." *Detroit Free Press*, October 22, 1977

Hall, Doug. "Did Miller See All Victims as One?" *Detroit Free Press*, July 19, 1979

Haskin, Carol. "Corpse Leaves More Questions Than Clues." *State Journal*, December 3, 1978

Haskin, Carol and Morello, Carol, "Miller Deal Reactions." *State Journal*, July 19, 1979

Heron, W. Kim. "No Clues to Missing Girl." *State Journal*, January 6, 1977

Heron, W. Kim, "Disappearance Unsolved." *State Journal*, January 8, 1977

Heron, W. Kim, "Prayer Vigil Starts for Missing Woman." *State Journal*, January 12, 1977

Heron, W. Kim, "Family of Missing Woman Posts Reward." *State Journal*, January, 19, 1977

Heron, W. Kim, "Clues Fade in Search for Coed." *State Journal*, July 18, 1978

Heron, W. Kim and Nixon, Mark, "Police Seek Link to Missing Woman." *State Journal*, August 17, 1978

Houk, Peter, "Miller Case Handled Right Way." Editorial, *State Journal*, September 3, 1979

Hughes, Mike, "Miller Case Gets National Spotlight." *State Journal*, January 7, 1999

Hyde, Justin, "Predator Bill Hits Obstacles." *State Journal*, May 20, 1998

Hyde, Justin, "Groups Debate Sex Offender's Bill." *State Journal*, May 20, 1998

Johnson, Malcomb, "Bill Would Extend Predators Prison Sentences." *Battle Creek Enquirer*, June 12, 1998

Knott, Louise, "Keep Miller in Prison, Group Says." *State Journal*, February 16, 1995

Knott, Louise, "Lansing Serial Killer Faces New Weapons Charge." *State Journal*, March 26, 1998

Knott, Louise, "Bills Would Quarantine Serial Sex Predators After Prison." *State Journal*, March 30, 1998

Knott, Louise, "Corrections Chief: Early Release Unlikely for Miller." *State Journal*, May 23, 1998

Knott, Louise, "Court Blocks Miller's Crimes as Trial Evidence." *State Journal*, August 13, 1998

Knott, Louise, "Miller Trial Reopens Old Wounds for Lansing Area Victims, Families." *State Journal*, August 15, 1998

Knott, Louise, "Murder Case Lingers in Minds of Lawyer, Former Prosecutor." *State Journal*, August 15, 1998

Knott, Louise, "Testimony Begins in Miller Trial." *State Journal*, August 26, 1998

Knott, Louise, "Doctor Testifies Against Miller." *State Journal*, August 27, 1998

Knott, Louise, "Miller is Guilty on Weapons Charge." *State Journal*, August 28, 1998

Leach, Hugh, "Victim's Mother Hopes Book on '70s Killings Helps Others." *State Journal*, September 22, 2005

LeBlanc, Beth, "County Prepares to Fight Killer's Release." *State Journal*, August 21, 2016

McDiarmid, Hugh, "Jailed Rapist Admits Slaying Two Women." *Detroit Free Press*, July 15, 1979

Morello, Carol, "Miller Trial Opens Today." *State Journal*, May 1, 1979

Nixon, Mark, "Disappearance Baffles Police." *State Journal*, January 4, 1977

Nixon, Mark, "Martha Sue Young Still Missing." *State Journal*, January 1, 1978

Nixon, Mark, "MSU Coed Still Missing." *State Journal*, July 15, 1978

Nixon, Mark and Poorman, Dan. "Police Hunt Missing Teacher, Fear Foul Play." *State Journal*, August 16, 1978

Nixon, Mark, "Police May Resume Miller Search." *State Journal*, August 18, 1978

Nixon, Mark, "Missing Women Probe Target." *State Journal*, November 3, 1978

Nixon, Mark, "Jury to Probe Disappearances." *State Journal*, November 3, 1978

Nixon, Mark, "Miller: 'Model Youth' in Jail." *State Journal*, December 3, 1978

Nixon, Mark, "Disappearance Capped Student's Impulsive Lifestyle." *State Journal*, December 3, 1978

Nixon, Mark, "Disappearances Probed." *State Journal*, December 22, 1978

Nixon, Mark, "Key Witness Saw Stuart Kidnapping." *State Journal*, February 19, 1979

Nixon, Mark, "Donald Miller Indicted in Murder of Two Women." *State Journal*, February 22, 1979

Nixon, Mark and Schneider, John. "Abduction Witness Expected to Testify." *State Journal*, April 2, 1979

Nixon, Mark, "Memory Unlocked, Stuart Witness Fingers Donald Miller." *State Journal*, April 4, 1979

Nixon, Mark, "Girls Unleashed Fury in Miller." *State Journal*, July 19, 1979

Ochberg, Frank, "Protect Mid-Michigan From Serial Killer Risk." Editorial, *State Journal*, April 25, 1998

Perry, Ellen, "Missing Coed's Mom Fears She is Dead." *State Journal*, July 20, 1978

Poorman, Dan, "Body Found Near Sleepy Hollow." *State Journal*, March 16, 1977

Poorman, Dan, "Police Ordered Not to Discuss Sleepy Hollow Stabbing Victim." *State Journal*, March 17, 1977

Poorman, Dan, "Skull Perplexes Police." *State Journal*, August 8, 1977

Poorman, Dan, "Police Say Skull That of Young Woman." *State Journal*, August 9, 1977

Poorman, Dan, "Hunters Find Martha Young's Purse." *State Journal*, October 21, 1977

Poorman, Dan and Nixon, Mark. "Hunters Find Clues to Missing Coed." *State Journal*, October 22, 1977

Poorman, Dan, "Cash Readied for Leads in Woman's Slaying." *State Journal*, August 10, 1978

Poorman, Dan and Lang, Bud. "East Lansing Woman Missing." *State Journal*, August 15, 1978

Poorman, Dan, "Stuart Family Asks Help." *State Journal*, August 19, 1978

Poorman, Dan and Nixon, Mark. "Miller Bound for Trial." *State Journal*, November 18, 1978

Schneider, John, "Mrs. Stuart's Husband Offering $8000 Reward." *State Journal*, August 30, 1978

Schneider, John, "Stain in Miller's Car Could Have Been Girlfriend's Blood." *State Journal*, April 7, 1979

Schneider, John, "Miller Trial to Begin in St. Joseph." *State Journal*, April 30, 1979

Schneider, John, "Prosecution Rests Case Against Miller." *State Journal*, May 3, 1979

Schneider, John, "Jury Hears Miller Called a Psychotic." *State Journal*, May 4, 1979

Schneider, John, "Miller Found Guilty of Attempted Murder; Rape." *State Journal*, May 9, 1979

Schneider, John, "Miller Given 30 to 50 Years in Prison." *State Journal*, May 31, 1979

Schneider, John, "Experts Defend Contradictory Testimony During Miller Trial." *State Journal*, June 10, 1979

Schneider, John, "Miller Faces Manslaughter." *State Journal*, July 15, 1979

Schneider, John, "Admits Two More Slayings." *State Journal*, July 18, 1979

Schneider, John, "Victim's Mother Outraged." *State Journal*, July 27, 1979

Schneider, John, "Miller Tells Details of Stuart Murder." *State Journal*, August 1, 1979

Schneider, John, "Miller Describes Killing of Women." *State Journal*, August 2, 1979

Schneider, John, "Murder He Wrote; Miller Case Becomes a Novel." *State Journal*, January, 12, 1986

Schneider, John, "It All Began New Year's Eve, 1977." *State Journal*, January 12, 1986

Weingarten, Gene, "Rape Suspect Faces 2 Murder Charges." *Detroit Free Press*, February 23, 1979

Westfall, Trudy, "Seek Clues of Mrs. Stuart." *State Journal*, August 27, 1977

Young, Sue, "Sexual Predator Law Constitutional, Right." Editorial, *State Journal*, June 7, 1998

Battle Creek Enquirer, 1978, "Suspect in Disappearances Declared Competent For Trial." October 25, 1978, 8

Battle Creek Enquirer, 1998, "Confessed Serial Killer Faces More Prison Time." August 19, 1998, 2

Battle Creek Enquirer, 1999, "Murder Case Gets National Spotlight." January 8, 1999, 4

Battle Creek Enquirer, 2016, "No Release for Killer." July 31, 2016, 4

Battle Creek Enquirer, 1977, "Parents Offer Reward for Return of Daughter." January 20, 1977, 3

Battle Creek Enquirer, 1978, "MSU Grad Held in Rape Attempt, Stabbing." August 18, 1978, 1

Battle Creek Enquirer, 1978, "Lansing Rape Suspect to Take Mental Exam." August 30, 1978, 6

Battle Creek Enquirer, 1979, "Store Detective Indicted in 2 Deaths Even Though Bodies Remain Missing." February 23, 1979, 12

Battle Creek Enquirer, 1979, "Confessed Slayer Miller to Appeal May Convictions." July 27, 1979, 10

Battle Creek Enquirer, 1979, "Miller Gets Two 10 to 15 Year Terms." August 29, 1979, 2

Battle Creek Enquirer, 1999, "Murder Case Gets National Spotlight." January 8, 1999, 4

Detroit Free Press, 1978, "Police Fear Teacher Abducted." August 17, 1978, 4

Detroit Free Press, 1978, "Rape Suspect Faces 2 Murder Charges." February 23, 1979, 1

Detroit Free Press, 1979, "Suspect in 2 Killings Convicted in Assaults." May 10, 1979, 78

Detroit Free Press, 1979, "Jailed Rapist Admits Slaying Two Women." July 15, 1979, 3

Detroit Free Press, 1979, "A Calm Demeanor and Deadly Rage." July 22, 1979, 8

Detroit Free Press, 1979, "Pain and Anger of Lost Love Led to Slayings, Killer Said." August 2, 1979, 3

Detroit Free Press, 1979, "Killer of Four Gets 15 Years; Judge Sorry it Isn't More." August 30, 1979, 2

Detroit Free Press, 1998, "Bills Would Extend Lock-ups For Some Killers." June 16, 1998, 1

State Journal, 1977, "East Lansing Hunts Missing Woman." January 3, 1977, 9

State Journal, 1977, "No Martha Young Clues." January 27, 1977, 6

State Journal, 1977, "Citizens' Help Sought in Search for Woman." February 14, 1977, 4

State Journal, 1977, "Police Ask Help in Search for Woman." February 18, 1977, 2

State Journal, 1977, "Reward Extended, Doubled." February 23, 1977, 12

State Journal, 1977, "No New Clues Found." October 23, 1977, 16

State Journal, 1977, "Young Search Hits Another False Trail." November 6, 1977, 16

State Journal, 1978, "Missing Coed worries MSU." July 5, 1978, 4

State Journal, 1978, "Miller Remains in Jail." August 20, 1978, 18

State Journal, 1978, "Fruitless Searches, Lack of Clues Stymie Missing Women Cases." October 6, 1978, 5

State Journal, 1978, "Rape Suspect Declared to be Mentally Competent." October 24, 1978, 1

State Journal, 1978, "Dead or Alive? What became of Loved Ones?" October 19, 1978, 1

State Journal, 1979, "'Missing Women' Area's Top Story." January 1, 1979, 15

State Journal, 1979, "Miller to Be Tried in Berrien County." January 27, 1979, 3

State Journal, 1979, "Young, Stuart Funeral Rites Scheduled." July 16, 1979, 3

State Journal, 1979, "New Approaches Needed." July 22, 1979, 17

State Journal, 1979, "Bush Memorial Service Slated." July 26, 1979, 10

State Journal, 1979, "An Injustice Done." August 31, 1979, 6

State Journal, 1992, "A Serial Killer's Bid for Freedom." June 14, 1992, 1

State Journal, 2005, "Notorious Crimes." April 28, 2005, 97

State Journal, 2016, "No Early Release for Killer." July, 31, 2016, 10

The Times Herald, 1978, "No New Leads in Hunt for Kristine." August 24, 1978, 2

The Times Herald, 1978, "Nightmare - Disappearances Puzzle Police." September 2, 1978, 6

The Times Herald, 1978, "Man Can Stand Trial." October 25, 1978, 10

The Times Herald, 1979, "Miller Leads Authorities to Kristine Stuart's Body." July 15 1979, 1

The Times Herald, 1978, "Secret Witness Reward Offered on Kristine." August 22, 1978, 2

The Times Herald, 1978, "Weekend Help Sought in Search for Stuart." August 25, 1978. 2

The Times Herald, 1979, "Judge Rules Change of Venue for Miller." January 10, 1979, 4

The Times Herald, 1979, "Miller Trial Moved to Neutral County." January 29, 1979, 2

The Times Herald, 1979, "Kristine's Family Hasn't Lost Hope." February 23, 1979, 1

The Times Herald, 1979, "Stuart's Accused Killer Has Hearing." April 8, 1979, 12

The Times Herald, 1979, "Miller Gets 30 to 50 Years in Prison for Attacking Two." June 1, 1979, 14

The Times Herald, 1979, "Miller Leads Authorities to Kristine Stuart's Body." July 15, 1979, 1

The Times Herald, 1979, "We Are Just Glad That It's Over." July 20, 1979, 2

The Times Herald, 1979, "Lawman Says Miller Had Been Main Suspect." July 31, 1979, 9

The Times Herald, 1979, "Judge Gives Maximum Sentence." August 30, 1979, 5

The Times Herald, 1979, "Crime Predator Bill Clears Senate." June 12, 1998, 5

The Times Herald, 1999, "Serial Killer Featured on 48 Hours." January 8, 1999, 6

The Times Herald, 2016, "Man Who Admitted to Killing 4 Michigan Women is Up For Parole." July 22, 2016, 4

The Times Herald, 2016, "Then There Was No Hope." August 1, 2016, 2

For More News About Rod Sadler,
Signup For Our Newsletter:

http://wbp.bz/newsletter

Word-of-mouth is critical to an author's long-term success. If you appreciated this book please leave a review on the Amazon sales page:

http://wbp.bz/killingwomena

 See even more at:
http://wbp.bz/tc

More True Crime You'll Love From WildBlue Press

 A MURDER IN MY HOMETOWN by Rebecca Morris

Nearly 50 years after the murder of seventeen year old Dick Kitchel, Rebecca Morris returned to her hometown to write about how the murder changed a town, a school, and the lives of his friends.

wbp.bz/hometowna

 BETRAYAL IN BLUE by Burl Barer & Frank C. Girardot Jr.

Adapted from Ken Eurell's shocking personal memoir, plus hundreds of hours of exclusive interviews with the major players, including former international drug lord, Adam Diaz, and Dori Eurell, revealing the truth behind what you won't see in the hit documentary THE SEVEN FIVE.

wbp.bz/biba

 SIDETRACKED by Richard Cahill

A murder investigation is complicated by the entrance of the Reverend Al Sharpton who insists that a racist killer is responsible. Amid a growing media circus, investigators must overcome the outside forces that repeatedly sidetrack their best efforts.

wbp.bz/sidetrackeda

 **BETTER OFF DEAD** by Michael Fleeman

A frustrated, unhappy wife. Her much younger, attentive lover. A husband who degrades and ignores her. The stage is set for a love-triangle murder that shatters family illusions and lays bare a quiet family community's secret world of sex, sin and swinging.

wbp.bz/boda

www.ingramcontent.com/pod-product-compliance
Lightning Source LLC
LaVergne TN
LVHW020305250325
806797LV00044B/1532